Interracial Intimacy

Interracial Intimacy

The Regulation of Race & Romance

Rachel F. Moran

The University of Chicago Press
Chicago & London

RACHEL F. MORAN is the Robert D. and Leslie-Kay Raven Professor of Law at the University of California School of Law, Berkeley.

The University of Chicago Press, Chicago 60637
The University of Chicago Press, Ltd., London
© 2001 by The University of Chicago
All rights reserved. Published 2001
Printed in the United States of America
10 09 08 07 06 05 04 03 02 01   1 2 3 4 5

ISBN: 0-226-53662-9 (cloth)

Library of Congress Cataloging-in-Publication Data

Moran, Rachel F.
    Interracial intimacy : the regulation of race and romance / Rachel F.
Moran.
        p.   cm.
    Includes index.
    ISBN 0-226-53662-9 (cloth : alk. paper)
    1. Miscegenation—Law and legislation—United States—History. 2.
Interracial marriage—United States. 3. United States—Race relations.
I. Title.
KF4757 .M667 2001
305.8′00973—dc21

                                                    00-011008

To my parents, who taught me how
to cross boundaries and how to love

You know quite well, deep within you,
that there is only a single magic, a single power,
a single salvation . . . and that is called loving.

—HERMAN HESSE

CONTENTS

During my career as a law professor, most of my work has focused on educational law and policy. So, you might well ask, how did an education law scholar wind up writing a book about interracial intimacy? Some years ago, I began a case study of desegregation and bilingual education in the Denver public schools. At the time, Denver was under a court order to integrate its school system, but city officials had been petitioning the federal district court to terminate busing remedies. In the course of interviews that I conducted, members of the community repeatedly told me that if the court ended the decree and schools resegregated, they would not be concerned so long as people could freely choose where to live. This popular view echoed the U.S. Supreme Court's jurisprudence, which held that school districts released from judicial oversight had no obligation to combat resegregation that arose because of private preferences and socioeconomic differences. Underlying these claims seemed to be a notion that a preference for members of one's own racial or ethnic group was neither racist nor ethnocentric if it did not reflect antipathy toward other groups. This distinction between ingroup solidarity and outgroup hostility fascinated me, and I determined to supplement my research by reading about interracial relationships in private life. What I discovered was a broad-ranging literature in law, history, and social science that had yet to be fully synthesized. To fill this gap, I set about writing this book, instead of the one on desegregation and bilingual education in Denver.

The book has special meaning for me because my father was Irish and my mother is Mexican. Throughout my life, I grew up in a household without racial or ethnic boundaries, only to enter an outside world that attached great significance to these dividing lines. I have always wondered why my family was so different, and this book has afforded me the opportunity to explore this personal history in what I hope has been a profitable way. As you will see, this is both a hopeful and cautious book. My own experience tells me that crossing boundaries can be difficult but also deeply rewarding. My parents' efforts to forge a family were not without pain and struggle, but their love survived. I still remember my father in the last days of his life. As he lay dying, a stroke had left him speechless and partially paralyzed. But he still had some use of his hands, and so he expressed his affection for my mother in the only way that remained available to him: He lovingly fingered the wedding ring she had worn for forty-two years and still wears now that he is gone. This book is a tribute to my parents' courage and resiliency.

In addition to my parents, I owe a debt to many others who have helped me over the years as I labored on this book. First, there are the colleagues who have taken the time to read all or part of the manuscript and provide me with thoughtful comments: Jesse Chaper, Carole Goldberg, Angela Harris, Joan Hollinger, Ian Haney Lopez, Carol McClain, Charles McClain, Judith Resnik, Dan Rodriguez, and Steve Sugarman. I owe a special thanks to Robert Post, who helped me to navigate the unfamiliar process of placing the book, and to Martha Minow, who read the entire manuscript on two occasions and offered extremely helpful suggestions each time. I also received valuable assistance in identifying and obtaining historical materials from Ginny Irving and Alice Youmans of the Boalt Hall Law Library. My assistant, Priscilla Battis, worked tirelessly on successive versions of the manuscript as well as on the index. I was also fortunate to work with able and dedicated research assistants, including Clark Freshman, Dana Johnson, Sujin Kim, and Jennifer Rochon. Clark has gone on to a career in law teaching and has become a treasured colleague and friend. I also benefited greatly from the opportunity to present portions of this manuscript at workshops at the University of California School of Law (Boalt Hall), California Western School of Law, New York University School of Law, and the University of Miami School of Law as well as at conferences sponsored by the Association of American Law Schools and the Law and Society Association. Last but not least, I must express a singular debt of gratitude to my editor, John Tryneski. He brought experience, intelligence, and integrity to this project. As a first-time book author, it has been a privilege (albeit sometimes a daunting one) to work with him and the other first-rate staff at the University of Chicago Press. John in particular has set a standard of excellence that undoubtedly made this a better book. To everyone who has helped along the way, I am profoundly grateful for your generosity, friendship, and faith.

ONE

Insights from
Interracial Intimacy

IN THE PAST few years, a spate of books has described the unique experience of growing up in an interracial family.[1] In *Life on the Color Line: The True Story of a White Boy Who Discovered He Was Black,*[2] Gregory Howard Williams (now dean at the Ohio State University School of Law) remembers life with a black father and white mother. In his earliest years, he believed that he was white and that his father was a dark-skinned ethnic. Later, when his parents' restaurant business failed, he discovered that his father was actually a light-skinned black man. Destitute and desperate, his father took Williams and his brother to live with their black relatives in Muncie, Indiana. His parents' marriage fell apart, and later, when his mother married a white man, she returned to ask Williams and his brother to live with her new family. Williams writes:

> The conditions for becoming part of her life became very clear to me.
> We could reenter her world if we rejected the one in which we had lived
> for the past ten years. . . . Gaining acceptance to her world required that
> we deny our black heritage and pretend that the people and circumstances
> of our life in Muncie did not exist. We were to forget we were "colored"
> boys. She expected us to move back into her life without a past, with-
> out roots, without feelings for the people who had sheltered and cared
> for us when our need was greatest. I knew that was something we could
> never do.[3]

But Williams was wrong. His brother did choose to share his mother's life, even though Williams himself declined an offer that had come "too late" and "felt farther away from [his] mother than [he] had at any time in [his] life."[4] The brothers made different choices, but each confronted the terrible riddle that a child's heart poses: How could a father's son not be his mother's little boy? Williams's story illustrates the unique lessons about race and intimacy that interracial intimacy can yield. Williams and his brother must struggle to form personal identities in a segregated world. Opposition to interracial marriage makes their parents' wedding a deviant act and their father's racial background a dirty secret. By degrading a black heritage, official policies of segregation diminish the children's own personhood. Neither Williams nor his brother is free to embrace a satisfying identity because enforced inequality and segregation limit their options for personal development. They confront these harms in an arena generally regarded as critical to the formation of self—their family.

In Williams's story, at least three ideas of race compete as ways to explain identity. First, Williams can rely on genotype, discovering his identity by tracing his ancestral racial affiliations. His mother is white, and his father is black. Under a one-drop rule that says that any trace of African ancestry makes him black, he too is black. Yet this approach leaves him feeling uncomfortable, for it erases his mother's contribution to his identity. Alternatively, Williams can look to phenotype—that is, his physical appearance. This approach also has limitations. Light-skinned enough to pass, Williams can be white with his mother, but if he returns to his father's side of the family, he becomes black. For Williams, phenotype, like genotype, yields an uncertain and contingent racial identity. Finally, Williams can rely on his sense of social connection, or loyalty, to decide his identity. In the end, he chooses to remain with his father as a "colored" boy, but the price of doing so is a deep estrangement from his mother. His brother opts to build social connections with his mother, but only at the cost of a loss of contact with his father. Once again, neither choice is clearly truer to the children's racial identity.

Williams's story also illustrates the problems that interracial relationships pose in defining racial equality. Advocates of colorblindness insist that the government must be indifferent to race in all its decision-making to ensure equality. In their view, even color-conscious remedial efforts like desegregation and affirmative action betray America's commitment to individual liberty and equal treatment. Proponents of color-consciousness, on the other hand, argue that the color line still exists and cannot be ignored. For them, the ideal of colorblindness has been betrayed by centuries of segregation and discrimination. Justice rings hollow when the principle is held up as inviolable mainly when remedial steps are at stake. For Williams, the debate is oddly misplaced. His parents have already crossed the racial divide. His family and he himself defy easy categorization in a world in which race is treated as an important and largely impenetrable social boundary. In a world in which race matters, it is hard to know how to establish the minimum conditions of personhood that will allow Williams to pursue a life unencumbered by the vestiges of past discrimination. Will a formal policy of colorblindness truly set Williams free? Will color-conscious remedies rigidify the hard choices he must make between the privileges of whiteness in his mother's world and the solidarity and community of his father's? If racial identity cannot be ignored, must Williams choose to be either white or black, even though the color line divides him to the bone? Or is it possible for him to forge a multiracial identity despite the fact that, by virtue of race, his mother and father occupy widely disparate worlds?

To treat Williams's account as a story only about race, though, is to do him an injustice. For his recollections also are about love. Americans prize the freedom to shape their closest relationships, for they understand that interpersonal associations play a critical role in shaping identity. Forced intimacy is frightening not just because friends or lovers may be incompatible but also because the arrangements violate a fundamental sense of self. Even as children, Williams and his brother are asked to choose between their mother and father, a choice that will be critical to the development of their identity. Although this freedom to choose is quintessentially individualist, there is no easy way to gauge which brother made the right decision based on personal development, racial loyalties, or filial love. If Williams's brother weighed the costs and benefits of living with his mother, does that make him an opportunist who capitalized on racial inequality? Or is his approach a rational way to evaluate parental fitness and his own best interest? Is Williams the better brother because he made his decision based on loyalty to those who cared for him in a time of need, or does his choice acquiesce in racial isolation? In the end, is the effort to compare the brothers' choices incoherent because each brother simply loved his parents in ways that were wholly subjective, immeasurable, and unique?

History, Law, and Interracial Relationships

The story of Gregory Howard Williams clearly shows how interracial relationships can shed light on questions of both racial equality and freedom to marry and build families. As the next three chapters will demonstrate, the freedom to love across the color line is a relatively recent phenomenon in American history. From colonial times until the mid-1900s, antimiscegenation laws banning interracial sex and marriage were a common feature of state law. Although the statutes typically criminalized interracial intimacy, penal sanctions served different functions at different times. During the colonial era, white indentured servants often worked in close proximity to black slaves, so that intermixing was bound to occur. Interracial relationships threatened to muddy the divide between black and white, slave and free. To keep these distinctions clear, antimiscegenation laws treated sex and marriage across racial boundaries as antisocial, dangerous acts. In the process, these laws defined both whiteness and blackness.

Eventually the challenge to the color line based on interracial sex and marriage was resolved by establishing a one-drop rule that mandated that any person with a trace of African ancestry was black. Yet even with the color line firmly in place, antimiscegenation laws persisted after the Civil War and Reconstruction, despite efforts to dismantle racial inequalities in public life. Indeed, laws prohibiting intermarriage were expanded to cover other groups, most notably Asian immigrants in the western United States. The racial identities of Asians had been clearly spelled out under federal immigration laws, which labeled the newcomers nonwhite and ineligible for citizenship. In these circumstances, antimiscegenation laws were necessary not to consolidate racial identity but to preserve racial hierarchy. By barring blacks and Asians from marrying whites, the laws ensured that these groups would have no access to white privilege through social contact and inheritance of family wealth.[5]

Although antimiscegenation laws sought to draw racial boundaries and preserve racial privilege, they also were markers of racial ambiguity. The blurring of some racial divisions expanded opportunities to marry across the color line and challenged racial hierarchies. For example, far fewer laws covered Native Americans, who often had mingled with white settlers during the early years of settlement when white women were scarce and tribal alliances highly advantageous. As a result, some prominent early American families had Native American ancestry. Virginia's antimiscegenation law, for example, contained a provision known as the "Pocahontas exception," so that descendants of the famous John Rolfe could be assured of their whiteness. Moreover, no antimiscegenation laws ever covered Latinos. Again, in the Southwest, substantial intermarriage occurred during the early years of contact between Anglo settlers and Mexican natives. Later, when the United States annexed portions of Mexico, the Treaty of Guadalupe Hidalgo assured former Mexican citizens of equal treatment if they remained and became American citizens. As a result, formal restrictions on intermarriage were not promulgated, although marriage registrars often used their informal discretion to deny marriage licenses to Latinos who appeared "too dark" to marry whites.[6] By criminalizing some forms of intermarriage and not others, antimiscegenation laws offered a flexible tool to contain and accommodate the ambiguity engendered by interracial relationships.

Although usually understood as racial legislation, bans on interracial marriage also sent a clear message that some members of the population could not be trusted to make responsible decisions about sex and marriage. Very often, fears of libertinism correlated with the arrival of newcomers who were perceived as degraded and different. During the late 1800s and early 1900s, for instance, urbanization broke down traditional means of regulating sexuality in small, rural communities. Newcomers, both immigrant and black, flocked to the cities, and white elites feared the collapse of social decency in the resulting hubbub. With increasing anonymity in urban centers, men could readily exploit poor, working women in factories and boardinghouses as well as patronize prostitutes in burgeoning sex districts. To contain this wayward sexuality, social hygiene reformers demanded increased regulation of sexual practices. As part of this reform effort, antimiscegenation laws proliferated. The statutes made clear that interracial sex and marriage remained highly deviant and dangerous even in a newly cosmopolitan America. Indeed, in redlight districts, the Black and Tan clubs serving patrons with a taste for sex across the color line were among the farthest removed from respectable residential and business districts. This way, no one could accidentally wander in to be corrupted by intimate interracial contact. Customers already had to be intent on pursuing illicit pleasures to find a Black and Tan.[7] Restrictions on sexuality and marriage during this period became a way to contain deviance and protect moral decency by defining the parameters of white respectability.

The central importance of the regulation of intimacy in defining racial identity, establishing racial inequality, and preserving moral propriety is evident from the longevity of antimiscegenation laws. As chapter 5 will show, these statutes endured from the colonial era until the twentieth century, despite efforts to promote racial equality and to deregulate sex and marriage. During Reconstruction, the state high court in Alabama declared a ban on intermarriage unconstitutional but reversed itself shortly thereafter.[8] The U.S. Supreme Court upheld an antimiscegenation statute in *Pace v. Alabama*[9] in 1883, thereby cementing the doctrine of "separate but equal" marriages and families. Only one state court declared antimiscegenation laws unconstitutional after the *Pace* decision. In 1948, the California Supreme Court in *Perez v. Sharp*[10] concluded that prohibition of interracial marriage violated the principle of racial equality and interfered with the liberty to choose a spouse. The U.S. Supreme Court did not reach a similar conclusion for another twenty years. In 1967, in an opinion by Chief Justice Earl Warren, the Court unanimously held in *Loving v. Virginia*[11] that antimiscegenation laws unconstitutionally discriminated on the basis of race in violation of equal protection and that they interfered with the fundamental right to marry under the due process clause.[12] Warren's opinion contained two distinct themes: a commitment to racial equality and a commitment to marital autonomy.

Over three decades have passed since Warren wrote the *Loving* decision. The question arises: Was the decision a success? Chapters 6, 7, and 8 of this book will try to answer this question by examining contemporary debates about interracial marriage, transracial adoption and interracial custody disputes, and multiracial identity. Those who advocate colorblindness in official policy about sex, marriage, and family will reply that *Loving* was an unambiguous success. Registrars no longer deny marriage licenses based on racial considerations, and some jurisdictions have even stopped keeping track of racial identity when granting licenses. The only problem with *Loving,* in their view, is that it has not swept broadly enough to bring an end to such practices as race-matching in adoption or racial recordkeeping on the census.

Yet others who look to contemporary patterns of marriage and family doubt that *Loving* has in fact been so successful in curing problems of racial discrimination. After three hundred years of antimiscegenation laws, it would be surprising if thirty years of official colorblindness have truly rendered race irrelevant in the choice of a marital or sexual partner. In fact, most Americans continue to choose a spouse of the same race. According to 1997 congressional testimony by Mary Waters, a sociology professor at Harvard University, over 93 percent of whites and blacks choose same-race partners, as do 70 percent of Asians and Latinos and 33 percent of Native Americans.[13] Because of these marital patterns, Americans generally grow up in racially homogenous families and report a single racial affiliation when asked to identify themselves. According to this view, race-matching in adoption and racial recordkeeping on the census simply reflect patterns of intimate behavior that remain highly color-conscious. The lawyerly response to this critique of *Loving* points out that the Justices addressed only official policy, not private behavior. But, for some Americans, the gap between formal rhetoric and informal practice is uncomfortable and disturbing. For every interracial romance that fails to blossom and for every interracial family that fails to form, there is the haunting possibility that the racial divide remains so wide that love is unfree.

Race and Equality

In evaluating the history of antimiscegenation laws, their judicial dismantlement, and contemporary controversies about interracial intimacy, this book will explore the meaning of race and racial equality and their relationship to personal autonomy. The three competing notions of race—genotype, phenotype, and social ties—that bedeviled Gregory Howard Williams in his search for a coherent identity are linked to inconsistent governmental policies regarding the relevance of race. Under a colorblind approach, officials must ignore race because it is presumptively irrelevant to individual merit. Race is nothing but an accident of birth, for children cannot choose their genealogy. As a matter of physical appearance, race manifests itself only in superficial differences like hair color and texture, skin color, and eye folds. Framed as a biological irrelevancy, race is no more germane to winning a government contract, getting a job, or gaining a seat at a public university than small ears or a freckled complexion. Yet, if race is defined in terms of its social consequences, its relevance to official decisions becomes complicated. If genotype and phenotype have been the basis for past state-supported discrimination, then these traits can be used to identify members of groups who have suffered historical wrongs. Race, defined in terms of ancestry or appearance, becomes a convenient proxy for victims of exclusionary policies and practices. As a result, in making amends for past harms, officials can adopt color-conscious policies that treat race as relevant.

Desegregation and affirmative action are the most common examples of color-conscious corrective justice. Precisely because these programs rest on a social rather than a biological understanding of race, they have been highly controversial. According to the programs' defenders, because race was wrongly used to segregate individuals in identifiable neighborhoods, schools, and workplaces, the government stands guilty of social engineering. These wrongs must be cured like a bad hangover with a "hair of the dog." That is, a massive reliance on race to do harm must be cured with a modest reliance on race to do good. Critics of desegregation and affirmative action allege that official demands for racial balance are as misplaced as folklore remedies: The programs do no more than replace one form of social engineering with another. A policy of forced separation is simply supplanted by one of forced togetherness.

For critics like constitutional scholar Herbert Wechsler, two wrongs do not make a right. Racial equality cannot be pursued through a sacrifice of personal freedom. As Wechsler himself put it: "[I]f the freedom of association is denied by segregation, integration forces an association upon those for whom it is unpleasant or repugnant. Is this not the heart of the issue involved, a conflict in human claims of the highest dimension . . . ?"[14] Wechsler did not believe this conflict could be resolved in favor of mandatory desegregation:

> For me, assuming equal facilities, the question posed by state-enforced segregation is not one of discrimination at all. Its human and its constitutional dimensions lie entirely elsewhere, in the denial by the state of freedom to associate, a denial that impinges in the same way on any groups or races that may be involved. I think, and I hope not without foundation, that the Southern white also pays heavily for segregation, not only in the sense of guilt that he must carry but also in the benefits he is denied. . . . Does not the problem of miscegenation show most clearly that it is the freedom of association that at bottom is involved, the only case, I may add, where it is implicit in the situation that association is desired by the only individuals involved?[15]

For Wechsler, then, respect for individual liberty is a surer way to healthy race relations than coerced contact, even if the cost is some degree of continuing segregation. *Loving*'s embrace of colorblindness offers a morally and legally appropriate solution to the problem of regulating race in marriage and elsewhere. According to Wechsler, the official pursuit of racial balance through desegregation and affirmative action is as improper as establishment of a state-run interracial dating service.

Yet, the commitment to colorblindness that seems indisputable in the area of marriage becomes murkier in areas like interracial custody and adoption. In these disputes, the government assumes a primary role in shaping families. Family courts and adoption agencies alike must decide whether race should play any part in placing a child. Based on the principle in *Loving,* any consideration of race in custody or adoption is argu-ably improper. In interracial custody disputes, family court judges have minimized their reliance on race by concluding that it has little or no bearing on which parent can better meet the child's needs. Disregarding race in these cases has seemed particularly appropriate because the cou-ples themselves have chosen to cross the color line to marry and procre-ate. In adoption, however, transracial placements have been engulfed in controversy. Far from treating race as mere genotype or phenotype, opponents of transracial adoptions characterize it as intricately linked to social ties. For these critics, placing black or Native American children with white adoptive parents amounts to "genocide" because it prevents these adoptees from identifying with their ancestry, culture, and racial community.[16]

In the adoption setting, Wechsler's invocation of freedom of associa-tion offers little guidance in fleshing out the meaning of racial equality. An adoption agency must decide whether to honor the affiliative prefer-ences of parents willing to adopt across the color line or of nonwhites who seek to keep a child within a racial community. In evaluating these conflicting claims, officials cannot readily identify a racially neutral prin-ciple of constitutional law. Race-matching in adoption arguably perpetu-ates and reinforces a principle of "separate but equal" families. Yet plac-ing children without regard to race may trivialize cultures and values associated with racially identifiable families. Even if segregated family structures are partly attributable to racial discrimination, individuals to-day assert the freedom to embrace the positive sense of community and culture that has come from resisting racial subordination. Far from using color-conscious policies to eradicate the effects of past wrongs, propo-nents of race-matching in adoption seek to value and affirm racial identi-ties, even those forged in a segregated society.

Eliminating a principle of "separate but equal" families may invade associational claims of racially identifiable communities. But accepting this principle can impede the development of new associational claims. For instance, racial categories on recent census forms have presumed that individuals have a single racial affiliation. Implicitly, this approach is predicated on segregation in marriage and family. The offspring of interracial marriages, sometimes called the "children of *Loving,*" have successfully challenged this classification scheme because it denies them full personhood. When single-race categories are used, the government fails to acknowledge the identity of multiracial persons and denies the legitimacy of interracial families. As a result, the children of *Loving* claim, the government has impeded racial progress and limited freedom to express a sense of self. Here, too, it is hard to find a neutral principle of constitutional law rooted in liberty or equality to guide the use of racial categories on the census. Any form of racial recordkeeping privileges some associations over others, yet a colorblind system arguably neglects the ongoing social importance of race in developing an identity.[17]

These preliminary explorations of interracial intimacy reveal the limitations of Wechsler's analysis, which pits liberty against equality. Wechsler treats liberty and equality as independent concepts that are in fundamental opposition. Even some of his harshest critics adopt the same view, contending that a formally colorblind approach privileges whites' desire not to associate over blacks' quest for equality.[18] In ordering desegregation of schools that were racially identifiable by law, however, the U.S. Supreme Court concluded that "separate educational facilities are inherently unequal."[19] In doing so, the Court suggested that if race is linked to social consequences, equality and association are integrally related. A person's very understanding of race comes through the experience of growing up in racially homogeneous families, schools, and neighborhoods. Wechsler, then, is wrong in treating racial equality and freedom of association as independent principles because associational preferences define racial differences, and racial differences in turn rigidify these preferences. In ordering desegregation, the Court concluded that racial boundaries could be broken down and racial hierarchy undone only through interracial contact.

When interracial contact leads to marriage and family, the very notion of race itself must be revisited. For opponents of transracial adoption, for instance, full-scale integration of families is a threat, not a means, to equality because it jeopardizes racial identity. *Loving* itself offers no clear answer to the question of how race or racial equality should be defined in this context. Its principle of colorblindness, far from being a definitive moral and legal solution, simply allows Americans to revise their assumptions about race, marriage, and family. In doing so, our nation must decide whether race is merely a shorthand for ancestry and appearance or whether it continues to serve as a useful proxy for certain social affiliations and conditions. Acknowledging these social consequences may be important in rectifying histories of discrimination. Moreover, respecting the social implications of race may be crucial to preserving cultures, customs, and values that have evolved in racially identifiable communities.

The regulation of interracial intimacy can yield new insights into the

debate over colorblind and color-conscious policies. By examining carefully the assumptions underlying race and marriage, it will be possible
to understand why *Loving's* strong and uncontroversial norm of colorblindness has persisted, even in the face of high rates of same-race marriage. Through a thorough exploration of basic beliefs about race and
family, it will be possible to see why strong norms of color consciousness
in adoption and on the census also have endured, even when "separate
but equal" policies have been discredited in other areas.

Love and Freedom

Like Williams's account of his childhood in an interracial family, the
Loving opinion turned on more than matters of race and equality. It
also relied on the right to marry free of government interference. This
right to marital freedom reflects the Court's view that intimate associations are integral to self-actualization. Throughout this book, the special
nature of sexual, marital, and family autonomy will shape the discussion
of interracial intimacy. Changing images of sex, marriage, and family
have played an integral role in redefining racial boundaries. A willingness
to harness intimate relationships in the service of the social good often
correlated with repressive racial regimes. The states have not always
adopted a "hands off" approach to sex, marriage, and procreation, nor
has the U.S. Supreme Court been a consistently reliable guardian of
these freedoms. In addition to its support for antimiscegenation laws in
Pace, the Court upheld other state controls on sex and reproduction
based on scientific claims about the dangers of unrestricted procreation.
During the late 1800s and early 1900s, new immigrants from southern
and eastern Europe flocked to America in search of economic opportunity. Their arrival prompted fears of lawless sexuality, which in turn
spawned the social hygiene movement. Social hygienists pressed legislators to regulate sexual conduct by cracking down on vice and prostitution. At the same time, the newcomers created anxieties about dilution
of American genetic stock. Eugenicists demanded that government officials take steps to avoid "race suicide" by limiting immigration and preventing the unfit from bearing children.[20]

The convergence of movements for sexual control and racial purity led
the Court to uphold extreme invasions of procreative freedom, including
mandatory sterilization of the feebleminded and criminals. The measures
were highly controversial, but in 1927, the Court upheld such a law in
Buck v. Bell.[21] Only when World War II demonstrated the perils of

Nazism's embrace of eugenic philosophy did the Court question the propriety of government intrusion into the sacred realm of procreation.[22] As sexual mores changed and racial fears subsided, the Court further distanced itself from its support for regulating sexuality. Beginning in the mid-1960s, the Justices used the doctrine of substantive due process to carve out a constitutionally protected realm of privacy and liberty. In *Griswold v. Connecticut,*[23] the Court struck down a Connecticut law that restricted married persons' access to contraceptives. In finding implicit protections for marital privacy in several constitutional provisions, the Court noted:

> We deal with a right of privacy older than the Bill of Rights. . . . Marriage is a coming together for better or worse, hopefully enduring, and intimate to the degree of being sacred. It is an association that promotes a way of life, not causes; a harmony in living, not political faiths; a bilateral loyalty, not commercial or social projects. Yet it is an association for as noble a purpose as any involved in our prior decisions.[24]

In *Eisenstadt v. Baird,*[25] the Court expanded its reasoning to include unmarried persons. In striking down a Massachusetts statute that prevented doctors from distributing contraceptives to unmarried adults, the Court explained:

> It is true that in *Griswold* the right of privacy in question inhered in the marital relationship. Yet the marital couple is not an independent entity with a mind and heart of its own, but an association of two individuals each with a separate intellectual and emotional makeup. If the right of privacy means anything, it is the right of the *individual,* married or single, to be free from unwarranted governmental intrusion into matters so fundamentally affecting a person as the decision whether to bear or beget a child.[26]

In a series of decisions, the Court made clear that matters related to childrearing and education,[27] family relationships,[28] and procreation, contraception, and abortion[29] were constitutionally protected areas of intimate association.[30]

It is no accident that *Loving v. Virginia* includes an endorsement of marital freedom alongside its discussion of civil rights advances. The refusal to regulate intimacy bolstered the Court's decision to strike down antimiscegenation laws. As its analysis of equal protection doctrine made clear, the state must act rationally when it engages in regulation. Arbitrary and capricious conduct is an abuse of discretion. Moreover, when a racial classification is at issue, the state has to prove that its behavior is "hyperrational": The classification must be necessary to promote a compelling state interest.[31] Without convincing evidence of race's relevance to the grant of a marriage license, the Court in *Loving* had to conclude that bans on intermarriage were irrational and hence impermissible.

The standard of rationality that controls government decisionmaking also rendered the government incompetent to second-guess most individual decisions about sex, marriage, and family. Precisely because the state cannot fathom the idiosyncratic influences that shape marital and sexual preferences, *Loving* treated official interference with intimate choices as suspect. Having required government to behave hyperrationally in matters of race and marriage, *Loving* refrained from any discussion of how individuals should responsibly choose a spouse. And that is as it should be if marital liberty is to be preserved. Keeping individual choice free is particularly important if a norm of rationality is misplaced in matters of the heart. Romantic individualism does not require a lover to weigh the assets and liabilities of a prospective mate. Indeed, someone who uses a résumé to select a spouse would likely be disdained as cold and calculating, perhaps something of a social-climbing opportunist. For this very reason, couples who meet through personal ads or dating services often keep the way that they found each other a secret. Somehow these methods of mating seem contrived: They require people to reduce both themselves and their prospective lovers to nothing more than lists of desirable traits.

The ideology of romantic individualism denies that prospective mates can be treated as the sum of their appealing characteristics. There must be something else, an *X* factor, that makes a person uniquely lovable. As Martha Nussbaum explains:

> [If the ideal lover can be captured through a list of ideal attributes, does]n't this view imply, after all, that one could in principle advertise for a lover, say, in the *New York Review of Books*? (Zeus-type soul, committed to philosophical and ethical values, seeks excellent man with similar aspirations. . . .) And if the list could be complete enough, and if there were in addition some reliable way of making sure that the applicant really had the virtues he purported to have, then didn't the view imply that the successful applicant would be her passionate lover? And wasn't this absurd? Plato['s advocacy of such an approach] is less crude than the advertisement on the epistemological issue, for he insists that real knowledge of habits and ways requires a context of intimacy. You cannot tell beforehand: you go by that trace; you allow yourself, in considerable

ignorance, to be melted. But it looked as if the real presence of these general traits was, in his view, sufficient for passionate love and sufficiently defined love's object. And this seemed bad or absurd enough. It was not only epistemology, surely, that prevented her from taking out such an advertisement.[32]

The *X* factor, as exemplified by romantic individualism, captures the popular commitment to intimacy as an affirmation of personal uniqueness: Relationships are unmediated, unquantifiable, and indescribable. Love and identity are beyond the reach of rational judgment, safe from its reductionist and dehumanizing effects. This humanistic model of decisionmaking has another important consequence: It renders a government that must aspire to rationality incompetent to enter the intimate domain. By regulating romance, a methodically rational state can threaten our very personhood and humanity.[33] Without rationality to provide the measure for evaluating intimate choices, officials are hardpressed to deal with race, sex, and marriage. If true love is like lightning, what can romantic choice have to do with racial justice:

> The light descends from nowhere.
> Why on these two and not on others?
> Doesn't this outrage justice? Yes it does.
> Doesn't it disrupt our painstakingly erected principles,
> and cast the moral from the peak?
> Yes on both accounts.[34]

For the romantic individualist, disproportionate rates of same-race marriage cannot be judged ill under a standard of colorblindness, nor can they be justified by some principle of color consciousness. Marital choices, interracial or not, are simply beyond the pale of rational analysis altogether.[35]

Confronted with the normative indeterminacy surrounding intimacy, officials find themselves at a loss when they must intervene in family matters like custody and adoption disputes. If parental like romantic love is imponderable,[36] how can a person's capacity to bond with a child be ensured, and what could race possibly have to do with such an elemental connection? The very effort to rationalize the placement process seems like an affront to the humanistic *X* factor at the core of marriage and family life. Yet, the state's only method of deciding is rooted in just such an objective evaluation. Precisely because government is an artificial construct and not a person, it cannot be lovestruck or bond with a child. Forced to rely on rational methods of decisionmaking, officials find few clear answers.[37] Should race be treated as irrelevant because differences in ancestry and appearance are no obstacle to the powerful bond between a parent and child? Or should the state use race-matching to enhance the compatibility of parent and child? Should the state abandon any attempt to make a hard and fast rule because the relevance of race turns on the particular individuals involved and their capacity to love across the color line? Can officials make room for the humanistic *X* factor by deferring to individual preferences in the placement process as much as possible? Or is this an abdication of the state's commitment to behave rationally?

Here, again, dilemmas of interracial intimacy demonstrate that the freedom to marry and build families is not independent of race but instead is integral to defining it. In deciding whether race should be relevant to placement, the state is navigating between two worlds: the segregated one we know today and the one that might have been in the absence of racial discrimination. Although the Court accords the freedom to marry and raise children to individuals, these liberties are in fact critical to the formation of communities.[38] As legal historian Robert Cover writes:

> Freedom of association is the most general of the Constitutional doctrinal categories that speak to the creation and maintenance of common life, the social precondition for a *nomos*. . . . Freedom of association implies a degree of norm-generating autonomy on the part of the association. It is not a liberty to *be* but a liberty and capacity to create and interpret law—minimally, to interpret the terms of the association's own being.[39]

In short, the choice of a spouse or the capacity to love a child may involve an impenetrable *X* factor, but our collective choices in turn determine the viability of particular identities and communities. These choices constrain our capacity to know the world. In evaluating the role of race in government decisions about marriage and family, officials have the power to preserve collective associations or destroy them.[40] In weighing the bonds of love in the racially divided world that we know against bonds that might have been in a world free of discrimination, the law of custody and adoption becomes "a system of tension or a bridge linking a concept of reality to an imagined alternative."[41] The bridge is a shaky one, subject to shifting understandings of both race and intimacy. As a result, legal standards remain highly contingent and contested, much like the wavering and uncertain connection of Gregory Howard Williams to his parents.

Conclusion

Williams's memoir reminds us of the power of race and intimacy. Looking back on his early years as a boy navigating uneasily between black and white worlds, he realizes that all of his later professional success cannot shield him from the impact of his racial heritage and family ties:

> I was fortunate to be able to achieve my goal of becoming a lawyer, and later my dream of being a law professor. I have held positions that even in my wildest fantasies during the nights at 601½ Railroad Street I could not envision for myself. Yet when I stand in front of students, my mind often wanders back to the pain and rejection of the Muncie years. Almost as if it were yesterday, I vividly recall watching Dad being beaten by the police, and the day we were chased from the "white" waiting room in Louisville. I never felt more impotent and powerless to control my life than I did in those days. When I think of those times, I remember what Dad used to say:
>
> "Son, one day this will all pale into insignificance."
>
> He was wrong. Muncie has never paled into insignificance. It has lived inside me forever.[42]

The time is long overdue to recognize the singular importance of interracial intimacy. It has not paled into insignificance, nor should it. Interracial intimacy is far more than an incidental consequence of racial equality or a particular proof of personal autonomy. As this book will show, those who choose love across the color line challenge the conventional wisdom that racial equality can be achieved in the absence of a rich network of interracial relationships and that love is truly free when it is cabined by pervasive segregation.

TWO

Antimiscegenation Laws and the Enforcement of Racial Boundaries

ANY HISTORY OF antimiscegenation laws must begin with the regulation of black–white intimacy, but it must not end there. Laws barring sex and marriage between blacks and whites had the longest history and the widest application in the United States. As one historian of intermarriage has pointed out, however, antimiscegenation "laws were enacted first—and abandoned last—in the South, but it was in the West, not the South, that the laws became most elaborate. In the late nineteenth century, western legislators built a labyrinthine system of legal prohibitions on marriages between whites and Chinese, Japanese, Filipinos, Hawaiians, Hindus, and Native Americans, as well as on marriages between whites and blacks."[1] At one time or another, thirty-eight states adopted laws regulating interracial sex and marriage. All of these laws banned black–white relationships, but fourteen states also prohibited Asian–white marriages and another seven barred Native American–white unions.[2] No state ever officially banned Latino–white intermarriage, though, presumably because treaty protections formally accorded former Spanish and Mexican citizens the status of white persons.

Antimiscegenation laws have played an integral role in defining racial identity and enforcing racial hierarchy.[3] To understand the distinctive ways in which antimiscegenation statutes were used to establish norms about race, it is essential to focus on the two groups that suffered the most onerous legal burdens: blacks and Asians. For blacks, the laws identified them as diminished persons marked with the taint of slavery and inferiority, even after they were nominally free. Although the statutes   *17* formally limited the freedom of blacks and whites alike, the restrictions clearly functioned to block black access to the privileges of associating with whites. For Asians, antimiscegenation laws confirmed their status as unassimilable foreigners. Already marked as racially distinct and unfit for citizenship by federal immigration laws, state constraints on intermarriage prevented Asian male immigrants from integrating into communities by thwarting their sexuality, hindering them from developing ties to the United States through marriage, and deterring them from having children who would be American citizens by birth. For both blacks and Asians, segregation in sex, marriage, and family was a hallmark of intense racialization and entrenched inequality.

The Black Experience: Drawing the Color Line and Keeping It in Place

The regulation of sex and marriage played a singularly important role in drawing the color line between whites and blacks. Antimiscegenation laws in the South laid a critical foundation for securing the full personhood of whites and entrenching the diminished status of blacks. Whenever racial ambiguity threatened the established social order, statutory restrictions on interracial sex and marriage were imposed to keep the color line firmly in place. During the colonial era, Southern states faced special challenges in drawing racial boundaries and establishing sexual norms. In New England, settlers were mostly farmers and artisans who arrived with families, settled in towns, and had strong religious traditions. In these homogeneous communities, same-race families were the norm and sex outside of marriage was relatively rare.[4] By contrast, in the Chesapeake world of Virginia and Maryland, settlers came from a wide range of backgrounds. Many arrived alone as indentured servants, who had contracted to work until they paid for their passage to America. No sense of community based on shared origins, townships, or religious beliefs bound the newcomers together. Men outnumbered women by four to one. In addition, the scarcity of marriageable women was exacerbated because indentured female servants could not marry until they completed their terms of service. Under these circumstances, rates of extramarital sex and out-of-wedlock pregnancy soared despite laws punishing fornication, adultery, and rape.[5]

When slavery began to replace indentured servitude as the primary source of labor in the upper South during the last decades of the seventeenth century, white indentured servants often worked in close proximity to black slaves. In some instances, coworkers became sexual intimates, and interracial sex and marriage began to blur the color line.[6] Antimiscegenation laws became a way to draw a rigid boundary between slave and free, black and white. Maryland enacted the first antimiscegenation statute in 1661, and Virginia followed suit one year later. Even before that, Virginia authorities in the 1630s and 1640s had whipped and publicly humiliated those who participated in interracial sexual liaisons.[7]

By punishing interracial sex severely, authorities in Maryland and Virginia sent a clear message that whites were not to adopt the sexual practices of slaves. Slaves typically did not enjoy access to the formal institution of marriage, although they did conduct their own slave marriage rituals. Some slaves practiced polygamy or polygyny, and many did not condemn premarital intercourse. Without social stigma, a woman might have sex and even bear children by a man before having been recognized by other slaves as "married" to him.[8] Legislation prohibiting interracial intimacy clearly condemned these alternative sexual and marital practices as heathen and unfit for right-minded, white Christians.

In the early settlement years, interracial marriage had been tolerated, presumably because of the uncertain racial status of blacks and the shortage of women. As the institution of slavery was consolidated in the late seventeenth century, marriages across the color line became anomalous and dangerous exceptions to the emerging racial hierarchy. Interracial unions enabled black women to control access to their sexuality through marriage, and it enabled black men to occupy a superior position to white women in a patriarchal institution that treated the husband as master. Marriages across the color line could give blacks and their mixed-race offspring access to white economic privileges by affording them the property protections that marriage and inheritance laws offered.[9] Black–white marriages threatened the presumption that blacks were subhuman slaves incapable of exercising authority, demonstrating moral responsibility, and capitalizing on economic opportunity. If whites could share their emotional lives and economic fortunes with blacks, how could blacks be anything less than full persons?

The Chesapeake colonies enacted statutes to ensure that, rather than benefit blacks, interracial marriages would simply degrade Whites. Under Virginia's 1691 law, a white spouse was to be banished from the colony within three months of an interracial wedding. In 1705, Virginia authorized jail sentences of six months for whites married to blacks or mulattoes. In Maryland, "freeborne English women" who married

"Negro slaves" were required to serve their husbands' masters during their husbands' lifetimes.[10] These laws stripped whites of racial privileges based on their intimacy with blacks.

Despite these harsh sanctions, some whites paid the price to marry across the color line. In Maryland in 1681, Nell Butler, known as "Irish Nell," fell in love with a slave known as "Negro Charles." When Nell, an indentured servant, informed Lord Baltimore, her master, of the planned marriage, he warned her that she and all her descendants would live as slaves. Unswayed and defiant, Nell replied that she would rather marry Charles than Lord Baltimore himself. She did marry Charles and spent the rest of her life working for his masters, probably as an indentured servant. Had she not married Charles, her contract of servitude with Lord Baltimore would have ended in four or five years. Nell reportedly died "much broken and an old woman." Still, Lord Baltimore was wrong about Nell's offspring. In the eighteenth century, a Maryland court held that neither Nell nor her descendants could be slaves. Subsequently, masters complained of runaway mulatto slaves who claimed to be "descendants of the famous Nell Butler."[11]

As the story of Irish Nell suggests, the problem of mulatto offspring was a serious one in a slave economy predicated on a clearcut boundary between whites and blacks. Despite laws punishing interracial sex, one-fifth of children born out of wedlock at the end of the seventeenth century were mulattoes.[12] Whether slave or free, these mulattoes complicated the enforcement of slavery and compromised its claims to moral authority. Mulatto slaves who could pass as white were considered particularly risky property because they could easily run away and escape detection. In 1835 in Virginia, whites refused to bid on one male slave because he was "too white" and might "too easily escape from slavery and pass himself as a free man." Later on, light-skinned mulatto slaves were used to call into question the very propriety of slavery. A favorite theme of abolitionist literature was the "white slave," who reminded white audiences that they too might be held in bondage.[13]

With widespread interracial sex that threatened the color line, the Virginia legislature had to define and ultimately confine the relevance of the mulatto. A 1705 law classified a mulatto as "the child of an Indian and the child, grandchild, or great grandchild of a negro."[14] During the Revolutionary era, high rates of emancipation coupled with Virginia's "one-fourth black" rule allowed some free mixed-race individuals to claim the privileges of whites, although they obviously had some African ancestry. Officials concluded that "[m]ulattoes must be made black, and the unfreedom of blacks must be defined and made universal."[15] To this end, the upper South adopted a one-drop rule, which defined as black any person with traceable African ancestry.

The adoption of a rule of hypodescent kept blacks from transmitting special privileges to the next generation through interracial sex or marriage. This racial tax on offspring precluded them from gaining official recognition of their white ancestry. By erasing their white heritage, the racial classification scheme converted mulattoes into blacks by a type of parthenogenesis: It was almost as though the child had been generated by a single parent without intercourse across the color line. As slavery hardened the lines between whites and blacks, the racial tax on mulattoes increased. Their curtailed privileges clearly identified them as nonwhite, and even the lightest mulattoes were denied the privileges of whiteness.

The imperative of consolidating racial boundaries was so great that Chesapeake authorities were willing to undo the legal tradition of paterfamilias. A long-standing English rule mandated that a child's status follow that of the father. Given the initial scarcity of white women in the Chesapeake, most interracial sex probably took place between white men and black women. As a result, the majority of mulatto offspring were free under the English approach. In 1662, Virginia departed from tradition by making a child's status follow that of the mother.[16] Under this matrilineal approach, children like Irish Nell's would be free, but most mulattoes would be slaves. Even mulattoes born to white mothers enjoyed only tenuous liberties. Under a 1691 Virginia law, they could still be sold as servants until the age of thirty. Mulattoes could not hold public office, and by 1723, free mulattoes were stripped of many of the privileges—including voting and the unrestricted right to bear arms— that white citizens enjoyed.[17] Virginia authorities also were concerned that doting white fathers might subvert laws that made their mulatto offspring slaves by emancipating them. To discourage manumission of mulatto offspring, masters had to send their freedmen out of the colony, and authorities were encouraged to eliminate roving bands of "negroes, mulattoes, and other slaves [perhaps Indians]."[18] In 1723, Virginia made private emancipation even more difficult.[19] Restricting the liberty of racially ambiguous mulattoes was essential to ensuring their definition as nonwhite.

Despite formal, legal restrictions, an influential and powerful white father sometimes could rely on his privileged position to win local—

albeit fragile and informal—acceptance of a mixed-race child. In 1805 in Campbell County, Virginia, Robert Wright, the mulatto son of a wealthy white landowning father and black slave mother, inherited his father's estate and became a well-to-do planter. Robert's father, a lifelong bachelor, was estranged from his white brothers and sisters and determined to pass on his substantial holdings to his beloved only son. With his father's support and guidance, Robert learned to manage the land and gained entry into the uppermost echelons of Campbell County's white society. One year after inheriting his father's property, Robert married a white woman. Although the county clerk and minister never recorded the marriage because of its illegality, Robert and his wife lived openly as a married couple and had a child together without being ostracized by their white neighbors.

Robert's troubles began when his wife ran away with a white man. In petitioning Virginia legislators for divorce so that he could marry another white woman, Robert sought formal acceptance of his white privilege, but the jerry-built, informal status of his father's making could not survive legal scrutiny. In his petition, Robert emphasized that he, his wife, and her lover were all free. He argued that despite the ban on interracial marriage, the union was "to all intents and purposes valid and binding between the parties" because they had obtained a marriage license and been married by a clergyman. Even if the minister had destroyed the marriage certificate, the marriage clearly had been recognized as valid for approximately a decade in the Campbell County community. White citizens in the community wrote in support of Robert's petition, noting his propriety, kindness to his wife, and reputation as "an honest, upright, and good citizen."[20]

Despite Robert's status in Campbell County, the state of Virginia could not permit its official ban on interracial marriage to be subverted. The Virginia House of Delegates decisively rejected Robert's divorce petition, making clear that "Robert Wright could be married to a white woman in his community, [but] he could not be married to her in law."[21] With the illusion of his whiteness destroyed, Robert lost standing in Campbell County. On tax rolls, his designation was changed from "White" to "M," for mulatto. When he persisted in living with the white woman he had hoped to wed, many of his neighbors condemned his public adultery. Humiliated and ostracized, Robert died at the age of 38, two years after the House of Delegates stripped away the pretense of his whiteness.[22]

Robert Wright's story is remarkable primarily because it demonstrates the privileges that white fathers could confer on mulatto offspring even in the face of antimiscegenation laws. Robert's father demonstrated his power as a white landowner in the community by subverting the legal restrictions on his mulatto son's ability to manage a white man's estate, mingle with the white elite, and marry a white woman. Yet even someone as influential as Robert's father could not create a foolproof escape from restrictions on personhood and identity that were essential to the preservation of racial inequality. Once Robert's wife left him for a white lover, the mulatto's manliness and his entitlement to the privileges of whiteness were called into question. Robert was no longer free to marry the woman of his choice, and his neighbors ceased to think of him as morally deserving or racially white. Robert's despoiled identity as mulatto was marked by incursions on his autonomy to associate with whites as he pleased.

In other instances, though, informal recognition of mulatto children reinforced racial hierarchy and subverted sexual mores that condemned incest and adultery. For example, in antebellum Loudon County, Virginia, a quadroon slave woman named Ary lived with her white paternal uncle. There she became the concubine of her young master, who also was her cousin. Far from challenging racial privilege, Ary's circumstances reinforced it: She avoided associating too closely with blacks, perhaps remembering her master's admonition not to get involved with "colored men" because they "weren't good enough" for her.[23] Nor did the situation trigger outrage at her sexual exploitation: Ary insisted that she was her father's favorite child, and she proudly described her elite white heritage and her young master's attentions to her. The price of Ary's sense of superiority to blacks was a complete dependency on white male relatives for validation of her racial and sexual worth. Because of their racial privilege, these men could define Ary's identity wholly in relation to their sexual needs, regardless of their relationship to her as father, uncle, or cousin.

In general, interracial relationships were tolerated only insofar as they left norms of racial and sexual privilege intact. By deprecating white women who cohabited or had intercourse with blacks, the affairs could be dismissed as indecent and depraved. According to historian Martha Hodes, local communities regularly turned a blind eye to black or mulatto men and poor white women who lived together as man and wife, so long as they remained on the outskirts of white society. These long-term liaisons as well as brief sexual encounters could be explained by characterizing the women as low-class and licentious.[24] For instance, in North Carolina in 1825, Polly Lane, a white indentured servant, accused Jim, a slave, of rape. Although Jim pleaded innocent, he was convicted and sentenced to death. As Jim awaited execution, white neighbors noted that Polly appeared to be pregnant, and they became suspicious of her claim of rape.[25] Four doctors submitted a statement that "without an excitation of lust, or the enjoyment of pleasure in the venereal act, no conception can probably take place."[26] When Polly gave birth to a child declared to be of "mixed blood," Jim was eventually pardoned "in part by invoking the white woman's bad reputation, thereby demonstrating that a poor and transgressing white woman could be worth less to elite whites than the profitable labor of a slave."[27]

Where the pressure to consolidate racial and sexual norms was less intense, sex across the color line was commonplace despite its racially ambiguous consequences. White men enjoyed ready and open access to black and mulatto women as a mark of their untrammeled freedom and privilege. In the lower South, for example, free mulattoes were rare and posed little threat to the system of slavery. The issue of interracial sex was openly debated in newspapers in South Carolina in the 1730s, and one anonymous poet wondered: "Kiss me black or white, why need it trouble you?"[28] This laissez-faire attitude toward sex across the color line allowed wealthy white planters regularly to indulge their appetite for black and mulatto women. In New Orleans and Charleston, there was a profitable "fancy trade" in mulatto women, who brought twice the price of a prime field hand. Free mulatto women went to quadroon balls in New Orleans to meet wealthy white men. Under a system of concubinage known as "placage," the men could make formal arrange-ments to support the women for a few years or for life in exchange for sexual services.[29] Without fear of social reprisal, plantation owners set up special residences for black and mulatto mistresses, and some slave owners even went so far as to bring concubines into their own homes, where their white wives had to endure the humiliation in silence.[30] At a time when the New England colonies and upper South frowned on extramarital sexuality, planters in the lower South openly flouted the norm of fidelity in marriage. Tolerance of concubinage commodified black and mulatto women, but it also damaged the status of white women. One northern visitor to the South in 1809 remarked that the "dull, frigid insipidity, and reserve" of southern women was one of the most insidious costs of slavery.[31]

The lower South's tolerance for interracial relationships was linked to an unwillingness to adopt hard and fast legal definitions of blackness. As Judge William Harper wrote in 1835:

> We cannot say what admixture of negro blood will make a colored person. The condition of the individual is not to be determined solely by distinct and visible mixture of negro blood, but by reputation, by his reception into society, and his having commonly exercised the privileges of a white man. . . . [I]t may be well and proper, that a man of worth, honesty, industry, and respectability, should have the rank of a white man, while a vagabond of the same degree of blood should be confined to the inferior caste.[32]

A flexible classification scheme permitted mulattoes to earn the privileges of whiteness through personal accomplishments and social connections. This reward system enhanced the mulattoes' value to whites as racial mediators: Mulattoes would not identify too closely with blacks, for fear of jeopardizing the benefits associated with their White heritage. Tolerance for mulattoes was so great in some parts of the lower South that they were able to establish themselves as a separate elite. In Louisiana, mulattoes amassed large estates and slaves to work their properties, educated their children abroad, and developed their own elegant, cultural traditions. Labeled "Creoles," these highly successful mulattoes kept their social distance from both whites and blacks by adopting a norm of endogamy, or in-marriage.[33]

By the 1850s, the industrial revolution had transformed the textile industry, and the demand for cotton had grown dramatically. Southern planters needed a growing number of slaves, and the proportion of mulattoes in bondage increased. As the slave population became "lighter," the free mulatto population seemed increasingly anomalous and dangerous. Grand juries were convened to identify the hazards associated with free mulattoes. As one jury concluded, "We should have but two classes, the Master and the slave, and no intermediate class can be other than immensely mischievous to our peculiar institution."[34] When the lower South found it necessary to rigidify racial boundaries, it followed the lead set in the upper South. States punished interracial sexual contacts, encouraged free people of color (of whom 75 percent were mulatto) to leave the jurisdiction, and adopted a one-drop rule that denied the relevance of mixed-race origins altogether. Vigilantes reinforced these legal changes by punishing those who had interracial sex and by threatening free people of color with violence.[35]

Although the one-drop rule had been consolidated in the South before the Civil War, the war and its aftermath threatened to undo racial boundaries. Nothing was better calculated than the prospect of inter-racial sex and marriage to stir up fears that the color line was crumbling completely. For this reason, when calling for emancipation, orthodox abolitionists shunned the issue of sex and marriage across racial bound-aries. Indeed, when freethinker Francis Wright established an interracial community and called for amalgamation of the races, she was promptly dubbed the "priestess of Beelzebub" and dropped by mainstream aboli-tionists who feared her radicalism would hurt the movement.[36] Similarly, after the war, most Reconstruction efforts focused on "political" equality, such as the right to vote, sit on juries, and hold office. Republican re-formers deflected concerns that political equality would lead to "social" equality, as typified by race-mixing in integrated communities. When southern Democrats coined the term *miscegenation* to ridicule the quest for racial equality during Reconstruction, Republicans chided their op-ponents for implying that cross-racial sexual liaisons were even tempt-ing.[37] The distinction between political and social equality made clear that the races would remain separate and distinct. Blacks would be for-mally rehabilitated as full persons before the law, but they would remain subordinate in informal and intimate spheres of life.

Although a few southern states did eliminate antimiscegenation laws after the Civil War, black–white intermarriage dropped sharply. The decline is particularly striking because of the strong incentives for white women to cross the color line. The ranks of white males had been deci-mated by the bloody conflict, and black men enjoyed newfound status and freedom of movement. Yet only in places with a particularly liberal view of race relations like New Orleans did some white women become involved with black men.[38] Presumably, the harsh pressures of public opinion prevented white women and black men from crossing the color line. Many white southerners blamed their defeat on the corrupting in-fluence of miscegenation:

> It does seem strange that so lovely a climate, and country, with a people in every way superior to the Yankees, should be overrun and destroyed by them. But I believe that God has ordered it all, and I am firmly of the opinion . . . that it is the judgement of the Almighty because the human and brute blood have mingled to the degree it has in the slave states. Was it not so in the French and British Islands and see what has become of them.[39]

To prevent further transgressions, self-appointed vigilante groups delivered swift and terrible punishment to black men suspected of consorting with white women. The Ku Klux Klan formed at about this time, and it sometimes lynched freedmen prominent in Reconstruction politics under the guise of retribution for the mistreatment of white women.[40] Through this clandestine attack on interracial relations, whites were able to send a clear message that political equality would not dismantle the color line. Restrictions on sex, marriage, and family would continue to be a cornerstone in defining racial difference.

Although black men suspected of having sex with white women could be lynched,[41] black women were unable to fend off the advances of white men. Ironically, once slavery ended, black and mulatto women found it more difficult than during the antebellum period to limit their sexual availability to only one white male. As a result, the number of mulatto offspring increased after emancipation. Reconstruction legislators did try to protect black and mulatto women from sexual exploitation. Efforts to outlaw concubinage failed, but some states adopted bastardy statutes that enabled black and mulatto women to file paternity suits so that white men would be forced to support their illegitimate mulatto children. These bastardy statutes eventually were repealed.[42]

Even though interracial marriages were exceedingly rare during Reconstruction, white southern males promptly reinstated antimiscegenation laws when they regained control of state legislatures in the post-Reconstruction era. With the one-drop rule of racial classification in place,[43] the color line could once again be officially consolidated by regulating sex and marriage. Under this regime, antimiscegenation laws became critical to conserving the integrity and purity of the white race. Without these prohibitions, blacks could gain access to white wealth and privilege through marriage. After all, in black–white marriages, the one-drop rule dictated that the heirs to white fortunes would be black.

Interracial sexuality outside of marriage became a means of establishing racial power and domination. White men could enjoy the sexual favors of black women with impunity, but black men would pay with their lives for sexual contact with white women. When white men impregnated black women, the offspring were illegitimate and generally could not even seek support from their fathers. The children of these black–white relationships threatened neither white identity nor privilege. By contrast, if black men had adulterous relations with married white women, any resulting offspring threatened the racial integrity of white men's families. After Reconstruction, then, antimiscegenation laws reaffirmed antebellum definitions of racial identity and reasserted the superiority of whites as marital partners. White men expressed their sexual dominance by policing access to white women and enjoying the favors of black women without obligations of marriage or support.

The Chinese and Japanese Experience: Racial Unassimilability and Sexual Subordination

Although antimiscegenation laws were used to draw racial boundaries between whites and blacks during the colonial era and early years of nationhood, the color line was well-established by the time Chinese and Japanese began to immigrate to the United States in substantial numbers during the mid- to late 1800s.[44] Definitions of blackness evolved through state legislation, but for Asians, federal immigration law made their status as nonwhite wholly unambiguous. Much of the racialization of Asians took place as successive waves of immigrants were labeled nonwhite, unassimilable, and unfit for citizenship. The Chinese were the first to arrive, coming in substantial numbers after 1848 when gold was discovered in California.[45] Early on, the U.S. government made plain that the Chinese were not white. Under a 1790 naturalization law, only "free white persons" were eligible for citizenship.[46] When Chan Yong applied for citizenship in 1854, a federal district court denied his application because he did not qualify as white, although newspaper accounts at the time stated that he was lighter-skinned than most Chinese.[47]

After the Civil War, race relations in America were contested. Congress amended the naturalization law to permit "aliens of African nativity" and "persons of African descent" to petition for citizenship. When the naturalization law was codified in 1875, the reference to "free white person" was dropped, leaving open the possibility that the Chinese could naturalize. Chinese immigrants quickly capitalized on the statutory uncertainty by filing petitions for naturalization in San Francisco.[48] Shortly thereafter, a federal court made clear that as nonwhites, Chinese immigrants continued to be ineligible for citizenship.[49]

A few years later, the federal government went even further in defining the Chinese as undesirable nonwhite aliens. In 1882, by an overwhelming margin, Congress passed the Chinese Exclusion Act, the first statute to ban a group from immigrating to the United States based solely on race or ethnicity. The Act prohibited any Chinese laborer or miner from entering the United States, and it barred any state or federal court from naturalizing any Chinese.[50] After passage of the Act, the Chinese population in the United States declined precipitously.[51] Periodically renewed and strengthened by Congress,[52] the law remained in force until 1952 when the McCarran-Walter Act nullified racial restrictions and substituted a quota system for immigration based on national origin.[53]

The Japanese began to arrive in the United States about twenty years after the Chinese. Most Japanese emigrated to Hawaii to work in the sugar industry, and their numbers were small because of restrictive Japanese emigration policies.[54] After 1890, two important changes in Japanese immigration occurred. First, the number of immigrants increased substantially so that by 1910, the Japanese outnumbered the Chinese; and second, Japanese immigrants began to arrive in the western continental United States, particularly California, to replace the dwindling numbers of Chinese laborers and to escape low wages and poor working conditions in Hawaii.[55] Having observed the mistreatment of the Chinese, the Japanese struggled to avoid occupying the same place in the racial hierarchy by distinguishing themselves from the Chinese under federal naturalization policy. Although the 1790 law permitted only whites to become citizens, the Chinese Exclusion Act of 1882 withheld the privilege of naturalization only from the Chinese. Several hundred Japanese successfully petitioned for citizenship in lower federal courts on the ground that they were not covered by legislation targeting the Chinese.[56] The federal government soon moved to clarify the status of the Japanese as nonwhite. In 1905, the U.S. attorney general informed President Theodore Roosevelt that the Japanese were and always had been ineligible for naturalization based on their race. One year later, the attorney general issued a formal opinion to that effect.[57]

Despite this setback, the Japanese continued to try to win favorable treatment under immigration laws by highlighting their capacity to assimilate to an American way of life. In a 1922 case, Takao Ozawa asked that his petition for naturalization be granted because the word *free* was more important than the word *white* in determining eligibility of "free white persons" for citizenship. Ozawa insisted that even though he was nonwhite, he should be allowed to naturalize because he could successfully shoulder the responsibilities of democratic freedom.[58] Despite Ozawa's proofs of good moral character and individual accomplishment, the U.S. Supreme Court denied his eligibility for citizenship. According to the Court, Ozawa's status as nonwhite barred him from naturalization, regardless of his ability to conform to an American way of life.[59] Race was a categorical stigma, one that did not permit individuals to escape through acculturation and achievement.

The federal government's treatment of immigrants from India cemented the racialization of Asians.[60] Unlike the Chinese and Japanese, Asian Indians were treated as Caucasian under the prevailing scientific taxonomy. Even so, the U.S. attorney general refused to find that Asian Indians qualified as "free white persons,"[61] but several federal district courts reached a different conclusion.[62] To remedy the confusion, the U.S. Supreme Court made clear in its 1923 decision in *United States v. Thind*[63] that Asian Indians were ineligible for citizenship because they were nonwhite. According to *Thind*, Congress used the term *white* rather than *Caucasian* because it was relying on popular, not scientific, conceptions of race. As the Court explained: "It may be true that the blond Scandinavian and the brown Hindu have a common ancestor in the dim reaches of antiquity, but the average man knows perfectly well that there are unmistakable and profound differences between them today. . . ."[64] Just as personal accomplishments could not save the Japanese, science could not save the Asian Indian from racialization. All Asians—whether Chinese, Japanese, or Asian Indian—had been definitively categorized as nonwhite. Any claims of racial ambiguity were decisively laid to rest by Congress, the attorney general, and the Supreme Court.

By labeling Asian immigrants unassimilable and unfit for citizenship, the federal government made them easy targets for racial discrimination in the western states where they settled. Bans on intermarriage were one of a number of state restrictions on Asian immigrants' liberties, all of which were designed to mark them as inferior and undesirable. With the color line clearly drawn by federal immigration laws, the statutes reinforced the temporary status of Asian sojourners, who came to the United States to work and then return to their home countries. Antimiscegenation laws marked the newcomers' marginal and subordinate status, prevented them from developing permanent ties to America through marriage and family, and severely restricted sexual options for Asian men in bachelor communities.

The racialized imagery that informed federal immigration policy dominated debates about the personhood of Asians. Popular accounts analogized the Chinese to blacks because of their willingness to work in conditions akin to slavery, their incapacity to handle freedom, and their distinctive physical appearance.[65] One politician compared the Chinese to Native Americans and recommended their removal to reservations.[66] These racial images in turn were linked to a degraded sexuality. One

California magazine confirmed the depravity of Chinese women by noting that their physical appearance was "but a slight removal from the African race."[67] As early as 1854, the *New York Tribune* characterized the Chinese as "lustful and sensual in their dispositions; every female is a prostitute of the basest order."[68] Other journals claimed that debauched Chinese males went to Sunday school only to ravage white female teachers. Readers were warned that Chinese men could not be left alone with children, especially little girls. Sexual anxieties about the Chinese were exacerbated by religious differences, as Christian missionaries sought to proselytize a people characterized as base and lecherous pagans.[69]

California's laws were particularly important because so many Asian immigrants resided there. During the convention to draft the 1879 California constitution, the chairman of the Committee on the Chinese warned: "Were the Chinese to amalgamate at all with our people, it would be the lowest, most vile and degraded of our race, and the result of that amalgamation would be a hybrid of the most despicable, a mongrel of the most detestable that has ever afflicted the earth."[70] To address these concerns, the delegates proposed an 1878 constitutional amendment to restrict intermarriage of Chinese and whites: "The intermarriage of white persons with Chinese, negroes, mulattoes, or persons of mixed blood, descended from a Chinaman or negro from the third generation, inclusive, or their living together as man and wife in this State, is hereby prohibited. The Legislature shall enforce this section by appropriate legislation."[71] The California electorate ratified the provision the following year, and the California legislature quickly moved to enact antimiscegenation statutes. The California Civil Code was amended in 1880 to prohibit the issuance of marriage licenses authorizing the union of "a white person with a negro, mulatto, or Mongolian."[72]

Although levels of interracial sex and marriage among whites and Chinese were quite low, the California legislature criminalized Chinese–white intermarriage in 1901.[73] That same year, the legislation was held unconstitutional based on a procedural defect.[74] California did not reenact the statute until 1905, primarily in response to intensified concerns about amalgamation with a new group of Asian immigrants, the Japanese.[75] As with the Chinese, Americans feared what they presumed to be Japanese immigrants' alien racial identity and unbridled sexual impulses. When the Japanese government successfully lobbied for its nationals to be exempted from laws that segregated the Chinese, political leaders warned of the dangers of white girls "sitting side by side in the school rooms with matured Japs, with their base minds, their lascivious thoughts, multiplied by their race and strengthened by their mode of life."[76] California's 1905 antimiscegenation law reflected fears of both racial difference and sexual deviance. The statute addressed eugenic concerns that Asian immigrants were a threat to the "self-preservation of [the white] race"[77] as well as anxieties about the lawless sexuality of Japanese immigrants.[78]

Even with state antimiscegenation laws in place, concerns about Asian intermarriage persisted. In 1907, Congress had passed an Expatriation Act,[79] which stripped American women of their citizenship if they married foreign nationals. In 1922, in response to protests from women's groups, Congress passed the Cable Act. In general, the Act did away with the practice of treating a woman's nationality as derivative of her husband's, thereby assuring a wife the freedom to choose her own allegiance. In the area of race, though, women who crossed the color line to marry Asian immigrants remained disempowered. The Cable Act continued to strip American women of their citizenship if they married aliens ineligible to naturalize. The marital autonomy of white women was sacrificed to preserve racial distinctions.

Moreover, the Cable Act made it more difficult than before for American men, usually native-born Chinese, to bring their wives from China. Because a woman's nationality was now independent of her husband's, the U.S. Supreme Court interpreted the Act as barring Chinese women from entering the country based on marriage to an American citizen. Previously, the women had been able to come to the United States but not naturalize. These provisions remained in effect for ten years.[80] Unable to bring wives from China and barred by antimiscegenation laws from marrying white women, even American-born Chinese had limited marital options. Citizenship by birth did not spare them from the adverse consequences of racial difference.

Restrictive immigration policies and state bans on intermarriage had particularly harsh consequences for the Chinese, who were denied access to wives of any race. Federal policy treated the Chinese as sojourners—temporary male workers who would eventually return to their homelands after fulfilling their labor contracts. Poor, unable to speak English, and unfamiliar with American customs, Chinese immigrants were ill-equipped to challenge their isolation. Many of them could not even afford their wives' additional passage. These obstacles were compounded by cultural tradition, which dictated that Chinese women join their husbands' extended families. This practice cemented the family's expectation that the men would return someday and send remittances in the meantime.[81]

Given this combination of federal policy, limited resources, and cultural traditions, the number of Chinese women coming to the United States during the 1800s was minuscule. In 1852, of 11,794 Chinese, only 7 were female. By 1870, Chinese men outnumbered Chinese women in the United States by 14 to 1. These severe imbalances in turn led to images of sexual deprivation and degradation. Men living without women in bachelor communities seemed deviant and dangerous. The few Chinese women in the United States were vulnerable to sexual exploitation, which reinforced the image of sojourners as predatory and debauched. According to the 1870 census, 61 percent of Chinese women were "prostitutes," while only 21 percent were "housekeepers."[82] Chinese women regularly worked in the sex trade after having been lured to the United States with promises of marriage, abducted, or sold into indentured servitude by needy families.

Antimiscegenation laws arguably played a more significant role in sending messages of racial inferiority than in thwarting interracial relationships. Anxieties about lustful Chinese bachelors harming white women appear to have been largely unfounded. Although interracial sex between blacks and whites remained relatively commonplace even under antimiscegenation laws, Chinese men were unlikely to cross the color line to cohabit and procreate with white women. During the early decades of Chinese migration, only the most affluent and powerful Chinese might dare to take a white wife or mistress.[83] The linguistic and cultural isolation of the Chinese, their segregation in immigrant enclaves, and their vulnerability to deportation—all of these factors undoubtedly made affairs with white women an unlikely prospect, and Chinese men frequently remained childless bachelors. Indeed, even as late as the 1920s and 1930s, many Chinese men chose to remain single rather than intermarry. According to Los Angeles County marriage records for 1924–1933, of the Chinese who married, only 23.7 percent had a non-Chinese spouse. Given that there were nine Chinese men for every two Chinese women at the time, the majority of Chinese men must have remained alone.[84] Although there is little evidence that the Chinese pursued white women for sex and marriage, western states continued to threaten the immigrants with criminal prosecution under antimiscegenation laws.

Far from alleviating the problems of bachelor communities, Congress consistently enacted immigration policies that worsened the gender imbalances. In 1875, the Page Law barred Chinese prostitutes from entering the country. Tough interrogation techniques were used to enforce the ban. In fact, the law was so intimidating that the number of Chinese women coming to the United States dropped by 68 percent between 1876 and 1882.[85] Shortly after the Chinese Exclusion Act was passed, a federal court in 1844 held that Chinese women assumed the status of their laborer husbands and were barred from entry. Only the wives of lawfully domiciled merchants could enter the United States.[86] Immigration laws were so effective in deterring family creation that, in 1890, only 8.7 percent of the Chinese in the United States were native born.[87] Restrictive immigration policies coupled with antimiscegenation laws confirmed the sojourner's status as a dehumanized and degraded laborer: "Permitted neither to procreate nor to intermarry, the Chinese immigrant was told, in effect, to re-emigrate, die out—white America would not be touched by his presence."[88]

The only relief that the Chinese had from harsh immigration policies came with the 1906 San Francisco earthquake. Because official records had been destroyed, Chinese men claimed to be native-born citizens who could bring their wives from China to the United States. Between 1907 and 1924, ten thousand Chinese women entered the country. By contrast, before 1900, only slightly more than forty-five hundred Chinese women lived in America.[89] This loophole was closed in 1924 when Congress restricted entry of Chinese women to students and wives of clergymen, professors, and government officials.[90] One year later, the U.S. Supreme Court upheld the law, even though it barred native-born Chinese from bringing their spouses to America.[91] The Chinese themselves felt the bitter sting of the federal government's efforts to restrict female immigration: "We were beginning to repopulate a little now so they passed this law to make us die out altogether."[92]

In contrast to the Chinese, Japanese immigrants were able to build same-race families in the United States. Although the Japanese also arrived as *dekaseginin,* or "men who go out to work," they soon were converted to *teiju,* or "permanent residents abroad."[93] Arriving in California in the midst of anti-Chinese hysteria, the Japanese quickly concluded that sojourner status would subordinate and humiliate them. With the support of the Japanese government, the newcomers embarked on a strategy of settlement to ensure economic independence, social standing, and self-respect.[94] Integral to this strategy was the immigration of Japanese women, who could help to build stable, self-sufficient families and communities. When the United States moved to restrict immigrant labor from Japan, a 1908 "Gentleman's Agreement" permitted Japanese residents to bring members of their immediate family to the United States.[95] The agreement protected the Japanese from the hardships of bachelor communities. In 1905–8, 16 percent of Japanese immigrants were women, but by 1909–14, the proportion exceeded 50 percent.[96] The ongoing arrival of Japanese women rapidly rectified gender imbalances in the immigrant community. In 1900, there were almost five Japanese men for every Japanese woman. By 1910, the ratio had dropped to 3.5 to 1, and by 1920, it was only 1.6 to 1. Moreover, nearly every adult Japanese female was married.[97]

Despite these important differences between the Chinese and Japanese immigrant experiences, both groups triggered anxieties about race-mixing. Fears associated with bachelor communities persisted for the Chinese, but the fears surrounding the Japanese arguably should have dissipated by the 1920s. The Japanese had built prosperous families and communities in the United States. Carefully screened by the Japanese government, immigrants arrived with higher rates of literacy and more material resources than their counterparts from Europe.[98] A number of Japanese became entrepreneurs, running successful farms and small businesses. In addition to their economic accomplishments, Japanese immigrants were able to forge stable, same-race families due to the steady influx of women from their home country.

Because the Japanese represented the anomaly of nonwhites with material resources, however, their self-contained communities sparked conflicting anxieties about their sexual and marital proclivities among whites. Some whites concluded that the Japanese settlements were proof of the immigrants' unassimilability and chauvinism. As one witness from California testified before the Senate Committee on Immigration in 1924:

> [W]ith great pride of race, they have no idea of assimilating in the sense of amalgamation. They do not come to this country with any desire or intent to lose their racial or national identity. They come here specifically and professedly for the purpose of colonizing and establishing here permanently the proud Yamato race. They never cease to be Japanese. They have as little desire to intermarry as have the whites, and there can be no proper amalgamation, you will agree, without intermarriage. In Hawaii, where there is every incentive for intermarriage, the Japanese have preserved practical racial purity. . . .[99]

At the same time, the Japanese immigrants' ability to establish farms and businesses raised fears that they would try to convert their economic success into sexual and marital privilege. One farmer worried that property and wealth would lead Japanese men to covet white wives with disastrous consequences:

> Near my home is an eighty-acre tract of as fine land as there is in California. On that tract lives a Japanese. With that Japanese lives a white woman. In that woman's arms is a baby. What is that baby? It isn't Japanese. It isn't white. I'll tell you what that baby is. It is a germ of the mightiest problem that ever faced this state; a problem that will make the black problem of the South look white.[100]

Concerns about the Japanese immigrants' sexuality were magnified by their integration into white schools and communities. Anti-Japanese propaganda warned that the Japanese were "casting furtive glances at our young women. They would like to marry them."[101]

Despite widespread fears that prosperous Japanese men would prey on white women, the rate of outmarriage among first-generation Japanese, or *Issei,* was quite low. Los Angeles County marriage records between 1924 and 1933 indicate that of *Issei* women who married, only 1.7 percent wed non-Japanese men; of the *Issei* men who married, fewer than 3 percent had non-Japanese brides. This was the lowest rate of outmarriage for any racial group in the area. By comparison, of blacks who married, 11.3 percent had nonblack spouses, and of Chinese who married, 23.7 percent wed non-Chinese.[102] Nor is there any evidence that the Japanese regularly evaded antimiscegenation laws through extramarital affairs with whites that produced illegitimate offspring.

The self-sufficiency and success of Japanese communities presented a singular challenge in interpreting the significance of antimiscegenation laws. Although bans on intermarriage could be interpreted as an unequivocal mark of racial subordination for blacks and Chinese, the same was not true for the Japanese. By building prosperous, autonomous communities, Japanese immigrants appeared to be exercising the freedom to forge a separate but equal society in the shadow of racial restrictions. Confronted with a nonwhite population that defied easy categorization as inferior or dependent, whites could no longer assume that low intermarriage rates automatically signalled a diminished status. To preserve a sense of white superiority, the lack of Japanese–white relationships had to be attributed either to Japanese chauvinism or to thwarted sexuality.

The Filipino Experience: Not Compliance but Defiance

Although the Chinese and Japanese generally abided by restrictions on intermarriage, one group of Asian immigrants refused to accept race-based limits on their sexual and marital autonomy. Unlike other Asian immigrants, Filipinos arrived in the United States steeped in the American democratic tradition. Convinced of their entitlement to full personhood, Filipinos fought vigorously for the freedom to date and marry as they saw fit.

Filipinos arrived on the West Coast, particularly California, in the 1920s and 1930s.[103] Like the Chinese, most Filipino immigrants were male: In 1930, there were 40,904 Filipino men but only 1,640 women. By 1940, of the Filipinos in the United States, there were still seven men for every woman.[104] They, too, formed bachelor communities and sparked fears of miscegenation.[105] Popular accounts portrayed the Filipinos as lascivious dandies with a taste for white women. One anti-Filipino spokesman described the immigrants as "little brown men attired like 'Solomon in all his glory,' strutting like peacocks and endeavoring to attract the eyes of young American and Mexican girls."[106] The president of the Immigration Study Commission warned of race-mingling between "Filipino coolie fathers and low-grade white mothers," whose numerous offspring could become "a serious burden."[107] Sexual anxieties reached such a pitch that race riots broke out in 1930 when white men became angry at Filipino men who were socializing with white women.[108]

Filipinos reacted defiantly to efforts to control their sexuality. Unique among Asian immigrants, Filipinos arrived not from a foreign country but from an American territory. As a result, they had been educated in American schools, spoke English, and were familiar with American history and civics. They felt that their discriminatory treatment betrayed the ideals taught in their classrooms: "In school in the Islands we learn from the Declaration of Independence that all men are created equal. But when we get over here we find people treating us as if we were inferior."[109] Filipinos confounded their critics by reveling in their depiction as sexually powerful and threatening. In 1936, a San Francisco municipal court judge wrote in *Time* magazine that Filipinos "have told me bluntly and boastfully that they practice the art of love with more perfection than white boys."[110] The Philippine Resident Commissioner responded dryly: "[T]he Judge admits that Filipinos are great lovers."[111] Another Filipino wrote to *Time* that "We, Filipinos, however poor, are taught from the cradle up to respect and love our women. . . . If to respect and love womenfolks is savagery, then make the most of it, Judge. We plead guilty."[112]

Filipinos in California strongly resisted the application of antimiscegenation laws. Most of California's Filipino population resided in Los Angeles County. California forbade marriages between whites and Mongolians, but the Los Angeles City Council announced in 1921 that Filipinos were exempt because they were not Mongolian. Eight years later, the California attorney general issued a contrary opinion, concluding that the term *Mongolian* included Filipinos as well as Chinese and Japanese.[113] Nevertheless, county clerks in Los Angeles continued to issue marriage licenses to Filipino–white couples.[114] In 1930, a lawsuit was filed to force the clerks to cease issuing licenses to Filipinos who were marrying whites. When a superior court judge held that the California attorney general's opinion was binding,[115] the Filipino community reacted with outrage.[116]

Filipino leaders promptly spearheaded efforts to fight the decision. By 1931, four cases were pending in Los Angeles superior courts on the legality of Filipino–white marriages.[117] Reversing itself after only one year, the superior court held that the term *Mongolian* did not include Filipinos. The California court of appeals agreed, affirming the lower court decision by a 3–3 vote. According to the court of appeals, the California legislature had not intended to cover Filipinos under the antimiscegenation law because anthropologists typically classified Filipinos as "Malays," not "Mongolians," and the legislature presumably had adopted this usage. Moreover, the original legislative debate was focused on Chinese, not Filipinos. The court added that the legislature could always amend the statute if it wanted to bar marriages between Filipinos and whites.[118] The California legislature did not take long to act on this suggestion. Nine days before the court's decision, a state senator introduced a bill that would amend the antimiscegenation statute to preclude Filipino–white marriages. Within a few months, California had adopted a new law to cover "negroes, Mongolians, members of the Malay race, or mulattoes."[119] The 1933 provision remained in effect until the California Supreme Court declared it unconstitutional fifteen years later.[120]

Faced with the ban on intermarriage, Filipinos did not concede defeat. Instead, they evaded California's antimiscegenation law by leaving the state to marry. Efforts to close this loophole met with limited success. In 1936, a California court of appeals ruled that a Filipino–white marriage that took place in New Mexico was valid in California. In that case, a white woman sought to annul her marriage on the ground that her Filipino husband had falsely represented himself to be "of Spanish Castilian descent." She testified that she would not have married him had she known he was Filipino because the marriage was illegal in California. The judge held that marriages between whites and Filipinos were legal in New Mexico, so "the ethnological status of the parties was not a ground of annulment."[121] In 1938, the California legislature passed a resolution calling on Utah to prevent whites and Filipinos from going there to evade the ban on miscegenation. Utah obliged by outlawing white–Filipino marriages that same year. Still dissatisfied, a California legislator introduced a bill to void interracial marriages that took place outside the state if they would be illegal in California. The bill died in committee.[122]

In addition to circumventing the law by going out of state, Filipinos married Mexican, Chinese, Japanese, and Eskimo women. In fact, most mixed couples in Los Angeles were Filipino–Mexican. There were some cultural affinities between Filipino immigrants and Mexican women because Spain had at one time colonized the Philippines. Consequently, many Filipinos spoke Spanish and were devout Catholics. Although Mexican-origin women were formally classified as white under California law, registrars seldom stood in the way of a marriage between a Mexican woman, particularly one who was dark skinned, and a Filipino man.[123] The prevalence of intermarriage among Filipinos was so great that by 1946, over half of the immigrants' children were biracial.[124] Far from accepting their relegation to bachelor communities, Filipino immigrants drew on their familiarity with American law and culture to challenge the ban on intermarriage. Unlike the Japanese who relied on separate settlements, Filipinos invoked their rights to freedom and equality before the law. When Filipino demands for recognition of their full personhood failed, they asserted their autonomy by using loopholes to circumvent racial restrictions.

Conclusion

Although antimiscegenation laws were identical in form, they served different functions at different times and for different groups. In the colonial era and during the early years of nationhood, bans on intermarriage were critical to drawing the color line between indentured white servants and blacks. Once the color line was in place, the statutes became a way to enforce racial hierarchy by barring blacks from assimilating through marriage to whites. Interracial sex continued to occur on a widespread basis, but it did not threaten white identity and privilege because the one-drop rule classified any illegitimate offspring as black. Nor did the extramarital liaisons jeopardize white superiority since white men could have their way with black women, but black men faced severe sanctions for having sex with white women.

Asian immigrants were subject to harsh restrictions on intermarriage, although their racial identities already were clear from federal immigration law. The use of antimiscegenation laws to subordinate the Chinese was in some ways harsher than their use to subordinate blacks. Blacks could form same-race families, but Chinese men often remained single and childless for life because of the shortage of Chinese women. Although forced to live in bachelor communities, Chinese men did not cross the color line to procreate. Linguistically, culturally, and economically isolated, Chinese men were ill-equipped to pursue extramarital liaisons with white women. Their emasculation reinforced their powerlessness, even as they were portrayed as sexually degraded and lascivious. The penalties for whites who became involved with the Chinese also were in certain respects more severe than for those who became involved with blacks. Although a white spouse in a black–white marriage remained white, American women who wed Chinese immigrants were stripped of their nationality, thereby taking on some of their spouses' unassimilable, alien qualities.

Enforcing racial subordination was particularly critical where the prosperous Japanese were concerned. The ability of Japanese immigrants to build stable, successful businesses, families, and communities threatened a sense of white superiority. In response, nativists insisted that the Japanese could not assimilate through naturalization or intermarriage, whatever their personal accomplishments. At the same time, though, nativists feared that Japanese racial pride made them spurn assimilation to a white way of life. While intermarriage remained a daunting prospect, the possibility that the Japanese might choose to remain a separate people also threatened white superiority. Just when proof of racial subordination was most urgently needed, antimiscegenation laws could no longer offer unambiguous evidence of white desirability and unattainability.

Although the Chinese and Japanese generally complied with antimiscegenation laws, Filipino immigrants defied the statutes. Rather than simply evade the restrictions through illicit liaisons, Filipinos demanded the right to cross the color line to date and marry women of their choice. Explicitly linking their masculinity to romantic and marital freedom, Filipinos were unwilling to forgo intimacy as the price of admission to the American workforce. Though economically marginal, Filipinos were not hampered by the linguistic and cultural isolation that doomed the Chinese to perennial bachelorhood. Often able to communicate in English and aware of American political ideals, Filipinos had a well-developed sense of democratic entitlement and acted on it. Their collective, confrontational approach to restrictions on sexual and marital freedom is unique in the annals of antimiscegenation law.

THREE

Subverting Racial Boundaries: Identity, Ambiguity, and Interracial Intimacy

Antimiscegenation laws inextricably linked racial identity and inequality to segregation in sex, marriage, and family. As a result, interracial intimacy often sowed subversive seeds of racial ambiguity. Typically relationships across the color line permitted people with some white ancestry to better their position in the racial hierarchy. Rather than undo a system of racial stratification, these individual strategies often reaffirmed the central importance of white privilege. For instance, mixed-race offspring could escape the harsh limitations of discriminatory laws by passing as white. Passing was a particularly important strategy for blacks with some white ancestry. The one-drop rule formally barred them from claiming any racial benefits based on their white origins, and the high rate of black–white extramarital liaisons prevented them from capitalizing on white family connections or wealth through marriage or inheritance laws. The only strategic racial advantage that these offspring gained from their white ancestry was an ambiguous and manipulable appearance.

In other instances, however, intermarriage conferred formal benefits on mixed-race offspring. For example, Native American women married white male settlers during the early years of contact and colonization. As a result, many states refrained from including Native Americans in their antimiscegenation laws, and people with some Native American ancestry were classified as white. Similarly, during the initial years of American settlement in the Southwest, white men married Mexican women to gain both emotional comfort and economic advantage. When formerly Mexican territory was annexed by the United States, Latinos were given the privileges of whites by treaty and were never included in antimiscegenation laws. In these instances, individuals came to enjoy the privileges of whiteness by suppressing the complexity of their origins.

Mixed-race persons were not always reclassified in a way that erased part of their ancestry. In some instances, their multiple origins were openly acknowledged by government officials. Typically this occurred when mixed-race people were living among nonwhite populations, and they could usefully serve as mediators or representatives in dealings with white authorities. Very often individuals with mixed origins could gain special privileges by virtue of their white ancestry, particularly if they were entrepreneurial in negotiating their relationships to whites. Again, though, the basic structure of racial division and inequality remained intact. Indeed, the advantages that mixed-race persons enjoyed as mediators depended on that very structure's perpetuation.

Ambiguous identities often revealed the central significance of race in organizing the everyday lives of Americans. For example, Latinos enjoyed official protections as white persons, but they regularly faced day-to-day discrimination based on their perceived nonwhite status. Their uncertain racial status often led to anomalous results under antimiscegenation laws. As whites, Latinos were barred from marrying blacks or Asians, but these weddings did take place. The marriages provided opportunities for the couples to circumvent or challenge discriminatory racial legislation. In some instances, this strategy proved successful in avoiding harsh restrictions. In others, however, the attempt to capitalize on intermarriage led to even harsher enforcement of the color line.

Passing and the Secret Stigma of Blackness

Slavery and segregation depended on a clearcut distinction between blacks and whites. Interracial sex undermined the legal regime by blurring the color line. Before the Civil War, a slave economy made it imperative to distinguish between the races, and mulattoes created undesirable racial ambiguity. Light-skinned slaves often ran away from their masters. When caught, the runaways insisted that their white ancestry entitled them to their freedom.[1] The intermingling of blacks and Native Americans further complicated racial identification. The two groups came into contact when they worked side by side as slaves or when blacks fled slavery and took refuge in tribal communities. Many tribes adopted runaway slaves as members, and even tribes that held slaves allowed blacks to become full and free members after intermarriage.[2] Like those with white ancestry, slaves with Native American ancestry were particularly apt to run away and escape detection. One 1747 announcement about a fifty-three-year-old escaped slave described him as having "some Indian blood in him" and as being accompanied by an adolescent who "was born of an Indian woman, and looks like an Indian." According to the advertisement, "they both talk Indian very well, and it is likely that they have dressed themselves in the Indian dress and gone to Carolina."[3]

Ties between blacks and Native Americans alarmed white settlers, who feared insurrection and revolt. A British officer warned in 1727 that "[t]heir mixing is to be prevented as much as possible."[4] These anxieties prompted efforts unique in the annals of American history, as steps were taken to limit interracial contacts among nonwhites. Black–Native American intermarriage was not formally prohibited, probably because neither slaves nor tribal members typically wed in an officially recognized, colonial ceremony. Instead, officials limited the freedom of movement of blacks and Native Americans in white settlements through curfews, restrictions on travel, and bans on carrying weapons.[5]

The end of slavery and the beginning of formal equality for black Americans after the Civil War did not put an end to fears that light-skinned blacks would wrongly gain access to white privilege. When efforts to rehabilitate blacks in the South during Reconstruction ended in the late 1800s, a racial caste system quickly reemerged. Once again, by law, race became an insurmountable barrier to full participation in American life, as states mandated segregation in schools, parks, libraries, courthouses, transportation, and other areas of daily existence.[6] The efficacy of these laws turned on the ease and accuracy of racial identification.

At the same time, industrialization was changing America's demography and way of life. Factories needed laborers in unprecedented numbers, and American cities welcomed immigrants from southern and eastern Europe as well as migrants from close-knit, rural communities in other states, including the South. Urban life was anonymous and impersonal: Newcomers could arrive without a past, remake themselves in the present, and know that the future offered chances to move on and start over if necessary. In this transient world, there were newfound opportunities for the clever or unscrupulous to redefine themselves and transgress traditional social boundaries.[7] Urbanization unsettled the norms of moral decency built in an agrarian society. City life enabled individuals not only to pursue the dream of a better life but also to fall prey to strangers with invented histories and false promises. In immigrant ghettoes, men proposed marriage to unsuspecting factory women, enjoyed their favors, and then disappeared. Even a wedding was not a complete safeguard against disappointment and desperation. During the late nineteenth and early twentieth centuries, rates of bigamy mushroomed, as men married a woman in one place and then moved on to marry again elsewhere.[8]

Just as individuals could manipulate their marital and sexual personae free of the constraints of small-town surveillance, they sometimes could alter their racial personae. Capitalizing on the influx of immigrants from southern Europe, light-skinned mulattoes passed themselves off as dark-skinned ethnics from the Mediterranean, whether Italian, Spanish, or Portuguese.[9] Passing could assume a variety of forms and serve a variety of purposes. Blacks sometimes passed permanently, forever concealing their African heritage. When they married whites, their children became involuntary passers, completely unaware that they were in fact black under the one-drop rule. Other blacks passed temporarily, working for a few years as whites to amass some savings before returning to the black community.[10] To contain the threat of "invisible blackness," northeastern cities began to employ rigid policies of residential segregation. These policies supplemented antimiscegenation laws by minimizing contact between blacks and whites outside the workplace. Ironically, though, segregated neighborhoods created the opportunity to pass on a part-time basis. Individuals could present themselves as white at work and then return home each day to black families and neighborhoods without fear of discovery. Part-time passing depended on the unwillingness of respectable whites to venture into a black section of town.[11]

Passing sometimes confounded efforts to apply antimiscegenation laws. Such cases usually involved a purportedly white spouse accused of being black. This claim could be used strategically to escape a marriage that had gone sour. For example, in 1910, a white husband in North Carolina sought to void a marriage on the ground that his wife was negro "within the prohibited degree." His wife denied his claim about her racial heritage and in turn alleged cruelty and abandonment. She asked for a divorce that would provide her with alimony and child support.[12] The court was not receptive to the husband's petition, finding that the trial court properly instructed the jury to focus on her genealogical ancestry, not rumors that had been circulated in the community.[13] The concurrence was even more explicit about his distaste for the husband's strategem:

> Years ago the plaintiff married a wife who, if she had any strain of negro blood whatever, was so white he did not suspect it till recently. . . . The plaintiff by earnest solicitation persuaded the defendant to become his

wife in the days of her youth and beauty. She has borne his children. Now that youth has fled and household drudgery and child-bearing have taken the sparkle from her eyes and deprived her form of its symmetry, he seeks to get rid of her, not only without fault alleged against her, but in a method that will not only deprive her of any support while he lives by alimony, or by dower after his death, but which would consign her to the association of the colored race which he so affects to despise. . . . The law may not permit him thus to bastardize his own children.[14]

Although a one-drop rule was the law, the judge refused to rely on an analysis of whether the wife "had any strain of negro blood whatever." Instead, the court examined both the wife's appearance and her substantial contributions to the marriage. In the judge's view, this woman had earned a white racial status for herself and her children through faithful execution of her domestic obligations.

On rare occasions a purportedly black spouse was accused of being white. In 1909, for instance, a judge in Richmond, Virginia, sentenced a man and his wife to eighteen years in prison for marrying interracially. Although the couple claimed to be black, the judge held that the husband was actually white.[15] Though whites rarely were prosecuted for passing as black, a 1945 study of black life in Chicago reported that some intermarried whites habitually passed as black "to gain some advantage or to avoid embarrassment."[16] As a white woman married to a black railroad waiter explained: "I have an annual pass with the railroad company my husband is with. I used it a couple of times. Yes, I was questioned when I used the pass and I said that although you might not think so, I have colored blood. I was telling the truth because I have red blood in my veins, and that's colored."[17]

After World War II, civil rights activists began to push for the elimination of state-mandated segregation. The horrors of the Nazi philosophy of racial superiority abroad and the ironies of a racial caste system at home forced Americans to reexamine the claim that separate racial facilities could be equal.[18] Despite the push to make government officials colorblind, concerns about passing persisted. Perhaps the most notorious example arose in Louisiana, where lenient attitudes toward race-mixing in the antebellum era greatly complicated later efforts to enforce racial classifications under a one-drop rule. The state's Bureau of Vital Statistics regularly identified individuals whose claims to whiteness were suspect. The bureau's efforts reserved to the state the power to define racial identity; individuals themselves were not free to choose whether to be black or white. When Naomi Drake became supervisor and deputy registrar of the bureau in 1949, she worked assiduously to investigate birth and death certificates that listed individuals as white when they had surnames common to blacks. The bureau checked these certificates against a "race list," and if the name appeared there, the bureau did additional genealogical study to determine whether the person had African ancestry. If the investigation identified a black ancestor, the bureau would issue a certificate only if the individual was designated as colored.[19]

As a result of race-flagging, the Louisiana Bureau of Vital Statistics denied at least forty-seven hundred applications for birth certificates and eleven hundred applications for death certificates between 1960 and 1965. A minimum of thirty-eight petitions for writs of mandamus were filed to force the bureau to issue certificates. By 1965 race-flagging had become controversial enough to lead to Naomi Drake's dismissal. Yet the practice persisted after her departure. As late as 1977, two full-time investigators dealt exclusively with questions of racial designation. In 1976 alone, the bureau devoted six thousand hours to investigating disputed racial identities.[20]

The Louisiana policy earned national notoriety in 1982 when Susie Guillory Phipps' case came to light. In 1977 Phipps applied for a passport and discovered that her Louisiana birth certificate listed her as "colored." Outraged, she insisted that "I was brought up white, I married white twice." She challenged the bureau's practice because race-mixing allegedly was so extensive in Louisiana that the entire native-born population would be considered black under its stringent definition. Despite her arguments, the Louisiana courts refused to designate Phipps as white when the bureau introduced genealogical records showing that her great-great-great-great-grandmother was a slave and some of her ancestors were classified as part black. Phipps lost in the courts but won in the forum of public opinion. Confronted with intensely negative publicity, Louisiana repealed its racial classification law and allowed individuals to designate their children's race freely.[21] Phipps could officially be white, rather than merely pass as white.

Individuals with any African ancestry traditionally were barred from all of the privileges associated with white identity. Passing became a way for some blacks to circumvent the color line without directly challenging it. Blacks used an ambiguous phenotype to integrate into white society and evade a genotypical definition of race. Yet those who passed never disabused whites of their beliefs about how blacks looked and acted. The work performed by a person who was passing did not demonstrate to white colleagues that blacks were in fact competent. Nor did passers who married whites change their spouses' minds about the lovability of people classified as nonwhite and inferior. Passing allowed individuals to escape racial limitations, but it offered no means for the collective improvement of the black condition. The power of the passer was that of the trickster or confidence artist. This brand of racial redefinition was a fraud, one that could be unmasked by an indiscreet remark, a black friend or relative, or a dedicated bureaucrat. The passer's limited power to steal but never own a white identity demonstrated how powerless blacks were to rehabilitate their stigmatized and degraded selves. By treating blackness as a damaging secret, those who passed actually showed that their racial identity was an inescapably inferior status.

The Alchemy of Intermarriage: Native Americans and Latinos

Although blacks with white ancestry could never formally cross the color line under a one-drop rule, other groups did gain the opportunity to assimilate to a white identity. In particular, some persons with Native American and Latino ancestry were able to identify themselves as white without being accused of passing. By doing so, these individuals participated in the benefits of white privilege while leaving a system of racial stratification otherwise intact. A key difference between the experience of Native Americans and Latinos and that of blacks was the degree to which intermarriage occurred. Officially recognized marriages and families played a critical role in the process of racial formation. When white men settled new frontiers and married Native American or Mexican women, their children were legally acknowledged and entitled to all of the privileges that family membership brought. By contrast, white slaveholders who had intercourse with black women bore no obligation to recognize the children, to support them, or even to rescue them from enslavement. Without the protection of marriage and family law, these mixed-race offspring were unable to claim the privileges of whiteness.

Native American Intermarriage and Identity

Of all the European settlers, the English were the most likely to bring women with them and hence least likely to intermarry with Native American tribes.[22] Still, some intermarriage did take place during the early days of British colonization. Most famous, perhaps, is the marriage of Virginia settler John Rolfe and Pocahontas, whose descendants went on to become members of Virginia's leading families.[23] Rolfe was not alone in forging early alliances with Native American women. To maximize white settlers' chances of survival, some leading colonists proposed measures that would encourage intermarriage. In the late 1700s, Patrick Henry offered a bill in the Virginia House of Delegates that would exempt marriages of whites and Native Americans from taxes. The bill offered monetary incentives for couples not only to marry but also to have children. The bill did not pass, but its philosophy continued to be influential.[24] In 1803 Thomas Jefferson suggested that there was only one solution to the "Indian problem": "In truth, the ultimate point of rest and happiness for them is to let our settlements and theirs meet and blend together, to intermix, and become one people. Incorporating themselves with us as citizens of the United States, this is what the natural progress of things will, of course, bring on, and it will be better to promote than to retard it."[25]

When white male settlers married Native American women, they found themselves in a position of dependency as their wives assumed the role of cultural mediator. The wives' importance conflicted with the settlers' sense of racial superiority and their patriarchal view of marriage. As a result, Native American women who became involved with white men were depicted in extreme terms. Sometimes their power and importance were denied by portraying them as sexually degraded victims, who were sold as slaves or leased for a period of years.[26] At other times their gifts were treated as unique: Indian women who married white men were regarded as heroines with exceptional courage and vision. The legend that grew up around Pocahontas is perhaps the best example. According to popular accounts, Pocahontas was an Indian princess who saved the life of Captain John Smith when he was sentenced to death by her father. Pocahontas went on to aid white settlers in a number of ways, converted to Christianity, and married a Virginia tobacco planter, John Rolfe. Pocahontas was portrayed as unusually beautiful, brave, and bright.[27]

The intermarriage of Native Americans and whites created doubts about the racial status of their offspring. In some instances, mixed-blood offspring became white. Virginia's antimiscegenation law, for example, contained what came to be called the "Pocahontas exception." It defined as "white persons" those "with one-sixteenth or less of the blood of the American Indian and . . . no other non-Caucasic blood. . . ."[28] Apparently, Rolfe's prominence and Pocahontas's characterization as a singularly remarkable individual enabled their descendants to escape completely the legacy of a nonwhite identity. Nor was Virginia alone in recognizing Native American descendants as white. In Louisiana, in the 1920s, the reclassification of Native Americans as white led to bans on their intermarriage with blacks. By the 1930s, Indians were permitted to marry whites under the state's antimiscegenation law.[29]

Mexicans in the Southwest

Like Native Americans in colonial times, Mexican women in the Southwest often intermarried with Anglo settlers during the early years of contact.[30] When French and English settlers arrived in the Southwest, they found a population with a long history of intermarriage. Although Spanish elites practiced racial endogamy, race-mixing was so common that the term *mestizaje* was coined to refer to the phenomenon.[31] Widespread miscegenation among Spaniards, indigenous tribes, and Africans created a "pigmentocracy" in which lighter skin correlated with social privilege and darker skin connoted manual labor and defeated peoples. Yet, even in a pigmentocracy, money lightened and permitted some dark-skinned people to improve their social standing through intermarriage.[32]

   In a society that prized light skin and treated matrimony as a vehicle for upward mobility, intermarriage was an attractive option when Anglo settlers arrived in the Southwest in the early 1800s. Mexico had just won its independence from Spain and hoped to capitalize on new frontier opportunities. Anglo settlers offered a way to develop a sparsely populated area, so long as they remained loyal to their new home. The Mexican government restricted the trade activities of foreigners, who otherwise might simply exploit the country's riches and leave with the spoils. Recognizing the bonds that Anglo settlers would forge to Mexican wives and families, an 1823 national colonization decree created opportunities to naturalize through intermarriage: "All foreigners who come to establish themselves in the Empire, and those who, following a profession or industry, in three years, have sufficient capital to support themselves with decency and are married, shall be considered naturalized; those who, under the foregoing conditions, marry Mexican women, acquire a special right to have their letters of citizenship given them."[33] The official naturalization law promulgated five years later did not make marriage to a Mexican national a prerequisite to citizenship, but apparently many Americans still believed that intermarriage would help their chances. In petitions for citizenship during this period, American men regularly mentioned their Mexican wives. In the late 1830s and early 1840s, the Mexican government tightened restrictions on foreigners' trade activities even further, but once again the policy exempted those married to Mexican nationals.[34]

Clearly, Mexican officials wanted American entrepreneurs to marry, have families, and settle permanently. These marriages frequently offered important benefits to both the Anglo settler and his new Mexican family. Anglo settlers could cement trade relations, obtain large tracts of land, and gain a foothold in the political life of the region through marriage to women from prominent families, while Mexican families gained the assistance of a son-in-law who could negotiate access to emerging markets in the United States. In a pigmentocracy, Mexican families also may have coveted the lightening of the skin that intermarriage with fair-haired whites produced in the next generation.[35] Sensitivities about the racial implications of intermarriage were reflected in the labels chosen for wives: Anglo men referred to their brides as "Spanish," while their male competitors remained "Mexican."[36]

Most Anglo settlers sought parental permission for their marriages with Mexican women, and as the Mexican government hoped, nearly 75 percent remained with their wives and families in the area. Still, some Americans did treat the unions as sexual dalliances. Matt Field, a journalist for the *New Orleans Picayune,* riveted his readers with the tale of Maria Romero, who was abandoned by a fickle Anglo settler named John. According to Field, John was

> a wild, dissolute young fellow . . . [who] had crossed the wilderness to hide himself from the world. He was a young man of very remarkable personal attractions, besides being possessed of an elegant address, and fascinating manners. He had but to smile and lift his finger, and poor Maria, the child of nature, and the charmer of the village, flew into his arms. His name need not be told. . . . Suffice it to say, that after a time he returned to the States, and Maria was told that he had been killed by the Comanches. This affliction the poor girl bore only in melancholy, bending over her infant [by John] in silent anguish; but when subsequently she heard that he had designedly abandoned her, and had gone forever back to the United States, her reason failed, and poor Maria, the beauty of Taos, became a lunatic.[37]

What is remarkable about this story is not simply the juxtaposition of John, the charming American con man, with Maria, the Mexican child of nature, but also the clear message that the social norm was for marriages between Anglo men and Mexican women to endure. Mexican women expected to be treated as wives, not used as mistresses or concubines.

As long as Mexico retained control over its territories, offspring of mixed marriages spoke Spanish, adopted Mexican cultural traditions, and usually married Mexicans. An American father's primary legacy was a non-Spanish surname, although even some of these last names were "Hispanicized."[38] Once the United States annexed formerly Mexican territories, Americans had few official incentives to marry Mexicans. As more Anglo women arrived in the area, intermarriage became increasingly anomalous. Still, immediately following the American conquest of Mexico's northernmost territories in the mid-1800s, some Mexican women from prominent families married soldiers to preserve their position and that of their children under the new regime.[39] Daughters of mixed marriages married Anglo men with increasing frequency after the American takeover as well.[40] In contrast to the earlier period, when offspring of intermarriages preserved their Mexican heritage, the children of the postconquest unions were apt to become Anglicized.[41]

The experience of Native Americans and Mexicans who intermarried is quite distinct from the black experience. No matter how phenotypically white or how many social ties to whites, a person with African ancestry was forever black. Any attempt to be reclassified as white was merely passing. By contrast, Native Americans and Mexicans could use their social ties to whites to identify their offspring as white. Admittedly white status sometimes depended on the remoteness of nonwhite ancestry, a criterion likely to ensure not only a rich network of white relatives and friends but also a phenotypically white appearance. The further in the past the Native American or Mexican heritage, the more likely that the individual had been fully integrated into white families and communities and had adopted a white way of life.

Why was intermarriage a successful strategy of assimilation for some Native Americans and Mexicans, but not for blacks? Those who favor biological explanations might claim that Native Americans and Latinos were more phenotypically similar to whites than blacks were. As a result, when Native Americans and Latinos had children with whites, their offspring were less likely to appear nonwhite than children born to black and white parents. Yet even light-skinned blacks who could pass were denied the privileges of a white identity. Perhaps of greater importance than phenotype was the ability to forge strong social ties to whites through interracial intimacy. As slaves, blacks could not intermarry at all. In the antebellum South and even immediately after the Civil War, most black–white sex was extramarital. These sexual liaisons were not promising ways to build social connections. As slaves, black women had little say in whether to have intercourse: They could be whipped and beaten for denying a white master's demand for sex. A white man had no need to make promises of love to his black slave, nor did he have to offer any special care or protection to their children. In fact, when a black–white relationship led to marriage or at least love and loyalty, it confounded the racial hierarchy and laws of marriage and inheritance.[42]

By contrast, when white settlers first encountered Native American and Mexican women, they often found themselves in a relationship of dependency rather than superiority. Long-term alliances were mutually beneficial, and intermarriage was a natural way to forge them. Men could not simply take these women by force. Indian women expected their white husbands to respect native customs about sex, marriage, and pro-creation. Mexican women, typically Catholic, expected to be treated as wives. They firmly believed in the sanctity of marriage and the sinfulness of adultery and fornication. Because unions between settlers and Native American or Mexican women often were enduring, the men developed strong attachments to their wives, children, and in-laws. A number of white settlers who intermarried became prominent members of their communities. For them, it was undoubtedly painful to think that their children, the heirs to their family name and fortune, would be relegated to a life of racial subordination. So the law accommodated these concerns by classifying the descendants as white with all the privileges that this identity entailed.

Official Recognition of Mixed-Race Identity

Although mixed-race persons often were forced to identify as either white or not, there were some instances in which their multiracial origins were openly acknowledged in an official classification scheme. Typically racial complexity was recognized when it was useful to identify members of nonwhite communities who would be particularly competent, trust-worthy, or useful. While these mixed-race individuals benefited from their ability to negotiate between racial categories, the very utility of these skills depended on the maintenance of the color line. At various times multiracial identity became relevant for all groups formally labeled nonwhite—whether black, Native American, or Asian.

In the antebellum period, the lower South adopted a complex set of racial categories that turned on degrees of black and white ancestry. A person who was three-quarters black was a "sambo"; seven-eighths black, a "mango"; one-sixteenth black, a "meamelouc"; and one sixty-fourth black, a "sang-mele."[43] This classification scheme recognized that the individuals were not white, yet accorded value to their white ancestry. In a slave economy, the labels could be linked to economic worth. A light-skinned male slave might bring a low price because he was particularly prone to run away, although a good-looking, fair-complected young boy could be a valuable commodity. An attractive female quadroon or octoroon also might bring a handsome price as a potential mistress or concubine.[44]

After emancipation, census takers continued to keep track of mixed-race origins. In 1870, when individuals of African origin were first counted as persons, mulattoes were identified separately from blacks. The 1890 census went even further, requiring enumerators to use visual inspection to estimate the amount of black and white ancestry that an individual had, whether one-half black (mulatto), one-quarter (quadroon), or one-eighth (octoroon). The distinctions were so unreliable, however, that the Bureau of the Census subsequently dropped them. Census takers continued to distinguish between mulattoes and blacks until 1920.[45] These distinctions were important during Reconstruction because mulattoes often were considered especially suited to leadership positions. Indeed, in Louisiana, Democratic legislators offered a "quadroon" bill that would have limited the franchise to light-skinned men of African ancestry.[46] With the decline of Reconstruction and the rise of Jim Crow segregation, the impetus to make distinctions among members of the black population declined. All blacks occupied a subordinate position, regardless of their mixed ancestry. The U.S. Supreme Court made this clear in *Plessy v. Ferguson*,[47] when it held that even a light-skinned octoroon could not ride in a railway car reserved for whites. Rather than identify mulattoes, the census in 1920 turned to a more pressing task: keeping track of the mixed European ancestries of immigrants who had swelled the ranks of urban America.[48]

Official attention to mixed ancestry was not limited to blacks. Among Native Americans, mixed-blood children often became tribal leaders because of their unique ability to negotiate with whites. As one Winnebago tale explained: "A person with French blood has always been the chief. Only they could accomplish anything among the whites."[49] At times, full-blooded tribal members distrusted mixed-bloods, fearing that they would readily capitulate to white interests.[50] In the late 1800s and early

1900s, for example, the federal government embarked on a campaign to "civilize" the Indian. As part of this campaign, the Dawes Act required reservation lands to be parceled out to individual tribal members.[51] When unscrupulous speculators used ingenious schemes to strip newly propertied Indians of their land, Congress prevented full-blooded Indians from selling or leasing their property for twenty-five years. Mixed-bloods, however, were exempted because they were presumed competent to manage their own affairs by virtue of their white ancestry.[52] Differential treatment of full-bloods and mixed-bloods spawned enmity and distrust among tribal members. Many full-bloods suspected mixed-bloods of colluding with whites to steal their property. One Cherokee complained that "they would send half-breeds around . . . and hunt for the names of the full-bloods without their consent, and they would take the names down and present them before the Dawes Commission . . . and take an oath on it . . . [Then, the full-bloods] would find a certificate of allotment sent to them at the post office."[53]

Government reliance on blood quantum to confer privileges on intermarried and mixed-race people is not confined to distant historical episodes. During World War II, when Japanese residents in the United States were sent to internment camps as potential saboteurs, the federal government gave special exemptions to some intermarried Japanese and their mixed-race offspring. Believing that Japanese who had married whites felt special ties of loyalty to the United States, relocation officials were concerned about consigning these couples and their mixed-race children to "infectious Japanese thought" in the camps.[54] As a result, officials devised a policy that allowed intermarried Japanese with children to avoid internment. A Japanese woman married to a white man could return with her children to the West Coast war zone, while a Japanese man with a white wife and children could leave the camps but could not go to the West Coast. Japanese who were intermarried but childless were not permitted to leave with one exception: A Japanese woman married to an American serviceman could return to the West Coast. Adult mixed-race offspring also could leave the camps upon proof that they had "fifty per cent, or less, Japanese blood" and that their prewar community ties had been to whites.[55] These rules clearly rewarded Japanese who had forged social connections to whites by treating them as loyal Americans despite their partial Asian ancestry.

In sum, mixed-race identity became a convenient mechanism for whites to manage relations with nonwhite populations. Partial white ancestry became a proxy for competency, trustworthiness, and receptivity to the cultivation of white social ties. In this instance, genotype and sometimes phenotype barred the mixed-race individual from becoming white. But some white ancestry coupled with social ties to whites could enable a person with mixed origins to escape the harshest consequences of racial discrimination. The special treatment enjoyed by mixed-race persons derived from a combination of racial distinctiveness and familiarity that enabled them to bridge the gap between whites and non-whites.

Racial Ambiguities and Alliances

The ambiguous identities of persons with mixed origins sometimes produced anomalous results under racially restrictive legislation. Very often, Latinos were the source of this racial confusion. When the United States annexed formerly Mexican territories in the Southwest, the Treaty of Guadalupe Hidalgo assured former Mexican citizens who remained in these areas that they would enjoy the full privileges of American citizenship. The treaty appeared to put Mexicans on a par with whites—at least under formal law.[56] Indeed, when Ricardo Rodriguez was denied the right to naturalize in 1896 on the ground that he was not a "free white person," a federal court quickly overturned the decision. The court concluded that under treaties with Spain and Mexico, Rodriguez could not be denied the rights and privileges of citizenship based on his allegedly nonwhite status, although he was still required to demonstrate his good character and ability to understand constitutional principles as other applicants were.[57]

Despite treaty protections, the racial status of Mexican-origin persons remained uncertain. Under the Latin American tradition of *mestizaje,* European ancestry was prized, but personal accomplishments and social standing could compensate for a dark-skinned, Indian appearance.[58] Former Mexican elites, like the Californios, tried to import this racial norm into the newly created U.S. territories with only partial success. For example, dark-skinned Californios struggled to be included in California's constitutional convention in 1849. They had to rely on their light-skinned counterparts and Anglo allies to defend their rights of participation. In arguing that those who were once citizens of Mexico should enjoy the privileges of whites despite their Indian ancestry, one sympathetic Anglo delegate noted that "some of the most honorable and distinguished families in Virginia descended from the Indian race."[59] The

Californios' position prevailed, and they took part in the drafting of official documents like the California constitution.[60]

The controversy surrounding race-mixing and politics persisted. Leading scholars during the mid-1800s warned that American democracy would be in jeopardy if the color line were compromised. They feared that a mixed-race population would convert the United States into "another Mexico" rife with political instability and economic insecurity.[61] Concerns about the impact of Mexican-origin persons on America's civic identity continued into the next century. In advocating restrictions on immigration from Mexico in the 1920s, Madison Grant contended that allowing "half-breeds" to enter the United States would undermine its racial purity.[62] During the early 1900s, academics in Texas concluded that the Mexican-origin population, neither black nor white, could never fit within America's traditional framework of race relations. For this reason, their presence threatened an always volatile and delicate racial balance. Professor William Leonard of the University of Texas wrote in 1916 that "[s]ociety in the Southwest cannot easily adapt itself to the handling of a second racial problem. . . . [F]or Mexican immigrants, there is no congenial social group to welcome them. . . . They are not Negroes. . . . They are not accepted as white men, and between the two, the white and the black, there seems to be no midway position."[63] Approximately fifteen years later, Max Handman, another Texas sociologist, wrote that "American society has no social technique for handling partly colored races. We have a place for the Negro and a place for the white man: the Mexican is not a Negro, and the white man refuses him an equal status."[64]

The contested racial identity of Mexican-origin persons often led to peculiar results under antimiscegenation laws, which were designed to draw a clear line between whites and nonwhites. Because individuals of Mexican descent were legally white, they were barred from marrying Asians or blacks. Yet local registrars sometimes permitted such marriages in ways that cemented the Mexican-origin spouse's nonwhite status. For example, in Imperial Valley, California, during the late 1920s and early 1930s, there were a number of Mexican–Punjabi marriages, despite a law that prohibited whites from marrying Asians. The Punjabis arrived unaccompanied by women because of restrictive immigration laws. When the men tried to marry, they found themselves in a quandary. They were barred by state law from marrying whites, and they had a strong cultural aversion to marrying blacks.[65] The Punjabis quickly tried to evade the ban on intermarriage to whites by traveling to a nearby state. However, this strategy proved to be untenable in a small, rural community. In 1918, when a successful Punjabi cotton farmer went to Arizona to wed the sixteen-year-old daughter of a tenant, a newspaper shrilly reported "HINDU WEDS WHITE GIRL BY STEALING AWAY TO ARIZONA," and wrongly concluded that the tactic was probably illegal.[66]

Another method of evasion was successful, however. Punjabis married women of Mexican origin, who satisfied the men's cultural standards and their white neighbors' racial sensitivities. Because Mexican-origin women were technically white, local officials made front-page news by issuing licenses for them to marry Punjabi farmers. When the first license was granted in March 1916, a reporter noted its questionable legality: "While in doubt as to their legal right to marry under the laws of this state, the clerk . . . issued the license, thereby passing the responsibility up to any authorized person who performs the marriage ceremony."[67] To address the community's racial concerns, registrars exercised some discretion in issuing licenses. Applicants might be listed as "white," "brown," or "black," depending on their skin color. Clerks tried to ensure that spouses had approximately the same pigmentation and denied a license if the Mexican-origin bride was "too white."[68] By regularly permitting Mexican–Punjabi marriages, registrars reinforced the nonwhite status of the Mexican-origin population. Their formal racial status became nothing more than a legal technicality that could be overcome by dark skin.

Mexican–Punjabi unions confused the application of not only the antimiscegenation law but also the Alien Land Law. Under the land law, a wife acquired her Asian husband's noncitizen status upon marriage and thus was ineligible to hold property for him. Because the Mexican–Punjabi marriages were anomalous, whites and Punjabis alike often erroneously believed that the Mexican wife could hold her husband's property.[69] Perhaps because a Mexican-origin wife was only technically white, local officials did not feel the same need to punish her marriage to an Asian through loss of the privileges of citizenship, including the right to hold property. The very malleability of the Mexican-origin wife's racial identity permitted the couples to escape the harsh consequences of restrictive laws aimed primarily at drawing the color line between whites and Asians.

Not all attempts to evade racially restrictive legislation by capitalizing on the ambiguous status of Mexican-origin individuals succeeded. In Texas, public schools were strictly segregated by race and interracial marriages were forbidden. Under the state's antimiscegenation law, people of Mexican origin were white and could not marry blacks. Because of the Mexican-origin population's informal status as nonwhite, however, officials generally turned a blind eye to the marriages. Still, the ban on intermarriage would come in handy when blacks tried to use their marriages to individuals of Mexican origin to claim new privileges. In Dimmit County in the 1920s, for example, black children were completely barred from the white public school. However, children of Mexican ancestry were permitted to attend the white school for first through third grade so long as they remained in separate classrooms. After that, a handful of Mexican-origin students deemed "clean" and "not like the others" were allowed to continue their education at the white school.

A black man married to a Mexican-origin woman tried to send his children to the white school on the ground that they were of Mexican ancestry. Shortly thereafter, he was prosecuted for violating the anti-miscegenation law. A judge in the county explained that "[t]he Negroes with Negro-Mexican children and the Mexicans wanted to send their children to the white school, so when that started . . . they just indicted them for violating the law against intermarriage. Then they tipped off the women that if they had nigger blood they could not put the men in jail."[70] When women of Mexican ancestry testified that they were part black to save their husbands from imprisonment, officials concluded that "all the Mexicans were black," and "we put the Mexicans and Negroes together in school and employed a part Negro to teach them."[71] Far from enabling the children of black–Mexican marriages to escape the impact of segregated schooling, this attempt to capitalize on an ambiguous Mexican identity resulted in all Mexican-origin persons losing their tenuous hold on whiteness.

Conclusion

Despite efforts to use antimiscegenation laws to draw the color line, interracial intimacy confounded racial boundaries. When whites had a stake in protecting children of intermarriage from discrimination, the scope of whiteness expanded to include those with some remote nonwhite ancestry. Yet when the color line was critical to preserving an established social order, the definition of whiteness became quite exacting, and those who transgressed racial boundaries were deemed antisocial and dangerous. Hysteria about "invisible passing" could become rampant under these circumstances. When race relations were in flux, mixed-race identities sometimes received official recognition. At times, such as during Reconstruction, greater equality was pursued, and mixed-race persons occupied a privileged position in the new regime. At other times, greater segregation took place through relocation to reservations or internment camps, and partial white ancestry could mitigate an individual's isolation from white society. Although an ambiguous racial identity might help in avoiding the sting of racially discriminatory laws, the most successful strategies were those of evasion, not confrontation. Officials would turn a blind eye to circumvention of the law when the violation reinforced community beliefs about how the color line should be drawn. But officials would not tolerate efforts to manipulate an ambiguous identity in a way that deliberately flouted racial privilege.

FOUR

Antimiscegenation Laws and Norms of Sexual and Marital Propriety

ALTHOUGH ANTIMISCEGENATION laws have been analyzed almost entirely as racial legislation, they also played an important role in defining the boundaries of sexual and marital propriety. Antimiscegenation laws established the norm that interracial attraction was pathological and deviant, not natural and loving. Practices that preserved racial separation and stratification were equated with moral rectitude, while sex and love across the color line were criminalized. Statutes characterized interracial sex as "forbidden fruit" and interracial marriage as a match so inappropriate that it jeopardized the social order. These messages were powerful enough to reach even those—like dance hall hostesses and prostitutes—on the margins of sexual respectability. The message was clear: Those who succumbed to interracial lust must pay serious consequences.

Less obviously but just as significantly, antimiscegenation laws created a norm of "separate but equal" marriages and families that made it possible to regulate nonwhite sexual and marital practices. By characterizing nonwhites as not only different but inferior, reformers could insist that their sexual and marital practices conform to those of white, middle-class Americans. As a result, racial separation did not lead to autonomy for nonwhites to marry and raise children as they saw fit. Instead, the assimilation of sexual mores and family values became integral to the racial rehabilitation of nonwhites and was offered as proof of their capacity to be equal.

Sex and Marriage across the Color Line: Disorderly and Deviant

Antimiscegenation laws became critical to the preservation of a sense of decency when sexual mores were in flux. During the late 1800s and early 1900s, industrialization and urbanization created newfound means of social mobility. In the turbulent, transient cities, people could experiment with a range of identities, including their sexual personae. Affluent white men dabbled in novel sources of erotic pleasure, as prostitution became increasingly commercialized and entrenched in red-light districts.[1] The enhanced sexual liberties of white men provoked fear and anxiety among middle-class, often female, reformers. The purity movement attributed sexual excess to unconstrained male urges. As one man who sought the comforts of a prostitute explained: "Perhaps I was wrong to go but 'a stiff prick has no conscience' as the proverb says, & I believe I would have gone crazy almost if I had not gone to her or to some other similar lady."[2] Crusades for purity required women not only to exercise self-control but to aid men in curbing their "animal instincts."[3] Middle-class, white men might seek an outlet for their sexual impulses by "raid[ing] the amusement parks or the evening streets in search of girls that could be frankly pursued for their physical charms," but these actions merely made them impure and in need of a "nice girl" to cleanse them and make them truly manly. During the late 1800s and early 1900s, the salience of prostitution led to a growing gap between sex on the one hand and love and marriage on the other. "Amorous ardors" were associated with "the vulgar, or worse, with the commonplace," rather than romance. While passion was important, marriage had to be based on a love rooted in "mutuality and companionship."[4] This ideology made sexual attraction an irrational impulse and marriage an act of mature deliberation and reflection.

During this period, social hygienists feared that the influx of immigrants from southern and eastern Europe was threatening the social order, including popular mores about sex and marriage. Researchers and reformers were shocked by the crowded conditions in urban tenements. To earn extra income, immigrant families often took in male boarders. These unmarried men lived in close proximity to young wives and daughters, and social hygienists were certain that widespread extramarital liaisons would result from such close, seemingly unsupervised, contact.[5] Moreover, immigrant women often went to work in factories, offices, or stores. Unchaperoned in their travels around the city and newly emboldened by the receipt of wages, the women seemed like easy targets for predatory men.[6]

The movement of women from Europe to America, from farm to city, and from home to work helped to explain the rise of white female prostitution, despite women's role as safeguards of moral purity. Prostitution grew rapidly in the late nineteenth century, and most prostitutes were young, foreign-born white women. Reformers typically assumed that unsuspecting girls were lured into the sex trade by false promises of love, marriage, or a glamorous and independent life. Alcoholism and economic need kept them in brothels or on the streets. Seldom did reformers attribute a life in prostitution to female sexual urges.[7] Crusaders for purity published lurid tracts about "white slavery" that detailed how naive girls left their small towns and villages to find romance and excitement in the big city but instead wound up as whores. Popular novels, plays, and movies in the early 1900s trumpeted the same theme.[8] The message was clear: The newfound freedom and mobility of urban life were a man's preserve but a woman's peril. Far from empowering women, industrialization and urbanization stripped vulnerable females of their dignity and self-respect, making them little better than slaves.

Although affluent white men were exhorted to exercise self-control over their base impulses, marginal and untrustworthy men were subject to criminal prosecution and deportation. To protect vulnerable young women from predatory pimps, the federal government passed legislation to deport sexually debauched immigrants, including the "large number of Jews scattered throughout the United States . . . [who] seduce and keep girls."[9] In addition, Congress passed the Mann Act, also known as the White Slave Traffic Act, in 1910. The Act made it a federal crime to transport women across state lines for immoral purposes.[10] Local law enforcement agencies also cracked down on prostitution.[11] These government efforts were supplemented by those of social hygienists, who sought to educate immigrants about sex and prevent the spread of venereal disease. Reflecting the view that men's unbridled sexual impulses were to blame for the growth of prostitution, reformers advocated male chastity before marriage. In *Ten Sex Talks for Boys,* a member of the Society of Sanitary and Moral Prophylaxis admonished his readers that sex should only take place as part of marriage. Otherwise, "THE SEXUAL RELATION IS ABSOLUTELY UNNECESSARY TO YOU OR TO ANY OTHER MAN."[12] In short, manliness did not require the exercise of one's "sexual muscle."[13]

The anxieties surrounding prostitution became complicated when blacks began their great migration from the rural South to northern cities in the second decade of the twentieth century. With their arrival, a new kind of sexual titillation was for sale: White men could enter segregated urban slums to sample the exotic pleasures of interracial dancing and sex in nightclubs. One white New Yorker described his experience with Harlem's nightlife in the 1920s as "an emotional holiday. Then, when the last ambiguously worded [and sexually suggestive] song is done, one puts on one's hat, coat, and niceties, and once again is staid, proper, and a community pillar."[14] In addition, with the rise in white prostitution, black men could buy the sexual favors of white women in red-light districts. For black male migrants, the white woman who had been taboo in the South could now be had for as little as five or six dollars.[15]

Despite the casual portrayal of interracial sex as "an emotional holiday," it presented new challenges in the early twentieth century. Extramarital sex across the color line was nothing new. White landowners had kept black and mulatto women as mistresses in the South, but these relationships were rooted in the power structures of slavery. Even when a New Orleans planter supported a free mulatto woman under a contract of placage, the transaction seemed only a slight remove from the white man who used his black female slaves for sexual pleasure. Interracial sex remained worlds apart from same-race relationships with white wives. With the spread of white prostitution in the late nineteenth and early twentieth centuries, however, interracial sex in red-light districts increasingly resembled the same-race sex trade. The clear line between morally respectable, intraracial relationships and degraded, interracial ones began to blur. After all, thriving businesses were being built on the taste for sex across the color line, even though antimiscegenation laws clearly marked these relationships as inferior and antisocial. To preserve sexual proprieties in the face of cross-racial liaisons, law enforcement authorities and sex trade workers alike had to establish that interracial sex remained inferior to same-race sex, that white men retained greater sexual liberty than nonwhite men, and that nonwhite women remained less appealing than white women.

To maintain the moral superiority of same-race sex, authorities condemned interracial sex as particularly vile and debauched. In Chicago, commissions to stamp out vice could not even bring themselves to describe the depredations of interracial Black and Tan clubs: "[N]o printable account could come within a mile of telling the depravity to which performers and patrons sank."[16] A prominent judge was outraged that "orgies of the jungle could have been permitted in a public café in

Chicago month after month."[17] A front-page headline in the *Pittsburgh Courier* trumpeted that "CHICAGO IS WORSE CITY THAN PARIS" because of the levels of interracial mixing in dance halls and clubs.[18] To avoid harsh scrutiny by local law enforcement, a club could establish its relative respectability by prohibiting black–white dancing altogether.[19]

Respectable blacks also disdained racial mixing, but for reasons that differed from those of Whites. Rather than emphasize sexual perils, black leaders cited the threat to racial peace. One black newspaper asserted that "dance halls wherein races mix are certainly the worst nuisances" because they "brought bad elements of the white and colored people together under inflammatory conditions and eventually that was certain to bring about a race collision, which might easily have the most terrible consequences."[20] Another black paper warned that the clubs were "a continuing menace of the most serious character, especially to our reputable colored residents who might be the chief sufferers from an outbreak of race passion."[21] Prominent blacks sometimes called for interracial cooperation to close down the clubs and dance halls where race mingling took place.[22] For blacks, interracial sex threatened their fragile hold on respectability and their freedom to build communities of color without fear of racial violence.

Dance hall operators and hostesses keenly appreciated the relevance of race to sexual respectability. They understood that sexual segregation was integral to racial identity and that racial privilege required special treatment of white male customers. Clubs that catered to white men's sexual appetites enjoyed a higher standing than those that indulged nonwhite customers' tastes. Dance halls could appease white authorities and patrons alike by allowing white men to choose black women as partners, but prohibiting black men from selecting white women. Other establishments excluded blacks, Asians, and Mexicans altogether for fear that they would drive away white customers. As one Chicago dance hall owner explained: "[Y]ou've got to look out for . . . the Chinks. The West-side guys [white ethnics] out there won't come. Once a girl goes with these Chinks they're too low down for any decent American guy to want to dance with."[23] Another successful operator remarked: "No really white guy is willing to go in and dance with these Chinks or Japs or whatnot. He's got to have a little nigger in him to be willing to do that."[24]

Black men who patronized clubs that catered to a taste for white women ran the risk of prosecution in states that criminalized extramarital sexual activities. For instance, in the 1920s, a black man was charged with pandering when he frequented a club where "white girls meet up with colored fellows." In his defense, he insisted that the prostitute was "passing as a colored girl. She was supposed to be colored when she was at 34th and State." Showing his respect for racial boundaries, he added: "If I knew she was white when I met her I never would have had anything to do with her." Despite his protestations, he was convicted and given the maximum penalty of one year in jail and a fine of one thousand dollars as well as court costs.[25] To preserve racial hierarchy in the face of changing mores, black men had to pay a penalty even for commodified interracial sex, a price that was not exacted from white men.

Precisely because interracial sex challenged the color line, it had to be carefully managed to avoid devaluing whiteness. White dance hall hostesses treated nonwhite patrons as inferior, although they were the source of lucrative tips and favors. White women referred to Asian men as "fish"—overly generous customers who could easily be reeled in because of their lonely lives in bachelor communities.[26] The women equated whiteness with respectability. A woman might trade on her racial desirability at a dance hall, but she could still salvage some sexual decency by refusing to act as though the interracial contact were pleasurable. To preserve their reputations, hostesses sometimes drew the line between dancing with nonwhite men for money and dating them outside of work: "The Flips [Filipinos] are all right for anybody that wants them. But they're not white, that's all. Of course, I'll dance with them at the hall. But I won't go out with them. I'm white, and I intend to stay white."[27]

Hostesses and prostitutes were well aware that their white allure could be lost through excessive familiarity with nonwhite patrons. Once a white woman's racial advantage was squandered, she would be little better than a nonwhite prostitute. Whiteness conferred a concrete market value. Compared to black prostitutes, white women were able to charge higher prices, limit more strictly the sexual services offered, and avoid arrest to a greater degree by working in brothels rather than on the streets. Even among black prostitutes, race privilege was commodified: Dark-skinned women generally earned less than light-skinned ones.[28] In the sex trade, race shaped perceptions not only of sexual desirability but also of femininity and moral worth. White prostitutes often were portrayed as victims of their own poor judgment and male lust, while black prostitutes were characterized as flagrant, aggressive, immoral, and wholly degraded.[29] As historian Hazel Carby has concluded, there were throughout this period "fears of a rampant and uncontrolled female sexuality; fears of miscegenation; and fears of an independent black female desire that ha[d] been unleashed through migration."[30]

A white woman who was too free with her favors could lose her market and moral advantage. The story of a Polish woman, Florence Klepka, is illustrative. She began as a burlesque performer at age nineteen but, after becoming pregnant, had to leave the shows to work in dance halls. There she served Greek and Italian men but lost her clientele when she developed a reputation for being promiscuous. She then began accepting dates from Filipino men but soon became too "common" for them. So she left dancing and turned to prostitution in Filipino rooming houses. Another woman followed much the same path but wound up as an independent prostitute who primarily served blacks and Chinese. Attempting to return to the Filipino dance halls, she was shunned for having "gone African."[31]

The new conditions of urban life intensified the line between sex and marriage in white, middle-class relationships, so that commercial prostitution could be treated as wholly distinct from romantic love and traditional matrimonial arrangements. No such distinction, however, kept the degradation of interracial sex from infecting images of intermarriage. With cross-racial sexual liaisons characterized as deviant and dirty, marriage across the color line seemed incomprehensible and indecent. In the early 1900s, for example, the black heavyweight champion boxer, Jack Johnson, became notorious for his affairs with white women. In 1912, he met a young white woman, Lucille Cameron, promised her employment at his interracial Chicago nightclub, and began having sex with her. Cameron's mother filed abduction charges against Johnson, but the prosecution collapsed when Cameron refused to testify. Although Johnson and Cameron later married, the law was not through with a flamboyant black man who openly flouted norms of sexual and marital propriety. Within a year of his marriage, authorities prosecuted Johnson under the Mann Act based on the testimony of a white prostitute with whom he had once had an affair. She alleged that Johnson had paid her to travel from Pittsburgh to Chicago for immoral purposes. Based on her evidence, an all-white jury convicted Johnson, and he was sentenced to one year in prison.[32]

Although Johnson was the most prominent black to be prosecuted under the Mann Act, he was not the only one. When black men attempted to travel with their white fiancees to states that permitted interracial marriage, they were sometimes charged with abduction or white slavery. White women who chose to marry black men were considered sexually immoral or incompetent.[33] Rife with illicit sexual connotations, interracial relationships seemed to offer no basis for a marriage predicated on ideals of tempered passion, mutual respect, and shared interests. The white woman seduced into marrying a black man clearly was not upholding middle-class standards of purity, and so she had to be adjudged a "white slave" to her misguided libido.

"Separate but Equal" Sex and Marriage: Assimilation to White Norms

By reinforcing views of interracial sex and marriage as pathological behaviors, antimiscegenation laws created a norm of "separate but equal" families. Segregated households did not guarantee autonomy for nonwhites, however. Instead, reformers found it necessary to assimilate nonwhites to white, middle-class mores as a way to cultivate the good character essential for healthy families and meaningful equality. Some groups escaped this reformist zeal either because they had already been saved or because they were not ripe for redemption. Mexicans in the Southwest had undergone a religious transformation when Spanish colonists converted the native population to Catholicism. As a result of this conversion, Mexicans had adopted the principle of lifelong, monogamous marriage and condemned adultery and fornication. Consequently, although there were some concerns about sexually libertine Mexican women, reformers for the most part found the families acceptably Christian in their beliefs and practices.[34] Chinese bachelor communities, on the other hand, did not provide an opportune site for reform because gender imbalances impeded the formation of same-race families. Missionaries could not urge Asian men to marry and have children when the immigrants were sojourners who were supposed to remain unattached until they returned home. In anticipation of that day, though, proselytizing reformers did try to convince Chinese men to abandon what they perceived to be a heathen polygamy in favor of a Christian, nuclear family structure. Yet these calls for change were largely abstractions and lacked the cachet of saving real-life families.[35]

Rather than focus on the moot question of family reform, white crusaders decried the sexual perversions of Chinatown and called for crackdowns on prostitution. In segregated immigrant enclaves, the sex trade flourished, in part because—as in red-light districts—the traffic in female bodies was discreetly hidden from the view of respectable whites. The plethora of Chinese men without women made prostitution highly lucrative. Asian men went abroad to find Chinese women who could be tricked, forced, or sold into prostitution. Once in the United States, these women were unable to escape their plight. Linguistically and culturally isolated in a foreign country, they were kept in cribs, small locked rooms that lined the alleyways of Chinatown. The women served large numbers of men, both Chinese and white, for a small fee and often with no other promise than their release from servitude.[36] Alarmed by the fate of these women, Presbyterian missionaries ran a home in California for escaped Chinese prostitutes from 1874 to 1939. Workers at the home rescued the women from cribs, gave them a safe place to live, and assisted them in court when owners attempted to enforce labor contracts for sexual services.[37] Yet these rescue attempts were not linked to any vision of family reformation as a cure for the ills of prostitution. Instead, the efforts reinforced the image of Asian male immigrants as immoral, depraved, and unfit for citizenship.

By contrast, black and Native American families offered ample opportunities for racial rehabilitation. For blacks, the process of uplifting families began in earnest with Reconstruction. During slavery, couples had not been able to marry. Black women regularly bore children out of wedlock, raised them without the father in residence, and turned to their parents or other relatives for help. These practices clearly deviated from white norms, which required couples to marry before bearing children and put men in charge of the household. To correct these unconventional practices, the Freedmen's Bureau required all former slaves to register their marriages or be prosecuted for adultery. In addition, the bureau empowered black men to act as heads of the household. Under sharecropping arrangements, men could sign contracts for the labor of the entire family. Black women were compensated at a lower rate than black men under the bureau's wage scales, and families without a male head of household sometimes received smaller land allotments than those with a man in charge.[38] The reconfiguration of black families was considered essential to full emancipation:

> All women were expected to defer to men, but for black women deference was a racial imperative. Slavery and racism sought the emasculation of black men. . . . Part of the responsibility of black men was to "act like a man," and part of the responsibility of black women was to encourage and support the manhood of our men. A woman should never intimidate him with her knowledge or common sense, let him feel stable and dominant.[39]

Although elite blacks readily conformed to this model of the family, the less affluent chafed at its confines. An informal system of separation and remarriage persisted among low-income blacks because they could not pay for a formal divorce. Authorities largely ignored the practice "[s]o long as [it] affects no one but Negroes."[40] Moreover, poor black women often found the new version of family imposed by the Freedmen's Bureau a bad bargain. Officially stripped of power and authority in the family, these women did not gain the privileges of domesticity accorded to middle-class wives. Low-income black women continued to work in the fields while managing the home. In addition, men often wanted their wives to bear more children to maximize the profitability of sharecropping agreements. Applying white, middle-class norms to the lives of low-income black families hardly proved a prescription for marital bliss. The Freedmen's Bureau received hundreds of complaints about wife-beating, adultery, and failure to pay child support. Angry women demanded that their husbands not be allowed to sign labor contracts on their behalf.[41] In the end, rather than reconfigure low-income black families, Reconstruction reformers did little more than stigmatize alternative strategies for coping with poverty and instability.

Concerns about blacks' sexual and marital practices reemerged with their migration from the rural South to urban centers in the North and West. An influx of immigrants from eastern and southern Europe already had prompted fears of casual sex, which in turn gave rise to the social hygiene movement. Crowded into tenements, black migrants sparked new anxieties about sexual and marital anarchy. Elite blacks created societies to educate poor, black migrant women about the hardships of raising children without the benefit of marriage.[42] These societies tried to wean black migrants from beliefs about sex and marriage that they brought with them from the rural South. Despite the efforts of Reconstruction reformers and the exhortations of affluent blacks, low-income blacks never fully conformed to images of white, middle-class respectability. One turn-of-the-century poem popular among black miners and railroad workers in Alabama made the point:

> White folks on the sofa
> Niggers on the grass
> White man is talking low
> Nigger is getting ass.[43]

Regardless of their personal beliefs about marriage, poverty often left blacks in low-income, urban ghettoes with few choices. In a study of Philadelphia Blacks in 1899, W. E. B. Du Bois found that many young adults lacked the financial resources to marry. Instead, they relied on cohabitation and serial monogamy.[44] Poor blacks in the city could not conform to the white, middle-class image of the ideal family. Black women worked long hours in domestic employment and had little time to supervise their own children. In the rural South, friends and relatives kept a watchful eye on the youth. But in impersonal urban neighborhoods, children often wound up as truants from school and were arrested for "improper guardianship."[45] Black men, perhaps humiliated by their inability to fulfill the role of breadwinner, deserted their families at a much higher rate than white men. As a result, black women often found themselves heading households and raising children alone, just as they had during slavery.[46]

During the 1950s and 1960s, the civil rights movement once again focused the nation's attention on questions of racial equality. At the same time, the sexual revolution was creating a new sense of personal freedom to experiment with sex outside of marriage, and the women's liberation movement was forcing America to reconsider the subordinated status of women in marriage and family life.[47] This newfound spirit of openness and experimentation did not extend to the black family, however. Instead, government authorities continued to apply deeply traditional norms of sexual and marital propriety. In 1965, Daniel Patrick Moynihan wrote a report for President Lyndon Johnson that attributed problems of welfare dependency, drug addiction, delinquency, and crime to the matriarchal structure of black families.[48] Echoing the approach taken by the Freedmen's Bureau, Moynihan urged officials to break through the "tangle of pathology" by making an effort to ensure that black males were fully employed. In this way, black men could assume their roles as breadwinners and approximate the norm that "presumes male leadership in private and public affairs."[49] The Moynihan report was engulfed in controversy for blaming blacks' problems on family inadequacies rather than racism. Even so, few questioned whether applying a traditional model of white, middle-class nuclear families to low-income blacks was appropriate.[50]

Much as urban segregation and antimiscegenation laws meant that black families would be racially separate, the removal of Native American tribes to reservations ensured that their families would be racially identifiable. Once again, reformers took steps to rehabilitate these tribal families so that they would become "equal" through assimilation to white norms. Some reformers doubted that isolated Indian families could progress without civilizing contact with whites, including intermarriage. In 1854, anthropologist J. C. Nott wrote:

It has been falsely asserted that the *Choctaw* and *Cherokee* Indians have made great progress in civilization. I assert positively, after the most ample investigation of the facts, that the pure-blooded Indians are everywhere unchanged in their habits. Many white persons, settling among the above tribes, have intermarried with them; and all such trumpeted progress exists among these whites and their mixed breeds alone.[51]

In the 1870s, influential anthropologist Lewis Henry Morgan advocated intermarriage as a way to solve the Indian problem. He believed that through several generations of intermarrying with whites, children would become respectable and attractive. He concluded: "This is to be the end of the Indian absorption of a small portion, which will improve and toughen our race, and the residue run out or forced into the regions of the mountains."[52] Morgan did worry that, in some instances, the admixture of Indians and whites could prove unpredictable and dangerous.[53]

Rather than undertake the seemingly risky experiment of widespread intermarriage, reformers turned their attention to assimilating Indians on isolated reservations by altering their patterns of kinship, family, and community life. Many tribes operated on communal principles. Instead of a system of individual property ownership and nuclear families, members held land and resources collectively and shared responsibility for raising children. Some tribes also practiced polygyny to make up for a shortage of men or to divide work in efficient ways.[54] White reformers considered these alternative ways of life antithetical to the Indian's progress. Polygynous arrangements led white Christian missionaries to conclude that Native American men were lazy, while Native American women were industrious but degraded. Missionaries believed that a woman was "robbed of [her] proper dignity and tolerated only as she was able to minister to the desires of the man called her husband. In our own land, as in the Orient, the heaviest curse of heathenism falls on women."[55] Others blamed the sexual degradation on the women themselves: They "were all courtesans; a set of handsome tempting women. . . . The curse of the Mandanes is an almost total want of chastity."[56]

The federal government set about reforming such sexual and marital lawlessness. An 1885 report to the Board of Indian Commissioners explained why reconstructing family life was essential:

> More than any other idea, consideration of the family and its proper sphere in the civilizing of races and in the development of the individual, serves to unlock the difficulties which surround legislation for the Indian.

> The family is God's unit of society. On the integrity of the family depends that of the State. There is no civilization deserving of the name where the family is not the unit of civil government. . . .
>
> But the tribal system paralyzes at once the desire for property and the family life that ennobles that desire.[57]

In 1883, the Secretary of the Interior reported that Indian agents must prevent Indian men from using casual divorces to abandon their wives and children. The secretary insisted that "[s]ome system of marriage should be adopted, and the Indian compelled to conform to it."[58] During the late 1800s and early 1900s, the U.S. Supreme Court and two state courts made clear that states had no jurisdiction to punish adultery, polygamy, or other violations of marriage laws on tribal reservations.[59] To fill the moral and legal vacuum and ensure the rehabilitation of Indian families, the Commissioner of Indian Affairs outlawed polygamy and authorized harsh penalties for adultery, cohabitation, licentiousness, bastardy, and fornication.[60]

By parceling out reservation land to Indian families and making Native American men the owners, Congress hoped that the Dawes Act[61] would inculcate an appreciation of property ownership and patriarchal nuclear families. As Merrill Gates, an Indian reformer, explained in 1896:

> We have . . . the absolute need of awakening in the savage Indian broader desires and ampler wants. To bring him out of savagery into citizenship we must make the Indian more intelligently selfish before we can make him unselfishly intelligent. . . . The desire for property of his own may become an intense educating force. The wish for a home of his own awakens him to new efforts. Discontent with the teepee and the starving rations of the Indian camp in winter is needed to get the Indian out of the blanket and into trousers,—and trousers with a pocket in them, and with a *pocket that aches to be filled with dollars!*[62]

When property was distributed, only single members of the tribe over age eighteen, orphans under eighteen, and married Native American men were eligible to receive an allotment. Married Native American women were completely excluded from receiving property in deference to their husbands' status as heads of the household.

To interrupt the transfer of Native American values from one generation to the next, the federal government separated children from their families so that they could be resocialized in settings dominated by whites. In 1904, the Superintendent of Indian Schools indicated that Indian children must give up their communal values in order to make progress against "inherited weaknesses and tendencies" that include "habits of aimless living, unambition, and shiftlessness."[63] White contact was deemed critical to this transformation. Indian children had to be adopted by white families or temporarily placed with them as part of a boarding school education.[64] Whether or not Indian parents consented, the Commissioner of Indian Affairs considered the removal necessary because Indian children otherwise would grow up "with fathers who are degraded and mothers who are debased." In such deficient homes, the children's "ideas of human life will, of necessity, be deformed, their characters warped, and their lives distorted."[65] The boarding school system was not dismantled until the late 1920s and 1930s.

Native American children often adopted the norms of white communities while at boarding school. For instance, some students chose to marry in disregard of clan relationships and traditional tribal enmities. Not all of these marriages survived the couples' return to reservations, but some did endure and demonstrated that Native Americans could choose romantic individualism over collective loyalties.[66] At times, boarding school pupils reverted to Indian customs when they rejoined their tribes, a practice referred to as "return to the blanket." Reintegration into the tribe at times was marked by a traditional Indian marriage. Sun Elk of the Taos Pueblo describes the way in which his wedding reaffirmed his connection to his people:

> My father brought me a girl to marry. Her name was Roberta. Her Indian name was P'ah-Tah-Zhuli (Little Deer Bean). She was about 15 years old and had no father. But she was a good girl and she came to live with me in my new house outside the pueblo.
> When we were married I became an Indian again. I let my hair grow, I put on blankets, and I cut the seat out of my pants.[67]

Throughout the decades of federal intervention to reform Indian families, officials used policies about sex, marriage, and childrearing to preserve racial difference as a biological matter while eradicating its social and cultural significance. As a result, Indian weddings often became a symbolic right of passage, proof of a tribal loyalty based not only on blood but also a common way of life.

In sum, by making families racially identifiable, antimiscegenation laws increased the salience of cultural differences in sex, marriage, and childrearing practices. Far from creating a safe haven for alternative family structures, segregation increased fears of dangerous and destructive differences. Often the urge to transform nonwhite families came as shifting racial boundaries provoked uncertainty and anxiety. When blacks were emancipated, Reconstruction reformers sought to remake black families in the image of white respectability without countenancing race-mixing. As blacks migrated to northern and western cities in the early 1900s, their place in the racial hierarchy once more became unsettled. The color line was challenged when the conditions of black migrants' lives converged with those of poverty-stricken immigrants from eastern and southern Europe. In response, middle-class reformers—both black and white—attempted to educate black migrants about the perils of interracial sex and the promise of traditional, same-race marriages and families. For Native American families, concerns about sex, marriage, and family arose when tribes were removed to reservations. Officials feared that the tribes would never become fully civilized because of their isolation from whites. To mitigate the danger of unassimilability, federal officials launched campaigns to build traditional nuclear families founded on Christian principles.

Conclusion

Most discussions of antimiscegenation laws have focused on their role in establishing racial hierarchies. What is often ignored, however, is the statutes' critical importance in building a normative hierarchy of sexual and marital practices. Just as the laws reinforced the racial superiority of whites, they placed their middle-class aspirations for love and marriage at the pinnacle of respectability. Whenever racial and sexual boundaries were contested, antimiscegenation doctrine provided a way to reassert the propriety of same-race sex and marriage. By criminalizing interracial relations, the law signaled the debauched and depraved nature of those who crossed the color line. Race-mingling meant ruin, not romance.

Perhaps even more perniciously, the statutes created a principle of "separate but equal" families that presumed that nonwhite couples should assimilate to white, middle-class norms. Demands for assimilation seldom took account of the limitations imposed by poverty and instability. Moreover, the insistence that nonwhites conform to white standards rejected the cultural worth of their alternative approaches to sex, marriage, and childrearing. Segregated by law, nonwhites could not capitalize on their isolated condition to build a distinct way of life. Instead, the pervasiveness of racial subordination was brought home by the imperative to assimilate, even in areas as deeply personal as sex, marriage, and family.

FIVE

Judicial Review of Antimiscegenation Laws: The Long Road to *Loving*

ANTIMISCEGENATION LAWS were designed to establish racial boundaries, contain racial ambiguity, and preserve sexual decency. When racial identities and sexual norms were in flux, the statutes were challenged, but they survived substantially intact until the 1960s. In upholding the laws, courts revealed the shifting significance of race, sex, and marriage. Race gradually became transformed from a genetic hierarchy to a biological irrelevancy. Laws mandating segregation were treated as a regrettable vestige of past discrimination, and eventually interracial intimacy ceased to be regarded as a subversive threat to the social order. Sexual and marital choices were no longer treated as an integral part of the formation of the state but instead became private matters primarily of concern to the individuals involved. The demise of antimiscegenation laws depended critically on the reconstruction of not only race but also of sexual and marital freedom. Racial equality in intimate affairs could be reconceived only when individuals were emancipated to experiment with alternative visions of sex and marriage.

Reconstruction and the Reconsideration of Antimiscegenation Laws

Before the Civil War, antimiscegenation laws were used to define racial identity and enforce racial inequality, particularly in southern states seeking to preserve a system of slavery. After the war, government officials faced a dilemma. Did full equality for blacks require the rescission of restrictions on interracial sex and marriage? As the federal government undertook to rehabilitate former black slaves during Reconstruction, the scope of the equality principle was limited to preserve antimiscegenation statutes. Officials were quick to distinguish between "political" equality, which related to formal access to the governmental process, and "social" equality, which related to informal relations among neighbors, friends, and family. Reconstruction was aimed at enabling blacks to vote, hold office, and serve on juries, but it did not necessarily try to promote "race-mixing" through interracial neighborhoods, friendships, and families. When foes of Reconstruction held up miscegenation as the bête noire of social equality, reformers laughed off the threat as extreme and implausible.[1]

Although defenders of Reconstruction often treated the dangers of miscegenation dismissively, some reformers did successfully challenge bans on interracial marriage. Six states—most in the North, and the rest in the Midwest and West—repealed antimiscegenation laws.[2] A few southern states also temporarily dropped restrictions on intermarriage.[3] State legislatures were responsible for most of the changes, but state courts could play an important role in evaluating whether antimiscegenation statutes were racially discriminatory. In 1872 in *Burns v. State*,[4] the Alabama Supreme Court declared a ban on racial intermarriage unlawful. Relying on the Civil Rights Act of 1866 and the Fourteenth Amendment, the court emphasized that marriage was a contract and that blacks now had the "right to make any contract which a white citizen may make."[5] By treating marriage as a contract, the *Burns* decision rejected the distinction between political and social equality as justification for an antimiscegenation law. Nor did the court accept the argument that the Alabama legislature had satisfied the requirement of equal treatment by imposing equivalent penalties on blacks and whites. In the court's view, the Civil Rights Act was not designed "to create merely an equality of the races in reference to each other. If so, laws prohibiting the races from suing each other, giving evidence for or against, or dealing with one another, would be permissible."[6]

After the end of Reconstruction, the Alabama high court reversed the *Burns* decision. In the 1877 case of *Green v. State*,[7] the court found that Congress did not intend the Civil Rights Act of 1866 to overturn antimiscegenation laws. After all, many congressmen who voted for the Act lived in states that banned interracial marriage. The Alabama court explicitly adopted the distinction between political and social equality in upholding restrictions on intermarriage. Unconvinced that marriage was simply a contract between individuals, the Alabama court considered it a civil status vital to the state's welfare. In the court's view, homes were "the nurseries of States," and public officials were entitled to regulate marriage to promote the general good. Miscegenation was a danger that states could prevent: "Who can estimate the evil of introducing into their most intimate relations, elements so heterogeneous that they must naturally cause discord, shame, disruption of family circles and estrangement of kindred?"[8] Nor did the antimiscegenation law violate federal protections against racial discrimination. So long as blacks and whites suffered comparable punishment, according to the court, the law was racially neutral. In any event, the state had no affirmative obligation to promote social equality among the races.[9]

The opinion in *Green* surely was proof that Reconstruction was limited in its reach, and that marriage and family law offered a way to preserve the color line despite a requirement of formal equality. In addition, *Green* reflected a growing belief that the state must restrict sexual and marital freedom to serve the common good. During the colonial period, the government's role in regulating marriage was unclear. In England, even though couples had to take certain formal legal steps to marry, informal marriages flourished as young lovers fled parental opposition.[10] During the early years of colonization, wedding banns and licenses offered a way for local communities to supervise and approve marriages. Still, decentralized colonial rule did not lend itself to vigorous enforcement of official requirements regarding marriage.[11]

After independence, states were generous in recognizing informal, or common law, marriages. Common law arrangements accorded primacy to individuals who were free to consent to marriage, regardless of formal community approval.[12] Until the mid-1800s, the freedom to marry steadily expanded as states "lowered fees and authorized a widening number of religious sects, municipal officials, and judicial officers to perform marriages."[13] Marriage licenses were used to register rather than regulate marriages, and parents found it difficult to use official channels to prevent children from marrying an undesirable spouse.[14] By the 1870s, a matrimonial reform movement had arisen to question this laissez-faire approach. Citing the rise of urbanization, reform advocates argued that the United States could no longer rely on informal controls in close-knit, rural communities to ensure that wise decisions were made about whom to wed. Sound marriages were considered essential to the community's well-being because families were the building blocks of good social order. States had a primary responsibility to regulate marriage because it was a civil status with far-reaching consequences, not just a private contract between two parties.[15]

The Alabama high court's approach to miscegenation in *Green* clearly reflected this shifting view of marriage. The court saw proper marital choices as vital to the state's future. Marriage was recharacterized as an instrument of the public good, but the result was not an endorsement of political equality at the altar. Instead, antimiscegenation laws assumed heightened importance as a way to avoid disruption of a segregated social order. As one southerner explained:

> Do away with the social and political distinctions now existing, and you immediately turn all the blacks and mulattoes into citizens, co-governors, and acquaintances: and acquaintances . . . are the raw material from which are *manufactured friends, husbands, and wives.* The man whom you associate with is next invited to your house, and the man whom you invited to your house is the possible husband of your daughter, whether he be black or white.[16]

By upholding the antimiscegenation law, the Alabama court explicitly recognized the state's power to advance a segregated vision of the good life, regardless of individual desires. Romantic impulses had to be subordinated to racial imperatives, and no formal principle of equality would stand in the way.

In *Pace and Cox v. State*,[17] the Alabama Supreme Court expanded on *Green* by allowing the state to punish interracial fornication and adultery more severely than intraracial fornication and adultery. Under Alabama law, a conviction for interracial adultery meant incarceration for two to seven years. By contrast, a first offense of same-race adultery was punished only by a fine of no more than one hundred dollars and, where appropriate, up to six months in jail. Although penalties for subsequent offenses were more severe, the maximum penalty for same-race adultery was two years in jail.[18] The Alabama high court concluded that the law did not discriminate against any person based on race because the discrimination was "directed against the offense, the nature of which is determined by the opposite color of the cohabiting parties."[19] Whether white or black, a person who crossed the color line to engage in illicit sex was subject to heightened punishment. The tough penalties were a justifiable means of preventing "amalgamation of the two races, producing a mongrel population and a degraded civilization, the prevention of which is dictated by a sound public policy affecting the higher interests of society and government."[20]

In 1882, in *Pace v. Alabama*,[21] the U.S. Supreme Court upheld the Alabama high court's decision, thereby institutionalizing a "separate but equal" principle in sexual and marital regulation. Before the Court, Alabama asserted that its antimiscegenation law "is a recognition of difference of races, but does not place upon either the badge of inferiority; they are based upon the idea of dissimilarity, which does not necessarily mean legal or civil inequality."[22] Writing for a unanimous Court, Justice Stephen J. Field adopted Alabama's reasoning: "[Interracial adultery or fornication] cannot be committed without involving the persons of both races in the same punishment. Whatever discrimination is made in the punishment prescribed . . . is directed against the offence designated and not against the person of any particular color or race. The punishment of each offending person, whether white or black, is the same."[23] In the Court's view, Alabama was entitled to treat desire across the color line as a more serious, criminal threat to the public welfare than desire that respected racial boundaries.[24]

The Court recognized the states' primacy in regulating sex, marriage, and family under a federalist system. Indeed, this proposition seemed so evident by the late 1800s that Pace himself conceded Alabama's authority in his brief and simply argued that Alabama could not use the criminal code to regulate intimate relationships in discriminatory ways. As Pace argued: "Legislative power may regulate how the lawful institution of marriage may be celebrated for the welfare of society, but legislative power may not say how crimes, in themselves penal, may be discriminately punished . . . according to the caste of the individual. . . ."[25] The Court rejected this effort to distinguish between the state's power to regulate marriage and its power to criminalize illicit sexuality. Once interracial relations were classified as a question of social rather than political equality, the federal government was not empowered to interfere with Alabama's efforts to promote the general welfare as it saw fit.

After *Pace*, antimiscegenation laws proliferated. Bolstered by the Court's approval, twenty states and territories added or strengthened bans on interracial sex and marriage between 1880 and 1920. Some states went so far as to amend their constitutions to include prohibitions on miscegenation.[26] Not only did the provisions forbid intermarriage of blacks and whites, some also addressed intermarriage with Native Americans, who had largely been ignored under earlier laws. At least one commentator even questioned the union of John Rolfe and Pocahontas, insisting that "no one will say that the experiment thus made of the intermarriage of the redman and the paleface was a success."[27] With the rise of Asian immigration, many western states added bans on white intermarriage with "Mongolians."[28] A 1910 study found that the increase in antimiscegenation laws "has not been confined to the South [and] has in large measure escaped the adverse criticism heaped upon other race distinctions."[29] Twenty years later, another study reported that statutes barring interracial sex and marriage commanded universal judicial approval.[30]

The legitimation of antimiscegenation laws presaged the emergence of a "separate but equal" doctrine in public life. Fourteen years after *Pace,* the Court extended this principle to public facilities and services in *Plessy v. Ferguson,*[31] a decision that sealed the fate of Reconstruction and endorsed the rise of a Jim Crow caste system. The Court found that equal access did not mean that facilities had to be racially integrated. Any coercive efforts to desegregate could violate the freedom to choose one's associates, an impermissible effort to enforce social equality.[32] *Plessy* focused on railway transportation and was quickly expanded to other areas, including public schools, courts, hospitals, libraries, and parks.[33] With the *Pace* and *Plessy* decisions, the line between political and social equality had become wholly manipulable and incoherent. Segregation in sex, marriage, and family could be coerced despite a norm of political equality because of a strong public interest in social stability. Yet the integration of schools, parks, courts, and railroads could not be mandated because it interfered with private, social arrangements.

Eugenics and the Regulation of Sexuality

Bans on intermarriage enjoyed unequivocal support not only because they reinforced racial segregation but also because they were consistent with efforts to reform marriage and control sexuality. In the late 1800s and early 1900s, urbanization and immigration prompted concerns about the genetic integrity of the American population. Reformers feared "race suicide" if desirable whites procreated at low rates while immigrants and blacks multiplied at alarmingly high ones. Eugenic reformers, including leading physicians and prominent citizens, demanded that immigration of weak-gened immigrants from southern and eastern Europe be stopped and that states prevent the genetically unfit from procreating.[34] The U.S. Supreme Court never explicitly endorsed a eugenic rationale for antimiscegenation laws, but it did accept this justification for invasive sexual control of those deemed genetically inferior. Between

1907 and 1931, twenty-seven states enacted mandatory sterilization laws, aimed primarily at the feebleminded and criminal. The statutes were quite controversial, and state courts declared them unconstitutional deprivations of due process and equal protection. Faced with doubts about the permissibility of forced sterilization, some state officials were reluctant to enforce the laws.[35]

In 1927, the Court resolved concerns about the constitutionality of these statutes in *Buck v. Bell*.[36] In an opinion by Justice Oliver Wendell Holmes, the Court held that Carrie Buck, "a feeble minded white woman" committed to a state institution, could be sterilized without her consent under a 1924 Virginia law. According to Holmes's opinion, Virginia could preserve the public welfare by preventing the state from being "swamped with incompetence."[37] Virginia officials might properly infer that "[i]t is better for all the world, if instead of waiting to execute degenerate offspring for crime, or to let them starve for their imbecility, society can prevent those who are manifestly unfit from continuing their kind."[38] Holmes believed that sterilization benefited the feebleminded because they could freely reenter society once fears that they would perpetuate their mental deficiencies were allayed.[39] The Court's decisions on race, marriage, and sexuality gave the states broad authority to regulate intimacy on eugenic grounds.

Although the Court was willing to tolerate gross invasions of marital and sexual autonomy, it took important steps to insulate families from government interference. In a series of cases in the early and mid-1920s, the Court used due process protections to preserve parents' freedom to bring up their children as they saw fit. In these decisions, the Court was concerned not with biological arguments about the genetically unworthy but with claims to social and cultural autonomy in a democracy. State legislatures had enacted laws that forbade foreign-language instruction in private schools to ensure that immigrant children, most often German-speaking ones, were loyal and patriotic.[40] As a result, parents could not remove their children from the public schools to place them in programs responsive to their special linguistic needs. In *Meyer v. Nebraska,* the Court found this restriction on parental freedom unconstitutional:

> [The liberty guaranteed by due process] denotes not merely freedom from bodily restraint but also the right of the individual to contract, to engage in any of the common occupations of life, to acquire useful knowledge, to marry, establish a home and bring up children, to worship God according to the dictates of his own conscience, and generally, to enjoy those privileges long recognized at common law as essential to the orderly pursuit of happiness by free men.[41]

By acknowledging a right to marry and raise children, the Court seemed to reject the view that states could regulate intimate relationships to promote a particular vision of the social order. Allowing government officials to usurp parental authority reflected "ideas touching the relation between individual and State [that] were wholly different from those upon which our institutions rest" and would "do[ ] violence to both letter and spirit of the Constitution."[42] Justices Holmes, in keeping with his willingness to regulate marriage and sexuality on eugenic grounds, dissented. Reflecting the view that families are the building blocks of society, Holmes believed that officials could reasonably restrict education to ensure that children assimilated to an American way of life.[43]

For two decades, cases like *Meyer,* which upheld a right to be free of state interference in marrying and raising a family, coexisted with *Buck v. Bell,* which permitted severe state-imposed limits on procreation. With the rise of Nazism in Europe in the late 1930s and early 1940s, Americans became increasingly fearful of eugenic policies. In 1942, the Court took steps to protect procreative freedom based on an explicit recognition of the dangers of racial engineering. In *Skinner v. Oklahoma,*[44] the Court struck down a statute that mandated sterilization of habitual criminals after two or more convictions for felonies involving moral turpitude. The law exempted those who committed "offenses arising out of the violation of the prohibitory laws, revenue acts, embezzlement, or political offenses."[45]

In overturning Skinner's sterilization order, Justice William O. Douglas announced that the "case touches on a sensitive and important area of human rights" because "Oklahoma deprives certain individuals of a right which is basic to the perpetuation of a race—the right to have offspring."[46] Finding that "[m]arriage and procreation are fundamental to the very existence and survival of the race," the Court had to apply strict scrutiny, the most stringent level of constitutional review, to "[a]ny experiment which the State conducts."[47] Otherwise, the power to sterilize "[i]n evil or reckless hands . . . can cause races or types which are inimical to the dominant group to wither and disappear."[48] The Court found that Oklahoma's law drew implausible distinctions among classes of criminals that could not survive exacting judicial review. The Court, for example, saw no reason why the criminal tendencies of an embezzler were less damaging to the state of Oklahoma than those of a chicken thief.

In spite of its stirring rhetoric, the *Skinner* decision did not completely resolve the tensions between the marital and procreative freedoms of individuals and the authority of the state to advance the general welfare.

The Court invalidated the Oklahoma statute because of the irrational distinctions it drew, but it refused to overturn *Buck v. Bell* because the Constitution did not absolutely prohibit states from regulating sex and procreation.[49] Even so, *Skinner* dealt a severe blow to eugenic justifications, including those underlying antimiscegenation laws. Rather than rely on the alleged biological dangers of race-mixing, officials would have to justify the statutes by asserting the social and psychological benefits of segregation. Yet, these claims would put state governments in the position of commandeering families to perpetuate a particular vision of the social good, a stance seeming antithetical to *Meyer* and its progeny. Despite the doctrinal conundrum that *Skinner* posed for bans on interracial sex and marriage, the Court did not declare these provisions unconstitutional for another twenty-five years.

Challenges to Antimiscegenation Laws after World War II

Just as World War II alerted America to the perils of eugenic policies, the conflict prompted a reconsideration of race relations. The United States had played a leading role in destroying a Nazi regime that espoused a doctrine of racial superiority, yet America continued to tolerate state-mandated segregation in education, transportation, and other public facilities. Nonwhite soldiers who had risked their lives to fight Nazism insisted on equal treatment in their own country, regardless of race. Building on this newfound sense of entitlement, the civil rights movement began to challenge an entrenched racial caste system.[50] As part of this effort, reformers undid some antimiscegenation laws during the postwar period. From the early 1950s to the mid-1960s, thirteen state legislatures located mainly in the West repealed bans on interracial sex and marriage.[51] Nevertheless, with one notable exception, state courts remained largely unmoved by arguments that antimiscegenation statutes were impermissibly discriminatory.

A Notable Exception: *Perez v. Sharp*

In 1948, the California Supreme Court in *Perez v. Sharp*[52] became the first and only state high court since Reconstruction to declare a ban on interracial marriage unconstitutional. The petitioners, Andrea Perez, who was considered white, and Sylvester D., who was black, challenged two California Civil Code provisions that prohibited registrars from issuing licenses for the marriage of "a white person with a Negro, mulatto, Mongolian, or member of the Malay race" and declared all such marriages illegal and void.[53] In striking down the law, Justice Roger J. Traynor contradicted the traditional view that the special nature of marriage made racial regulation constitutionally permissible. Most state courts had concluded that the government's unique stake in promoting strong, stable families justified antimiscegenation laws. In Traynor's view, though, the unique burden on the right to marry made the laws especially pernicious. When the U.S. Supreme Court upheld separate but equal facilities, a person still could enjoy the benefits of, for example, railroad transportation, even if the cars were segregated.[54] However, "[s]ince the essence of the right to marry is freedom to join in marriage with the person of one's choice, a segregation statute for marriage necessarily impairs the right to marry."[55]

Because an antimiscegenation statute created race-based classifications, it was subject to the most searching scrutiny under the equal protection clause.[56] Here, too, Justice Traynor relied on the special nature of marriage to undo the Supreme Court's reasoning in *Pace*. For Traynor, the issue was not whether whites as a group and nonwhites as a group suffered equal penalties under the law. Instead, the question was whether a person who wished to marry someone of a different race was treated in the same way as a person who wished to marry someone of the same race. The commitment to an individualistic principle of non-discrimination was especially apropos in the area of marriage: "The right to marry is the right of individuals, not of racial groups."[57]

The California Supreme Court definitively rejected the state's eugenic justifications for the ban on interracial marriage.[58] Justice Traynor dispensed with eugenic rationales by noting that "[m]odern experts are agreed that the progeny of marriages between persons of different races are not inferior to both parents."[59] Even if the law was designed to deter unfit marriages that would weaken the robustness of the state's population, its provisions were poorly tailored to accomplish this goal. The statute was both over- and underinclusive because "a tubercular Negro or a tubercular Caucasian may marry subject to the race limitation, but a Negro and a Caucasian who are free from the disease may not marry each other."[60] Moreover, the miscegenation ban extended to some, but not all, racial groups,[61] and it permitted marriages between persons of mixed ancestry, even though the dangers of amalgamation were the same.[62] Nor did the statute address extramarital relations across the color line, even though they too presented comparable dangers of race-mixing.[63]

The California Supreme Court in *Perez* also dismissed the state's concerns about the social and psychological welfare of children born to inter-married couples. There was no reason to presume that "persons wishing to marry in contravention of race barriers come from the 'dregs of society' and . . . their progeny therefore will be a burden on the community."[64] Moreover, even the "dregs of society" enjoyed a fundamental right to marry, and there was no basis for concluding that the "dregs" could be identified solely based on their willingness to cross the color line.[65] Nor was the statute necessary to mitigate racial tensions and prevent the birth of children who would become "social problems." As Traynor noted: "It is no answer to say that race tension can be eradicated through the perpetuation by law of the prejudices that gave rise to the tension."[66] The children of interracial marriages faced obstacles not because of their parents, but because of "prejudices in the community and the laws that perpetuate those prejudices by giving legal force to the belief that certain races are inferior."[67] Traynor observed that with the rising number of persons of mixed ancestry in the United States, the barriers they faced would steadily diminish.[68]

Having rejected all of the state's proffered justifications, the California Supreme Court then called into question the very foundations of the state's racial classification scheme. Traynor asserted that the antimiscegenation law was void for vagueness because it failed to indicate how persons of mixed ancestry should be categorized. California law referred to mulattoes but did not define the term and made no other attempt to classify mixed-race persons. In the majority's view, officials could not rely on ad hoc determinations of race in an area as momentous as the regulation of marriage.[69]

The *Perez* decision was 4–3. Justice John W. Shenk wrote a lengthy dissent joined by Justices B. Rey Schauer and Homer R. Spence. Shenk emphasized the state's prerogative to regulate marriage, the long-standing judicial approval of antimiscegenation laws, and the need to defer to legislative judgments regarding the threat to health, safety, morals, and the general welfare posed by interracial unions.[70] The dissent believed that reform should come from the legislature, not the judiciary.[71] Until then, public officials should be free to regulate some dangers of interracial mixing and not others. In the dissent's view, the adequacy of the law's racial classification scheme was simply not an issue because the petitioners conceded that the bride was white and the groom black.[72]

In justifying the ban on intermarriage, Shenk relied on both biological and social concerns. However, the dissent conceded that the eugenic underpinnings of the law were heavily disputed, so that social rationales assumed increasing significance. Shenk's opinion noted that "much that is best in human existence is a matter of social inheritance, not of biological inheritance. Race crossings disrupt social inheritance. That is one of its [*sic*] worst features."[73] As expert support, Shenk quoted Father John La Farge's 1943 work *The Race Question and the Negro* at length. La Farge contended:

> [I]dentification with the given [racial] group is far-reaching and affects innumerable aspects of ordinary daily life. . . .
> Where marriage is contracted by entire solitaries, such an interracial tension is more easily borne, but few persons matrimonially inclined are solitaries. They bring with them into the orbit of married life their parents and brothers and sisters and uncles and aunts and the entire social circle in which they revolve. All of these are affected by the social tension, which in turn reacts upon the peace and unity of the marriage bond.[74]

According to Shenk's dissent, the California legislature could regulate marital choices to promote same-race families in a segregated world. Stripped of a eugenic rationale, though, the antimiscegenation law appeared to be nothing more than social engineering to preserve the racial status quo. The U.S. Supreme Court had made plain in cases like *Meyer* that state governments could not interfere with marriage and family simply to advance a favored social or political agenda. Under the Court's substantive due process rationale, it was unclear why California could foster racially discrete identities by regulating the right to marry when it could not foster Americanized ones by regulating parental decisions about a child's education. Yet the dissenters in *Perez* made no attempt to distinguish *Meyer* and its progeny, presumably because they continued to defer to legislative judgments about the merits of eugenics.

Despite the clarity and comprehensiveness of the majority decision in *Perez,* it did not immediately prompt other state courts or the U.S. Supreme Court to strike down antimiscegenation statutes as unconstitutional.[75] Indeed, other states continued to enforce the laws vigorously. One year after the *Perez* decision, a man in Ellisville, Mississippi, was sentenced to five years in prison for marrying a white woman. He "had lived his life as a White in the White part of town and came from a family that had been considered White for the seventy years that older residents of Ellisville could recall." Although the husband appeared phenotypically white, "rumors had circulated, and trial and conviction followed."[76] That same year, in Roanoke, Virginia, officials tried a man for miscegenation because his mother-in-law dreamed that he was black. The Baptist minister who married the couple reported that the groom "seemed to be a white man. . . . He seemed to be very genteel and nice and I invited them to join my Bible class if they settled in Roanoke."[77] When the marriage soured, though, the bride's parents found that their son-in-law was not only growing increasingly vulgar and coarse but also was "getting darker and darker."[78] A few weeks later, the mother-in-law had her dream, and the man was arrested. In the South, then, antimiscegenation laws continued to pose a substantial threat to the freedom to marry, especially when a spouse could be criminally prosecuted based on speculative claims of a hidden black identity.

Perhaps states like Mississippi and Virginia considered California's stance on interracial marriage unique. Even before *Perez,* California had taken an extremely lenient approach to miscegenation. No criminal penalties attached to interracial marriages, to attempted interracial marriages, to interracial cohabitation, or to entry into the state by miscegenous couples.[79] The California Supreme Court therefore had arguably done little more than formally eliminate a law already largely eviscerated in practice. Even in this relatively tolerant environment, though, local registrars insisted on obtaining the race of applicants for marriage licenses after *Perez.* When one Caucasian couple wrote "human" in the space provided, they had to threaten a California registrar with a lawsuit to overcome his objections.[80]

A Reluctant Reformer: The U.S. Supreme Court
and Antimiscegenation Laws

In the mid-1950s, the U.S. Supreme Court began to dismantle the legacy of the Jim Crow caste system in *Brown v. Board of Education*[81] by declaring state-mandated segregation in public schools unconstitutional. In a unanimous opinion by Chief Justice Earl Warren, the Court held that official separation of the races was "inherently unequal" and therefore denied black students equal protection of the laws. The Court subsequently expanded this approach to cover other public services and facilities, including transportation, parks, and swimming pools. Faced with intense southern political opposition to school desegregation, the Justices were reluctant to address the constitutionality of antimiscegenation laws. Only six months after *Brown,* the Court without dissent refused to hear an appeal from Linnie Jackson's conviction under an Alabama statute barring interracial marriages.[82] Shifting their position on the nature of marriage once again, Alabama officials characterized it as a private contract, rather than a civil status fundamental to public order. As a result, they contended that *Brown* did not apply because its reach was limited to public services and facilities. *Perez* was dismissed as an aberration.[83] By refusing to hear the case, the Court sidestepped a potentially explosive issue. As one of Chief Justice Warren's law clerks that term recalled, "the denial of cert[iorari] was totally prudential, totally based on a high-level political judgment."[84]

The Court's reluctance to hear a challenge to antimiscegenation laws was not limited to statutes regulating black–white intermarriage. One year after the *Jackson* case, the Court had the opportunity to hear an Asian man's challenge to Virginia's enforcement of a ban on interracial marriage. In *Naim v. Naim*,[85] a Chinese seaman and Caucasian woman evaded Virginia's law by marrying in North Carolina. They then returned to their home in Virginia.[86] The marriage offered Naim new-found opportunities to participate in the American dream. In 1952, Congress had eliminated racial restrictions on naturalization, a key victory for previously ineligible Asian immigrants. Naim now could use his marriage to apply for an immigrant visa and become a U.S. citizen. Approximately fifteen months after the wedding, Naim's wife filed for an annulment because Virginia did not recognize interracial marriages. Naim moved to dismiss his wife's petition on the ground that the marriage was valid in North Carolina. For Naim, the stakes were high: If the annulment was granted, his immigration petition would fail and he would be deported.[87]

When a state trial court in Virginia annulled the marriage, Naim appealed. He argued that the Virginia courts lacked jurisdiction to invalidate a North Carolina marriage. In addition, he contended that Virginia's antimiscegenation law infringed on his fundamental right to marry and discriminated against him on the basis of race.[88] The Virginia Supreme Court upheld the annulment, emphasizing the primacy of the state's role in regulating marriage. While Alabama had defended its statute based on the private, contractual nature of marriage, Virginia's high court emphasized the role of marriage in preserving the social order:

> The institution of marriage has from time immemorial been considered a proper subject for State regulation in the interest of the public health, morals and welfare, to the end that family life, a relation basic and vital to the permanence of the State, may be maintained in accor-

dance with established tradition and culture and in furtherance of the
physical, moral and spiritual well-being of its citizens.

   We are unable to read in the Fourteenth Amendment to the Constitution, or in any other provision of that great document, any words or any
intendment which prohibit the State from enacting legislation to preserve
the racial integrity of its citizens, or which denies the power of the State
to regulate the marriage relation so that it shall not have a mongrel breed
of citizens. We find there no requirement that the State shall not legislate
to prevent the obliteration of racial pride, but must permit the corruption
of blood even though it weaken or destroy the quality of its citizenship.
Both sacred and secular history teach that nations and races have better
advanced in human progress when they cultivated their own distinctive
characteristics and culture and developed their own peculiar genius.[89]

The Virginia high court cited numerous precedents upholding antimiscegenation statutes and duly noted the U.S. Supreme Court's unwillingness to overturn these decisions.[90]

   When Naim appealed to the Supreme Court, four Justices—Earl
Warren, Hugo Black, William O. Douglas, and Stanley Reed—were
ready to decide the case. However, Felix Frankfurter feared that any
decision in *Naim* would jeopardize the Court's ability to implement
school desegregation. To avoid confronting the antimiscegenation issue,
Frankfurter worked with Justice Tom Clark to draft a per curiam opinion asking the Virginia court to clarify the factual basis for its jurisdiction
to annul Naim's marriage. Without further effort to clarify the record,
the Virginia Supreme Court flatly declared that Naim could not escape
Virginia law by marrying in North Carolina, an act it characterized as
an intentional evasion.

   Applauding this act of defiance, the *Richmond Times-Dispatch* com-
mended the Virginia court for rebuffing the Justices in an "area of
State affairs over which [the U.S. Supreme Court] has no jurisdiction."[91]
Warren, who had opposed the request for additional facts, concluded:
"That's what you get when you turn your ass to the grandstand."[92] Faced
with the Virginia high court's intransigence, Warren and Black wanted
to hear the case and overturn the Virginia ruling. Frankfurter nevertheless prevailed in convincing the Justices to decline the case for failure to
present a question of federal law, a rationale that has been characterized
as an "absurd fictitious ground."[93] Although Warren and Black believed
the Court had evaded its responsibility and Warren characterized the
Naim opinion as "total bullshit," another Justice summed up the rest

of the Court's view with respect to desegregation and antimiscegenation: "One bombshell at a time is enough."[94]

The U.S. Supreme Court did not review the constitutionality of antimiscegenation laws until the 1960s. By then, Congress had enacted the Civil Rights Act of 1964,[95] lending strong legislative and administrative support to the Court's efforts to desegregate schools and other public facilities.[96] No longer an isolated voice for racial reform, the Court could press ahead in addressing questions of equality, including the propriety of prohibiting interracial marriage.[97] At the same time, the Court was reconsidering its approach to the regulation of sex, marriage, and family. In *Skinner,* the Court did not invalidate the state's power to interfere in decisions about procreation but instead emphasized the irrational distinctions among habitual offenders that Oklahoma's compulsory sterilization law had made. *Skinner* coexisted uneasily with cases like *Meyer* that recognized a fundamental right to marry and bring up children free of government interference. By the mid-1960s, the Court was ready to resolve this conflict by adopting strong constitutional protections in the area of reproductive choice.

Relying on *Meyer* and related decisions,[98] the Justices in *Griswold v. Connecticut*[99] struck down a Connecticut statute that limited the use by married couples of contraceptives. The 1965 decision by Justice Douglas declared that marriage was an institution "intimate to the degree of being sacred," the very vitality of which depended on "privacy and repose."[100] According to the Court, the right of privacy in marriage was "older than the Bill of Rights," and the freedom inherent in the marital relationship was "an association that promotes a way of life. . . ."[101] In rejecting the Connecticut law, the Court noted that both the legislative philosophy and enforcement regime threatened "the sacred precincts of marital bedrooms [while police search] for telltale signs of the use of contraceptives."[102] Rejecting Douglas's claim that some liberties were so fundamental that they transcended textual provisions, Justices Hugo Black and Potter Stewart dissented because they could find no clear language in the Constitution to support rights of marital autonomy and privacy.[103]

Seven years later, the Court abandoned *Griswold*'s distinction between married and unmarried persons when it struck down a Massachusetts statute that denied single people access to contraceptives.[104] Writing for the Court, Justice William Brennan found that the legislature had overstepped its bounds in trying to discourage extramarital intercourse. Under Massachusetts law, fornication was a misdemeanor punishable by a fine of thirty dollars or three months in jail. Surely then, an unwanted pregnancy was a disproportionate penalty for this offense.[105] Refusing to distinguish between marital and extramarital sex, the Court insisted that the right in *Griswold* was that "of the *individual,* married or single, to be free from unwarranted governmental intrusion into matters so fundamentally affecting a person as the decision whether to bear or beget a child."[106] With Black's retirement from the Court and Stewart's decision to join the majority, only Chief Justice Warren Burger dissented. He chided the Court for its activism in using the Constitution to veto the states' political decisions.[107]

Strengthened norms of racial equality and emerging tenets of sexual and marital freedom—these judicial developments made antimiscegenation laws appear increasingly anomalous. If sexual and marital choices were protected, then why should decisions about the race of one's partner be regulated? If bans on intermarriage enforced racial segregation in sex, marriage, and family, why didn't the statutes violate norms of equal treatment? The Court finally began to tackle these questions in 1964 in *McLaughlin v. Florida.*[108] After watching through the window of a Miami Beach apartment, a landlady reported to police that Dewey McLaughlin, allegedly black, was living with her lessee, a white woman named Connie Hoffman.[109] Under Florida law, as a man and woman of different races habitually occupying the same room, McLaughlin and Hoffman were presumed to be having sex and thus were guilty of adultery and lewd cohabitation.[110] Had McLaughlin and Hoffman been of the same race, however, local prosecutors would have been unable to impose criminal penalties without proving intercourse. When arrested, Hoffman protested that "she never heard of any law that a Negro and a White woman couldn't live together and she didn't believe it." Later, she vowed to "go to the Supreme Court," a statement that proved prophetic.[111]

McLaughlin, on the other hand, sought to defend himself on the ground that he was not black but Latino. At trial, Hoffman's landlady described McLaughlin as "a Spanish fellow." Moreover, McLaughlin spoke fluent Spanish and identified himself as being from Lacieba, Honduras.[112] Nevertheless, the arresting officers concluded that McLaughlin was black based on "the physical presence and certain features that are predominant in colored males."[113] Despite defense objections to the officers' rough visual judgments,[114] a trial court convicted the couple of having illicit extramarital sex across the color line.[115]

On appeal to the Florida Supreme Court, McLaughlin contended that the penalties for interracial adultery were particularly unfair because of the ban on interracial marriage. Unlike same-race couples, interracial couples could not defend themselves from adultery charges based on a common law union. The state replied that punishing interracial adultery and fornication was necessary to prevent couples from contemplating interracial marriage.[116] Despite McLaughlin's efforts to link his case to the ban on intermarriage, the Florida Supreme Court limited itself to applying the U.S. Supreme Court's analysis in *Pace* to the adultery statute. On this basis, the state high court rejected McLaughlin's equal protection challenge to the adultery law because whites and blacks received the same punishment for extramarital sex across the color line.[117] The state court urged the Supreme Court to uphold the conviction despite new-fangled notions of racial equality:

> [T]his appeal is a mere way station on the route to the United States Supreme Court where defendants hope that, in the light of supposed social and political advances, they may find legal endorsement of their ambitions.
>   This Court is obligated by the sound rule of stare decisis and the precedent of the well written decision in *Pace.* . . . The Federal Constitution, as it was when construed by the United States Supreme Court in that case, is quite adequate but if the new-found concept of "social justice" has outdated "the law of the land," . . . it must be enacted by legislative process or some other court must write it.[118]

The Florida court was not alone in calling for restraint. While the *McLaughlin* case was pending before the U.S. Supreme Court, renowned constitutional law scholar Alexander Bickel urged the Justices to confine themselves to the cohabitation issue and not to create a controversy over the validity of interracial marriage, "an issue that is, after all, hardly of central importance in the civil rights struggle."[119] Following Bickel's suggestion, the Court limited its decision to the adultery statute and left intermarriage to another day.[120] As a result, *McLaughlin* focused on racial equality in the criminal justice system without addressing the relevance of the fundamental right to marry.[121]

Overruling *Pace v. Alabama,* the Court unanimously concluded that the Florida law discriminated on the basis of race in violation of equal protection and reversed McLaughlin's conviction.[122] In an opinion by Justice Byron White, the Court found that "*Pace* represents a limited view of the Equal Protection Clause which has not withstood analysis in the subsequent decisions of this Court."[123] Equal protection required not simply that members of legislatively defined classes be treated equally but also that the legislative classifications themselves be neither arbitrary nor invidious. Because the classification here was race-based and applied in a criminal context, it was subject to strict scrutiny under equal protection law.[124] As the first Supreme Court decision to apply this standard to strike down a racial classification, *McLaughlin* stood squarely for the proposition that officials must be colorblind unless they can offer compelling reasons for differential treatment based on race.

McLaughlin was a strong endorsement of a principle of nondiscrimination, but it did not deny the state's authority to regulate sexual conduct. Justice White concluded that Florida's purpose of "prevent[ing] breaches of the basic concepts of sexual decency"[125] was a concededly legitimate objective but did not justify singling out interracial cohabitation for special treatment. There was simply no reason to characterize promiscuity across the color line as especially disruptive or dangerous.[126] Because of the dangers of racial discrimination, the Court held that Florida's legislature could not exact severe penalties for interracial adultery as a first step in getting tough on extramarital sex in general. Legislators had no compelling basis for beginning with a category of sexual activity so fraught with dangers of abusive treatment based on race.[127] Moreover, there was no evidence that "a white person and a Negro are any more likely habitually to occupy the same room together than the white or the Negro couple or to engage in illicit intercourse if they do."[128] Although Frankfurter privately expressed skepticism that couples who lived together refrained from having sex, he joined the *McLaughlin* opinion.[129]

Echoing concerns raised by the California Supreme Court in *Perez,* McLaughlin also contended that the Florida statute was unconstitutionally vague because "Negro" was defined as "every person having one-eighth or more of African or negro blood," but there was no such thing as "Negro blood" and "white blood." Even if the term *blood* referred to African ancestry, the officers relied only on a subjective, ad hoc evaluation of the defendant's appearance.[130] Florida's counsel argued that McLaughlin was estopped from raising the vagueness claim because it had not been presented at trial or on appeal to the Florida Supreme Court. In any event, Florida defended McLaughlin's classification as black because he had "the external physical characteristics of a 100% full-blooded member of the Negro race." According to the state, the sin of Florida's fractional definition was "over-exactness . . . not ambiguity."[131] Although Florida's defense appeared to conflate genotype with rough judgments based on phenotype, the U.S. Supreme Court declined to reach the issue. The Court thereby left intact the racial classification scheme necessary to make Florida's ban on intermarriage intelligible.[132]

Immediately following the *McLaughlin* decision, Court watchers began to speculate that bans on interracial marriage would soon be declared unconstitutional.[133] These predictions were confirmed three years later when the Supreme Court struck down Virginia's statute criminalizing interracial marriage in *Loving v. Virginia*.[134] Richard Loving, a white man, and Mildred Jeter, a black woman, had grown up in Caroline County, Virginia, and had known each other since childhood.[135] Informally, racial lines in the county were malleable. Indeed, Caroline County had been called "the passing capital of America" because of the number of light-skinned blacks who were taken for white.[136] As one of Mildred's cousins put it: "Richard isn't the first white person in our family."[137] The Lovings were married in Washington, D.C., in June 1958 and immediately returned to Caroline County. Less than six weeks after the marriage, the justice of the peace issued arrest warrants for the couple. The Lovings eventually pleaded guilty to violating the antimiscegenation law and were each sentenced to one year in jail in January 1959. The sentence was suspended on condition that the Lovings leave Virginia and refrain from returning together for twenty-five years.[138] The Lovings then moved to Washington, D.C.[139]

Over four years later in November 1963, with representation from the American Civil Liberties Union (ACLU),[140] the Lovings went to state court to vacate the judgment against them and set aside their sentences. They argued that their punishment was cruel and unusual, violated the due process and equal protection clauses, and was a burden on interstate commerce. A little over a year after the Lovings filed their case, the Virginia trial court rejected all of their claims. According to Judge Bazile, the cruel and unusual punishment clause did not apply to anything as mild as the Lovings' sentences, and their conviction had nothing to do with interstate commerce because marriage was a domestic arrangement that was primarily a state and local concern.[141] After rejecting due process and equal protection challenges to the antimiscegenation statute, the trial court went on to argue that enforcement was a moral as well as legal obligation. According to the judge, "Almighty God created the races white, Black, yellow, malay, and red, and he placed them on separate continents. And but for the interference with his arrangement there would be no cause for such marriages. The fact that he separated the races shows that he did not intend for the races to mix. . . ."[142] Endorsing a curious blend of eugenics and divine authority, the trial court upheld Virginia's antimiscegenation statute.

The Lovings then filed suit in the federal district court for the Eastern District of Virginia, asking that a three-judge panel decide the constitutionality of the Virginia law. After hearing arguments in the case, the three-judge panel held that the Lovings must pursue their state remedies before seeking federal relief.[143] The federal court, however, retained jurisdiction over the case should the Virginia Supreme Court reject the Lovings' appeal.[144] The Lovings immediately sought review of Bazile's decision before the Virginia Supreme Court, arguing that the antimiscegenation statute violated due process and equal protection. The Virginia Supreme Court was unpersuaded by either claim, although it modified the sentence so that the Lovings could return to Virginia simultaneously as long as they did not cohabit.[145]

In rejecting the Lovings' appeal, the Virginia high court relied on its earlier decision in *Naim v. Naim.* In the court's view, subsequent decisions in *Brown v. Board of Education* and *McLaughlin v. Florida* did not undermine the validity of the state's antimiscegenation law. *Brown* dealt with public services like education, rather than the domestic institution of marriage. *McLaughlin* dealt with the criminalization of interracial adultery without reaching the regulation of marriage, where states had an admittedly vital interest.[146] The Virginia high court concluded that challenges to the law should be addressed to the legislature, rather than the judiciary.[147]

The Lovings' attorneys then sought and obtained direct U.S. Supreme Court review, again asserting that the Virginia statute violated due process and equal protection under the Fourteenth Amendment.[148] Although counsel on both sides offered arguments about the language and legislative history of the amendment, the Court found this evidence inconclusive and turned to other claims regarding the propriety of bans on interracial marriage.[149] Each side addressed the scientific justifications for restrictions on interracial marriage. On behalf of the Lovings, the ACLU cited a wide array of authority discrediting the eugenic rationale for the statute. Virginia responded by introducing evidence from non-southern scientific experts documenting the dangers of race-mixing.[150] In its brief, Virginia warned the Court not to usurp the state legislatures by entering "a veritable Serbonian bog of conflicting scientific opinion on the effects of interracial marriage. . . ."[151]

Recognizing the limitations of a strictly eugenic defense, Virginia's counsel, R. D. McIlwaine, justified the statute on social and cultural as well as biological grounds. As McIlwaine explained to the Court:

> We start with the proposition . . . that it is the family which constitutes the structural element of society; and that marriage is the legal basis upon which families are formed. . . . Text writers and judicial writers agree that the state has a natural, direct, and vital interest in maximizing the number of successful marriages which lead to stable homes and families and in minimizing those which do not.
>
> It is clear, from the most recent available evidence on the psychosociological aspect of this question that intermarried families are subjected to much greater pressures and problems than are those of the intramarried, and that the state's prohibition of interracial marriage, for this reason, stands on the same footing as the prohibition of polygamous marriage, or incestuous marriage, or the prescription of minimum ages at which people may marry, and the prevention of the marriage of people who are mentally incompetent.[152]

Citing a textbook by Dr. Albert Gordon, McIlwaine sought to persuade the Court that "intermarriage is definitely inadvisable; that they are wrong because they are most frequently, if not solely, entered into under present-day circumstances by people who have a rebellious attitude toward society, self-hatred, neurotic tendencies, immaturity, and other detrimental psychological factors."[153]

Yet McIlwaine's social and psychological claims left him on shaky ground with the Court. When Chief Justice Warren (whose daughter had married a man of a different faith) asked whether problems of interracial and interreligious marriages could be distinguished, McIlwaine eventually conceded that they could not.[154] Justice White pressed McIlwaine about whether the special problems facing intermarried couples and their children stemmed in part from laws like Virginia's antimiscegenation statute. Refusing to recognize a link between law and social attitudes, McIlwaine could only reply: "I don't find anywhere in this that the existence of the law does it. It is the attitude which society has toward interracial marriages, which in detailing his opposition, [Dr. Albert Gordon] says, 'causes a child to have almost insuperable difficulties in identification,' and that the problems which the child of an interracial marriage faces are those which no child can come through without damage to himself."[155]

In a unanimous opinion written by Warren, the Court rejected Virginia's justifications for its antimiscegenation law and declared race a biological irrelevancy. Because the Virginia law utilized a racial classification, the Court applied strict scrutiny as it had in *McLaughlin*.[156] Scientific claims about the perils of interracial marriage were not sufficient to uphold the statute under the searching review that race-based classifications triggered. Stripped of dubious scientific support, "the racial classifications must stand on their own justification, as measures designed to maintain white supremacy," particularly since only interracial marriages involving whites were the object of the Virginia legislature's concern.[157]

Although most of the brief opinion in *Loving* focused on equal protection, Warren included a short discussion of due process and the fundamental right to marry.[158] In finding that the antimiscegenation law violated due process, the Court characterized marriage as "one of the vital personal rights essential to the orderly pursuit of happiness by free men."[159] The Justices insisted that "the freedom to marry, or not marry, a person of another race resides with the individual and cannot be infringed by the State."[160] The social and psychological dangers cited by Virginia's counsel could not negate this fundamental liberty. In the original draft of Warren's opinion, the due process analysis was lengthier and cited *Meyer* as support. In deference to Justice Black's concerns about conjuring constitutional rights out of whole cloth, though, the passage was trimmed to preserve unanimity.[161] Still, the Court did rely on principles of both liberty and equality in striking down the statute.

Although tacked on to its equal protection analysis, the Court's due process discussion was critical in reinforcing a norm of colorblindness. Critics of the school desegregation cases had argued that the federal courts were coercing whites to associate with blacks in the name of racial equality.[162] For any who feared that the principle of equality in *Loving* would lead to efforts to promote interracial marriage, the Court's analysis of the fundamental right to marry was reassuring. The right to marry, after all, required officials to adopt a hands-off approach in the area of intimate choices. Any attempt to foster interracial marital relationships would violate due process and therefore presumably could not be required under equal protection law.[163]

In *Loving*, the Court once again refused to address the legitimacy of racial categories. Both the National Association for the Advancement of Colored People (NAACP) and the Japanese American Citizens League had attacked racial classification schemes as vague, unscientific, and insupportable in their amicus briefs.[164] Although the Court used scientific evidence to undermine Virginia's claims about the dangers of race-mixing, it was unwilling to find that the categories themselves were incoherent and outmoded. The Court's adoption of a colorblind approach may have made this issue seem irrelevant. In fact, though, states continued to keep track of race. When couples applied for marriage licenses, for example, registrars could still ask them to identify themselves by race. Even more importantly, the Court was aware of the critical role that racial classifications could play in the enforcement of *Brown*'s mandate to dismantle a separate and unequal system of public education. The NAACP was also sensitive to this concern. For the first time, its brief omitted any argument that racial classifications were inherently invidious or per se unconstitutional, even though it had advanced this very claim in *McLaughlin* only a few years before. The prospect of color-conscious remedies undercut the NAACP's traditional demands that race be treated as wholly irrelevant to government decisionmaking.[165] Rather than launch a wholesale attack on all official racial classification schemes, then, the NAACP focused on the deficiencies of the particular scheme used to enforce Virginia's antimiscegenation law. Ironically, then, the *Loving* decision's resounding and enduring endorsement of colorblindness concealed a growing ambivalence about the explicit use of race in law and policy.

Conclusion

Antimiscegenation laws played a critical role in defining racial difference, enforcing racial inequality, and establishing the boundaries of proper sexual and marital practices. The *Loving* decision lifted formal restrictions on intermarriage, but it would be naive to think that the Court could instantly undo the informal assumptions and practices that developed during three centuries of a "separate but equal" principle in sex, marriage, and family. *Loving* treated race as a biological irrelevancy by discrediting eugenic theories, but the decision did not take a position on the ongoing social and psychological significance of race in choosing a sexual partner, selecting a spouse, or raising a family. Instead, the Justices gave ordinary Americans the freedom to rethink the role of race in their intimate relationships.

As might be expected, this newfound liberty to experiment has led to uncertainty and conflict. After all, *Loving* aspired to change the law, but the human heart lay beyond its reach. While some Americans believe that race should be irrelevant to sex, marriage, and family in a colorblind society, others contend that race correlates with cultural heritage and social contacts in a country in which housing, education, and employment remain highly segregated. Those who accept color consciousness in intimate relationships believe that ignoring race trivializes the importance of historical discrimination, persistent racial division, and distinctive cultural practices. Although the struggle to find the meaning of racial equality continues, the transformative power of the Court's decision has been considerable. In the chapters that follow, *Loving*'s influence and its limits are explored in the context of Americans' rethinking of romantic love, the good family, and racial identity itself.

SIX

Race and Romanticism:
The Persistence of Same-Race
Marriage after *Loving*

AFTER THE U.S. SUPREME COURT struck down antimisce-
genation statutes in *Loving v. Virginia*[1] in 1967, the decision was imple-
mented with surprising ease. Registrars in some states engaged in ob-
structionist tactics, but others readily complied. In fact, less than two
months after *Loving,* the first modern interracial union in Virginia occurred without incident when a black man married a white woman in a
Jehovah's Witness ceremony in Norfolk.[2] Today, *Loving*'s normative
ideal of colorblindness in the regulation of marriage is well established.
Legal barriers have fallen, but interracial marriages, particularly between
blacks and whites, remain an anomaly over thirty years after the decision. Because the Court envisioned race as a biological irrelevancy but
was unwilling to coerce intimacy, it has never been clear whether *Loving* succeeded because official behavior changed or whether it failed because marital behavior remains substantially unchanged.

The task of reconciling a colorblind ideal with high rates of same-
race marriage has fallen to ordinary Americans. For them, the challenge
has been to understand whether a preference for dating and marrying
people of one's own race is necessarily racist. Before *Loving,* the role of
race in marital choice was explicit. Scholars treated marriage as a market,
one in which devalued racial status could rationally be considered in
selecting a mate. After *Loving,* the relevance of race to romantic preference gradually became obscured. Now, love and desire are treated as
imponderables not subject to rational evaluation. The relevance of race is
submerged in romantic complexity: Love cannot be based on a person's
résumé, and no single attribute, including race, can be dispositive of an   *101*

<u>individual's lovability</u>. Because the roots of compatibility are myriad and mysterious, high rates of same-race marriage are not equated with racism. To the extent that people remain color conscious, they often attribute racist attitudes about dating and marriage to others. Individuals who say that they have no objection to marrying across the color line still fear that friends, family, and coworkers will condemn the match. Concerns about hostility to interracial marriage make it seem like a fragile, dangerous, and ill-advised experiment.

Reconciling *Loving*'s colorblind ideal with high rates of same-race marriage yields important lessons about the definition of racial equality in marriage. Because of the complex nature of romantic choice, many Americans have concluded that high rates of same-race marriage are beyond both legal intervention and moral reproach. For these Americans, disparate racial outcomes are not tantamount to racist outcomes. That is, people can prefer same-race spouses without discriminating against those of other races. According to this view, same-race marriages arise out of legitimate concerns about compatibility that incidentally correlate with the color line. Race happens to relate to culture and values, traits important to healthy relationships, and resulting concerns about compatibility are not tantamount to racial antipathy.

The Disparity between Principle and Practice: The Persistence of High Rates of Same-Race Marriage after *Loving*

Interracial marriage patterns have changed since *Loving*, but the shifts have differed for blacks, Asian Americans, Native Americans, and Latinos. Immediately following the *Loving* decision, most studies focused on black–white intermarriage.[3] Only in the late 1970s and 1980s did marital patterns among other racial and ethnic groups begin to receive significant scholarly attention.[4] Ironically, *Loving* piqued researchers' interest in interracial marriage at the same time that it made the phenomenon harder to study than ever before. In the spirit of colorblindness, a number of states eliminated racial identifications from their marriage statistics after 1967.[5]

Still, available research yields some consistent insights into patterns of white intermarriage with blacks, Asian Americans, Native Americans, and Latinos.[6] These findings provide three types of evidence that race continues to matter in marriage decisions. First, although intermarriage rates have risen since *Loving,* all groups continue to marry out at rates lower than would be predicted at random. Over 93 percent of whites and blacks marry within their own group, while 70 percent of Asians and Latinos and 33 percent of Native Americans do.[7] Second, outmarriage patterns within groups differ for men and women, depending on how racial and sexual stereotypes interact. Blacks and Asian Americans are the two groups with the most intense history of racialization through vigorous application of antimiscegenation laws. These groups show strong gender differences in outmarriage, arguably as a result of ongoing racialized images of sexuality. Third, the assimilative power of intermarriage also varies by group. For example, marrying across the color line is least successful as an assimilative device for blacks because children of black–white marriages typically cannot claim the privileges of a white racial heritage. To understand *Loving*'s impact, then, it is necessary to examine the experiences of blacks, Asian Americans, Native Americans, and Latinos separately.

Blacks

Even before *Loving* and perhaps in response to the nascent civil rights movement, the rate of black–white intermarriage increased somewhat between 1950 and 1960 but remained low.[8] After the elimination of laws making miscegenation a crime, the rate of black–white intermarriage rose steadily, although the overall number, about 65,000 couples, stayed small.[9] By 1982, there were 155,000 black–white couples, about 2.5 percent of all married couples with at least one black partner.[10] In 1990, there were 211,000 black–white marriages in the United States, which amounted to four out of every thousand married couples in the country.[11]

Blacks, whether male or female, who marry out are better educated than those who do not. In addition, white men who marry interracially are more likely to have a college education than those who marry within their race. This pattern suggests that integration of higher education and white-collar workplaces has produced increasing contact between blacks and whites who are highly educated. When students or coworkers of different races interact on a daily basis, they sometimes come to see one another as suitable marriage partners. Even with advances in integration, however, the increase in intermarriage remains quite modest.[12]

As was true of marriages between whites and blacks during the first half of the twentieth century, most couples consist of black men and white women.[13] In previous periods, such as the early 1900s in Boston, when black–white intermarriage rates grew, black men married out at higher rates than black women.[14] Similarly, after *Loving,* most of the increase in intermarriage has been attributable to a significant rise in the number of black men who marry white women.[15] From 1982 to 1990, marriages between black men and white women accounted for about 70 percent of black–white unions.[16]

The difference in outmarriage rates for black men and women is particularly striking because most race-mixing historically took place between white men and black women. These interracial contacts usually involved illicit liaisons, not formal marriages.[17] Still, if there was a strong sexual attraction across racial lines, one might expect that with the end of antimiscegenation laws, marriages of white men to black women would increase. Moreover, black women have stronger incentives and more resources to marry out than black men do. There are substantially fewer marriageable black men than black women in the population. If black women are limited to black male partners, a significant number will forgo marriage altogether. Because black women attain higher levels of education and employment than black males, those who marry a same-race partner may have to choose one with less education or a lower-status occupation. Under these circumstances, black women could use their superior educational and occupational attainment to attract a white husband.[18]

Instead, black women marry out at a substantially lower rate than black men. This paradoxical outcome reflects in part the impact of ongoing racialized sexual imagery. Both black men and women have been stereotyped as hypersexual and promiscuous.[19] Unlike the image of the "black macho," however, the myth of the "black Jezebel" is countered by another view of black women. Because they often have played the role of caretaker in white homes, black women have been portrayed as asexual and motherly.[20] As the black poet Nikki Giovanni writes:

> it's a sex object if you're pretty
> and no love
> or love and no sex if you're fat
> get back fat black woman be a mother
> grandmother strong thing but not woman
> gameswoman romantic woman love needer . . .[21]

When black men achieve educational and economic success, they become suitable marriage partners for white women. Their accomplishments "lighten" and "masculinize" them.[22] Success does not have the same impact on the appeal of black women. Black "superwomen"— who are resourceful, self-sufficient, and employed outside the home— are labeled "sub-feminine" and "castrating."[23] Black women are caught in a double bind: They must be at least as submissive and dependent as a traditional white woman to be attractive, yet they must be self-sufficient to survive in the black community.[24] Strikingly depressed rates of outmarriage coupled with persistent gender asymmetry in marital patterns are strong evidence that black Americans remain a deeply racialized people in the realm of sex and marriage.

This racialization is further confirmed by the limited power of interracial marriage to assimilate blacks. They are less able than any other group to transmit the privileges of white identity to their children through outmarriage. Children of a white mother and black father are identified as black nearly 70 percent of the time. Another 8 percent are identified as "Other" and only 22 percent as white. By contrast, when white women marry Native American men, 50 percent of the children are considered white. Children born to white mothers and Japanese fathers are labeled white at a rate of 43 percent, and the rate for children of white mothers and Korean fathers is even higher at 58 percent. Only one group approximates the low rates of transmission of white identity in black–white marriages: A mere 35 percent of children of white mothers and Chinese fathers identify as white.[25]

Asian Americans

Asian American outmarriage to whites increased steadily well before the Supreme Court declared antimiscegenation laws unconstitutional in *Loving*.[26] Rates of marriage to whites for Chinese men increased from 3.2 percent in 1940–49 to 7.2 percent in 1950–59 and 11.5 percent in 1960–70. The corresponding rates of marriage to whites for Chinese females rose from 2.6 percent to 6.7 percent and then to 12.8 percent.[27] Intermarriage between Japanese and whites grew even more dramatically during this period. Of marriages in the United States involving one Japanese partner, 14.9 percent were intermarriages in 1940–49, 53.1 percent in 1950–59, and 53.3 percent in 1960–69.[28] At least one researcher has argued that the dramatic upsurge in Japanese outmarriage rates in the 1950s was a direct result of the internment experience during World War II. Relocated to concentration camps, the Japanese received an object lesson in the dangers of racial isolation. Intermarried Japanese received special privileges during wartime, and exogamy became an important strategy to guard against future discrimination and segregation.[29]

Rates of intermarriage of Asian Americans to whites have remained high in the more than thirty years since *Loving*. One study of Korean intermarriage in Los Angeles County based on marriage statistics for 1975, 1977, and 1979 found that of all marriages involving one Korean partner, 26.0 percent were to non-Koreans in 1975, 34.1 percent in 1977, and 27.6 percent in 1979. Of these outmarriages, approximately three-quarters were to non-Asians. The overall rates of outmarriage for Koreans were lower than for Chinese and Japanese in Los Angeles County included in the same study.[30] Today, one out of five Asian Americans who are married has a non-Asian spouse.[31] Asian American outmarriage rates increase intergenerationally, regardless of whether the group is Chinese, Japanese, or Korean.[32] As Asian Americans become acculturated, they not only become receptive to intermarriage but also are perceived as suitable partners by whites.[33] In fact, outmarriage among the Japanese has become so commonplace that some observers believe this group will become fully absorbed into the white community and lose its distinctive culture and identity altogether.[34]

Asian American women marry out at higher rates than Asian American men. Again, this pattern holds true for all groups, whether of Chinese, Japanese, or Korean ancestry.[35] The disparity is particularly striking because Asian immigrant men historically outnumbered Asian women by a significant margin. Under the circumstances, these men had strong incentives to marry white women, although racial restrictions kept them from doing so. White men, however, had little reason to consider Asian women as partners because they were few in number and typically highly sought after by Asian men.[36] Today's differences in outmarriage between Asian American men and women cannot be explained by an imbalance in the gender ratio because the number of marriageable Asian men and women is about equal. Moreover, Asian American men and women enjoy comparable socioeconomic status.[37] Finally, the difference cannot be attributed to marriages between American servicemen and Asian women overseas.[38]

These gender disparities in outmarriage once again reflect racialized images of sexuality. Asian American women often are depicted as "hyper-feminine" out of a belief that they will be more submissive and deferential than white females.[39] The sexual images of the exotic Asian woman are so powerful that they can even infiltrate professional relationships in the workplace. For this reason, Asian American women may be particularly vulnerable to racialized sexual harassment.[40] And there is preliminary research to suggest that Chinese American women who wish to be taken seriously as career women must control their fertility to a greater degree than white women.[41]

Asian American men, on the other hand, are characterized as weak and effeminate. One Asian American explained: "In this society, they took away the black male's mental and gave him his physical. The Asian male has been denied the physical and given the mental."[42] Another Japanese American man has described his struggle since adolescence to overcome a sense of sexual marginalization: "I pressed harder to prove my uniqueness, my difference from other Asian Americans. I wanted to star in football and basketball, wanted to make it in the glamour sports, not in fencing or golf, where the few Asian American athletes played. Rather than dress like a science geek nerd, I was one of the first jocks to sport bell-bottoms. . . ."[43] Although Asian Americans have high rates of intermarriage, persistent gender asymmetry in marriage patterns indicates that Asian Americans like blacks remain a racialized people.

Despite ongoing racialized sexuality, Asian Americans are far better able than blacks to assimilate through intermarriage. Still, gender asymmetry for Asian Americans influences even their ability to transmit the privileges of whiteness by marrying out. The assimilative impact of intermarriage is particularly strong when Asian American women wed white men. For example, when the father is white and the mother is Japanese, only 25 percent of the children are labeled Japanese. The same holds true for the children of white men and Chinese women: Only 26 percent of the children are identified as Chinese. The assimilation of children to a white identity is astonishingly high for white–Asian Indian marriages. When the mother is Asian Indian and the father is white, 93 percent of the children are considered white. By contrast, when a Japanese or Chinese man weds a white woman, fewer than half of the children are labeled white.[44]

Native Americans

In contrast to blacks and Asian Americans, Native Americans have not faced pervasive legal barriers to intermarriage.[45] As a result, rates of marriage between Native Americans and whites were relatively high even before the *Loving* decision in 1967. According to the 1960 census, over 15 percent of Native American men were married to white women, as compared to 1 percent of black men.[46] Since then, rates of intermarriage between Native Americans and whites have increased steadily. The 1970 census showed that 33 percent of married Native American men and 35 percent of married Native American women had white spouses. According to a 1976 survey, over 40 percent of Native American men between the ages of twenty-four and fifty-four were married to white women. Using 1980 census data, another study found that in states with large, relatively concentrated Native American populations, approximately 40 percent of Native Americans were married to whites, while over 60 percent of Native Americans in states with small, dispersed Native American populations were.[47] The census data for 1990 revealed that, nationally, 59 percent of Indians were married to non-Indians.[48]

Part of the substantial increase in intermarriage rates since 1960 probably is an artifact of people's decisions to change their identification from white to Native American. Early intermixing of white and Native American populations has blurred personal racial identifications, so that people readily shift their identities in response to changing policy, such as preferential treatment under affirmative action programs. Between 1960 and 1970, 67,000 individuals converted from a white to Native American identity, and another 358,000 did so between 1970 and 1980.[49] As a result, from 1950 to 1990, the Native American population in the United States grew over fivefold from 377,000 to 1.96 million.[50] Because of the inconstancy of self-reported Native American identification, intermarriages in this category undoubtedly include spouses without a strongly rooted Indian identity. Indeed, some couples may be identified in their communities as white rather than intermarried. Data on Native American–white intermarriage therefore are not necessarily comparable to findings for other groups with self-reported racial identities that are relatively stable.[51]

Exogamy rates do not differ significantly for Native American men and Native American women, whether they live in states with concentrated or dispersed Indian populations.[52] This gender symmetry is consistent with the relatively nonracialized identities of many Native Americans. If highly assimilated individuals have chosen to embrace their Native American ancestry, their suitability as marital partners is unlikely to be influenced by this optional and largely symbolic identity. Unless men and women choose to self-identify as Native American at different rates, intermarriage rates should be symmetrical by gender. It would be interesting to determine whether there are gender differences in outmarriage for Indians living on reservations. Unlike their assimilated counterparts, these Native Americans could be racialized in ways that affect the perceived desirability of men and women as sexual and marital partners.

The identification of children born to intermarried Native American and white couples bolsters the conclusion that racialization is weak and ambiguous except perhaps for Indians with strong tribal affiliations. In areas with high rates of intermarriage, Native American–white couples are very likely to classify their children as white. These areas have Indian populations that are highly dispersed and relatively urban. Many of these self-identified Native Americans undoubtedly have remote ancestry and treat their Indian identity as optional. By contrast, in areas with low rates of intermarriage, Native American–white couples are apt to categorize their children as Indian. In these areas, the Indian population is concentrated, readily identifiable, and likely to treat its identity as fixed and important.[53]

Latinos

Latinos have never been subject to antimiscegenation laws, but exogamy is not as high as one would expect if race and ethnicity were irrelevant to marital choice. Still, Latino intermarriage has increased steadily, and Latino intermarriage rates are notably higher than those for blacks.[54] Based on 1980 census material, Richard Alba and Reid Golden concluded that of Latino men born after 1950, 35 percent married out, while only 18 percent of Latino men born before 1920 did so.[55] Like Asian Americans, each succeeding generation of Latinos marries out at a higher rate than the one before. As Latinos become acculturated, they are viewed as suitable marital partners, and they become receptive to intermarriage.[56] Researchers also have found that rates of outmarriage for Latino males increase as their socioeconomic status improves.[57]

There are some variations in Latino outmarriage patterns based on country of origin. Rates of exogamy are very high for those of Cuban, Mexican, Central American, and South American origin. Puerto Ricans and Dominicans, however, have lower rates of intermarriage than other Latinos.[58] This disparity may relate in part to the racial identification of these groups. Compared to other Latinos, Puerto Ricans and Dominicans have higher proportions of members who are dark-skinned and therefore considered black, a racial identity that could depress their outmarriage rates.[59]

Among the Latino population, women historically have married out at a higher rate than men, a pattern that persisted until recently.[60] Again, gender asymmetry in outmarriage rates probably correlates with racialized images of sexuality. Like Asian American women, Latinas often have been characterized as submissive and deferential, even when they were well educated and pursued careers. Alicia, a Chicana graduate student at Berkeley, was surprised and disappointed when she discovered that her ex-husband believed that she would prove to be a traditional woman in spite of all her accomplishments:

> One of the things my ex-husband said that really attracted him to me was the fact that I was strong, that I had a mind, that I had things to say. So he was apparently attracted to a strong woman. But when it came down to the daily reality of it all, it just wasn't quite attractive to him.[61]

Latino men also have become the objects of racialized sexual stereotyping. Like blacks, but unlike Asian Americans, Latinos typically have been characterized as domineering machos with a sexual swagger. One Cuban American recounts how his ethnic identity became eroticized:

> I began advertising my exotic condition with a redolent Ricky Ricardo accent—actually, I mimicked my parents' accent and broken grammar, not the clownish Desi. I started smoking cigars. And, as I vaguely recall, I even came up with a genetically flavored, jargon-laced explanation for that equine quality all males from Cuba most certainly enjoyed. At this point, of course, I had unwittingly surrendered to self-parody—I was becoming Desi Arnaz—but the more *cubanazo* I became, the more effortless dating games became. God only knows how much better I might have made out if only I had brought a Santa Barbara medal on a thick gold chain and a decent pair of bongos.[62]

Despite the self-mocking humor, the ache of the unassimilated permeates these ethnically loaded dating games: "With the Anglo women, you are reminded of your exile not just from Cuba but from effortless cultural participation of any kind. . . . [I]t has been in matters of love where I have felt the pain of double exile the strongest."[63]

Notwithstanding this history of racialized images of Latino sexuality, rates of exogamy for Latino men and women appear to be evening out, as Latino outmarriage increases. In fact, the rate for women may even be slightly lower than for men.[64] This shift raises the intriguing possibility that as Latinos acculturate, they are becoming a less racialized population than was historically the case. The ambiguities surrounding Latinos' racial identity, which enabled them to escape formal restrictions on intermarriage altogether, also may have made their sexual stereotypes more malleable than those of blacks or Asian Americans. Whether this trend in marriage patterns continues could depend in part on whether high rates of immigration reinforce racialization and retard the impact of acculturation for all Latinos, not just the newly arrived. For example, Latinos may have depressed patterns of outmarriage in states with high proportions of immigrants, even after controlling for recency of arrival and the demographic makeup of the pool of eligible mates. So far, no definitive research has been done on the interplay of immigration, racialization, and marital choice in the Latino community.

The weak racialization of Latinos, particularly those who do not identify as black, is further demonstrated by their ability to transmit the perquisites of whiteness through intermarriage. Their offspring may maintain a voluntary and symbolic connection to their Hispanic origin without forgoing a white identity. According to a study of eighty-four Mexican-origin individuals married in Los Angeles County in 1963 to non-Mexican spouses, Mexican-origin women sometimes reported that an advantage of intermarriage was obtaining a non-Spanish surname, and fewer Mexican-origin women than Mexican-origin men gave their offspring Spanish names or nicknames.[65] Although Mexican-origin partners "maintain[ed] cultural ties, an ethnic identity, and an ethnic social network," the marriages "appear[ed] to be flexible enough to allow each spouse to maintain ties with their culture of origin, to transmit both cultural orientations to their offspring and to be relatively free of intercultural conflict."[66]

Reconciling the Colorblind Ideal and the Persistence of High Rates of Same-Race Marriage

Statistics on interracial marriage indicate that race remains a powerful influence in the choice of a mate. At first glance, the persistence of racial endogamy seems at odds with the ideal of colorblindness set forth in *Loving*. One straightforward response to this concern is that the U.S. Supreme Court mandated only that the government cease to use race as a basis for regulating marriage. The Court did not require that individuals ignore race in making marital choices. On the contrary, *Loving* made clear that public officials could not reform decisions about romance, even racist ones, because of Americans' fundamental freedom to make sexual and marital choices for themselves. This formalistic rationale is unsatisfying to those who believe that selection of a spouse must not be a racist act. For them, *Loving* should have prompted voluntary changes in attitudes and behavior related to interracial marriage. Regardless of the Court's power to coerce, it at least had the power to educate.[67] In fact, *Loving* arguably has transformed attitudes toward intermarriage. In 1991, a Gallup poll found for the first time that more Americans approve of interracial marriage than disapprove of it.[68] However, this change in attitude has not led to comparable shifts in behavior, as the data on interracial marriage show.

The gap between attitude and behavior is a problem only if color-blindness means that marriages should take place at random with respect to race. Before *Loving*, race was recognized as an immutable trait that was clearly germane to marital choice in a caste system based on color. As part of the jurisprudence that dismantled this official racial hierarchy, *Loving* stood for a new proposition: Race is immutable, but it is a biological irrelevancy. In a setting like the workplace, a rational assessment of an individual's qualifications should mean that, other things being equal, patterns of hiring would be random with respect to race.[69] Yet, for many Americans, selection of a spouse defies rational explanation. A wife is not like a business associate or coworker whose qualifications can be reduced to a résumé. Attraction is ineffable, desire is unpredictable, and love is not held to the standard of an equal opportunity employer.[70] As a result, even after *Loving*, most Americans do not equate high rates of same-race marriage with racism. Once the assumption of rational choice is discarded, they see no reason to assume that marital choice will be random with respect to race, even if people consciously refrain from discriminating on that basis.

How Race Was Weighed in Marital Choice before *Loving*

Before *Loving*, antimiscegenation statutes made clear that race was an immutable status presumptively relevant to marital choice. When inter-marriage did occur, it was regarded as a vehicle for assimilating the racially subordinate spouse to the norms and standards of the dominant one.[71] Consequently, both social science research and popular accounts attached explicit and profound significance to race in explaining intermarriage. Because marriage was a rational act designed to promote upward mobility, race could be weighed against other personal attributes in choosing a spouse. Otherwise, intermarriage had to be a departure from rational behavior driven by pathological impulses, usually sexual. This defiance of conventional norms was necessarily a deviant and dangerous act.

*Social Science Research on Intermarriage: Marriage Markets
and Racial Determinism*

Researchers in the pre-*Loving* era openly acknowledged that any rational
person would weigh race in selecting a marriage partner. In a 1941 article,
leading sociologist Robert K. Merton looked at how blacks and whites
traded off racial status against class standing in a racial caste system.[72]
Merton treated marriage as a kind of market. Each partner preferred
hypergamy, or marrying up, based on caste and class, and each partner
tried to avoid hypogamy, or marrying down. Unfortunately, if one partner married up, the other married down, so the preferred state for both
partners was endogamy, or marrying within one's caste or class. In Merton's view, interracial marriage should be rare and would occur only
when one partner traded class status for racial status.[73] For instance, a
white woman with low class standing might marry a black man with
high class standing.[74] On the few occasions when individuals married
without any benefit to their class or racial position, Merton characterized
their behavior as antisocial: They were either rebelling against social
norms or succumbing to lusty impulses.[75]

Research on intermarriage of groups other than blacks adopted a similar conception of race as a status attribute. In a study of couples who
married between 1940 and 1959 in Hawaii, researchers found that nonwhite men and women who married across racial and ethnic lines scored
higher in dominance, aggression, and autonomy and lower in deference
than those who married within their racial or ethnic group, suggesting
perhaps that they were particularly ambitious and upwardly mobile. Unlike Merton, however, these researchers posited that white men who married out were especially open, tolerant, and noncompetitive. The authors
argued that those men and women who were willing to disregard racial
and ethnic stereotypes in marriage might also be prone to reject sexual
stereotypes and produce a more egalitarian husband–wife relationship
than was traditionally the case.[76] This characterization of white spouses
hinted at a more flexible and dynamic idea of race and marriage, one
not captured by rigid caste lines and marital social climbing. This study
held out the promise of a pluralistic marriage, but this vision was only
realized in therapeutic literature on intermarriage in the 1970s and 1980s,
not in discussions of marital choice.

Even at the time *Loving* was decided, researchers continued to treat
race as an immutable and highly relevant social characteristic in marriage.
During the 1960s and 1970s, black sociohistorians rejected the traditional

view that "[i]f marital assimilation . . . takes place fully, the minority group loses its ethnic identity in the larger host or core society. . . . Prejudice and discrimination are no longer a problem. . . ."[77] For the sociohistorians, race was an unbridgeable divide, and blacks would not be assimilated in the way that immigrant ethnic groups had been. In a racially divided world, interracial sex and marriage were necessarily pathological, indelibly tainted with irrational fears and prejudices. Blacks' attraction to whites was a form of self-hatred, a betrayal of black identity and an acceptance of whites as the romantic ideal.[78] Far from being motivated by love, black men chose white women to exploit them and thereby avenge past racial injuries.[79] White women who involved themselves with black men were painted as masochists or rebels, who irrevocably severed their ties to white society.[80] This bleak view of racial determinism hardly comported with *Loving*'s notion that race was nothing more than a biological irrelevancy.

Popular Accounts of Intermarriage: Exceptionalism and Exoticism

Popular accounts of intermarriage echo these social scientific accounts, juxtaposing rational calculation with irrational lust. One popular explanation for intermarriage is "exceptionalism," which harkens back to Merton's market model of marriage. Someone with a devalued racial status becomes exceptional by acquiring unusually attractive characteristics through good fortune, hard work, or both. These characteristics permit the gifted individual to cross racial boundaries by marrying a white person. Exceptionalism is a popular ideology with a long pedigree. One of the oldest examples is the biblical legend of Esther's marriage to King Ahasuerus. Dissatisfied with Queen Vashti's lack of deference, Ahasuerus decides to replace her with someone more suitable. His search produces Esther, who unbeknownst to him is a Jew. Eventually, Esther's roots are revealed, but through her feminine virtues, she is able to triumph over her Jewish heritage to preserve her place as queen and lift up her people. For the king, Esther's outstanding feminine virtues as well as her intelligence and accomplishments compensate for her status as a despised minority.

The exceptionalist account assumes that the person with a devalued racial status aspires to assimilate through intermarriage. Desirous of the privileges of white identity, the nonwhite partner has everything to gain and nothing to lose by marrying a white person. Very little attention is paid to the sacrifices that exceptional mates must make in minimizing their racial backgrounds to assimilate through marriage. Or as Michelene Wandor puts it in recounting Esther's story:

> there is something missing
> from this story:
> someone
> somewhere
> doesn't bother to say
> whether Esther
> actually liked
> King A[81]

By treating intermarriage as a vehicle of assimilation and upward mobility, the exceptionalist account tightly circumscribes the pool of eligible mates. Because marriage is an avenue to white privilege, a nonwhite partner must earn this opportunity through extraordinary effort. Only the most talented and deserving nonwhite can win the affection of even an average white person. Because race matters, upward mobility through marriage is limited to the privileged few and leaves the color line largely intact. If race were not an important social boundary, perfectly ordinary nonwhites could marry perfectly ordinary whites and experiment with forging new identities. Not only would intermarriage become more commonplace but the notion of separate and stratified racial identities would begin to crumble.

Another popular explanation of interracial attraction is exoticism, which treats racial difference as a source of sexual titillation. Because the ephemeral state of lust is not considered a satisfactory basis for the permanent commitment of marriage, exoticism makes interracial marriage inappropriate. Interracial sex in the exotic tale is an experiment that keeps racial privilege firmly in place:

> Compared with racism, exoticism is merely decorative and superficial. It doesn't build death camps. It doesn't exterminate. Exoticism cares mostly about its own amusement and tends to find differences of color amusing where racism finds them threatening. Exoticism is frivolous, hangs out at nightclubs, will pay anything to have the black singer or pianist sit at its table. Racism is like a poor kid who grew up needing someone to hurt. Exoticism grew up rich, and a little bored. The racist is hedged around by dangers, the exoticist by used-up toys.
>
> If one is to be treated as a thing, one would rather be treated as a rare and pretty thing than as a disgusting or dangerous one. But that is still to be treated as a thing.[82]

Like exceptionalism, exoticism leaves little room for intermarriage to become an everyday phenomenon. Interracial relationships are exotic precisely because they are unusual. Their allure comes from their forbidden nature. Crossing the color line to engage in sexual experimentation is no basis for a long-term marriage built on steady love and companionship. Those who marry impulsively based solely on exotic attraction not only defy sexual conventions but also flout the traditional wedding vow to love, not lust after, one another.

How Race Has Become Submerged in Romantic Complexity

After the *Loving* decision, race could no longer be reduced to a devalued and inescapable status conferred at birth. Now officially treated as a biological happenstance, race occupied an increasingly peripheral place in accounts of romantic choice. At the same time, rational accounts of marital choice and histories of racial determinism were replaced by images of romantic complexity. For romantic individualists, the choice of a spouse could not be justified simply on the basis of a weighing of costs and benefits. Indeed, an excessively rational approach to marriage was likely to be considered cold, calculating, and slightly immoral: "It should be at least questioned whether we do not overrationalize the whole process of mate selection. Our emphasis upon free marital choice seems to imply that one chooses a mate as rationally as one buys a garden tool or a tube of toothpaste."[83]

In contrast to Merton's market model of marriage, today's researchers focus on the individual's ineffable commitment to love for love's sake. Precisely because romanticism is not a rational strategy, its influence is hard to measure; some nevertheless have tried. Professor Zick Rubin, a social psychologist, constructed a "romanticism scale" that asks people how strongly they agree with such statements as "A person should marry whomever he loves regardless of social position" and "As long as they at least love one another, two people should have no difficulty getting along together in marriage."[84] Rubin's romanticism scale captures the popular notion that love and commitment are not entirely motivated by self-interest and are perhaps even inexplicable acts. The rise of romanticism permits individuals to rely on love to explain their marital choices without ever thinking very hard about the characteristics that make their partners lovable.

Under a model of romantic individualism, love can be not only blind but colorblind, even when high rates of same-race marriage persist. The catchall term *love* is used to minimize the significance of race, now a formally irrelevant biological trait, in selecting a mate. Consider, for example, the reasons that friends give for marrying someone. All of them are likely to say that they chose someone they loved. If pressed for additional reasons, they may cite similarities in background, interests, education, religion, and occupation. For instance, a man might say that he wanted to marry someone who was a college graduate so she would fit in with his friends, family, and business associates, or a woman might say she wanted a husband who grew up in a large Catholic family so that he would understand her ideas about marriage and children.

It is probably highly unlikely, however, that one of your white friends would say "I chose my wife because she is white." Such a statement comes perilously close to being a racist remark because it implies that he would not have chosen his wife if she were black. This claim in turn sounds very much like "I would not marry a black person." An a priori judgment that no black would be an acceptable spouse seems racist insofar as it presumes that blacks invariably are inferior to whites as marriage prospects.[85] The preferred way of explaining high rates of same-race marriage is to treat them as happenstance: "I chose a wife who happens to be white."[86] In this way, people can love same-race partners without being accused of hating people of other races. Yet, when over 93 percent of whites and blacks marry someone of the same race, and approximately 70 percent of Asian Americans and Latinos do, patterns of endogamy appear to be more than romantic accidents. If pressed to explain these patterns, whites may reply that they don't hate members of other races, but they simply aren't attracted to them.[87] By equating outright antipathy with racism and lack of interest with race-neutral behavior, these individuals reject the view—expressed by Elie Wiesel, Holocaust survivor and winner of the Nobel Peace Prize—that "the opposite of love . . . is not hate, but indifference."[88]

Significantly, the profession of colorblindness required of whites is not always required of nonwhites.[89] A black acquaintance may openly say "I definitely want to marry someone who is black." This color-conscious statement is not necessarily understood as racist because blacks are allowed to escape societal prejudice by marrying endogamously and creating spaces in their home where they can be totally at ease.[90] Just as small religious groups can use inmarriage to preserve their way of life, blacks can commit themselves to conserving their identities through same-race marriages. Norms of endogamy for small, vulnerable racial groups are considered consistent with racial equality and fairness because these groups otherwise might disappear completely through marital absorption.[91] Colorblindness is not required for nonwhites because race is no longer a mere biological accident, as it is in white accounts of marital choice. Instead, race is a fundamental source of social identity and belonging.

When whites and nonwhites intermarry, they often justify their decision on the ground that love is indifferent to color. Race once again is relegated to a trivial artifact of ancestry and appearance, and social differences are explained in cultural and personal terms. According to one interracially married person:

> I guess when you fall in love you sort of become colorblind. I guess I don't believe in loving somebody just for their culture, . . . but I don't believe in not liking them because of that either. . . . [F]alling in love is the thing that really makes the difference. And then you have to face yourself and say "Is this love strong enough to withstand what our families might think, what the world might think, our friends might think?"[92]

A study of North American servicemen who married or planned to marry Filipinas while stationed at Subic Bay Naval Base demonstrates how powerful the tendency is to discount race in explaining romantic attraction. An overwhelming number of these men and women gave "romantic love" as their reason for marrying, even though the question was phrased "In addition to love, why did you marry someone from another culture?"[93] When the men were pressed for additional reasons, they denigrated North American women as "too selfish," "too self-centered," and "too aggressive," while they praised the womanliness and femininity of their Filipina spouses or fiancees.[94] At the same time, the servicemen denied any significant cultural differences between themselves and the Filipinas, noting, for example, that the women were "really . . . American underneath."[95]

The Filipinas gave different reasons for marrying American servicemen. Once romantic love was not available as a complete explanation, Filipina wives and fiancees cited economic security and the desire for "a better future for myself and my children" as their primary motives.[96] At the same time, though, Filipina wives gave an explanation at odds with the very concept of strategically choosing a mate. The women mentioned "fate," saying "[i]t is my fate to marry an American." This concept is probably closely linked to that of romantic love, but it may also reflect the fact that only six out of one hundred Filipina hostesses escape poverty by wedding a serviceman.[97] Notably, neither husbands nor wives cited race as a factor in their choice of a spouse. Femininity, acculturation, class mobility, and fatalism were the social characteristics used to frame their decisions.

The focus on romantic individualism not only suppresses the significance of race in personal decisionmaking but also deflects attention from structural factors like segregation that limit a person's ability to meet, date, and marry someone of another race. Demographic research has clearly demonstrated the impact of these factors.[98] Using marriages that are random with respect to race as the benchmark of racial equality,[99] demographers have found that intermarriage is seriously impeded by socioeconomic differences, which in turn correlate with segregation in housing and education.[100] Blacks, Native Americans, and Latinos who marry exogamously are younger and better educated than those who marry endogamously.[101] People of approximately equal socioeconomic status are well represented among the intermarried and tend to marry cross-racially after contact in integrated institutions of higher education.[102] Rather than accord independent significance to these structural factors, however, researchers reconcile them with a model of romantic individualism by concluding that factors correlated with higher rates of intermarriage—such as age, education, and income—reflect declining racism and increasing social compatibility.

In fact, acknowledging the role of structural influences in a choice as deeply personal as marriage subverts the very notion of romantic individualism. As Japanese American writer David Mura explains:

> The meanings and valuings of our sexual desires are not just subjective, they are societally created. Of course, to argue this goes against certain public notions of individual liberty which maintain that whom I desire is a private matter, while whom I hire is not. There is a separation, as it were, between the bedroom and the boardroom. You don't want the government or its laws meddling in your private life, what you do behind closed doors is your own personal matter, etc. But, of course, this does not mean that there isn't a relationship between whom I desire and whom I hire, or between whom I want my children to desire and whom I hire. And I suspect that America's squeamishness in examining this fact comes in part from a realization that the lines of race run deeper than we want to acknowledge and occupy a more intractable area of psyche than we're able, at this point in time, to deal with.[103]

How Responsibility Has Been Displaced by Focusing on Other People's Racism

Although people submerge race in romantic complexity, they do sometimes admit that racist beliefs about intermarriage persist. Typically, individuals insist that they themselves have nothing against interracial marriage, but that other people do.[104] Because social ostracism creates special hardships for intermarried couples and their children, choosing a spouse of another race is a risky decision. In her work on how white women come to understand their racial identity, Professor Ruth Frankenburg asked about their attitudes toward interracial marriage. These women often claimed that race didn't matter because "[t]he more you meet different people, the more you realize people are all the same."[105] Even so, the women were concerned about racial boundaries in marriage, especially when nonwhite groups were seen as separate and stigmatized. A politically conservative, forty-year-old white woman remarked:

> It's funny that the stigma always seems to be with Blacks and . . . to a certain extent the Chicanos, the Mexicans. Those seem to be the two, because people will accept a mixed marriage between an Oriental and a Caucasian much more readily . . . I guess because the skin tones are more similar . . . and maybe—it's known fact—Orientals are bright people, the brightest in the world, if you want to categorize them intellectually.[106]

The women often equated marriage with procreation, and they couched their concerns about race in terms of the welfare of the couple and their mixed-race children. In response to a question about whether interracial marriage would cause problems for a couple, one working-class white grandmother in her forties replied:

> Mostly it's not so much for them as for the children, because they are half and half. I have a friend right now who married . . . a Black guy and had a baby with him, and she can't go with a white guy [with whom she was in love] because he would mistreat her son. . . . She didn't want to marry into the Black again but said she felt she had to because of her son. . . . And that's where I don't think it's right because the kids have to pay for it. . . . I've seen too many little kids has to pay for something their parents has done. . . . When the kids get older and are ready to marry, they can't get a Black or a white, because they are mixed.[107]

These views were by no means confined to white women of a certain class or age. A working-class woman in her late twenties worried that "You see a Black and white couple together and they have a child, and you know the whites'll say 'ugh' and the Blacks'll say the same."[108] And according to a woman in her sixties who was married to a business executive in the Silicon Valley, "I don't think it'd be as hard to be all Chinese as it is to be half Chinese in an all-white, rural city, because they don't fit either place. They don't have a culture they can identify with. To me, that's the problem."[109]

These concerns about mixed-race couples and their children are eerily reminiscent of the justifications for antimiscegenation laws that were invoked in the post-World War II era. In defending the statutes in California and Virginia, advocates cited the dangers to stable families and identities that intermarriage posed. The social pressures on interracial couples threatened their capacity to stay together and raise well-adjusted children.[110] Today, whites like those in Frankenburg's study see these dangers as the regrettable legacy of racist thinking and urge individual responsibility rather than government regulation. In their view, race is far more than a superficial biological characteristic for intermarried couples and their children. The anomaly of crossing the color line makes race a salient feature in the development of social ties and personal identity. Precisely because of other people's racism, intermarriage leads to color-conscious consequences, not a liberating state of colorblindness. As a result, these whites question the prudence of pioneers who break out of racially segregated marriages and families.

Race and Culture in Pluralist Accounts of Intermarriage

By submerging race in romantic complexity, Americans have been able to reconcile high rates of same-race marriage with a formal norm of colorblindness that treats race as irrelevant to marital choice. Racism, to the extent that it persists, is attributed to other people. Interestingly, though, after the choice to marry interracially is made, the salience of race grows. Precisely because marriages across the color line remain so unusual, the 3 percent of American marriages that are interracial present special challenges that make race hard to ignore.[111] Once people intermarry, they often chafe at assimilationist models that require one spouse to suppress a racial identity in deference to the other's. Far from being colorblind, these couples must confront the impact that growing up in racially segregated and culturally distinct worlds has on their relationship. No longer a biological irrelevancy, race becomes a proxy for social ties and cultural attributes of paramount importance to building a successful marriage. Researchers who adopt a pluralist vision emphasize the need for intermarried spouses to acknowledge and respect their differences:

The goal of cultural pluralism, broadly speaking, envisages a society where ethnic groups would be encouraged to maintain their own communal social structure and identity, and preserve certain of their values and behavioral patterns which are not in conflict with broader values, patterns, and legal norms common to the entire society.[112]

When couples marry across the color line, dangers arise if one spouse must efface a personal history and identity to make the relationship work. For instance, when a white woman marries a black man, she may integrate into the black community and sever ties to whites. But the process of separating from the white community can create intense feelings of alienation.[113] According to one case study:

> [Mr. and Mrs. S, a black man and white woman] had met while they were in the military service; following discharge they had moved to a large industrial city where Mr. S had been raised. They soon had four young children. Mr. S was of little help around the house, and Mrs. S was developing feelings of isolation. Their social contacts had been essentially with blacks. Mrs. S had begun to resist these contacts, as she felt that black women resented her. Mr. S denied this and stated that her reaction was a result of her thinking that she was better than blacks. Mrs. S strongly denied this.[114]

Divisive racial conflicts are not limited to black–white couples. Korean women married to American servicemen have reported feelings of loneliness and isolation, in part as a result of linguistic and cultural barriers. These women expected their husbands to help them by taking an active interest in their heritage, and serious difficulties resulted when the men assumed that their wives would simply assimilate to an American way of life.[115]

Research on interracial marriage demonstrates the delicate balance between assimilation and pluralism that couples strike. In a study of seventeen Native American women married to white men in the New York metropolitan area in 1971, intermarriage sometimes facilitated but did not guarantee acculturation. White husbands on occasion were attracted to Native American ways, and several women described their spouses as "like an Indian" or "very Indian."[116] In other instances, the women were well aware of the assimilative implications of their marital choices. One woman who was fully acculturated and married to a white man reported that her father "had placed two restrictions upon her in regard to dating—no Indians and no Mexicans. Her father insisted that she date only White boys in order to 'get somewhere in this world.'"[117]

Although much of the research on intermarriage has racial overtones, contemporary therapeutic literature emphasizes cultural differences. As a result, marriage counselors and social workers can address social ties that correlate with race without accusing spouses of being racially insensitive or hostile. Under this therapeutic, culturally pluralistic model, "[t]o marry an individual from another culture is to marry that culture as well."[118] The greater the spouses' cultural differences, the more difficulties they can expect to encounter in adjusting to marriage.[119] Although an assimilationist model treats marriage as a fixed institution defined by the dominant partner's values, the pluralist model treats it as contingent. In some cultures, marriage is the beginning of a new family separate from the extended family, while in others, the couple merges into the extended family. Depending on their cultural traditions, husbands and wives assume different roles and resolve conflicts in distinct ways. In intermarriages, couples must engage in a complex process of cultural exchange to resolve differences in their conception of marriage.[120]

Intermarriage often unmasks the cultural assumptions underlying matrimony in unsettling ways. Neither partner can be sure of the "rightness" of beliefs about home and family:

> Mary, an only child who had been raised alone by her Norwegian mother, married Jaime, a Puerto Rican, one of several children with a large extended family living nearby. Initially, she saw his relatives as the family she had never had but always wanted. Although Jaime's family had welcomed Mary into their home and seemed to like her, they spoke no English and she spoke no Spanish, so she always felt disconnected from them. Not only did she look different from them and act differently, but without a common language, developing intimacy with them was an impossible task. The couple spent a lot of time with Jaime's relatives since he enjoyed socializing with them. In contrast, Mary had no relative to visit except her mother, whom Jaime viewed as authoritarian, cold, and difficult.
>
> As time went by their differences began to affect their relationship. . . .
>
> In therapy they began to understand that their views about family were very different. . . . Marriage in Jaime's family mean[t] that more relatives would be added to the system. To Mary it meant that now she could separate from her mother and form a new family.[121]

The pluralist model challenges traditional conceptions of both race and marriage. Pluralists openly question the assumption that nonwhites want to assimilate through intermarriage. Instead, whites and nonwhites must share a common interest in one another's culture and heritage.

This egalitarian approach reduces the racial and cultural dominance of the white spouse. Pluralists recognize that far from being a biological irrelevancy, race can correlate with important differences that influence the health of a marriage. Among these differences are distinct notions about the significance of marriage and family. Marriage cannot be taken as a given, a uniform vehicle for assimilating the nonwhite partner. Instead, spouses must negotiate their identities through day-to-day household interactions. In short, the racial identities of the parties, as expressed through culture, can influence the nature of marriage, and the marital relationship can transform the couple's sense of themselves. Race and marriage are not independent but integrally linked to one another.

Pluralist accounts of marriage, however, limit the relevance of race by focusing exclusively on intermarried couples and by characterizing their differences as cultural rather than racial. As a result, pluralists ignore the impact of same-race marriage on racial identity and the roles of husband and wife. These claims about pluralism suggest that inmarriage not only rigidifies racial difference but also entrenches an unduly narrow conception of marital life. Nor do pluralists acknowledge the role that segregated marriages and families play in perpetuating the cultural disparities that trouble interracial couples. Intermarriage exists in the shadow of the overwhelming norm of endogamy. Crossing the color line is challenging precisely because it creates ambiguities about race and marriage for whites and nonwhites alike. Intermarried whites can no longer count on nonwhite spouses to adopt their way of life. And those nonwhite partners in turn must confront doubts about whether cultural exchange in a pluralist marriage can ever be equal in a society dominated by whites. The uncertainties inherent in an interracial marriage do not derive so much from the partners' personalities but from a world in which segregation in marriage and family defines distinctive ways of life.

Conclusion

The most striking feature of the aftermath of *Loving v. Virginia* is how readily people have accepted segregation in marriage, so long as it is not officially mandated. Despite compelling evidence that race continues to matter in affairs of the heart, Americans embrace a colorblind ideal. Same-race marriages are not considered evidence of racism, nor are they seen as a barrier to racial equality. Americans overwhelmingly believe that so long as people do not despise members of another race, they are free to love members of their own race without legal interference or moral reproach. *Loving* treated marital autonomy almost as an afterthought rather than a compelling constitutional justification. Yet the decision's legacy is a triumph of the freedom to love, even if romantic choice is complex, ineffable, and even irrational. The vindication of autonomy is so complete that romanticism must prevail, even if respect for this irrational preference makes it hard to stamp out another—namely, racism.

Still, the tension between equality and autonomy is not wholly resolved. Although *Loving* targeted its mandate of colorblindness at official conduct, individuals still feel some compunction about making private choices that are racist. To mitigate the perception that high rates of same-race marriage are a product of racism, the pattern is explained on the basis of shared cultural experiences. Cultural affinities are a socially acceptable and indeed desirable consideration in choosing a mate. When cultural preferences lead to racial endogamy, the pattern can be seen as an innocent by-product, a kind of racial coincidence. Cultural compatibility regularly leads to the selection of a spouse who happens to be of the same race.

The shift to a cultural explanation ignores the role of racial segregation in producing distinct ways of life. The color line has served not only as a marker of alleged biological differences but also as a boundary between separate worlds. Each of these worlds has generated its own folkways and traditions. Although unified by a common political heritage, Americans living in a segregated society have been culturally as well as economically divided by race. Segregation in marriage has contributed to this fragmentation, not only by perpetuating a sense of biological distinctiveness but also by reproducing disparate social and cultural practices.

The solution is not to trample marital autonomy. The federal government cannot coerce love across the color line any more than it can forcibly prevent it. Instead, the answer lies in enabling Americans of all races to recognize the fundamental error of romantic individualism. The choice of a mate is not entirely individual because romantic preferences are highly contextualized. While love itself may seem like an irrational impulse, that most intimate of feelings is a product of social forces that transcend the individual. For love to be intelligible, it must occur within accepted cultural parameters. For *Loving*'s promise of marital freedom and racial equality to be realized, Americans must confront the ways in which race has distorted social boundaries rather than retreat into the easy and unreflective innocence of romantic individualism.

SEVEN

Race and the Family: The Best Interest of the Child in Interracial Custody and Adoption Disputes

IN GENERAL, the government does not directly structure families, but on occasion it must. When a family breaks up through divorce, judges have to decide which parent will have primary custody of the children. When rights of the biological parents are relinquished or terminated, agencies must try to place a child in a new adoptive home. In interracial custody and adoption cases, courts and agencies directly confront the role of race in the family. Unable to rely on the laissez-faire approach to intimate choices about marriage, the state must make difficult normative judgments about which family bonds to acknowledge, nurture, and preserve. In doing so, officials struggle to reconcile a colorblind ideal with the reality that the overwhelming majority of families in the United States are of the same race.

Throughout most government programs and activities, the constitutional norm is colorblindness. Because race is considered an irrelevant biological trait, officials have no reason to give it any weight in decisionmaking. When courts encounter race-based classifications, they apply the most stringent level of review—strict scrutiny. Under this standard, the government must show that its use of race is necessary to promote a compelling state interest.[1] This level of review is so hard to satisfy that one scholar has characterized it as "strict in theory and fatal in fact."[2]

Yet, when courts and agencies deal with interracial placement decisions, they typically treat race as relevant in assessing the "best interest of the child."[3] These color-conscious placement decisions have reflected a societal judgment that same-race families are not only statistically commonplace but normatively desirable. Race is pertinent because agencies try to replicate "naturally occurring" biological families. The vast majority of these families are racially homogeneous. In addition, race matters because it is linked to social and cultural differences that affect a parent's competency to raise a child. A white adoptive parent in a white neighborhood may not be prepared to meet the psychological needs of a black child, for example.

The dilemma posed by the role of race in custody and adoption cannot be easily resolved by resorting to largely unfettered, private choices. The closest approximation to the laissez-faire approach to marriage is the independent adoption in which biological parents relinquish their rights to an adoptive couple through an intermediary, typically an attorney, without substantial government involvement. Even here, the state has a normative obligation to prevent the commodification of children, whose interests may not be adequately safeguarded by the adults who negotiate their transfer. Assuming that the dangers of commodification could somehow be overcome, the state would still have a role to play for those children and prospective adoptive parents left out by an expensive process of private placements.

At present, healthy white infants are most likely to find a home through private agencies or independent adoptions. These babies are apt to wind up with affluent white couples who can afford the substantial costs associated with private placements. This system leaves many children, whether nonwhite, older, or disabled, without adoptive homes. Moreover, less affluent couples, who are ready and willing to offer a loving home to a child, are unable to make their needs and wishes known in a private system. As a result, the state will continue to play an important part in child placement policy, and given the limitations of the private adoption process, officials will devote a considerable amount of time to finding appropriate homes for nonwhite children.

The Shifting Relevance of Race in Custody and Adoption

Although the ideal of colorblindness is well entrenched in civil rights rhetoric, the role of race in child placement policy has been hotly debated. Courts and agencies have struggled to decide how much weight to give race in assessing a child's best interest. The inability to resolve the conflict has prompted Congress to intervene to eliminate race-matching policies in adoption. At the same time, though, Congress continues to support placement of Native American children with Indian families to protect tribes from extinction. In short, placement policy generates serious inconsistencies about the relevance of race, if any, to a child's well-being.

The Controversy over Race-Matching

Race historically was a decisive factor in both custody and adoption disputes. In a 1950 custody case, for example, the Washington Supreme Court found that the daughters of a black father and white mother "will have a much better opportunity to take their rightful place in society if they are brought up among their own people [in their father's home]."[4] Adoption experts made similar claims about the benefits of race-matching:

> The hypothesis of matching was one of equalization. If all possible physical, emotional, intellectual, racial, and religious differences between adopter and child could be reduced, hopefully to zero, the relationship stood a better chance of succeeding. So ingrained was the matching idea that its assumptions, especially those relating to religion and race, were operationalized into law under the rubric of a "child's best interests."[5]

The consensus about the benefits of race-matching began to break down as the civil rights movement forced a reconsideration of the significance of race. Courts started to question the practice of treating race as dispositive in custody cases as early as the 1950s.[6] In the mid-1950s and 1960s, adoption agencies also became fairly open to transracial placements.[7] Although the shift in child custody law met with little resistance and continued to evolve in the 1970s,[8] agencies came under intense attack for permitting white parents to adopt black children. In 1972, the National Association of Black Social Workers (NABSW) drafted a position paper opposing interracial placements and likening them to genocide.[9] Fearful of being attacked as racist, agencies grew reluctant to approve transracial adoptions. Despite efforts to recruit black adoptive parents, agencies still could not place all black children in same-race homes, and many spent long periods of time in foster care or institutions. Meanwhile, prospective white parents remained childless because of a shortage of white children available for adoption.[10]

Although opinion polls indicate that many Americans, black and white, support transracial placements, some social workers are still vehemently opposed to them.[11] As a result, adoption across the color line continues to be a rarity, especially for black children who are not racially

mixed. Historically, though, the most common form of transracial placement in the United States has been the international adoption of a Korean child by a white family.[12] When transracial placements of blacks
do take place, they typically involve children with some white ancestry.
Latino children, whose racial identity is more ambiguous than that of
blacks, have a better chance of being adopted transracially and spend
less time in foster care than black children.[13] In fact, the small number
of transracial adoptions that occur generally involve nonblack children.
According to a 1993 report, 92 percent of adoptions involve same-race
families. Only 1 percent of all adoptions involve a white mother adopting
a black child, 5 percent involve a white mother adopting a child who is
neither black nor white, and 2 percent involve nonwhite parents adopting a white child. Because these figures include adoptions of foreign-
born children, the rate of transracial adoption of children born in the
United States is quite low.[14]

Despite the statistical rarity of transracial adoption of black children
by white parents, these placements generate the most controversy, pitting
racially divided Americans against one another in disputes about parental
competency.[15] Race-matching in custody and adoption clearly conflicts
with a colorblind ideal, but the U.S. Supreme Court refrained from
addressing the issue until 1984 in *Palmore v. Sidoti.*[16] Although—or perhaps because—controversy surrounding transracial adoption was more
intense, the Court chose to focus on an interracial custody dispute.
When Linda and Anthony Sidoti, a white couple, were divorced, a Florida court awarded Linda custody of their daughter, Melanie. One year
later, Anthony filed a petition to win custody of Melanie because Linda
was living with a black man, Clarence Palmore, whom she later married.
Anthony also alleged that his ex-wife was not properly caring for Melanie.[17]

Despite Anthony's allegations of improper care, the Florida trial court
concluded that "there is no issue as to either party's devotion to the
child, adequacy of housing facilities, or respectability of the new spouse
of either parent."[18] A court counselor, however, had reported that "[t]he
wife has chosen for herself and for her child a life-style unacceptable to
the father and to society. . . . The child . . . is, or at school age will be,
subject to environmental pressures not of choice. . . ."[19] In awarding
custody to the father, the trial court agreed:

> The father's evident resentment of the mother's choice of a black partner
> is not sufficient to wrest custody from the mother. It is of some signifi-
> cance, however, that the mother did see fit to bring a man into her home

and carry on a sexual relationship with him without being married to him. Such action tended to place gratification of her own desires ahead of her concern for the child's future welfare. This Court feels that despite the strides that have been made in bettering relations between the races in this country, it is inevitable that Melanie will, if allowed to remain in her present situation and attains school age and thus more vulnerable to peer pressures [*sic*], suffer from the social stigmatization that is sure to come.[20]

The Florida district court of appeal affirmed the decision to award custody to Anthony without opinion, and the U.S. Supreme Court granted certiorari.[21]

The Supreme Court concluded that the trial judge had relied solely on race in taking Melanie away from her mother and would have decided the case differently if Clarence Palmore had been "a Caucasian male of similar respectability."[22] Writing for a unanimous Court, Chief Justice Warren Burger found that this race-based approach was subject to strict scrutiny under the equal protection clause. Race was a suspect basis for government action, and Florida could not reinforce a parent's personal prejudices or other private biases through its custody determinations. The placement decision did not pass constitutional muster because the lower court's exclusive reliance on race was not necessary to promote Florida's compelling interest in protecting Melanie's welfare.[23]

In spite of the decision in *Palmore,* Melanie was not immediately returned to her mother. The family court judge was reluctant to disrupt a stable placement with her father, one that admittedly had occurred only because of the trial court's illicit consideration of race.[24] Not only did *Palmore* fail to alter Melanie's placement, but its impact on other custody disputes remains uncertain. Family courts now evaluate race as one but not the sole factor in custody disputes. Judges still enjoy considerable discretion to give race as much or as little weight as they deem appropriate.[25] Sometimes, courts have been accused of sneaking illicit racial considerations into a custody case under the guise of a neutral and objective analysis of the child's best interest. For example, white mothers complain that they have been denied custody of their children based on moral unsuitability, even though their real sin is not cohabitation but cohabitation with a black man.[26]

Nor can race be the sole basis for making or denying an adoptive placement.[27] Relying on *Palmore,* adoption agencies continue to consider race as one factor among many in the placement process.[28] In truth, though, public and private agencies alike have treated interracial placements as a last resort.[29] Agencies keep minority children, particularly blacks, in long-term foster care or institutions while they await a home with parents of the same race, despite overwhelming evidence that adoption at an early age is key to a child's successful adjustment.[30] Even after efforts to recruit black families under relaxed criteria for defining acceptable placements, the shortfall in black adoptive homes persists. Critics allege that the preference for same-race placements has exposed children to greater risks of instability and hardship than transracial placements would. Black children must bear the uncertainty of temporary care, and even when adopted, they are more likely to wind up in a single-parent or low-income household than white children are.[31]

Race-matching policies are also attacked because they impede recognition of ties of love and dependency that develop across the color line. Most notably, white foster parents have been denied the opportunity to adopt nonwhite children, despite evidence that the children have thrived in their care.[32] Even when foster parents and children have bonded as a psychological or de facto family, they have no constitutional right to preserve their relationships. Foster parents are considered nothing more than temporary caretakers working under contract with a child welfare agency. Although a parent has a due process right to bring up children without government interference, foster care providers do not have any legal rights as parents. Without the formal approval of adoption agencies and courts, foster parents can not convert a short-term, paid service contract into a constitutionally protected, permanent family. Even if a lengthy relationship in a foster family were to trigger some legal protections, social workers and judges would still be obligated to ascertain the child's best interest in any placement proceeding. This process of evaluation could include racial considerations as one factor.[33]

Critics also allege that the preference for same-race placements has resulted in heavy reliance on nonwhite, especially black, relatives who will never adopt the children in their care. When the number of children in foster care grew dramatically in the 1980s, a system of "kinship care" evolved, especially in large urban areas.[34] Under kinship care, relatives qualify as foster parents or take children into their homes without being licensed by the foster care system. The arrangement builds on extended family networks, particularly in the black community.[35] In 1979, the U.S. Supreme Court laid the foundation for this approach to the foster care crisis when it found that under federal funding provisions, states could not pay relatives less than strangers if both provide comparable services to children in their homes.[36]

Kinship care has received mixed reviews among researchers and policy-makers. Supporters argue that placement with relatives minimizes the children's trauma of separation from parents. Opponents criticize the system for placing children in homes that do not meet foster care licensing requirements and that may suffer from intergenerational patterns of abuse and neglect.[37] Some evidence suggests that children in kinship care are less apt to be reunited with their parents or to be adopted than are children placed with strangers. Because children in kinship care are with extended family, they may see their parents on an informal basis, even when no official reunification takes place. As a result, reuniting with a parent may seem less urgent than when a child is in a stranger's care. Moreover, financial exigencies in low-income communities can make adoption difficult. In fact, the chances of reconciliation or adoption may decline as the size of the government subsidy for kinship caregivers goes up.[38] Those who support reliance on extended family networks argue that the placements should be formalized as long-term arrangements by using guardianships that provide ongoing financial support from child welfare agencies.[39]

Because of the burdens that race-matching imposes on nonwhite children, some adoption law experts have argued that the policies violate equal protection.[40] Courts generally have been reluctant to agree, and lawsuits to strike down race-matching have been rebuffed. The experience in the District of Columbia demonstrates the limited success of litigation designed to enforce a colorblind placement policy. Two years before the *Palmore* decision, the District of Columbia court of appeals boldly announced that race-matching in adoption was unconstitutional unless necessary to promote a child's best interest.[41] Insisting that strict scrutiny was the appropriate standard of review, the judges refused to apply a more lenient test based on an adoption agency's allegedly benign purposes. As the court of appeals explained, "even if [a more lenient] standard were applicable in the context of affirmative action to remedy past discrimination . . . , I would not find it applicable in a family-law context, where racial classifications over the years have resulted in particularly vivid examples of invidious discrimination."[42]

In 1985, one year after the Supreme Court's decision in *Palmore,* the court of appeals reversed itself and applied a less demanding standard than strict scrutiny to interracial adoption cases.[43] The court justified its decision based on the substantial discretion granted to judges in placement hearings and the lack of any statutory mandate to consider race. The court's quick about-face reflected the widespread judicial reluctance

to interfere with complex assessments of a child's best interest by imposing a strict principle of colorblindness.[44]

Federal Efforts to Reform Race-Matching

Because of the reticence by the courts to interfere with race-matching
policies, Congress addressed the issue in 1994. Senator Howard H.
Metzenbaum introduced the Multiethnic Placement Act (MEPA) to address concerns that nonwhite children were being warehoused in long-
term foster care and institutions to avoid transracial adoptions.[45] MEPA
also sought to resolve marked disparities in state law. Florida and Texas
had eliminated race-matching policies that delayed placement, but other
states like Minnesota maintained an explicit commitment to the practice.
The Uniform Adoption Act recommended speedy, permanent placement over race-matching, but state law remained in flux.[46]

MEPA was quickly engulfed in controversy,[47] and its final language
was a compromise between the colorblindness advocated by proponents
of transracial placements and the color consciousness advocated by proponents of race-matching.[48] The Act reiterated the clear constitutional
mandate that agencies cannot flatly bar parents from adopting a child
of a different race.[49] To prevent race from exercising an undue influence
in individual placement decisions, MEPA provided: "An agency, or entity, that receives federal assistance and is involved in adoption or foster
care placements may not . . . delay or deny the placement of a child
for adoption or into foster care, or otherwise discriminate in making a
placement decision, solely because of the race, color, or national origin
of the adoptive or foster parent, or the child, involved."[50] MEPA allowed
an agency to consider a child's cultural, ethnic, or racial background and
the prospective parents' ability to meet the child's needs if these factors
were relevant to the child's best interest and were considered along with
other factors.[51]

As Congress mandated,[52] the Secretary of Health and Human Services
issued guidelines under MEPA for public and private adoption agencies.[53] Using strict scrutiny as the benchmark, the guidelines declared a
number of policies that place special burdens on transracial adoptions
impermissible. These included: (1) time periods in which an agency
would seek only a same-race placement; (2) formal placement preferences
based on race, culture, or ethnicity; (3) requirements that caseworkers
justify transracial placements; and (4) policies that delayed placements
in order to find families of a particular race, culture, or ethnicity.[54] Under

the guidelines, a child's cultural, ethnic, or racial background could be considered only on an individualized, case-by-case basis. Agencies might properly assess prospective parents' attitudes and skills in bringing up a child of a different cultural, ethnic, or racial background. One factor to consider was the parents' own express preference for a child of a particular race or ethnicity.[55] Agency assessments had to focus on individual traits, not "generalizations about the identity needs of children of a particular race or ethnicity or . . . generalizations about the abilities of prospective parents of one race or ethnicity to care for, or nurture the sense of identity of, a child of another race, culture, or ethnicity."[56]

In 1996, MEPA was amended by the Removal of Barriers to Interethnic Adoption Act.[57] The amendment strengthens the prohibition against race-matching policies by prohibiting delay or denial of a placement based on race, regardless of whether race is the sole factor. In a memorandum dated June 4, 1997, federal officials announced that adoption agencies could not consider "race, culture, or ethnicity" in placing a child.[58] Within a year, these officials revised their stringently colorblind interpretation. In a series of questions and answers on federal adoption law, enforcement experts advised adoption agencies that they could not routinely consider race, national origin, or ethnicity in finding a suitable home for a child unless special circumstances required these factors to be weighed on an individualized basis.[59] The experts noted that Congress did not address the relevance of culture and that "cultural needs may be important in placement decisions, such as where a child has specific language needs."[60] Although federal officials did not define "culture," they made clear it could not be used as a proxy for race, color, or national origin.[61] Generalizations based on race, national origin, and ethnicity were forbidden in the adoption process, but agencies could consider the attitudes and preferences of prospective parents to decide whether placement was in a child's best interest.[62] Shifts in the official interpretation of federal adoption policy left colorblindness a contested and uncertain principle, despite recent congressional action.

The Special Case of Native American Children

Although Congress has embraced colorblindness in adoption decisions to a greater degree than ever before, its treatment of Native American children remains highly color-conscious.[63] During congressional hearings in the 1970s, tribal leaders testified that abusive child welfare practices by state agencies had decimated their communities and deprived Native American children of their cultural birthright.[64] Witnesses testified that 25–35 percent of all Native American children in the United States had been separated from their families and placed in adoptive homes, foster care, or institutions.[65] Experts reported that these placements had a detrimental impact on Native American children, their families, and their tribes.[66]

In the 1960s and 1970s, Congress endorsed a policy of self-determination for tribes. The Indian Child Welfare Act (ICWA) of 1978[67] explicitly recognized that tribes could not survive as semisovereign peoples if their constituencies were decimated through family separation.[68] As a result, ICWA not only protects the best interest of Native American children by shielding them from a culturally insensitive adoption system but also promotes the "stability and security of Indian tribes and families."[69] In creating these dual objectives, Congress did not consider whether the best interest of children and the tribe's interest in self-preservation sometimes conflict.[70]

ICWA confers jurisdiction on tribal courts to decide placement cases involving Indian children. A tribal court has exclusive jurisdiction when children reside on or intend to return to the reservation or when children are wards of the tribal court, regardless of where they live.[71] The tribal court has such complete authority in these cases that it can veto an Indian parent's preference to process the adoption in a state court. As the U.S. Supreme Court explained in 1989 in *Mississippi Choctaw Band of Indians v. Holyfield,*[72] ICWA's purpose goes "beyond the wishes of individual parents" out of a commitment to advancing "long-term tribal survival" and preventing "damaging social and psychological impact on many individual Indian children."[73] ICWA therefore gives tribal courts the power to enforce their jurisdictional claims over Indian children who live on the reservation. Three Justices dissented, asserting that Congress did not intend to allow tribes to usurp the rights of Native American parents to choose a forum for adoption that better reflected their values and desires for their children.[74]

A tribal court has concurrent and presumptive jurisdiction over children who are either tribal members or eligible for tribal membership, even though they are not domiciled on a reservation. To enable tribal courts to exercise their jurisdictional prerogatives, state courts must notify tribes of involuntary proceedings involving an Indian parent and child, but need not advise tribes of voluntary proceedings.[75] So, for example, a state court has to tell the tribe that an Indian parent's rights are being terminated without consent but need not tell the tribe when the parent agrees to relinquish a child for adoption. When jurisdiction is concurrent, ICWA requires transfer to a tribal court unless a parent objects, the tribal court declines the case, or the state court finds good cause to keep it.[76] If parents object to the transfer, their objections usually are respected, regardless of whether the dissenting parent is Indian.[77] So long as neither parent objects, tribes almost always accept the transfer of custody cases from state court.[78] If a state court keeps the case, federal law imposes a preference for placement with a member of the Native American child's extended family, other members of the same tribe, or other Native American families, unless there is good cause to choose a placement with non-Indians.[79] Tribes retain the right to intervene in the proceedings if an Indian child is involved.[80]

In most instances, when a state court retains jurisdiction, it has found good cause based on the child's best interest. Some Native American advocates have argued that the good cause exception to tribal jurisdiction in effect continues the practice of placing high numbers of Native American children in white homes.[81] When a child has developed a bond with white foster parents and has little contact with Native American culture or customs, the state court is particularly likely to find good cause to retain jurisdiction and to opt for placement with a non-Indian family.[82] Alternatively, some state courts have found an "existing Indian family" exception to ICWA. That is, unless a placement disrupts an already established Indian family, ICWA does not even apply. Under this approach, courts have concluded that ICWA does not cover adoption of a child born out of wedlock to a non-Indian mother and Indian father, even when the father and tribe object to the placement, because no Indian family ever existed.[83]

State courts are especially reluctant to apply ICWA when there is no existing Indian family and bonds formed with an adoptive family will be disrupted. In *In re Bridget R.,*[84] an Ohio couple adopted twin girls after the biological parents had voluntarily relinquished their rights to the children. During the adoption proceeding, the biological father did not reveal his Indian heritage on his relinquishment form, although he told his attorney he was one-fourth Indian. In fact, the girls' father was three-sixteenths Pomo, and when his mother learned of the impending adoption, she enrolled herself, her son, and her twin granddaughters in the tribe. The girls' grandmother then contended that the adoption could not be finalized without considering ICWA's applicability.[85]

The Califiornia court of appeals found that because the twins had lived with their adoptive white parents for a substantial length of time, both parents and children had a substantive due process right to be free of government interference with their family life. In the court's view, due process rights arose in de facto families, regardless of whether family members were biologically related. Such constitutionally protected, psychological ties could outweigh biological ties to Indian parents or relatives. The court, in a startling departure from earlier precedent, concluded that any official intervention in the affairs of a de facto family would trigger strict scrutiny. Because the twins' Indian parent neither resided on the reservation nor had significant ties to the tribe, ICWA provided no compelling justification for infringing on an adoptive family's right to keep its psychological bonds intact.[86]

The *Bridget R.* case went on to attack the racialization of adoption policy under ICWA. The court of appeals concluded that ICWA does not apply to Native American parents living outside the reservation if they have no "significant social, cultural or political relationship with their tribe."[87] Because the twins' father had no substantial connection to the tribal community, his membership was based solely on his biological ancestry. This race-based classification violated equal protection because awarding custody to fully assimilated Indians, such as the twins' father and grandmother, was unlikely to promote the objective of conserving Native American families and tribes.[88]

Cases like *Bridget R.* have generated considerable concern about ICWA's scope. Members of Congress have tried unsuccessfully to codify the California court's holding. The Indian Child Welfare Improvement Act of 1995[89] would have amended ICWA to limit tribal jurisdiction to cases involving "those living on a reservation and their children and those who are members of an Indian tribe."[90] Tribal membership would have been evaluated on the date of the child's birth, so that a parent's subsequent enrollment in a tribe could not retroactively bring the child under ICWA's coverage.[91] Similarly, the Adoption Promotion and Stability Act of 1996 proposed that ICWA not apply to child custody proceedings in which neither the biological parents nor the child maintained an affiliation to an Indian tribe. To find an affiliation, a court would have had to conclude that one of the child's biological parents is "of Indian descent" and that the parent or child "maintains significant social, cultural, or political affiliation with the Indian tribe."[92]

In addition, Congress has been troubled by the balance struck between parental and tribal rights under ICWA. Echoing the concerns about parental autonomy that were expressed by the *Holyfield* dissenters, the Voluntary Adoption Protection Act of 1997 would have exempted proceedings in which an Indian child's parent or guardian consents to the placement.[93] Those who want to strengthen tribal rights have introduced legislation that would require notification of voluntary as well as involuntary proceedings that involve an Indian child. Under these bills, a tribe would be entitled to intervene in the proceeding within a specified period. If no notice were provided, the tribe would retain the right to intervene at any time. The proposed amendments would authorize criminal penalties when parties to a placement proceeding intentionally conceal the Indian identities of parents or children to escape ICWA's strictures. The legislation also would authorize courts to order that birth parents, extended family members, and tribal members have enforceable visitation rights or other forms of continued contact with a child after an adoption.[94] So far, ICWA remains intact, a fragile compromise between tribal sovereignty and traditional adoption law and policy. Still, the tensions have taken their toll. ICWA's provisions are regularly attacked as a wrongful invasion of Indian parents' autonomy, a perpetuation of racist ideology, and a bureaucratic nightmare that unsettles the stability of adoptions based on remote claims of Indian ancestry.

Contested Images of Race in Custody and Adoption Disputes

The debate over interracial custody and adoption disputes is linked to changing conceptions of race and family. Colorblind policy assumes that race is a biological irrelevancy, a trivial artifact of ancestry and appearance. In determining whether a placement will serve a child's best interest, however, courts and agencies often have treated biology as highly relevant to family formation. Through their placement decisions, family court judges and social workers have tried to mimic "naturally" occurring families, which are overwhelmingly homogeneous in terms of race.[95] As a result, color-conscious policies traditionally have dominated placement cases. With the rise of a civil rights jurisprudence that minimizes the relevance of skin color to public life, race-matching based on ancestry or appearance has become increasingly anomalous. To reconcile this contradiction, courts and agencies are struggling to redefine the role of race in nonbiological terms.

Shifting Definitions of Race: Genotype, Phenotype, and Social Ties

The meaning of race has evolved differently in interracial custody and adoption cases. In custody battles, courts now minimize the weight given to ancestry and appearance because both parents typically have biological ties to the child. By defining race as a function of ancestry rather than appearance, each parent has an equivalent claim to the child, and race is not helpful in making a placement decision.[96] Courts therefore focus on the competency of each parent to meet the child's social and emotional needs. Here, too, race is not likely to be a decisive factor insofar as each parent chose to cross the color line to build a family. Presumably, both parents were willing to take on the challenges of parenting in an interracial household, and no matter what the court decides, the child will live in a multiracial home. Custody cases therefore treat race not only as a biological irrelevancy but also as a complex social phenomenon that precludes any facile resort to stereotypical judgments.

Ironically, ancestry and appearance remain quite important in adoption, even though most prospective adoptive parents have no biological connection to the child.[97] Agencies have been eager to produce families that do not give away the "secret" of adoption based on an outsider's casual inspection of the parents and their children.[98] A child's skin tone, hair color and texture, and facial features have been meticulously recorded to determine the propriety of a placement. One mixed-race transracial adoptee describes the notes about her as an infant in foster care in 1963. Social workers carefully chronicled changes in her skin color from "white and clear" to "somewhat dusky" and "definitely dusky" to "quite dark." They punctiliously described her hair as "sparse, black, and tend[ing] to curl," her eyes as "brown," and her nose as "broad." She was labeled "negroid in appearance."[99] The rise of the permanency movement, which emphasizes placing children in loving homes, dissipated some of this focus on phenotypical matching, but these concerns persist.[100] Even today, black children with some white ancestry are more apt to be placed transracially than those without white ancestry.[101]

A shift from phenotype to genotype has not minimized the biological significance of race in adoption cases as it has in custody disputes. Instead, the change has simply restructured the inquiry into whether a placement creates a family that appears biologically compatible. In *Reisman v. Tennessee Department of Human Services*,[102] white foster parents wanted to adopt a child in their care. The child was defined as "bi-racial" or "mixed-race" because "her father was a black person and her mother was a white person based upon community standards of identifying race."[103] The Department of Human Services denied the adoption petition because it preferred to place mixed-race children in black families. The Tennessee federal district court held that this policy denied the child's right to equal protection because changing social conditions required that "bi-racial children in the custody of the Department shall be classified as bi-racial children with a bi-racial culture and a bi-racial heritage." The court rejected the characterization of mixed-race children as black as "the automatic invocation of race stereotypes."[104] To meet the special needs of mixed-race children, the district court ordered an elaborate system of race-matching:

> [B]i-racial children shall be placed in foster homes and in adoptive homes with bi-racial families, if possible. If not, they shall be placed in the most suitable home based upon the availability and suitability of the adoptive parents or parent with a goal of providing for the children appropriate love and nurture with a commitment to assist the children in solving as much as possible problems created by members of society in either the black or white race or both.[105]

To address the complex role of race in the placement process, the judge created a special placement committee with racially diverse membership.[106]

The *Reisman* case makes plain that a shift from appearance to ancestry is no panacea for dealing with racial issues in adoption. By focusing on a genotypical conception of race, the court redefined the naturally occurring, biological family for a biracial child as a mixed-race, not black, couple. As a result, the decision simply refined rather than eliminated a system of race-matching. Because interracial marriages remain rare, the pool of mixed-race adoptive couples is probably quite small. The real question, then, is whether *Reisman* forces agencies to abandon their preference for black rather than white adoptive homes once it becomes clear that no mixed-race home can be found. Depending on the special placement committee's answer, *Reisman* may do little more than delay the placement of biracial children. Certainly, the case does nothing to dispel color-conscious practices in adoption.

The quandary over the relevance of biological definitions of race is further illustrated by debates over the meaning of "Indianness" under ICWA. In contrast to concerns that black adoptees and white parents look too dissimilar to be members of the same family, ICWA reflects a fear that white parents see Indian children as phenotypically similar enough to be adopted and absorbed into white society.[107] Widespread intermarriage has made Indianness turn on distant genotypical ties, and state courts have chafed at treating this ancestry as anything other than a biological irrelevancy. For example, the *Bridget R.* decision criticized ICWA for reducing race to a blood quantum requirement without regard to social, cultural, and political manifestations of Indian identity.[108] Defenders of ICWA's color-conscious policies insist that tribes must be allowed to use remote biological ancestry to define Indianness because social ties have been artificially disrupted. Far from being a biological irrelevancy, tribal representatives see fractional blood quantum requirements as a legacy of the impact of early contact and forced assimilation.

Congress, courts, and tribes continue to struggle with the balance between rules of descent, which make eligibility for membership an involuntary status, and social, cultural, and political affiliations, which convert membership into a voluntary choice. Striking the balance is especially difficult because policymakers must weigh a tradition of individual liberty against a promise to respect the communal claims of tribes. When courts try to minimize the significance of biological ties, tribes insist that blood quantum identifies individuals who would have been actively involved with the tribe but for the impact of past discrimination. The semisovereignty of Indians as peoples therefore depends on giving tribes the power to define membership, regardless of state court judges' concerns about manipulation and abuse. When judges express concern about disregarding Indian parents' wishes about a child's placement, tribal leaders reply that this is the price of rectifying past official efforts to disrupt Indian families. The fear that some parents will pass as white and then use their hidden Indianness to disrupt an adoption is treated as a cost of racial ambiguity that comes from partial but not complete assimilation.

Just as state courts have questioned a strictly genotypical definition of Indianness under ICWA, they have grown increasingly skeptical of race-matching policies in adoption based solely on the need to create phenotypically similar families. Because civil rights jurisprudence envisions race as a biological irrelevancy, courts have turned to the impact of race on social attitudes and cultural practices to uphold color-conscious adoption policies. Judges occasionally have acknowledged the relevance of race to parental competency: "However unpleasant, it would seem that race is a problem which must be considered and should not be ignored or minimized."[109] Some judges have permitted adoption agencies to consider race so long as it is not used in a way that amounts to a racial slur or stigma.[110] In deciding how race should be weighed, however, most courts have focused on the general attitudes and cultural awareness of adoptive parents.[111]

When evaluating parental attitudes and skills, courts confront the dilemma of deciding which perspectives and practices promote healthy racial socialization. Consider, for example, the DeWees, white foster parents who petitioned to adopt Dante, a biracial child who had been in their care since he was two months of age. Mrs. DeWees initially expressed some concerns about taking in a biracial child, but both she and her husband came to love Dante during the two years that he lived with them. Dante had made a good adjustment in the DeWees's home and had bonded with them.[112] In spite of this favorable evidence, the expert who evaluated the DeWees's parental fitness was concerned that they believed that "race had 'no impact' on developing a child's identity and self-esteem, that addressing racial issues was not important in raising a minority child; and, that they would not prepare [the child] to deal with racial discrimination but rather would address the problem if and when it occurred."[113] In addition, the DeWees lacked contacts in the black community, and Mrs. DeWees had remarked that she would "not manufacture black friends."[114] When the DeWees's petition was denied, however, the couple offered to take any course of action necessary to meet Dante's needs and to participate in a support group of transracial adoptive families.[115]

The court upheld the denial of the petition, presumably because the adoption agency properly concluded that the DeWees's refusal to engage in color-conscious parenting reflected unhealthy racial attitudes.[116] Yet the court also recognized that its decision subverted the principle of colorblindness:

> In making adoption decisions, state agencies cannot ignore the realities of the society in which children entrusted to them for placement will be raised, or the affect [*sic*] on children of those realities as documented by professional studies. The court would hope, however, that these agencies also will be mindful of the possibility that an overemphasis on racial issues may retard efforts to achieve a color blind society, and of the need to avoid even the appearance that an adoption decision may have been based on race per se.[117]

In a society in which interracial families are anomalous, the relevance of race to socialization remains unclear. Once race is no longer simply used to create phenotypically similar families, courts find its significance in forging bonds of love, support, and guidance quite mystifying. Indeed, judicial uncertainty is so great that an expert's opinion could override concrete evidence that Dante had thrived in his white foster parents' care and that they were permanently committed to his welfare.

Administrative interpretations of MEPA and its subsequent amendments do little to clarify this ambiguity. Although the law is designed to establish a norm of colorblindness, enforcement officials continue to acknowledge the social and cultural relevance of race to family formation. Race is considered in evaluating parental competency at two levels. In the first place, the placement process can accommodate a prospective parent's preference for a child of the same race. Equality requires not that these preferences be disregarded but that preferences for children of a different race or a complete indifference to the child's race be accorded equivalent respect. By deferring to these subjective preferences, the new federal adoption provisions rely on an approach similar to *Loving*'s treatment of interracial marriage.[118] Once again, the task of deciding whether to forge interracial families is left to the predilections of ordinary Americans.

After personal preferences are ascertained, race enters the process again when adoption agencies make objective evaluations of parental fitness. Because culture is presumptively relevant even though race is not, federal law leaves considerable room for same-race placements to persist out of concern that adoptive parents are not competent to raise children from a different background. By failing to define culture yet forbidding its use as a proxy for race, official interpretations hardly clarify which parenting strategies are desirable and which are disqualifying. Federal officials do not say whether colorblind parenting is culturally insensitive or racially neutral. Nor do they tell adoption agencies whether color-conscious parenting is culturally competent or racist. Far from making a norm of colorblindness clear, current federal law leaves the mystery of what constitutes healthy racial socialization unsolved.

Clarifying the Nature of Race in Custody and Adoption Cases

The traditional justifications for a norm of colorblindness are confounded by the debate over interracial custody and adoption. In general, proponents of a colorblind jurisprudence have assumed that once they demonstrate that race is a biological irrelevancy, there can be no other basis for officials to consider it. In family matters, however, experts and policymakers in recent decades have increasingly focused on social and emotional bonds, rather than blood ties. Because the best interest of children is at stake, race cannot be dismissed as an unimportant or impermissible factor simply to promote equality. Once race's irrelevance is no longer axiomatic, those who advocate colorblind placement policy must demonstrate that this trait is unrelated to forging functional families, even in a society that remains highly segregated. This task is difficult, if not impossible. Once race is deemed germane, however, it is unclear how it should be weighed. For while placements should not harm children, laws also should not entrench segregation and racism. The result is an inescapable indeterminacy, as officials navigate between the world that might have been in the absence of racial discrimination and the world that exists after centuries of racial separation and subordination.

The Irrelevancy of Biological Definitions of Race

Race is properly deemed a biological irrelevancy in custody and adoption cases. Biological conceptions of race, whether they turn on genotype or phenotype, should play no role in placement decisions. In custody disputes, genetic ties are already irrelevant because each parent usually has an equivalent tie to the child. In adoption decisions, genotypical claims should be ignored for the opposite reason. Prospective parents typically have no genetic ties to the children, whatever their race. So genotype alone offers no insight into whether a white parent is more fit to raise an unrelated white child or an unrelated black child. Moreover, the bedrock assumption underlying adoption is that biological kinship is unnecessary to form a strong parent–child bond. According to this view, adoption can lead to healthier relationships than blood ties when a birth parent is unfit. Given this philosophy, genetic ties should be equally beside the point for same-race and transracial placements.

When race is defined as phenotype, it again should be treated as irrelevant. In custody battles, a child's physical resemblance to one parent rather than another is a strange basis for evaluating parental fitness. In same-race marriages, for instance, family courts do not find that a child with his father's blue eyes and pug nose should be taken from his mother because she has brown eyes and a classic Roman nose. Parents have no control over the physical appearance of their children, and siblings can look remarkably different. When choosing to marry and conceive, most couples presumably would not want a future custody decision to turn on a throw of the genetic dice that determines eye color, hair color, and other phenotypical traits. Rather, they would prefer that the decision be based on actions that they can control—in particular, the parenting strategies that they use to bond with the child. So far, there is little evidence to suggest that adults and children who look alike bond better than those who look different. Past parenting strategies, however, do appear to be a good basis for predicting future fitness.[119] Under these circumstances, phenotype should carry no weight when a court has specific evidence about parental involvement with the child.

Phenotype should be irrelevant in adoption as well. There is no evidence that adoptive parents form weaker bonds to dissimilar looking children than to similar ones.[120] Consequently, the principal justification for phenotypical race-matching must be that it permits families to keep the fact of adoption a private matter and to avoid the hardships of being an anomalous, interracial family. Transracial placements should not be disfavored because they make a family's nonbiological ties obvious. Assuming that adoptive parents are comfortable with an arrangement in which the adopted status of their children is apparent, officials have no reason to keep adoption a hidden condition unless its visibility interferes with an adoptee's well-being. At present, there is no persuasive evidence that such harm generally occurs.[121]

The hardships of being an interracial family relate to the social consequences of race rather than to phenotype per se. Race-matching is based on the assumption that interracial families will encounter hostility and prejudice in a racially divided world. At present, social science data indicate that despite the special challenges posed by transracial adoption, children in interracial homes are as well adjusted as those placed with same-race families. Moreover, adoptive parents report that the experience of raising a child of another race is highly rewarding.[122] In the face of this evidence, agencies cannot invoke phenotype alone to justify race-matching without a thorough assessment of the social and cultural implications of race in the family.

The Complexity of Social and Cultural Conceptions of Race

In civil rights jurisprudence, the conclusion that race is a biological irrelevancy has been viewed as a necessary and sufficient basis for colorblind policy. In custody and adoption cases, however, race may matter, even when its biological significance is rebutted. Race marks important social and cultural boundaries that can hardly be ignored in determining a child's best interest. These boundaries are relevant even when the placement involves an infant who has yet to form a racial identity, rather than an older child who already identifies racially. The child's racial designation can influence how adoptive parents understand their responsibilities. Prospective parents already have well-developed notions about race that can empower or stigmatize a child. In addition, a racial designation can be a proxy for future social experiences, both positive and negative, for which the child needs to be prepared. A black infant will probably encounter discrimination later in life that a white infant is unlikely ever to experience. Conversely, the black adoptee may have opportunities to express a sense of racial solidarity that the white child will never know. For all of these reasons, the social and cultural implications of race are undeniably relevant to placement policy.[123]

In placement decisions, courts and agencies must put a child's welfare first, while respecting principles of racial equality and family or parental autonomy to the extent possible. In the custody setting, for example, courts should consider an interracial couple's desire that children retain a sense of their dual heritage after divorce, so long as the arrangements do not interfere with the children's welfare. In one comparison of Anglo couples, Latino couples, and couples with one Anglo and one Latino partner, men who had intermarried spent more time with their children after a marital breakup than those who had not. The difference was especially great for Latino fathers divorcing Anglo women. In part, the fathers' extra commitment of time reflected a desire to maintain the children's sense of their Latino and Anglo identities.[124] Joint custody arrangements were especially attractive to these fathers. So long as these arrangements are not detrimental to the children, they should be permitted.

In adoption, agencies should be allowed to accommodate parental preferences about race where necessary to protect a child's best interest. Agencies must be able to protect children from adoptive parents who label themselves unwilling or unfit to raise a transracial adoptee.[125] This principle of accommodation may raise concerns that agencies will simply endorse whatever preferences prospective parents have when they walk in the door. These concerns are both legitimate and unavoidable. Adults seeking to adopt a child are likely to have well-entrenched views about race. These views are unlikely to be transformed by agency programs of "re-education" that urge parents to consider the benefits of transracial adoption. These programs are best directed at adults who are open to but uncertain about adopting a child of another race.[126]

Moreover, cracking down on independent adoptions solely to hamper the expression of same-race preferences seems misguided. At present, those who can bear children are free to implement their preferences by choosing mates of the same race.[127] If this choice is deemed beyond the reach of regulation, it is unclear why infertile couples' preferences should be condemned on this ground—at least so long as they ask the state to do no more than grant the adoption petition just as it would issue a marriage license.[128] In addition, adoption agencies are still permitted to consider racial preferences as a way to protect children from placement in unsuitable homes, so same-race preferences could still be expressed even if independent adoptions were curtailed. If parents are willing to pay the substantial costs of independent adoption to obtain a "designer child" of the same race, forcing them into a regulated agency process seems unlikely to cultivate their taste for transracial placements.[129] Rather, these prospective parents are apt to use their resources to flee to other deregulated systems—such as international adoptions—that permit them to indulge, among other things, their preference for a child of the same race.[130]

Independent adoptions, whether domestic or international, should be regulated based on the need to protect the best interest of the child. At some point, the freedom to express preferences for a particular kind of baby becomes the power to commodify children in demeaning and inappropriate ways. Children may be devalued based on a number of characteristics, including age, race, gender, or disability. A child's ties to biological parents can be wrongly disrupted through financial overreaching or other forms of coercion. When independent adoptions fall prey to this pathology of autonomy, that is, the dehumanizing objectification of children, then regulation is appropriate.[131]

Agencies cannot realistically transform racial attitudes of prospective parents during the screening process, but officials must make clear that in responding to patterns of demand among prospective adoptive parents, they are not endorsing their preferences.[132] Placement policies can accommodate preferences for same-race families, but officials also must accord equal respect to preferences for interracial families. Nonwhite children should not spend long periods in foster care or institutions when white parents are willing and able to adopt them. These delays or denials of placement send a message that forming an interracial family is an untrustworthy and perhaps pathological choice.

Moreover, as federal law mandates, agencies cannot impose unique burdens of justification on transracial adoptions. However, agencies tend to distrust adoptive parents who express a preference for a child of a different race and commonly make extensive inquiries about their racial attitudes. Questions about racial attitudes should be tailored to assist those contemplating a transracial adoption to be effective parents, rather than to pass judgment on the preferences. Moreover, parents who express an intense, rigid preference for a child of the same race may harbor prejudices that also merit investigation.[133] Otherwise officials will create a presumption that with respect to racial socialization, same-race families are universally functional, while interracial families are likely to be dysfunctional.[134] In fact, researchers have found that children in interracial families have more flexible attitudes about race and are more receptive to friendships and romance with individuals of other races than children in same-race families are.[135] Under these circumstances, it is not clear why concerns about racial socialization should be limited to transracial placements.

Although agencies cannot endorse racist ideologies, they must be open to a range of views about racial socialization and equality—so long as these ideologies are not detrimental to a child's best interest. Like the DeWees, some parents in interracial families are strongly committed to colorblind caretaking and to teaching their children that they are "human above all else—color is totally irrelevant."[136] But many of these parents express frustration that society insists on attaching oversimplified racial labels to children with complex individual identities.[137] These parents believe that so long as they provide a loving home and are not racist, they should be able to adopt a nonwhite child.[138] For them, race-matching and color-conscious parenting are politically correct requirements that exact a high cost from nonwhite children who remain in foster care or institutions.[139]

On the other hand, experts like the one in the DeWees's case believe that color-conscious parenting is essential to a child's healthy socialization in a society deeply divided by race. These experts equate colorblind caretaking with cultural insensitivity and ethnocentrism. In their view, white parents who disregard nonwhite children's racial identities fail to prepare them for the experience of racism and neglect to inculcate pride in and awareness of their unique heritage.[140] As a result, transracial adoptees raised by colorblind, white parents lack a well-developed sense of themselves as racialized persons.

In the absence of consensus about the meaning of healthy racial socialization, agencies should deem both colorblind and color-conscious parenting strategies acceptable. So far, there is no persuasive evidence that either approach harms an adoptee's self-esteem, adjustment at home, or performance in school. Agencies should accord substantial weight to a prospective parent's flexibility about childrearing practices, however. An adoptive parent ideally should be willing to modify socialization practices, including those related to race, if they are not meeting an individual child's needs.[141]

When evidence of successful parenting is available, moreover, this should be a weightier consideration than abstract views about racial so-cialization.[142] In the DeWees's case, they overcame reservations about a biracial child to give Dante a loving home. Dante's ability to thrive in their care should have counted more than Mrs. DeWees's expressed be-lief in colorblind caretaking.[143] Similarly, when black foster parents suc-cessfully nurture a white child, their adoption petition should not be denied simply because a white placement might be available.[144] Even if same-race placements are the overwhelming statistical norm for white children,[145] prospective white parents must not automatically be treated as superior to black foster parents solely because of their racial identity. Otherwise, federal efforts to lift the special burdens on transracial adop-tions will produce at best a squint-eyed ethic of colorblindness.

The uncertainty surrounding the propriety of different approaches to racial socialization reflects a larger dilemma. Policymakers are still struggling to decide what racial equality means. In doing so, they must balance a speculative vision of what America might look like absent racial discrimination and the reality of what America looks like in the wake of racial segregation and subordination. Proponents of colorblindness focus on the ideal: Race should be nothing more than happenstance in the formation of family bonds. Advocates of color-conscious placement policies emphasize the real: In a society that remains racially segregated, the color line shapes parental attitudes and abilities, which in turn influ-ence children's welfare.

Reconstructing Family Autonomy to Escape Racial Complexities

Policymakers have yet to strike a stable balance between racial ideals and realities. In the face of uncertainty about what racial equality means, courts and agencies can turn to principles of parental and family auton-omy in formulating placement policy. Officials should accord equal re-spect to family ties, regardless of whether they conform to the image of a traditional, same-race nuclear family. This principle of equal respect is especially appropriate in light of the unsettled nature of family in recent years. Any rigid definition of the "good family" is now openly challenged, given the increasing diversity of arrangements for child-rearing.[146] Not only are some families interracial, but parents often di-vorce and remarry, leading to complicated "blended" families. More and more, women find themselves raising children alone, and support from relatives, friends, and professional caretakers is critical to their families' survival.

Under a principle of equal respect, courts should not devalue de facto family ties solely because they cross the color line. When white foster parents attempt to adopt black or biracial children in their care, courts refuse to accord their psychological bonds as a family constitutional protection. The lack of protection for these intimate relationships reflects not only the view that foster parenting is a temporary, contractual arrangement but also the belief that interracial placements are a last resort. When white parents petition for adoption of a child of the same race in their care, they may be rebuffed because there is no guarantee of permanency. Yet their petition will not be denied because the child's race makes any expectation of building a permanent family, however healthy the emotional ties, seem misplaced and peculiar.

Nor should courts create special protections for de facto families simply because they are putatively same-race arrangements. In *Bridget R.*, the court took the unusual step of according due process rights to white parents who had bonded as a de facto family with children believed to be white as well. When the white parents subsequently learned that the children were "retroactively" Indian, the court found that the family was burdened by unfair surprise. By holding that the de facto family was exempt from ICWA and even constitutionally protected, *Bridget R.* validated the white parents' expectation that their same-race household would be free of government interference. In reaching this conclusion, *Bridget R.* even went so far as to suggest that the children were not really Indian because they had no ties to Indian people. In this way, the court permitted the adoptive family not only to stay intact but to stay intact as a white family.

In addition, courts and agencies should not devalue alternative family structures because they correlate with a nonwhite identity. ICWA is the clearest endorsement of alternative definitions of family. It recognizes that children can be political and cultural resources for tribes facing extinction. Even transracial adoption supporters who denounce blacks for treating children as communal property rather than people[147] often tacitly acquiesce in ICWA's goal of tribal preservation. Very often, ICWA is justified as a concession to both the unique power of tribes as semi-sovereign peoples and their unique weakness as vanishing ones. For each of these reasons, tribes are allowed to conscript members who would have belonged but for a history of coerced assimilation. The House Report on the Act reached precisely this conclusion: "One of the effects of our national paternalism has been to so alienate some Indian [parents] from their society that they abandon their children at hospitals or to welfare departments rather than entrust them to the care of relatives in the extended family."[148] The ideal of racial equality in ICWA, far from being colorblind, envisions a world in which tribes remain distinct from white society.

Upon closer inspection, however, ICWA's provisions belie an account based purely on corrective justice for racial wrongs. If ICWA is designed to cure the false consciousness of assimilation, it seems to focus its incentives on the wrong members. Indians who are arguably least assimilated to a white way of life, as evidenced by their decision to reside on reservations, are also least able to exercise parental discretion about their children's future. Meanwhile, Indians who are most assimilated and have the fewest contacts with a tribe are most able to escape ICWA's strictures. If the law is intended as a corrective for tribal alienation, surely the jurisdictional provisions are precisely backwards.

Rather than a cure for false consciousness, ICWA should be seen as a way to accord equal respect to alternative definitions of family in tribal life. ICWA empowers tribes to recognize extended families and tribal communities as caretaking units that are just as plausible as nuclear families. As a result, children are as connected to tribes and collateral relatives as they are to biological parents, and there is no reason to give the parents' wishes primacy in the placement process. When parents submit to tribal authority by living on a reservation, they presumptively accept alternative definitions of family. By contrast, nonreservation Indians do not necessarily endorse the tribe's vision of the family, so they can demand that their parental prerogatives be respected. Rather than counteract the incursions of assimilation, ICWA serves primarily to preserve alternative conceptions of family in Indian communities that remain vital sources of social and cultural meaning for their members.[149]

ICWA's protections should apply whenever an eligible member demonstrates acceptance of the tribe's norms for family formation. Living on the reservation is one way to assent, but it is not the only way. Nonreservation Indians may register as members, observe tribal customs, or maintain contact with the tribe, for example.[150] Moreover, courts should not presume that simply because Indian parents consent to a placement with white parents, they have chosen a non-Indian model of the family. Judges should assure themselves that Indian parents are fully informed about the relevance of their tribal identity to placement proceedings before accepting consent as a rebuff of ICWA's concerns.[151] By focusing on whether parents have demonstrated a commitment to tribal authority over family, courts can avoid far-ranging examinations of the authenticity of parents' and children's Indianness. Even when nonreservation Indian parents reject tribal authority over the family, they can still regard themselves and their children as Indian in other ways. The *Bridget R.* decision unnecessarily invades a person's freedom of self-definition when it finds ICWA inapplicable by denying parents and children even a symbolic kind of Indian identity.

Because ICWA permits tribes to implement alternative definitions of the family, courts should not feel constrained to use adoption to create a nuclear family that completely replaces the biological one. Under ICWA, courts could consider arrangements that build on Indian traditions of extended, communal families. For instance, courts might approve an open adoption in which a white family has custody of a Native American child, but the Indian parents and extended family members retain generous visitation rights. Rather than relinquish a Native American identity through adoption, the child then could remain eligible for tribal membership and preserve connections to Indian relatives and traditions.[152]

Like Native Americans, African Americans have a well-developed history of relying on extended family networks. Yet the kinship care system does not fully legitimate these networks because they do not conform to the traditional model of the white nuclear family. Rather than emphasize strict race-matching policies to preserve black identity, blacks should demand equivalent respect for their alternative family structures. The proposed Kinship Care Act of 1997[153] could have begun to validate extended black families by authorizing projects on the viability of long-term kinship care. Although the legislation did not pass, Congress did enact the Adoption and Safe Families Act of 1997, which requires the Secretary of Health and Human Services to report on kinship care. The Act also provides for grants to fund demonstration projects, some of which will address kinship care.[154] Despite these recent initiatives, efforts to recognize and support black caregiving arrangements remain tentative, exploratory, and uncertain in comparison to ICWA's endorsement of alternative tribal family structures.

Conclusion

The government cannot respect racial equality in the family by espousing simplistic norms of either colorblindness or color consciousness. In a country in which racial segregation is a reality, officials must be careful not to reinforce "separate but equal" families as an ideal. Yet courts and agencies also must protect the best interest of children who are racially identified in a divided society. Undoubtedly there is a fine line between acknowledging that segregation exists and acquiescing to it as desirable or inevitable. Still, that is the line that officials must walk if they are to strike a balance between the world that is and the one that might be in the absence of racial discrimination. Courts and agencies must not denigrate the parenting strategies and family structures that have evolved to cope with racism, poverty, and adversity. At the same time, though, policy cannot enshrine these responses in ways that perpetuate racial difference and division, even when some Americans are willing to build families across the color line.

EIGHT

Race and Identity:
The New Multiracialism

ANTIMISCEGENATION LAWS historically were used to define racial difference and enforce racial inequality. When the U.S. Supreme Court struck down restrictions on intermarriage as unconstitutional in *Loving v. Virginia*,[1] it refrained from attacking racial classifications themselves. In recent decades, interracial marriage has been on the rise, though race continues to be a significant factor in predicting marital choices. Still, the growing number of interracial couples with mixed-race offspring challenges conventional definitions of race. Members of interracial families have flexible conceptions of race that collide with inflexible racial categories. Lately, those who crossed the color line to marry and have a family successfully demanded that the U.S. government recognize multiracialism on the 2000 census. Although the multiracial movement unsettles racial boundaries, it has not yet contested the meaning of race itself. As a result, multiracialism may be a diversion from the dilemmas that race poses if it equates the experiences of nonwhite groups as diverse as blacks, Asian Americans, and Native Americans.

The Riddle of Mixed-Race Identity in a World of Racially Separate Families

Race is a pervasive feature of everyday life that organizes people's experience. Neighborhoods remain segregated by race, and same-race families and friendships are still the norm.[2] Because racial boundaries are clearly marked in the earliest relations with family, friends, and strangers, children become aware of these differences at about three to five years of age.[3] Kindergartners already understand that phenotypical traits are markers of racial identity. Children rely on skin color to distinguish blacks from whites and eye folds to identify Chinese and Japanese people. Interestingly, though, when children are asked to define "Spanish people," they emphasize the use of the Spanish language and state that "[a] Spanish person could be white, kind of white, and darker white, but never brown or black."[4] Young children already appreciate that some groups are racialized based on involuntary traits, while others are defined by their choice of linguistic and cultural practices.

The segregation of intimate life bounds a child's sense of racial possibilities. At a remarkably early age, children in same-race families sense that interracial marriages are not just unusual but undesirable. These children say that "mommies and daddies should be the same color" and "if they're different colors, then everybody would laugh at you." A child would feel "sad" if her parents were of different races because "[p]eople could make fun of me, and they would hurt my feelings and everybody's feelings." A sense of racial separation in the family is so deep-seated that children in same-race families insist that parents cannot produce a baby of a different race. When shown a picture of a black woman holding a white infant, they conclude that she must have adopted the child or be babysitting.[5]

When couples cross the color line to form a family, their children develop flexible notions of race. Children born to interracial couples readily accept the possibility that parents can be of different colors. They are generally comfortable with their parents' racial differences. When pressed about whether these differences matter, a child may emphasize emotional attachments that transcend color: "[Parents] should be nice to each other and pick up their own kids and be[ ] nice to them." Children of interracial unions also agree that a parent and child can be different colors. When shown the picture of an African American woman with a white baby, one boy explained that the child "came out of her tummy" and was white " 'cause he had a white father." When children have some contact with interracial couples, they become more open to the possibility of racial differences within families than those who do not.[6]

Although children in interracial marriages seem comfortable with racial differences, they often struggle to find their place in a world that presumes that families are racially segregated. Their freedom to forge an identity is limited by ongoing uncertainties about the relevance of race. Interracial couples themselves disagree about what healthy racial socialization means: "Some parents say their child is a human above all else—color is totally irrelevant; other parents teach their children to have a Black identity or the identity of the parent of color and to learn minority survival skills; the third group teaches its children that they are interracial and should have an interracial identity."[7] To maximize the chances that children develop an appreciation of their complex heritage, interracial families often live in integrated neighborhoods or in neighborhoods near large universities or cosmopolitan cities. These families report enjoying a "comfort factor" in that they "don't have to think all the time about differences—you just accept them."[8] Although some interracial families live in all-black neighborhoods and participate in all-black activities, one couple contended that this strategy was not "any more healthy for biracial children than being segregated in an all-white area."[9]

In a world in which race matters, parents sometimes find it difficult to ensure that a biracial child is treated as "just a human being." One white man married to a black woman expressed dismay about his daughter's inevitable racialization:

> [My daughter] will be considered black in this society, regardless of how her parents view her or how she views herself. And yet, she has a lot of contact with both my side of the family and her mother's, and she will be culturally black *and* white. It seems to me that to merely label her "black" is not an accurate reflection of her true identity and it angers me that my own heritage is blotted out in society's view of my daughter's background.[10]

The literature on biracial children chronicles the dangers of overidentification with one parent's heritage over another's. Based on counseling work with biracial adolescents, Jewelle Taylor Gibbs concluded that teenagers who emphasize their black heritage to the exclusion of their white background often embrace what she terms "lower-class" black culture by engaging in extreme social and sexual behaviors, such as promiscuity. On the other hand, those who focus on their white background to the detriment of their black origins are frequently ambivalent about their racial identification and become socially withdrawn and sexually repressed. Two biracial females who had grown up in privileged homes had trouble building friendships when they arrived at college. One expressed anger at her parents "for treating me like I was white and not preparing me for the real world as a black person."[11] The other complained that she could not fit in with either whites or blacks: "When I'm with the white students, I think like a black person and when I'm with the black students, I think like a white person."[12]

Despite these difficulties, most children in mixed marriages become well-adjusted adults with a healthy racial identity.[13] They have a sense of their pluralistic origins that is flexible and functional. For instance, a study of families with an Anglo parent and a Mexican-origin parent found that the children functioned well and expressed a strong and positive sense of their Mexican heritage. About 40 percent spoke some Spanish, although they knew relatively little about traditional Mexican culture. The children often had a white best friend, and the vast majority viewed intermarriages as being as successful as in-group marriages. Of the sixty-three subjects in the study, thirty-four expressed no racial preference regarding a spouse. Of those who had a preference, 51.7 percent wanted a white spouse, and 44.8 percent wanted a Mexican-origin spouse. One wanted an Asian spouse.[14] These children were less likely to view race and ethnicity as rigid, insurmountable social barriers to marriage than their peers in either all-Anglo or all-Mexican-origin families.[15]

Precisely because race is an important social boundary for most Americans, multiracial individuals present a unique challenge to racial separation in the family. As Michael Omi and Howard Winant, two prominent researchers on the meaning of race, explain:

> One of the first things we notice about people when we meet them (along with their sex) is their race. We utilize race to provide clues about who a person is. The fact is made painfully obvious when we encounter someone whom we cannot conveniently racially categorize—someone who is, for example, racially "mixed." . . . Such an encounter becomes a source of discomfort and momentarily a crisis of racial meaning.[16]

This dangerous ambiguity is an inescapable feature of mixed-race identity. As the son of a white mother and black father writes, "[C]onflict was a part of our lives, written into our very faces, hands, and arms. . . ."[17] Judy Scales-Trent, a light-skinned black of mixed racial origins, echoes this sense of embattled identity:

> The crossroads is . . . a difficult place to be in a society like ours, which is defined by internecine warfare. We pit women against men, the able-bodied against the disabled; we create ethnic, racial, and religious groups, and set them to fight. Because we are in a constant state of war, there is enormous pressure to choose up sides, to pledge allegiance to one side

or the other. It is politically unpopular to be on both shores at once when there are opposing armies on each shore. It is also disorienting.[18]

Multiracial individuals embody the anomaly of interracial intimacy in a world of segregated families. The presumption of racial separation leaves little room for multiracial persons to define themselves on their own terms. If people with multiple racial origins identify as white, they can be accused of rejecting their nonwhite heritage. Consider, for example, the case of Anatole Broyard, a long-time literary critic who wrote for the *New York Times.* Broyard made a conscious decision to conceal his black origins because he "wanted to be appreciated not for being black but for being a writer."[19] Despite the eager anticipation surrounding the release of his first novel, Broyard never finished the work. To break his writer's block, Broyard sought the counsel of literary friends. One told him that the writing in his memoirs was stilted and distant because he wasn't telling the truth. Still, rather than write an honest and compelling autobiographical account, Broyard carried his secret to the grave. Henry Louis Gates Jr., Harvard professor of African American Studies, asserts that "[Broyard] lived a lie because he didn't want to live a larger lie: and Anatole Broyard, Negro writer, was that larger lie."[20] According to Gates:

> [Broyard's] perception was perfectly correct. He would have had to be a Negro writer, which was something he did not want to be. In his terms, he did not want to write about black love, black passion, black suffering, black joy; he wanted to write about love and passion and suffering and joy. We give lip service to the idea of the writer who happens to be black, but had anyone, in the postwar era, ever seen such a thing?[21]

If people with multiple racial origins identify themselves as nonwhite, the authenticity of their identity is still open to question. For example, in 1994, the Northwestern University Law School had to decide whether to offer a tenured position to Professor Maria O'Brien Hylton as part of an effort to retain her husband on its faculty. O'Brien Hylton was the daughter of an Australian father of Irish ancestry and a black Cuban mother.[22] The Black Law Students Association insisted that O'Brien Hylton "should not be counted as Black," but the Hispanic Law Students Association concluded that she "should not be counted as Hispanic, either, because she 'seems to identify more as a Black.'"[23] Ultimately, the law school appointments committee concluded that it could not offer O'Brien Hylton a tenured position, purportedly because she was "not black enough" to hold herself out as a minority candidate.[24]

According to one account of the controversy, O'Brien Hylton fell prey to a pervasive tendency among African Americans to exclude as not black enough those who are "too light-skinned, too middle class, too refined, too conservative politically, or too well-educated."[25] Moreover, "[p]eople can also be excluded if they are foreign-born or have too many White affiliations, such as a spouse or friends."[26] As a multiracial person, O'Brien Hylton could not be black, white, or even Hispanic. In a segregated America, she was a woman without any accepted racial identity.[27]

Even when people like O'Brien Hylton try to escape the dilemma of identifying as either white or nonwhite by calling themselves multiracial, they are still apt to be accused of trying to minimize their nonwhite background. The uproar surrounding champion golfer Tiger Woods's insistence on being labeled "Cablinasian" as a reflection of his white, black, Native American, and Asian ancestry provides a good example. One editorialist complained:

> Tiger's mix of impulses around race is a muddy stew of his mere 21 years on the planet and an almost Star Trekian brand of humanism. Woods thanks black golf pioneers after his Masters win, yet expresses anger at being called African American. Woods brags in interviews that he reads all his racist hate mail, yet says he has no interest in being the great black hope. . . .
> . . . Certainly [Woods] has a right to claim whatever racial moniker he prefers. But his Cablinasianism reads more like a privilege ploy than a healthy empowerment strategy for mixed-race identity. Indeed, Cablinasianism constructs multiracialism as a teacher's note excusing Tiger and others like him from the race debate. And it definitely doesn't challenge race and class hierarchies. (Note which ethnic prefix leads Tiger's nom de plume: Caucasian.)[28]

In contrast to this harsh treatment of those on the margins of racial categories, mixed-race individuals are sometimes celebrated as ideal mediators between different races. In criticizing derogatory terms like *mulatto* that have been applied to mixed-race persons, Judy Scales-Trent urges:

> America could have . . . created a name to celebrate this union:
> "people-who-link-us-together"
> "people-who-join-our-families"
> "people-who-bind-us-in-friendship"

> Or, America could have seen these people as the forerunners of a new world, a world where all are linked through kinship:

"new people"
"people-of-the-future"

Or indeed, America could have looked at all the new, glorious skin colors created through the union of so many different kinds of people and celebrated the display of beauty:

"people-of-the-rainbow" . . .[29]

Yet there are those who chafe at the special burdens of being a bridge. They long for an identity that "doesn't want explanations," that doesn't have to "make it right for others," that doesn't strive to "be a non-statistic."[30]

Indeed, the challenges of forging a healthy identity have prompted one mixed-race scholar to issue "A Bill of Rights for Racially Mixed People." This proclamation invites multiracial people to assert the right "not to justify my existence in this world, not to keep the races separate within me, not to be responsible for people's discomfort with my physical ambiguity, and not to justify my ethnic legitimacy."[31] In pursuit of these rights, the bill insists that multiracial people be free to forge a unique identity, regardless of what strangers expect or how other family members define themselves. This identity should be flexible, so that multiracial people can openly express their loyalty to more than one group and freely cross racial boundaries to choose whom to befriend and love.[32]

The Debate over Classification of Multiracial Persons

As "A Bill of Rights for Racially Mixed People" makes clear, it is often hard for multiracial persons to express a sense of self through available racial labels. The battle over labeling is exemplified by recent debates over how to deal with racial categories on the U.S. 2000 census.[33] Since its inception, the Bureau of the Census has kept track of racial differences, but the categories changed as the social and political relevance of race was transformed.[34] The earliest census counts focused on the enumeration of free whites, slaves, and free colored.[35] Increasingly thorough racial categorization was considered an outgrowth of the late-nineteenth-century professionalization of the census. After the Civil War, the 1870 and 1880 census counts kept track of race-mixing between whites and blacks by adding the category "Mulatto." In 1890, before officials became preoccupied with the demographic impact of immigra-

tion, census enumerators sought to distinguish among mulattoes, quadroons, and octoroons based on visual inspection.[36] Beginning in 1890,
the Bureau of the Census began to keep track of the small numbers of
Chinese and Japanese living in the United States.[37] Census officials also
started to count all Indians, not just those who were taxed and included
in the apportionment of congressional representatives.[38] Perhaps because
of their ambiguous identity, Latinos were not identified as a racial group
on the census with one exception. In 1930, at the height of the Great
Depression when many Mexicans were being deported, this category
appeared on the list of racial classifications. However, it was dropped
by 1940.[39]

In 1970, the Bureau of the Census ceased to use enumerators to classify people racially. Instead, individuals were asked to identify themselves
as members of a single race.[40] Since then, the racial options have been
"American Indian or Alaskan Native," "Asian or Pacific Islander," "Black
or African American," "White," and "Other." The 2000 census, however, offers six options instead of five because the Asian or Pacific Islander
category has been split in two.[41] Beginning in 1970, the census also added
a question about Hispanic origin, which is treated as an ethnic category
independent of race.[42] In addition, individuals have been able to mark
multiple ethnic affiliations in response to a question about ancestry.[43]

Until recently, the concept of race in the United States has been
rooted in the black experience. In the 1960s and 1970s, when the Bureau
of the Census adopted its current racial classification scheme, only about
10 percent of Americans considered themselves nonwhite, and of these,
nearly all identified themselves as black. Today the concept of race is
under increasing strain not only because of changes in intermarriage but
also because of the explosive growth of Asian American and Latino populations. As a result, at this time one of four Americans identifies as black,
Asian American, Latino, or Native American. Of these, only about half
are black.[44] Projected increases in the number of Asian Americans and
Latinos mean that blacks in the coming decades will constitute a progres-
sively smaller proportion of the nonwhite population in the United
States.[45] Asian American and Latino experiences with integration and
intermarriage diverge from the black experience in significant ways. So
far, both Asian Americans and Latinos seem better able than blacks to
assimilate through marriage to whites and inclusion in white neighborhoods.[46] Because of these disparities, the notion of race will grow increasingly uncertain and contested.

By making racial designations a self-reported status, the 1970 census

began to blur the line between "race" and "ethnicity." Race traditionally
has been understood as a biological difference, while ethnicity describes
social and cultural differences linked to country of origin. Race is an
involuntary status, an accident of birth that can be readily ascertained.
Because a person cannot alter a racial identity, it is stable and unchanging. In a world divided along racial lines, race shapes a person's life
chances, affecting everything from educational opportunity to income
to the choice of a spouse. Ethnicity, though also a product of ancestry,
is seen as voluntary and malleable. Because white ethnic origins are not
central to a person's everyday life in America, individuals can decide
whether to celebrate their heritage or ignore it. Even those who embrace
their origins can do so in ways that do not significantly alter their lives.
Eating corned beef and cabbage or wearing green on St. Patrick's Day
is a largely symbolic and ritualistic commitment to being Irish.[47] When
the social isolation of a group begins to break down through integration
and intermarriage, its members appear less racial and more ethnic. Social
mobility converts an involuntary racial status into an ethnic option. In
short, growing equality means growing freedom to shape an identity.

The debate over multiracialism indicates that the distinction between
race and ethnicity is being challenged. Based on the recommendations
of a federal task force, the 2000 census permits individuals to report
multiple racial origins just as they have multiple ethnic ancestries.[48] Based
on concerns about divisiveness, government officials rejected a new
catchall classification labeled "multiracial" because "[h]aving a separate
category would, in effect, create another population group, and no doubt
add to racial tension and further fragmentation of our population."[49] By
allowing mixed racial ancestry to be recognized just as multiple ethnic
ancestry is, the census enables multiracial persons to demonstrate that
race is a fluid concept and that families are not rigidly segregated.[50] For
some, though, the opportunity to check more than one box is a poor
substitute for a multiracial category. As Susan Graham, president of Re-
classify All Children Equally (RACE), complained: "My children are
multiracial, not 'check all that apply.'"[51] During discussions of the new
approach to reporting racial identity, she insisted that refusal to include
a multiracial category is a form of discrimination, and she won powerful
allies like former Republican Speaker of the House Newt Gingrich. According to Gingrich, a multiracial category "will be an important step
toward transcending racial division and reflecting the melting which is
America."[52]

The 2000 census allows people to convey complex, personal understandings of racial identity.[53] However, when individual responses are aggregated into categories for use in reapportionment of voting districts, monitoring of equal employment opportunity, and tracking of racial trends, federal officials must balance the need to express a racial identity with the demands of programs that require continuity in their statistical reporting techniques. These techniques have been built around single-race distributions that can not now be dramatically altered.[54]

The process of reaggregating people who select multiple racial origins remains complicated and tentative. In a working draft, the Tabulation Working Group of the Interagency Committee for the Review of Standards for Data on Race and Ethnicity offered provisional guidelines on reaggregation to federal agencies. These guidelines use methods that depend on the purpose behind collecting the data. The Working Group has yet to decide how to report data for voter redistricting, although it is considering the use of two counts: one based on all individuals who mark a single racial category (for example, a person who chooses only the designation "Black"); and one based on all individuals who choose a racial category, regardless of whether they choose more than one (for example, anyone who chooses "Black" as at least one racial origin). This approach provides the upper and lower numerical boundaries of any given racial population. The provisional guidelines assume that these boundaries will not diverge greatly, so they do not make clear what to do if a substantial disparity arises. In other words, the Working Group is relying on the continuing power of impermeable racial boundaries to solve this potential problem.[55]

In the employment setting, the Working Group offers not only the method of using upper and lower boundaries but also two additional methods. One requires employers to reassign individuals who mark more than one racial affiliation to a single category, the largest nonwhite group chosen. The size of nonwhite groups will be based on population statistics in the local employment area. The other method asks employers to collect a microdata file on each employee, which includes all racial designations selected. This file would then be forwarded to agencies responsible for monitoring and enforcing equal employment opportunity to use as they deem appropriate.[56] Again, with both the upper and lower boundary approach and the reassignment approach, the agencies will be assuming that single-race categories remain so dominant that little distortion will result from their treatment of multiracial responses. The microdata approach preserves information about multiple racial designations, but the use of the data remains wholly uncertain and discretionary.

A little over a year after the Working Group released its report, the Office of Management and Budget issued a bulletin on how racial data should be reaggregated for civil rights monitoring and enforcement. Once again noting that the guidelines were provisional, federal officials chose an approach that was "straightforward and easy to implement" and did not require "either fractional or double counting of individuals, or arbitrary allocation of responses to one minority group versus another."[57] Under the guidelines, state and local government agencies as well as businesses must report responses of individuals who choose only one of the racial categories as well as responses of individuals who choose one of the four most common "double race" combinations. These are "American Indian or Alaska Native and White"; "Asian and White"; "Black or African American and White"; and "American Indian or Alaska Native and Black or African American." In addition, agencies and businesses must report any other combinations that represent more than 1 percent of their workforce or population and the balance of individuals reporting more than one race.[58]

Single-race responses are not allocated, while those who report one minority race and white are allocated to the minority race. If an individual marks two or more minority races, the reaggregation depends on how the statistics will be used. If a federal agency's enforcement action is prompted by a discrimination complaint, the individual is included with the racial group alleging mistreatment. If the enforcement action is based on a disparate impact claim, the individual will alternately be included with each minority group chosen in order to determine how the patterns of discrimination are affected.[59] In each instance, reaggregation resurrects single-race classifications, and only those with no nonwhite ancestry are treated as white. Although some critics are concerned that the new system is "byzantine" and "cumbersome," civil rights groups have praised the guidelines as a first step toward ensuring that the new racial categorization scheme does not undermine enforcement of antidiscrimination laws.[60]

Adding to the complexity and confusion surrounding racial recordkeeping, federal officials have yet to determine how census data will be reported so that researchers can make comparisons to earlier population reports and estimates. Because individuals can now mark up to six racial categories, there are sixty-three potential responses, ranging from a single race to a combination of up to six races. Separately, individuals can mark whether or not they are of Hispanic origin. When the answers to the race and Hispanic origin questions are combined, there are 126 potential categories. It simply will not be possible to tabulate data for all these categories in each census report, but how the categories will be pared down remains an open question.

The likely methods are to report the number of single-race responses, the number of responses for each race alone or in combination, and the total number of responses that list more than one race. The data on those who indicate Hispanic origin would be reported as well. So a person who marked "Black or African American" and "Hispanic origin" would be included in the single-race category "Black or African American," in the category of "Black or African American alone or in combination," and in the category "Hispanic origin," but not in the category of "Two or more races." Only certain detailed population reports for census tracts will likely contain information on all 126 categories and only insofar as the statistics do not violate the confidentiality of responses from members of numerically small racial combinations.[61] In short, except at the most localized level, official reports generally will continue to highlight racial boundaries rather than racial mixing. The only question is which side of the line people who mark multiple responses will occupy.

The Unequal Promise of Multiracialism

The methods for reaggregating data suggest that the most immediate impact of the change in recording racial categories will be the individual's newfound freedom to mark multiple boxes. It would be a mistake, however, to assume that all racial groups share the same perspective on this opportunity. Not all races are equally able to mix in the marital melting pot. Most non-Hispanic whites intermarry with an Asian, Latino, or Native American. Rates of intermarriage between blacks and whites remain quite low. Moreover, Americans are more likely to oppose intermarriage between blacks and whites than other forms of intermarriage.[62] When blacks, Asians, Latinos, and Native Americans marry out, they typically choose a non-Hispanic white partner. In 1987, 93 percent of interracial marriages involving an Asian, Latino, or Native American were to white partners, and only 7 percent were to black partners. Of blacks who intermarried, 83 percent had a white partner and only 17 percent had a partner of another race who was nonwhite.[63] These differential rates of intermarriage mark yet another important truth: While most Asian Americans, Latinos, and Native Americans now have at least a distant white relative through marriage, blacks are much less likely to report a kinship relationship to any other group.[64]

Disparities in intermarriage patterns undoubtedly help to explain the very different reactions among blacks, Asians, Latinos, and Native Americans to proposals to acknowledge multiracial persons on the census. Blacks arguably have little to gain and much to lose through adoption of a multiracial category. Blacks are the most racially isolated group in America based on measures of residential and marital segregation. They have the greatest difficulty in converting economic gains into access to integrated neighborhoods or families.[65] Many blacks who can claim some white ancestry do so based on illicit and often involuntary sexual contacts that took place during slavery. These liaisons gave them little or no access to white privilege or kinship networks.[66] By contrast, the strongest proponents of a multiracial category are spouses like Susan Graham, the president of RACE, who recently married interracially. For them, the new category gives their children a way to claim the privileges of access to white heritage and kinship networks, privileges regularly denied to blacks before *Loving*.[67]

Yet acknowledging the few who have gained a multiracial identity through intermarriage should not obscure the many who have not. For some blacks, particularly those with remote white ancestry, multiracialism harkens back to the late 1800s and early 1900s when the census labeled them as mulattoes, quadroons, and octoroons based on perceived amounts of black and white blood.[68] The push to recognize multiple racial origins seems to create yet another opportunity for blacks to further stratify themselves internally based on degree of white ancestry without ever being fully accepted as equals. As Arthur A. Fletcher, chairperson of the U.S. Commission on Civil Rights, testified at congressional hearings on changes to the census racial classifications:

> I can see a whole host of light-skinned Black Americans running for the door the minute they have another choice. And it won't necessarily be because their immediate parents are Black, White, or whatever, but all of a sudden they have a way of saying—in this discriminatory culture of ours, they have another way of saying, "I am something other than Black."[69]

Despite Fletcher's prediction, blacks' ambivalence about their multiracial origins has manifested itself in a reluctance to use the category. In a survey conducted by the Bureau of the Census, those most likely to choose a multiracial identification were not blacks, but Asian Americans.[70]

For Asian Americans, the option to identify as multiracial could offer substantial advantages. In their case, multiracialism does connote intermarriage in the last few generations. As a result, Asian Americans have gained access to the benefits associated with white kinship networks. Indeed, Asian Americans have been so successful at using intermarriage to assimilate that some, like the Japanese Americans, are in danger of losing their distinctive identity altogether.[71] An approach that recognizes multiple racial origins allows Asian Americans to begin converting their racialized status into one that approximates an ethnic identity. This approach recognizes that race, for them, is not a rigid barrier to integration and intermarriage. At the same time, an acknowledgment of their multiple origins enables Asian Americans to preserve some sense of their heritage despite high rates of exogamy. By converting from a racial to an ethnic identity, Asian Americans can sustain a symbolic recognition of ancestry, reflected in choice of foods or observation of holiday rituals, without giving up the privileges of whiteness through intermarriage.[72]

Latinos, too, have high rates of intermarriage, but the gains for them of instituting some form of multiracial identification are more ambiguous than for Asian Americans. Latinos today can be of any race, and Hispanic origin is already treated as an ethnic identity.[73] When Latinos select a racial category, most identify themselves as white without forgoing the opportunity to acknowledge their Hispanic background. It is not clear that they will be better off by marking multiple racial boxes.[74] Even if a multiracial approach better reflects Latinos' mixed-race ancestry, the cost might be the loss of hard-won and already tenuous privileges of whiteness. Depending on how multiple responses are reaggregated, all Latinos who list some white, black, and Native American ancestry might be lumped together, even if they previously had chosen different racial designations. This reaggregation could conceal significant racial divisions within the Latino community. The color line between Latinos who have identified themselves as white and those who have identified themselves as black marks real differences in social, educational, and economic opportunity. Latinos who describe themselves as white principally associate with whites, while Latinos who describe themselves as black principally associate with blacks.[75] Latinos who prize a white identity and the associations it engenders would reject a multiracial approach that equates them with Latinos who live in a nonwhite world.[76]

Moreover, the option to select multiple racial affiliations still leaves many Latinos without a way to express their identity accurately. Although Latinos can now mark multiple racial affiliations, they cannot indicate mixed Hispanic and non-Hispanic origins.[77] Moreover, they may not even be able to identify their multiple racial origins properly. A substantial number of Latinos currently mark "Other" when asked to provide a racial identification. In part, this choice reflects discomfort with single-race categories that deny a tradition of *mestizaje,* or race-mixing, in Latin America. Latinos who have recently arrived in the United States are most likely to mark "Other" for this reason. For these Latinos, racial mixing primarily involved Spaniards and the indigenous peoples of South and Central America. The census, however, does not recognize indigenous ancestry outside of the United States. So, even with a chance to mark multiple boxes, a number of Latinos will still have to mark "Other" to describe their Indian origins in Mexico as well as Central and South America.[78]

Native Americans also have found it difficult to express their identities on the census because of extensive and long-standing mixing through intermarriage. According to a study of 1980 census data, those who identify as Indian respond in three ways. Some indicate that they are Indian in response to both the race and ethnicity questions; others identify themselves as Indian racially but list some non-Indian ancestry on the ethnicity question; and still others give a non-Indian race but list Indian ancestry as part of their ethnic background. Of the 7.4 million individuals who in some way identified themselves as Indian in 1980, 84 percent considered themselves ethnically Indian but racially non-Indian.[79] This figure may be influenced by census reclassification techniques. When people report being Native American without a tribal affiliation, the census reclassifies them as white.[80] This reclassification strategy suggests that in the absence of strong social, cultural, and political ties to a tribe, Indian identity has been wholly converted from a racial to an ethnic affiliation. When large numbers of individuals switched their affiliation from white to Indian beginning in the 1960s, they treated their Native American ancestry as voluntary and malleable, not stable and unchanging. Far from feeling that Indianness was an immutable racial trait, these people seemed to view it as a symbolic ethnicity, a remote affiliation that could be altered at will.[81]

The debate over multiracialism is in many ways most peripheral to Indians, the group with the most extensive intermarriage to whites. For Native Americans, the critical struggle is over how to preserve a distinct identity when widespread outmarriage threatens to reduce Indianness to nothing more than a symbolic ethnic affiliation. Tribes must draw lines between "mixed-bloods" and "full-bloods" in determining who is a member. If only full-bloods can identify as members, the tribe will be tiny. Yet, if mixed-bloods can join, some tribal leaders worry that those with remote ancestry who treat their affiliation as largely optional will be lumped together with those who have more immediate roots and strong ties to Indian communities.[82] One possible solution might be to treat Indian identity as primarily political rather than racial or ethnic. The U.S. Supreme Court adopted this view when addressing eligibility for jobs and benefits based on Indian status.[83] Federal officials and some tribal leaders, however, continue to treat Indian identity as a function of ancestry by insisting on minimum blood quantum requirements for membership.[84]

According to the federal government, tribes should require that individuals have at least one-quarter Native American ancestry to join.[85] This threshold would greatly circumscribe eligibility. Based on current patterns of intermarriage, only 8 percent of the American Indian population during the next century will have a blood quantum of one-half or more. The proportion with less than one-fourth blood quantum will increase to about 60 percent.[86] As a result, tribes have reduced reliance on tests based on biological ancestry and instead have turned to evidence of cultural, social, and political ties. Of the 317 federally recognized tribes, only 21 require more than one-quarter blood quantum, and of these 85.7 percent are reservation-based. Almost one-third of the tribes have no minimum requirement at all; of these, only 63.9 percent are reservation-based. Tribes without communal lands have been less able than reservation-based tribes to preserve a distinct Indian identity through endogamy.[87]

Tribal attempts to redefine membership have turned symbolic ethnicity on its head. Instead of characterizing remote ancestry and limited cultural practices as a malleable identity, some tribes are trying to convert them into eligibility for legally recognized, permanent membership. Presumably, these tribes hope that formalizing membership will enhance a sense of allegiance and commitment. Whether these efforts will succeed is unclear, particularly if nonreservation tribes are loosely structured entities with few tangible benefits to offer members. Attempts to draw in those with attenuated biological and social ties will widen the gap between the meaning of membership in a nonreservation and a reservation tribe. Tribes with reservation lands and substantial membership benefits are likely to adopt practices that encourage inmarriage and close ties to tribal life. Membership requirements will not only limit eligibility for benefits, but also promote close-knit, culturally distinctive, and politically cohesive tribal units.[88] As disparities in the meaning of tribal membership grow, so will controversy about the significance of Indian identity. Already, under the Indian Child Welfare Act, state courts are struggling to decide whether a parent's remote Indian ancestry justifies tribal authority over a child's placement.[89]

In sum, the current debate over census categories is most relevant for groups historically subject to restrictions on intermarriage that clearly marked them as racial. Both blacks and Asian Americans have a substantial stake in the outcome for different reasons. For many blacks, multiracialism seems divisive and self-defeating because it diverts attention from the persistence of segregation and inequality. For Asian Americans, though, a multiracial approach could signal their increasing integration and declining racialization in America. Groups with ambiguous racial identities like Latinos and Native Americans are generally less concerned with multiracialism and more concerned with the incoherent line between race and ethnicity that has resulted from widespread intermarriage. The impact on Native American tribes is especially severe as they struggle to define membership in semisovereign and often vanishing Indian nations.

Responsible Recordkeeping and the Realities of Race

The debate over multiracialism directly addresses the impact of intermarriage on the meaning of race, an issue that the U.S. Supreme Court declined to reach when it struck down antimiscegenation laws as unconstitutional in *Loving v. Virginia. Loving* stood for a principle of official colorblindness in the regulation of marriage, but the Court left to ordinary Americans the task of ascertaining the relevance of race to marital choice. So, too, the Court has left the process of defining race to a system that mixes scientific expertise and bureaucratic management with demographic politics. The result has been ongoing uncertainty about whether the government should engage in racial recordkeeping and, if so, how it should be done.

Although spokespeople like Susan Graham who advocate multiracialism have received most of the media attention, some intermarried couples have expressed discomfort with efforts to fine-tune racial recordkeeping. They are leery of efforts to fractionate people into racial components and to highlight the significance of their mixed origins. As one woman in a black–white marriage explained:

We're really careful I think in the last few years about the terms that we use . . . ; like, *biracial* bugs me, *mulatto* bugs me, *race* bugs me. I quit checking race on forms that I fill out. The only time I do it is like for the census, 'cause I wanted them to know that there are married couples like us that are happy and living together. . . .[90]

These individuals support a colorblind policy, in accordance with which the government would cease keeping track of race altogether.[91]

Despite concerns about overweening color consciousness, the federal government seems to be refining its processes of racial recordkeeping, even as the push for colorblind policy and practice in other areas like adoption intensifies. One straightforward explanation for color-conscious recordkeeping is that influential interest groups support it. Both civil rights organizations and researchers who study race have a powerful stake in maintaining racial data. Because advocates of color-blindness find it awkward to oppose keeping track of racial problems and progress, they direct their attacks at programs that confer racial preferences, such as race-matching in adoption, or they question the accuracy of current racial classifications.[92] Far from dismantling racial recordkeeping, all sides seem to welcome its improvement.

The demand for a multiracial classification, though color conscious, also is touted as a way to mark racial progress. Keeping track of the rise of multiracial persons provides perhaps the strongest proof that whites are willing to accept nonwhites as equals. Recent intermarriage rates suggest that if each white person has sixteen relatives, "potentially one-sixth of white Americans now have a nonwhite affinal relative and are likely to have a racially mixed kinsperson, the offspring of the interracial marriage."[93] The multiracial option is offered as a way to loosen social boundaries and lessen social distance:

> Government recognition may lead to significant positive inter-group consequences in which mixed individuals may act as sensitive, objective negotiators of inter-group racial conflict. . . . With biological, psychological and sociological attachments to multiple racial heritages, multiracial[s] possess unique credentials for mediating racial conflict. Governmental recognition could facilitate and legitimize the multiracial individual's assumption of this negotiator role.[94]

Some even believe that intermarriage will eventually resolve America's racial problems. As Ward Connerly, the principal force behind California's dismantlement of affirmative action, put it: "In 10 to 15 years, intermarriage will make this entire debate [over racial and ethnic preferences] a moot one . . . and we'll wonder why we didn't see it coming."[95]

Despite this optimism, there is strong evidence that race-mixing will not be an immediate antidote to racial division. Census officials estimate that only 1–2 percent of Americans will take advantage of the multiracial option.[96] Blacks, who have the lowest rates of intermarriage, will be particularly unlikely to provide multiple responses. Regardless of their scientific accuracy as measures of biological difference, racial categories continue to express important truths—albeit partial and imperfect ones—about fundamental social boundaries. For those who live within the confines of a segregated world, "the idea of Rationality and Truth completely replacing the irrationality of racial identity is an idea whose time has not yet come, particularly for the oppressed who require their own irrationalities to fend off the irrationalities of the powerful."[97] Race remains one of the few ways to name the reality of segregation, a nomenclature critical to those on the wrong side of the color line. Because race is still a key marker of social identity, the census must continue to record racial difference. Ignoring race will not undo it, but dismantling racial recordkeeping will wrongly imply that segregation is no longer relevant to the life chances of Americans.

Although the continuing significance of race should be recognized, the Bureau of the Census also must acknowledge the growing reality of multiracialism. This step is not necessitated simply by personal desires to express a complete identity.[98] Although the census relies on self-reporting, it is not a process of self-actualization.[99] General categories necessarily limit an individual's capacity to report a unique identity, and the question is not whether the categories circumscribe self-expression but whether they fail to advance social and political objectives. The push for multiracialism is justified because current categories are out of step with emerging truths about the permeability of racial boundaries. As the chairman of the House subcommittee responsible for reviewing the census classifications explained: "We don't want our standards of measurement to distort the intricacies of ethnic identity. We have to avoid over time the hardening of categories that don't inform us as well as they might, and become, as a result, increasingly irrelevant to many of the people whom we seek to enumerate."[100] Multiracialism should accomplish more than descriptive accuracy for individual respondents. It should capture a new collective understanding about the significance of crossing the color line.

Census officials must not institutionalize a norm of racial segregation in the family when it is undergoing change. By insisting on monolithic racial categories, the Bureau of the Census has elevated same-race over interracial families, even as barriers to intermarriage begin to break down. Techniques that uniformly presume racial segregation in house-holds and neighborhoods exacerbate the problem. For instance, when Latinos mark "Other" as a racial affiliation, bureau officials use "hot-decking" to reassign them. This technique first looks at the racial desig-nation of another person in the household who self-identified as Latino and assigns the same designation to the respondent. If no one else in the household has provided a racial designation, the bureau assigns a Latino neighbor's racial designation to the respondent.[101] Although racial segregation remains a pervasive feature of American life, hot-decking is used even when other census data indicate that a particular neighbor-hood is racially integrated or that there are high rates of intermarriage for couples in a particular locale. Monolithic racial categories and tech-niques like hot-decking overstate the rigidity of the color line. By min-imizing the visibility of those who cross racial boundaries, the census is not only descriptively inaccurate but also bolsters a norm of racial segre-gation in the family.

There is no perfect way to gather racial and ethnic data because the categories of race and ethnicity are currently in flux. At present, the decision to allow respondents to mark multiple affiliations rather than a single multiracial category seems sound.[102] This approach permits indi-viduals to express complex personal conceptions of identity and does not assume that all mixed-race persons share the same experience, regard-less of their origins. With all of the focus on reaggregation of multiple responses, however, there has been little attention to what each origin means. Individuals whose immediate relatives are predominantly white but have remote Indian ancestry may mark two boxes more readily than those who have immediate relatives who are predominantly black but have some remote white ancestry, for example. People of mixed black and white ancestry might typically check off two boxes only if their parents are intermarried.[103] Currently, the census leaves the underlying social meaning of race undefined.[104] Rather than instruct respondents that remote ancestry counts or that recent intermarriage is required, the form simply asks them to indicate how they define themselves.

The burdens of uncertainty associated with multiple racial responses do not fall evenly on all groups. Because neither Latinos nor Native Americans have been understood in strictly racial terms, officials have already dealt with ambiguities related to remote ancestry and inter-marriage by relying on responses to questions about Hispanic origin or tribal membership, rather than race, in fashioning programs to remedy discrimination and disadvantage.[105] Moreover, Asian Americans generally have not been the focus of programs aimed at remedying racial disadvantage.[106] On average, Asian Americans have achieved high levels of education and income.[107] Moreover, remote non-Asian ancestry is not really an issue for most Asian Americans. Their arrival in the United States is relatively recent, and widespread intermarriage is an even newer development. Asian Americans who report multiple racial origins are generally children of intermarriage to whites. Their Asian American parents typically will not be recent immigrants, but instead will be highly acculturated, well-educated, affluent, and integrated into white neighborhoods.[108] The multiracial option is unlikely to harm efforts to reach less advantaged Asian subgroups, who generally are newcomers to the United States, live in enclaves isolated by language and culture, and encounter barriers to education and employment as a result. By dint of their segregation in immigrant communities, these Asian American residents generally do not marry out and hence would not be removed from a single-race category.[109]

For blacks, however, the new ambiguities associated with multiple racial responses are unsettling. Even today, blacks have the lowest rate of intermarriage to whites, and when they do intermarry, their mixed-race children are least able to claim the privileges of white identity. Blacks continue to find that race is a mark of permanent and indelible difference, inescapable even through outmarriage. Racial segregation has been a social requirement so powerful in defining black–white relations that the one-drop rule denied the very possibility of multiracialism, regardless of mixed ancestry or individual preferences.[110] While other groups equate multiracialism with integration and assimilation, blacks have discovered that white parentage cannot fully shield them from racial isolation. As a result, multiracial status at best offers an uncertain promise that the children of *Loving* can soften racial boundaries and escape the box of race itself.[111]

After all, redefining racial categories is not the same thing as undoing a legacy of racial discrimination and segregation. Blacks are least able to escape race as a marker of segregation and social distance, regardless of how official categories are constructed. Even though most blacks in the United States have some white ancestry,[112] they remain intensely segregated both in choice of residence and marital partner. For a substantial number of blacks, multiracial status is a mark not of freedom but of oppression. As Malcolm X wrote: "I was among the millions of Negroes who were insane enough to feel that it was some kind of status symbol to be light-complexioned—that one was actually fortunate to be born thus. But, still later, I learned to hate every drop of the white rapist's blood that is in me."[113] For those blacks who share this ambivalence about their white ancestry, multiracialism seems less a strategy of empowerment and more an act of self-degradation.

Even when individuals with mixed black and white ancestry try to disregard racial boundaries, the overwhelming reality of segregation reinstates them. Take, for example, the case of W. E. B. Du Bois, who had both Dutch and African ancestry. Kwame Anthony Appiah has claimed that Du Bois might as easily have chosen to be Dutch as to be black. In his view, "the choice of a slice of the past in a period before your birth as your own history is always exactly that: a choice."[114] Yet, as legal scholar Christine B. Hickman has persuasively argued, Du Bois was not free to acknowledge his Dutch and African origins interchangeably because he was trapped in social and political circumstances:

> [H]istory placed far greater restrictions on Du Bois's ability to choose to identify with his Dutch side. In Tennessee, for example, history dictated that if he had married a Dutch woman, the marriage could have been annulled and he could have been jailed as a felon; and that if he had made unwelcome romantic overtures toward a Dutch woman, he would have placed himself in danger of being beaten, castrated, or lynched. Thus, if Du Bois had "chosen" to identify with his Dutch ancestors, he would have needed to enjoy this choice as a closet Dutchman.[115]

Even today, Ward Connerly, a prominent foe of color-conscious policies in California, reports that people laugh if he tries to identify himself as Irish based on the fact that he is 37.5 percent Irish, 25 percent French, 25 percent black, and 12.5 percent Choctaw.[116]

The quest for multiracialism cannot address the growing asymmetry of the underlying racial categories on the census. If current patterns of intermarriage persist, there will be one group, blacks, who remain maritally isolated from all other groups. Race will mark a significant social divide, one that does not exist to the same degree for Asian Americans, Latinos, and Native Americans. As the Asian American and Latino populations continue to expand, blacks will become an increasingly small and isolated group, even among nonwhites. As a result, the color line itself could shift. The critical divide may no longer be between whites and nonwhites but between blacks and nonblacks.[117] Because underlying racial categories remain unchanged, multiracialism does not necessarily help Bureau of the Census officials to address this potentially fundamental transformation of American race relations.

The opportunity to describe oneself in 126 ways with respect to race and Hispanic origin seems an almost overwhelming tribute to individual autonomy to define an identity. Indeed, the options are slightly greater because a person who does not believe in racial labels can decline to respond altogether. From the standpoint of equality, however, the critical issue will be how data are reaggregated. Blacks, in particular, must be concerned about whether the unique barriers to intermarriage and integration that they face will be lost in the multiracial shuffle. A chart with 126 different statistics on race and Hispanic origin could make it seem that racial designations are finely parsed and fungible when this is not the case. On the other hand, merely reallocating multiple responses to single-race categories defeats the purpose of marking racial progress and treating racial boundaries as flexible.

Currently, the Bureau of the Census is struggling with how to balance the increasing permeability of some racial boundaries with the ongoing rigidity of other racial barriers, especially for blacks. Reaggregation techniques should focus on three goals: (1) preserving a sense of the internal diversity of those who select a particular racial identification; (2) maintaining an awareness of the multiple racial boundaries that have arisen due to demographic change; and (3) acknowledging the dangers of discrimination and stereotyping, which lead to a denial of diverse identities, often through overreliance on the color line between whites and nonwhites or blacks and nonblacks.

The provisional guidelines accomplish some but not all of these goals. First, by tabulating single-race responses and responses that include that race alone or in combination, agencies will be able to use the gap between the upper and lower boundaries of a racial group as a rough measure of its internal diversity. The gap may reflect access to intermarriage, willingness to acknowledge remote ancestry, or both. What this gap will not reveal is the precise source of this internal diversity. So it will not be possible to say which racial groups are mixing and whether the contact is recent or remote. Even so, this method can help to identify racial rigidities. The higher the proportion of single-race responses for any given group, the more inflexible racial identity is likely to be and the greater will be the dangers of segregation and exclusion.

Second, by calculating both single-race responses and responses for a race alone or in combination, officials can mark a multiplicity of racial boundaries. Some separate single-race respondents from multiple-race respondents. Others mark the lines among racial groups, which may vary depending on whether the upper or lower boundaries of the groups are used. In addition to noting divisions among those who mark a single racial affiliation, agencies can distinguish between those who select a category alone or in combination and those who do not select it at all. This multiplicity of plausible boundaries diffuses the power of the white/ nonwhite and black/nonblack divide. Again, this process has some limitations. It continues to dichotomize race rather to identify the complex ways that multiple racial identities intersect. Although the dichotomies have multiplied, the richly textured nature of multiracial identity remains impossible to capture through these statistics.

One danger posed by the use of multiple racial boundaries is that unique problems of stereotyping and discrimination based on particular racial affiliations will be ignored. As a result, when discrimination is alleged, the federal government has reverted most strongly to a system of single-race categories that emphasize the line between whites and nonwhites. Yet the government's own catalog of the most common dual racial responses shows that this line is not always the most intractable one. The combinations that are reported show that most nonwhites who cross the color line marry whites. The only common dual combination that involves nonwhite groups is American Indian or Alaskan Native and black or African American, intermingling that is probably due to remote ancestry rather than recent intermarriage. Under the circumstances, it seems ironic that intermarriage between whites and nonwhites is nullified by the invariable assignment of mixed-race persons to a nonwhite category.

Presumably, this approach reflects the view that discrimination reifies all persons with nonwhite ancestry. Yet it seems entirely possible that in a shifting, multiracial society, individuals could be penalized for being less assimilated, as evidenced by lack of white ancestry, while more assimilated, mixed-race persons are not. At present, the provisional guidelines recognize racial ambiguity only when an individual has multiple nonwhite origins. Then, the person can be alternately assigned to the different nonwhite groups listed in determining whether an employer's practices have a disparate impact based on race. Arguably, though, the same racial ambiguity exists when a person has both white and nonwhite ancestry, so that alternate assignments would also be appropriate under these circumstances. The reassignment would have little effect when mixed-race persons comprised a small percentage of the population in question, but the alternative calculations might yield critically important differences when their numbers are substantial.

One concern that arises is that such alternative reassignments will greatly complicate discrimination claims. In fact, it seems likely that discrimination occurs most readily in environments where racial lines are drawn in bright-line, inflexible ways. If so, the greater the racial diversity of the workforce, including the presence of mixed-race persons, the less likely discrimination will be. As the proportions of different racial groups grow and as a greater number transect racial boundaries, the concept of race will become more flexible and less available as a tool for exclusion. As a result, reassignment of mixed-race persons to a nonwhite category is probably appropriate where they are an anomalous presence, but this technique will be misdirected as their numbers grow and they truly bridge racial worlds. As a result, alternative reassignments are most important when they complicate received racial wisdom, for they are signaling that the traditional notions of race that undergird the enforcement regime are breaking down.

Conclusion

By crossing racial boundaries, multiracial persons demonstrate the power of racial segregation at the same time that they challenge it. Their struggle to express multiple racial origins reveals just how deeply entrenched the norm of racially segregated families is. Race is a way to name the reality of separation in marriage and family, and the freedom to choose one's spouse is the power to define a people isolated by race. Multiracialism, however measured, is an important barometer of racial progress, but it should not be used to minimize the continuing reality of racial separation. The idea that intermarriage will serve as a natural melting pot for the races is an insidious myth, one that masks the magnitude of the marriage gap for blacks as compared to Asian Americans, Latinos, and Native Americans.

Relying on the marital melting pot to solve racial problems can lead to misplaced optimism and dangerous complacency. The responsibility for bridging racial divides is a heavy burden to place on multiracial people, who did not even choose their mixed identities. The children of *Loving* are a small, emerging, youthful population, and many of them are not even situated to bridge the widest racial gap—that between blacks and whites. So multiracialism is apt to work best at mediating race relations where it is needed least. Groups already intermarrying in substantial numbers will produce offspring who can bridge an ever narrowing social divide. Far from being a sign that America's racial problems are now solved, today's tiny multiracial population is a mark of progress that has just begun.

NINE

The Lessons of
Interracial Intimacy

THIS BOOK BEGAN with Gregory Howard Williams's story about growing up as the son of a black man and white woman to illustrate the dilemmas that interracial intimacy poses. It seems fitting to return to his experiences in this final chapter to see how questions about racial identity, the meaning of racial equality, and the nature of intimacy can be answered. Interracial relationships today are more widely accepted than they were when Williams was a child growing up in Muncie, Indiana. But they remain anomalous and in need of explanation. Despite the progress that has been made in race relations, Williams is still likely to find that his identity is contested and uncertain. These contested meanings complicate efforts to pursue racial justice through either colorblind or color-conscious strategies. Most discussions of interracial intimacy have focused on how race shapes choices about neighbors, friends, and family. Just as importantly, however, patterns of intimacy have the power to give race meaning.

The Definition of Race

The subtitle of Williams's book—*The True Story of a White Boy Who Discovered He Was Black*—reveals the racial boxes that circumscribed his quest for a personal identity.[1] Clearly, as a child, Williams believed that he must be either white or black but not both. Indeed, those in his community agreed with him. When Williams obtained his school records, he found that his designation as "White" had been changed to

"Colored" and a handwritten entry duly noted that "Father is colored—
mother is white. . . ."[2] When Williams became interested in going out
with a white classmate despite his school's policy against interracial dating, friends warned her about dating a " 'colored' basketball player" and
her parents received anonymous telephone calls reporting that their
daughter was going out with a "nigger."[3] Today there are more opportunities for Williams to acknowledge his mixed origins. As a man in his
mid-fifties, Williams can mark multiple racial affiliations for the first
time on the 2000 census. Able to express the complications of his ancestry, Williams perhaps can write a sequel about "The Man Who Discovered that He Could Be Multiracial."

Despite a newfound appreciation for genotypical complexity, Williams may find that many of the difficulties of defining his racial identity
persist. Reporting his multiple origins on the census provides a way for
him to communicate his own sense of self. But on a day-to-day basis,
many of Williams's racial experiences will depend on encounters with
strangers, people who know little or nothing about his past, and draw
their inferences about him based largely on a superficial acquaintance.
These informal judgments will have little to do with how Williams answers a formal questionnaire. Because Williams appears phenotypically
white, he will be treated as a white person in most casual encounters
and consequently will enjoy the privileges of a white identity when he
travels to a strange city, hails a cab, or goes shopping. In this respect, one
could say that however many boxes Williams checks off on the census, he
is still in some sense white.

If Williams decides to disclose his black heritage to strangers, he can
put them on notice that he is not white. Imagine, for example, that
Williams is riding on a plane and having a conversation with the white
passenger sitting next to him. The passenger begins to describe how
much he resents affirmative action, particularly since he just lost a promotion to a less qualified black. Williams can break in at this point and
explain that he himself has a black father as well as a white mother. At
this point, the fellow traveler is likely to stop talking freely about the
dangers of reverse discrimination. Instead, he may ask how it felt to grow
up with parents who married interracially. The conversation that ensues
will probably explore Williams's racial experiences or his identity.[4] At
the end, the fellow passenger may emerge thinking of Williams as black
or as multiracial, but he will certainly not leave the plane thinking of
him as white. Nor is he likely to feel that he can confide his racial resent-
ments as freely. Even though Williams has a white mother, his capacity

to empathize with the problems of whites will be suspect. After the conversation with Williams, the traveler is apt to conclude that Williams's black heritage shaped him in ways that make it impossible to "think like a white person." And, that conclusion may be justified.

Now, imagine that Williams is on his connecting flight. This time, he is seated next to a black woman who asks him why so many whites fail to appreciate the need for affirmative action. This time, Williams replies that he cannot answer the question because he is not white. His father is black, so he knows the experience of racism firsthand. This passenger, too, may ask Williams what it was like to grow up in a mixed-race family, and he may share stories of the discrimination he suffered growing up in Muncie. Still, based on Williams's phenotypically white appearance, the woman may doubt openly or privately that he really can understand the situation of dark-skinned blacks whose racial origins can not be concealed.[5] Indeed, in his book, Williams describes the doubts that some blacks in Muncie harbored about his nonwhite identity. When Williams was being considered for a job in the sheriff's department, a local black minister opposed his appointment because he believed that the sheriff was "planning to pay off the black community . . . , while preserving the outward appearance of a 'lily-white' department."[6] Although Williams eventually got the job, it is not clear that the minister ever really thought of him as black. And, even today, at the end of the trip, the black passenger may leave the plane believing that Williams is really white because of the way he looks, really multiracial because of his ancestry, or really black because of his heritage and childhood experiences.

This brings us to the final way that race can be defined. Rather than being an artifact of ancestry or appearance, race can be a function of social experiences and ties. For example, when Williams confided in a black cousin about his feeling of betrayal upon learning that the minister had questioned his racial identity, he received this reply:

> That old preacher don't know a damn thing about who you are and what you can do. . . . Let the politicians worry about who's black and who isn't. Nobody in Muncie ever gave you any breaks just because you looked white. You've had to take just as much crap as anybody I know, black or white. You deserve that job just as much as anyone. If you're in a position to arrest some brothers, you are gonna be fair—not like some of the hillbillies they got on the department. You always gonna have people crackin' about you bein' black or sayin' you ain't black enough. Damn, cousin, you paid your dues![7]

This answer reassured Williams of the authenticity of his blackness because he "paid [his] dues" by experiencing racism.

The definition of race offered by Williams's cousin, however, poses a serious dilemma. If the key correlates of race are segregation and discrimination, it seems doubtful that it is a social category worth preserving. Advocates of colorblindness often want to do away with race because they believe it reinforces interpersonal distance and hostility. What this analysis overlooks, however, is the way race is used to express special ties of intimacy. Williams and his cousin could have this conversation not only because they are blood relatives but also because they both think of themselves as black. It seems unlikely that Williams could speak so frankly with a white cousin from his mother's side of the family. The sense of solidarity that comes from the shared experience of racism is so great that Williams's cousin refers to other black men as "brothers," whether or not they are related to him. For Williams and his cousin, the sense of familiarity and connection associated with blackness provides a sense of community worth keeping, even if it originated as a response to the hardships of racial exclusion.

Solidarity may be a particularly important value for blacks, who have suffered extreme residential and marital isolation. Like blacks, Indians living on reservations undoubtedly value the distinct sense of community that their geographical separation brings. Reservation Indians, however, have a significant advantage when they demand respect for their tribal way of life. They are formally recognized as a semisovereign people, entitled to live apart from white society to preserve their customs and values. Blacks, by contrast, have been characterized as a racial minority that should assimilate to American life.[8] When blacks insist on maintaining a unique identity, they can be accused of separatist tendencies and misplaced nationalism. When they insist on their distinctiveness, blacks are likely to be compared unfavorably to Asian Americans, nonreservation Indians, and Latinos, who have been able to integrate and intermarry with greater ease.

Blacks may want to use race to mark their unique experience of social isolation because they understand their culture as one of resistance. With a notion of community that is rooted in the experience of segregation and discrimination, blacks cannot be sure that their sense of shared heritage will survive full-scale integration and intermarriage. Blackness has historically been defined by separation in marriage and family. From colonial times, antimiscegenation laws played an integral role in drawing the color line between whites and blacks. The one-drop rule made clear that not only whites but also Native Americans, Latinos, and Asian Americans who intermingled with blacks would doom their children to racial unassimilability. Indeed, blackness is so inextricably linked to the experience of isolation and exclusion that the flight of middle-class blacks to the suburbs has been blamed for sapping the vitality of black urban neighborhoods.[9]

No other racial or ethnic group has a racial identity as tightly tied to bans on intermarriage and integration.[10] Asian Americans come closest, but their racialization was embedded primarily in federal immigration laws that barred them from citizenship. Once Congress labeled Asians as undesirable and unfit aliens, antimiscegenation laws played at most an ancillary role in defining their racial identity. When racial restrictions on immigration to the United States were lifted after World War II and when Asian immigration exploded in the 1970s and 1980s, the image of the unassimilable foreigner began to break down. Asian Americans have increasingly come to be seen as an immigrant population that will acculturate to American life intergenerationally. The balance between race and ethnicity for Asian Americans is revealed by the census' asking those who mark the category to indicate their country of origin.[11] This record-keeping practice highlights Asian Americans' immigrant history and ethnic origins. In fact, the category of "Asian American" is often labeled "panethnic" as well as racial.[12]

The racialization of Native Americans and Latinos is the most ambiguous and uncertain. Already having experienced a substantial amount of intermarriage, nonreservation Indians and Latinos often designate themselves as white rather than nonwhite on the census. These individuals find little in the term *race* to help explain their sense of distinct identity. Nor does a racialized status seem to help them preserve their unique heritage. Terms like *language, culture, national origin,* and *ethnicity* often appear to be superior alternatives, particularly since they do not automatically conjure up the inequalities associated with race.[13]

Many Asian Americans, nonreservation Indians, and Latinos understand their ethnicities and cultures as flexible and capable of accommodation. Latinos, for example, emphasize that they are bilingual and bicultural. Native Americans without a strong tribal affiliation describe themselves as ethnically but not racially Indian. Asian Americans have spoken about their multiple consciousnesses and global identities.[14] Perhaps because many Asian Americans and Latinos are relatively recent arrivals to the United States, their distinct heritage seems to be generated primarily in their countries of origin. Languages and cultures will thrive in the homelands they left behind, regardless of whether the immigrants integrate and intermarry. Urban Indians also may believe that they can assimilate because Native American traditions will be carried on by tribal members on reservations. Symbolic ethnicity is a meaningful option because the cultures and heritages these individuals embrace will remain vital without their direct participation. Whether or not they assimilate, they will retain access to the traditions that have made them distinctive.

Blacks may not feel that their unique social and cultural practices will survive without their ongoing loyalty and participation. Precisely because theirs is not a traditional immigrant story, blacks cannot look as readily to home countries for perpetuation of their way of life. Even if some African traditions did survive the devastating impact of slavery, blacks had to build new social networks and cultural practices to endure in a society that oppressed them as a people, rather than as a congeries of African nationals.[15] The result is a heritage that mere symbolic ethnicity may not preserve.

The Meaning of Racial Equality

If the population of Asian Americans and Latinos continues to grow while the isolation of blacks remains largely unchanged, battles over the meaning of race are likely to become increasingly intense and divisive. These struggles over labels will determine whether the black experience continues to dominate paradigms of opportunity, or whether alternative images of fairness and equality emerge. In fact, this debate over terminology reveals a fundamental weakness in forcing Americans to choose between colorblindness and color consciousness: The very choice is framed as though color is the only relevant criterion for understanding the meaning of equal treatment based on race. The term *color* focuses on a phenotypical notion of race, a set of superficial differences in appearance that should be irrelevant. By treating race as color, blindness seems to follow almost inevitably. In fact, it is hard to imagine color consciousness as anything but an awareness of racism and its consequences.[16]

In some ways, the book by Gregory Howard Williams illustrates this very point. It is a story of a fall from grace. Once his parents lose their restaurant, Williams's father tells him and his brother that "[l]ife is going to be different from now on. In Virginia you were white boys. In Indiana you're going to be colored boys. I want you to remember that you're the same today that you were yesterday. But people in Indiana will treat you differently."[17] Williams is plunged into instability and poverty, he is subject to racist treatment, and the only balm for his affliction is the affection he receives from black relatives, friends, and neighbors. As a result, when Williams's father later tells him he should pass as white, Williams realizes that "I hadn't wanted to be colored, but too much had happened to me in Muncie to be part of the white world that had rejected me so completely."[18] In the racially divided world of Muncie, color consciousness is inherently tainted, a concession that race is inescapable because of pervasive discrimination.

Perhaps it is no surprise, then, that when social differences are valued, they often are labeled in nonracial terms. In explaining marital choices, for example, Americans focus on similarities in background and experience without characterizing them as racial distinctions. Correlations between race and wealth, income, education, and residence are treated as coincidences, not predictable consequences of a society in which race still separates us. We do not admit when we fall in love that

> Every beginning
> is only a sequel, after all,
> and the book of events is always open halfway through.[19]

We prefer to believe in the spontaneity of that moment of connection. We choose not to think about how our personal histories have endowed us with the characteristics that make us suitable or unsuitable, lovable or unlovable. That heady inattention permits us to insist that colorblindness has been achieved. Yet, no matter how a romantic impulse may seem to overwhelm reason, love's power is circumscribed by pervasive patterns of segregation, so commonplace that they are taken for granted. These patterns in turn determine who seems familiar, who is available, and whose personal stories "open halfway through" are likely to be on the same page as our own.

Still, setting aside the moment when people are carried away by romance, most of them will say in a more deliberative mood that they do not oppose interracial marriage. Neither vigilantes nor public officials will bar a couple's way to the altar because they crossed the color line. Those who insist that high rates of same-race marriage are a sign that the legacy of racism persists can seem shrill, demanding, and, truth be told, excessively color conscious. Proponents of colorblindness say that we should not be keeping such close racial accounts thirty years after *Loving v. Virginia*[20] struck down antimiscegenation laws. People must be treated as individuals, not racial beings, in romance as elsewhere. In short, the characterization of race as a discredited biological difference makes it hard to name some racial disparities as racism.[21] The point of these observations is not to argue that marriages in an ideal world would take place at random with respect to race. No one can imagine America's racial utopia with complete confidence. Rather, the point is that the equation of race with superficial accidents of ancestry and appearance has impoverished our capacity to imagine racial utopias, to build a bridge between the world that is and the one that might be in the absence of discrimination. Somewhere between the present pattern of 97 percent same-race marriages and an image of strict racial proportionality must lie some space for acknowledging the social consequences of race.

The realm of intimacy may provide unique opportunities for Americans to reconsider the vocabulary of difference. Virtually all Americans understand the challenges of forging healthy relationships, and they are able to make their choices largely free of direct government interference. People can name differences as they see fit, without fear of upsetting delicate political compromises. After all, there are no programs of affirmative action in marriage to be defended, and no vested interests have developed around government-run interracial dating services. Already, romantic individualists have found ways to explain the roots of attraction in terms of class, religion, culture, and old-fashioned sex appeal.

Yet, the imperatives of colorblind rhetoric lead some people to understate the relevance of race by submerging it in romantic complexity.[22] Those who name race explicitly as a factor in their marital decisions fear being labeled racists; consequently, same-race marriage is relegated to the status of a happenstance, albeit a highly reliable one. By reducing the informal pressures to characterize race as irrelevant, Americans might be able to address its place in romantic choice openly. In doing so, they need not rely on the rigidities of an earlier era. Race does not have to be reduced to a caste-like status that is weighed in the marital market. Nor must it be the pathological detritus of a sociohistorical account of racism. Instead race might be used to identify social differences, like customs and culture, that influence marital choice. Alternatively, people might conclude that the baggage of racial language is so cumbersome that other, less charged terms are more constructive ways to mark important social boundaries.

Although hemmed in by bureaucratic inertia and the vested interests of social worker constituencies, the debate over transracial adoption provides a glimpse of the dialogue that interracial intimacy can prompt about the meaning of race. The controversy first reveals the importance of whether a group is characterized as a separate people or a racial minority. The Indian Child Welfare Act (ICWA)[23] sets forth a fundamental principle: To preserve a distinctive way of life, tribes should play an integral role when Indian children are placed in foster care or adoption. Although there have been disputes about who should qualify as Indian, no one has challenged the right of tribes to assert their rights as a semi-sovereign people. By contrast, when black social workers demand race-matching to maintain the identities of black children, they are met with charges of holding children captive to a misguided nationalist agenda.[24] Because blacks are considered a racial minority rather than a separate people, their doubts about the possibilities for assimilation through transracial placements are met with skepticism if not scorn.

Precisely because interest groups have mobilized around the principle of race-matching in adoption, the notion of race has become reified. Agencies look to a child's physical appearance to determine an appropriate placement. Light-skinned black children with some white ancestry are deemed better prospects for transracial placements than dark-skinned black children without white ancestry. While phenotype is critical to the chances that a black child will be placed in a white home, the notion that appearance is all important for a successful placement does not apply equally to other groups. Asian children are readily placed in white homes because the international adoption process allows prospective parents to bypass the rigidities of race-matching. If asked, these parents are likely to describe the adoption as international, not transracial, thereby emphasizing the foreignness rather than the race of their child.[25]

Precisely because race has become reified in the placement process, Congress has demanded that a standard of colorblindness be imposed. To break through the racial politics of adoption, federal legislation has largely accepted the agencies' characterization of race as phenotype. New laws that break down barriers to transracial placements conclude that once race is nothing more than color, blindness follows automatically. The agencies' argument that they should be able to mimic naturally occurring, biological families is rejected as an illicit form of color consciousness. Faced with a congressional determination that race is irrelevant, federal enforcement officials have struggled to find alternative terms to identify pertinent social differences. In an early interpretation of federal law, officials prohibited an adoption agency from considering race, culture, or ethnicity. Later on, they conceded that culture might be germane to placement decisions. Still uncertain of the precise implications of the congressional mandate, these officials refused to define the term *culture,* leaving agencies to sort out which differences are permissible considerations and which are impermissible proxies for race.[26]

Critics of race-matching have focused on the policy's adverse effects on black children who spend long periods in foster care or institutions while awaiting placement in a black home. Despite this concern with the impact of agency decisions, the federal demand for colorblind placement policy may not change these outcomes dramatically. Most prospective parents are white, and the overwhelming majority express a preference for a white child. Agencies cannot second-guess parental attitudes without jeopardizing a child's best interest. So long as agencies can defer to these preferences, nonwhite children will continue to face substantial delays in placement. As a result, the harms that nonwhite children suffer may be more a function of a widespread and largely unexamined desire for a child of the same race, rather than of an agency's race-matching policy. Until these parental preferences are reconsidered, substantial levels of same-race placement will persist.

Moreover, race-related concerns about parental competency are likely to continue to influence agency assessments of fitness. Even if phenotype is no longer treated as relevant to placement, race correlates with cultural and social distinctions that could be germane to a child's best interest. Because federal officials have declined to define what culture means, agencies may engage in wide-ranging cultural matching that replicates race-matching to a significant degree. In fact, much as with marital choice, these practices will relegate race to a biological irrelevancy by unlinking it from cultural and social heritage. As a result, agencies will be able to form families that are overwhelmingly homogeneous with respect to race, while at the same time abiding by the colorblind standard imposed by the federal government. So long as culture is not used deliberately to circumvent the ban on race-matching, agencies will not run afoul of the new law.

The debate over colorblindness and color consciousness in adoption also demonstrates the extent to which racial considerations obscure other implications of the placement process. Agency decisions about adoption send messages about what the "good" family looks like. Even so, efforts to analyze the transracial adoption dispute and the ICWA's unique placement provisions as arguments about the nature of family are invariably overshadowed by the polarizing rhetoric of race-matching. For example, kinship care offers a way to respect extended family networks in black communities. Yet efforts to bolster kinship care opportunities have been decried as a way to subvert the principle of colorblindness in adoption and to perpetuate race-matching.[27] These accusations further marginalize the extended family structure by denying that public officials could value kinship networks that happen to be black. Instead, policymakers are indicted for manipulating these networks because they are black and serve racial ends.[28] The traditional conception of the good family reifies race, and the reification of race in turn intensifies the debate over colorblind and color-conscious policies.

Similarly, in criticizing how Indians are defined under the ICWA, state courts insist that tribes are wrongly racializing individuals based on remote Native American ancestry. Seldom do these judges explore alternative definitions of family that might mitigate conflict by permitting children to be placed in white families without losing contact with their Native American roots. Because courts assume that children must be placed with either a white nuclear family or an Indian nuclear family, judges rarely consider open arrangements that permit Indian parents and relatives to maintain contact with a child after placement in a white home. This rigid conception of family ignores the possibility that children can grow up with dual white and Native American identities.[29] Once again, narrow conceptions of the family limit a sense of racial possibilities.

The Relationship of Intimacy to Race and Identity

Gregory Howard Williams's account of *Life on the Color Line* illustrates the ways in which images of family can complicate a sense of racial loyalties and identities. When Williams's mother wants to see him and his brother after a ten-year absence, Williams is reluctant to meet her. He is sick at heart at the same time that he aches to be reunited with her:

> I had waited ten long, lonely years for this call. In those first few years in Muncie not a day passed that I didn't fall asleep hoping she would call or write. Yet we heard nothing, day after day, month after month, year after year. The pain of rejection, of begging my cousins for small bits of information about her, of having my hopes dashed time after time, had nearly cauterized me. Now, when she seemed gone forever and when we accepted we would never see her again, she came back.[30]

In answer to Williams's doubts about seeing his mother again, his brother says simply: "Greg, you're right. She let us down, but she's still our momma."[31] The Williams brothers finally do meet with their mother. Williams chooses to stay with his black friends and family, while his brother joins his mother in her new home. Later, Williams receives a note from Miss Dora, a black woman who, though not related, had helped care for him. Miss Dora calls Williams her "dear son" and signs the note "your truly mother."[32] Although Miss Dora is comfortable describing herself as Williams's mother, his school finds the arrangement so strange that it enters a special comment in his record: "He lives with Mrs. Dora Terry whom he says is no relation to him."[33]

Implicit in Williams' torment over his identity is the assumption that he should have grown up in a traditional nuclear family. But his black father is unreliable and his white mother disappears from his life when he is ten years old, so Williams must rely on the kindness of strangers. Through the years, these strangers become family. Despite the school's difficulty in recognizing these extended networks of kin, Williams can have more than one mother: his white biological mother who was with him the first ten years of his life, and Miss Dora, the black woman who cared for him later. Neither woman has to qualify as his "truly mother" so far as psychological bonds are concerned, even if the law recognizes only one as his "real" parent.

Williams also struggles with how to build his own family because he is not sure how his racial identity should influence his romantic choices. At his ninth-grade graduation, he must bring a female companion or walk at the back of the procession. He "dread[s] arousing the curiosity of white parents when [he] marche[s] in front of them with a black companion."[34] When he chooses one of his classmates to accompany him, his father explodes: "Why in the hell would you pick her? She's black as coal." His father tells him that "A rich white girl is what I see in your future. You might have to live in the ghetto, but you don't have to subsist on its food. Life is going to be easier if you have a white wife."[35] Defending his choice, Williams replies: "You're the one who wants to be white, Dad, not me."[36] Later, Williams is attracted to just the kind of white girl his father said was right for him. Once her family finds out about the relationship, they reject Williams based on his black ancestry without even meeting him. When the young woman continues to see Williams, her family severs all ties to her. As Williams and his girlfriend drift apart under the strain, Williams tries to please her by becoming "more malleable." Still, they decide to part ways, unable to withstand the conflict. Six years later, they are reunited and married. At this point, Williams no longer feels that he has to be white to marry a white woman, nor does his wife feel that she must abandon her whiteness to be with him. They later adopt two Honduran boys, and neither feels that this jeopardizes their status as a normal or good family.[37]

In struggling with choices about whom to date and marry, Williams clearly sees the decisions as linked to his own sense of identity. He understands what research on pluralistic marriages has begun to show: Far from believing that he will be black if he marries a black woman and white if he chooses a white wife, Williams comes to appreciate that his identity will evolve in the relationship. Rather than relinquish part of his identity to marry, he will be testing his sense of self through the close attachments he forms. Race is not a fixed characteristic, but a contingent form of personal identity. It depends on the reactions of family, friends, and strangers, every bit as much as it does on laws about segregation and discrimination.

Although antimiscegenation laws are no longer in place, informal pressures can be nearly as effective in discouraging intermarriage. When 95 percent of all marriages in America take place between people of the same race, race shapes marital choice; but just as importantly, marriage shapes racial identity. When legal scholars treat racial equality and freedom of association as independent constitutional values,[38] their focus on legal abstractions blinds them to a fundamental truth: The freedom to select our intimates is also the power to define racial difference. Interracial families remain unusual, but even so, they provide a unique opportunity to reconsider whether race is truly an immutable trait beyond our control. These brave new families demonstrate that race is a contingent concept, not a fixed and natural truth.

This phenomenon is probably most clearly illustrated by the current push to recognize multiracial origins on the census. Until recently, officials of the Bureau of the Census presumed that families were segregated and that individuals therefore had only one racial affiliation. Those with multiple racial origins could either choose one race or identify themselves as "Other." The proportion of marriages that are interracial remains quite small, but in the three decades since *Loving* these unions have grown increasingly respectable. As a result, the children of *Loving* have been empowered to demand recognition as multiracial people. New patterns of intimacy are redefining the way that Americans think about race, but this is a fragile experiment that has only just begun.

While some have ignored the links between race and intimacy in addressing constitutional concerns, others have trumpeted interracial marriage as the melting pot that will naturally heal America's racial divide.

In their view, formal legal distinctions are secondary to the power of informal relationships to transform race. Despite this optimism, changes in marital choice have been modest at best. Moreover, when nonwhites marry out, they overwhelmingly choose whites as partners. This pattern preserves images of racial desirability because marriage to whites remains the sure path to integration, assimilation, and acceptance. A sense of racial stratification is reinforced by the ongoing marital isolation of blacks. They have low rates of outmarriage not only to whites but to Asian Americans, Latinos, and Native Americans. So far, then, race has not readily dissolved through intermarriage, and here as elsewhere, blacks remain separate to a significant degree.[39] The growth in intermarriage undoubtedly reflects a softening of racial boundaries, as proponents of the marital melting pot suggest. However, high rates of same-race marriage, the predominance of outmarriage to whites, and the marital isolation of blacks—all indicate that marital patterns reflect racial differences as much as reform them.

The persistence of high rates of same-race marriage is by no means a basis for the government to coerce interracial intimacy. As Martin Luther King Jr. explained at the height of the civil rights movement: "The law may not be able to make a man love me, but at least it can keep him from lynching me."[40] King understood that public officials could restrain racist acts, but they could not alter the way that people think and feel about race.[41] Given the limits of government intervention, the most that advocates like King could hope for was a world in which whites and nonwhites accorded one another respect in impersonal settings like the school and workplace, if not love and friendship at home and at play. In separating the impersonal realm of rationality from a personal world of emotion, King and his followers built on a doctrine with a long pedigree in American race relations. After the Civil War, the federal government appeased concerns in the South regarding interference with racial traditions by making clear that the sole objective of Reconstruction was to establish political equality. That is, blacks would enjoy equal privileges of citizenship, including nondiscriminatory access to public education, public facilities, and the political process. At the same time, the federal government eschewed any effort to foster social equality through forced association of the races. The worst charge that critics of Reconstruction politics could level was that Congress was trying to promote miscegenation.[42]

After Reconstruction, the doctrine of "separate but equal" facilities inscribed the distinction between political and social equality on impersonal spaces. As the U.S. Supreme Court explained in the 1896 case of *Plessy v. Ferguson,* political equality did not require "a commingling of the two races upon terms unsatisfactory to either."[43] In challenging the "separate but equal" doctrine, the modern-day civil rights movement seemed to strike at the heart of the distinction between political and social equality. Demands for integration of public schools, public transportation, and public facilities all seemed to require forced sociability by subordinating freedom of association to the quest for racial equality.[44] In fact, however, civil rights activists merely remapped the distinction between political and social equality by inscribing it on the psyche of the individual. People were to be judged by their conduct in the impersonal realm of public life. Yet they were free to preserve status distinctions through their private beliefs about race. The closet bigot committed no cognizable wrong as long as his beliefs did not lead to racist acts.[45]

Under the kind of racial equality that King described, individuals had to treat people with equivalent respect, regardless of race, in impersonal settings. Racist acts reflected a detestable intrusion of irrational emotion into places like courts, schools, and workplaces that ought to be operating on principles of rationality and efficiency.[46] As a result, in evaluating whether wrongful acts had been committed, courts looked at whether individuals were motivated by discriminatory intent. An innocent and therefore presumably rational decision could not be punished just because it had an adverse effect on some racial groups.[47] Because of the civil rights movement's emphasis on rational norms in impersonal spaces, the intimate realm has remained largely beyond the purview of demands for racial equality. Although racist sentiment must be masked on the bus or train to work, at the job, and in school, people are free to express these views behind closed doors in their homes. Friends and family provide a refuge from the demands of "political correctness." In fact, Congress made this distinction clear when it exempted even quasi-intimate settings like small businesses, boardinghouses, and private clubs from the reach of civil rights mandates.[48]

Today, this distinction has serious consequences for civil rights reform efforts. Increasingly, the emphasis on intentional discrimination by public officials has obscured the significance of links between racial identity and personal choices about neighbors, friends, and lovers. As a legal matter, courts have concluded that resegregation of schools and workplaces can be race-neutral. So long as educators and employers have rectified any past wrongdoing and no longer act with discriminatory intent, their behavior is formally colorblind. Resegregation then is an incidental consequence of private decisionmaking, not a direct result of public action.[49] For example, one public official in Denver emphasized personal choice in explaining why the city's black mayor supported terminating a federal desegregation order, even though the public schools again would become racially identifiable:

> [E]ven in situations where the price of the housing stock is not a factor, the mayor chooses to live in a black area of Denver. He doesn't want to live in southeast Denver where the majority of people are Anglo. . . . [The mayor and other prominent black officials] can afford to live in other areas, but [they] like living in the black community. And this is true with Hispanic people, too, according to the people I've talked to. So, we don't expect a random distribution [of racial and ethnic groups across neighborhoods]. We expect people to live in areas where they want to live. . . . [Concentration of Hispanics in west Denver is] consistent with what the mayor believes are people's voluntary choices, that it isn't the forces of discrimination that are dictating where Hispanics live.[50]

For reasons like these, certain forms of segregation increasingly appear to be beyond the reach of law and policy.

Whatever the formal legal definition of colorblindness, there is no such thing as race-neutral resegregation as a social matter. So long as we live in segregated neighborhoods, attend segregated schools, and choose same-race marriages and families, race will be a significant social boundary. The government cannot directly interfere in personal choices about where to live, whom to befriend, and whom to love and marry. After all, the freedom to shape our identities by forming close relationships is central to our very humanity.[51] Yet there is a difference between coercive government action and policies that expand the range of options that individuals can consider. Zoning policy, home loan programs, integration of schools, and affirmative action in workplaces—all of these can help individuals to rethink their assumptions about a good place to live, good working conditions, and a quality learning environment. Color-conscious programs can heighten awareness of race in the short run, but over time they may reduce its significance if they enable individuals to think differently about racial boundaries.

It is perhaps no accident that the U.S. Supreme Court has been most explicit about the benefits of contact with people from a range of racial backgrounds in settings in which people are forging a sense of personal identity. In *Regents of the University of California v. Bakke*,[52] for example, Justice Powell allowed public colleges and universities to consider racial diversity as one factor in building a heterogeneous student body. In doing so, he emphasized the free exchange of ideas necessary to create an atmosphere of "speculation, experiment, and creation."[53] Powell's opinion recognized that academic freedom and racial equality are not independent values but mutually related concepts. Distinct racial experiences are relevant to a robust exchange of ideas, and this interchange in turn can lead to a reconceptualization of racial differences. In reaching this conclusion, *Bakke* recognized that much of what a student learns in school comes from interaction with peers. Our associations mold us and make us who we are. The identities we form are contingent, and one of the factors that influences them is our racial contacts.

Today, programs of affirmative action are under increasing attack.[54] In challenging these programs, critics argue that the only rationale for color-conscious intervention is corrective justice. Once past harms have been rectified, public officials have no independent interest in promoting interracial exchange.[55] In fact, however, so long as America remains pervasively segregated by neighborhood, marriage, and family,[56] the government has a unique and important role to play in enabling us to imagine the world that might have been in the absence of racial discrimination. Particularly in areas that shape personal identity, a commitment to building racially diverse environments can be an important way to permit individual Americans to reconsider the significance of race. Without such opportunities, we will be denied the "chance to enrich [our] perceptions, [our] experience, and learn that most valuable of all human lessons, the ability to call the established conditions of [our lives] into question."[57] Instead, we will succumb to "fantasies of collective life parochial in nature":

> Who "we" are becomes a highly selective act of imagination: one's immediate neighbors, co-workers in the office, one's family. . . . The more local the imagination, the greater becomes the number of social interests and issues for which the psychological logic is: we won't get involved, we won't let this violate us. It is not indifference; it is refusal, a willed constriction of experience the common self can permit in.[58]

Studying interracial intimacy demonstrates the impact that increased racial contact has had on Americans' ability to imagine and accept interracial marriages, transracial adoptions, and multiracial identities. Yet these incremental changes in beliefs about the color line could disappear if segregation intensifies in America's neighborhoods, schools, and workplaces. Without programs to diversify higher education and employment, whites, Asian Americans, blacks, Latinos, and Native Americans will be far less likely to mingle in everyday settings.[59] In the absence of regular interaction, racial boundaries are once again apt to become rigid and reified. By resegregating ourselves, we will remake race.

Conclusion

This analysis of interracial intimacy is meant as both a hopeful and a cautionary tale. Individuals who cross the color line to marry, build families, and form identities show us that race need not be an insurmountable divide. At the same time, the rarity of interracial marriages, families, and identifications demonstrates that race remains a powerful social barrier. Even the modest changes in racial boundaries since *Loving v. Virginia* are fragile and could be lost if they are swamped by the rise of resegregation. Imperiled though interracial intimacy may be, it holds out a seductive promise. We can undo race before it undoes us.

CHAPTER ONE

1. See, e.g., Shirlee Taylor Haizlip, *The Sweeter the Juice: A Family Memoir in Black and White* (paperback ed. 1994); Judy Scales-Trent, *Notes of a White Black Woman: Race, Color, Community* (1995); Lisa See, *On Gold Mountain: The One-Hundred-Year Odyssey of My Chinese-American Family* (paperback ed. 1995). Indeed, such narratives are so popular that one of them recently topped the best-seller list. Paperback Best Sellers: *N.Y. Times,* June 15, 1997, at § 7, p. 36 (Book Review) (describing best-seller status of James McBride, *The Color of Water: A Black Man's Tribute to His White Mother* [1996]).

2. Gregory Howard Williams, *Life on the Color Line: The True Story of a White Boy Who Discovered He Was Black* (1995).

3. Id. at 281.

4. Id. at 282.

5. For a fuller discussion of these historical issues, see chapter 2.

6. For a complete analysis of these differences, see chapter 3.

7. For a treatment of these concerns, see chapter 4.

8. *Burns v. State,* 48 Ala. 195 (1872). The decision was reversed in *Green v. State,* 58 Ala. 190 (1877).

9. 106 U.S. 583 (1883).

10. 32 Cal. 2d 711, 948 P.2d 17 (1948).

11. 388 U.S. 1 (1967). The evolution of the legal regulation of interracial sex and marriage is fully analyzed in chapter 5.

12. Before that, in *McLaughlin v. Florida,* 379 U.S. 184 (1964), the Court had held that states could not impose differential penalties for same-race and interracial adultery.

13. House Committee on Government Reform and Oversight, Subcommittee on Government, Management, Information and Technology, *Hearings on Federal Measures of Race and Ethnicity* (May 22, 1997) (prepared testimony of Professor Mary C. Waters, Department of Sociology, Harvard University).

14. Herbert Wechsler, "Toward Neutral Principles of Constitutional Law," 73 *Harv. L. Rev.* 1, 34 (1959).

15. Id. at 34–35.

16. For a fuller discussion of these issues, see chapter 7.

17. For an in-depth treatment of the census debate, see chapter 8.

18. See Dorothy E. Roberts, "The Priority Paradigm: Private Choices and the Limits of Equality," 57 *U. Pitt. L. Rev.* 363, 366–67, 379–91 (1996).

19. *Brown v. Board of Education,* 347 U.S. 483, 495 (1954).

20. For a fuller discussion of the forces leading up to state regulation of procreation, see Stephen Trombley, *The Right to Reproduce: A History of Coercive Sterilization* (1988).

21. 274 U.S. 200, 207 (1927); see also Paul A. Lombard, "Three Generations, No Imbeciles, New Light on *Buck v. Bell,*" 60 *N.Y.U. L. Rev.* 30, 31 (1985).

22. *Skinner v. Oklahoma,* 316 U.S. 535 (1942).

23. 381 U.S. 479 (1965).

24. Id. at 486.

25. 405 U.S. 438 (1972).

26. Id. at 453.

27. *Meyer v. Nebraska,* 262 U.S. 390 (1923); *Pierce v. Society of Sisters,* 268 U.S. 510 (1925); *Wisconsin v. Yoder,* 406 U.S. 205 (1972).

28. *Moore v. City of East Cleveland,* 431 U.S. 494 (1977).

29. *Roe v. Wade,* 410 U.S. 494 (1977); *Carey v. Population Services International,* 431 U.S. 678 (1977).

30. The Court's initiatives in this area waned in the late 1970s and early 1980s, but its basic commitment survives intact. There are some areas of sexual and marital conduct that remain open to regulation, however. Most notably, the Court has upheld a state ban on sodomy as applied to homosexual acts on the ground that this conduct has long been prohibited and therefore does not qualify as a fundamental right "implicit in the concept of ordered liberty" or "deeply rooted in this Nation's history and tradition." *Bowers v. Hardwick,* 478 U.S. 186, 191–94 (1986). The majority tied constitutional protections to family, marriage, and procreative sex. Id. at 191. The dissent countered that an individual's right to engage in intimate acts in the home meant little if the choice to be different was not protected. Id. at 204–8, 210–13 (dissenting opinion of Blackmun, Brennan, Marshall, and Stevens, JJ.). Some commentators have analogized proscriptions on homosexual activity to antimiscegenation laws, but that discussion is beyond the scope of this book. See, e.g., Mark Strasser, "Family, Definitions, and the Constitution: On the Antimiscegenation Analogy," 25 *Suffolk U. L. Rev.* 981 (1991).

31. See Michael W. Dowdle, "The Descent of Antidiscrimination: On the Intellectual Origins of the Current Equal Protection Jurisprudence," 66 *N.Y.U. L. Rev.* 1165, 1165–66 (1991).

32. Martha Nussbaum, "Love and the Individual: Romantic Rightness and Platonic Aspiration," in *Love Analyzed* 13–14 (Roger E. Lamb ed., 1997) (paperback ed.).

33. Martha Nussbaum has refused to label emotions irrational and has argued that decisionmaking processes that allow emotional attachments to be weighed in certain circumstances are not only consistent with but essential to a norm of public rationality. Martha C. Nussbaum, *Poetic Justice: The Literary Imagination and Public Life* 78 (1995). I have chosen not to use her phrase "rational emotion" because I do not believe it necessary in the intimate realm to label a decisionmaking process rational to render it legitimate. In addition, I am not convinced that the complex, humanistic considerations that enter into intimate connections can be fully or appropriately incorporated into public processes. Nussbaum's suggested approaches often leave the role of these emotional influences open-ended and ill-defined, which exacerbates fears that such methods would be open to abuse. See Thomas Morwetz, "Empathy and Judgment," 8 *Yale J. L. & Hum.* 517, 520 (1996) (characterizing Nussbaum's proposals in *Poetic Justice,* supra, as "more hortatory than analytical").

34. "True Love," in Wislawa Szymborska, *View with a Grain of Sand: Selected Poems* 89 (paperback ed. 1995).

35. The problems of evaluating racial equality in the context of romantic choice are dealt with in chapter 6.

36. See Barbara Bennett Woodhouse, "Of Babies, Bonding, and Burning Buildings: Discerning Parenthood in Irrational Action," 81 *Va. L. Rev.* 2493 (1995).

37. Wechsler himself recognized the need to preserve bodily integrity and dignity, but he believed that empirical data were critical to the regulation of sexuality, such as the criminalization of adultery and incest. Norman Silber and Geoffrey Miller, "Toward 'Neutral Principles' in the Law: Selections From the Oral History of Herbert Wechsler," 93 *Colum. L. Rev.* 854, 869–70 (1993).

38. See Roberts, "The Priority Paradigm," 57 *U. Pitt. L. Rev.* at 403–4 (questioning whether freedom of association is a meaningful right for individuals who are members of groups with few, if any, resources to support collective development).

39. Robert M. Cover, "Foreward: Nomos and Narrative," 97 *Harv. L. Rev.* 4, 12–13 (1983).

40. Id. at 53, 60–68.

41. Id. at 9.

42. Williams, *Life on the Color Line* at 284–85.

CHAPTER TWO

1. Peggy Pascoe, "Race, Gender, and Intercultural Relations: The Case of Interracial Marriage," 12 *Frontiers* 5, 6 (1991).

2. Robert J. Sickels, *Race, Marriage, and the Law* 64 (1972); Paul R. Spickard, *Mixed Blood: Intermarriage and Ethnic Identity in Twentieth-Century America* 374–75 (1989).

3. For a collection of historical essays that describe interracial relationships and their impact on race relations, see Martha Hodes (ed.), *Sex, Love, Race: Crossing Boundaries in North American History* (1999).

4. Fewer than 10 percent of brides in colonial New England were pregnant when they married. John D'Emilio and Estelle B. Freedman, *Intimate Matters: A History of Sexuality in America* 9–10 (1988).

5. As many as one-third of all brides in the Chesapeake were pregnant when they married. Id. at 9–13.

6. A. Leon Higginbotham Jr., *In the Matter of Color: Race and the American Legal Process: The Colonial Period* 22 (paperback ed. 1980) ("Some scholars have argued that for at least half a century the status of blacks in America remained incompletely defined—socially somewhere at the bottom of the white servant class perhaps, but nowhere near chattel slaves.").

7. H. R. McIlwaine (ed.), *Minutes of the Council and General Court of Colonial Virginia, 1622–1632, 1670–1676 with Notes and Excerpts from Original Council and General Court Records, into 1683, Now Lost* 477, 479 (1924) (citing *Re Davis* (Sept. 1630)); I Helen Tunnicliff Catterall (ed.), *Judicial Cases concerning American Slavery* 77–78 (1926); Joel Williamson, *New People: Miscegenation and Mulattoes in the United States* 7–10 (1980); Higginbotham, *In the Matter of Color* at 23–24.

8. D'Emilio and Freedman, *Intimate Matters* at 13. For differing views of the nature of black families under slavery and the impact of slavery on contemporary black family

structure, see Herbert G. Gutman, *The Black Family in Slavery and Freedom, 1750–1925* (1976); John Blassingame, *The Slave Community: Plantation Life in the Ante-Bellum South* (1972); Eugene Genovese, *Roll, Jordan, Roll: The World the Slaves Made* (1974); Robert Fogel and Stanley Engerman, *Time on the Cross: The Economics of American Negro Slavery* (1974); E. Franklin Frazier, *The Negro Family in the United States* (1939); Abram Kardiner and Lionel Oresey, *The Mark of Oppression: Explorations in the Personality of the American Negro* (1951); Kenneth Stampp, *The Peculiar Institution in the Ante-Bellum South* (1964); Stanley Elkins, *Slavery: A Problem in American Institutional and Intellectual Life* (1968).

9. For discussions of how antimiscegenation laws deprived unmarried sexual partners and their children of the benefits of marriage and inheritance law, see Virginia R. Dominguez, *White by Definition: Social Classification in Creole Louisiana* 56–84 (1986); Emily Field Van Tassel, "Personal Liberty and Private Law: 'Only the Law Would Rule between Us': Antimiscegenation, the Moral Economy of Dependency, and the Debate over Rights after the Civil War," 70 *Chi.-Kent L. Rev.* 873, 876, 895, 904–9 (1995).

10. Williamson, *New People* at 8–10.

11. Martha Hodes, *White Women, Black Men: Illicit Sex in the Nineteenth-Century South* 19–38 (1997).

12. D'Emilio and Freedman, *Intimate Matters* at 14.

13. Hodes, *White Women, Black Men* at 120; Martha Elizabeth Hodes, "Sex across the Color Line: White Women and Black Men in the Nineteenth Century American South" 10–36 (Ph.D. diss., 1991).

14. Williamson, *New People* at 10.

15. Id. at 14.

16. Id. at 8; Higginbotham, *In the Matter of Color* at 43–44.

17. Williamson, *New People* at 8, 10; Higginbotham, *In the Matter of Color* at 45, 47.

18. Williamson, *New People* at 9–10; see also Higginbotham, *In the Matter of Color* at 47–48.

19. Higginbotham, *In the Matter of Color* at 48.

20. Thomas E. Buckley, S.J., "Unfixing Race: Class, Power, and Identity in an Interracial Family," 102(3) *Va. Magazine of History and Biography* 349, 361 (July 1994).

21. Id. at 363.

22. Id. at 364–67.

23. Brenda E. Stevenson, *Life in Black & White: Family and Community in the Slave South* 241 (1996).

24. D'Emilio and Freedman, *Intimate Matters* at 103–4; Hodes, *White Women, Black Men* at 48–50, 65; Hodes, "Sex across the Color Line," at 63–66.

25. Hodes, *White Women, Black Men* at 38–48.

26. Id. at 48.

27. Id. at 61.

28. Williamson, *New People* at 17.

29. Id. at 22–23; D'Emilio and Freedman, *Intimate Matters* at 102–3.

30. Williamson, *New People* at 67–71; D'Emilio and Freedman, *Intimate Matters* at 102. By contrast, penalties for sex across the color line were imposed on white male servants, white males who did not own slaves, and white women. Higginbotham, *In the Matter of Color* at 158–59.

31. D'Emilio and Freedman, *Intimate Matters* at 94.

32. II Helen Tunnicliff Catterall (ed.), *Judicial Cases Concerning American Slavery* 269, 359 (1929); Williamson, *New People* at 18.

33. Williamson, *New People* at 20–22. For a description of racial tensions that arose over the use of the term *Creole* in Louisiana to identify both blacks and whites, see Dominguez, *White by Definition* at 140–48.

34. Williamson, *New People* at 22–23.

35. Id. at 71–75; Hodes, *White Women, Black Men* at 148–65; Hodes, "Sex across the Color Line," at 177–79.

36. D'Emilio and Freedman, *Intimate Matters* at 113–14.

37. Hodes, *White Women, Black Men* at 143–48, 166–75; Hodes, "Sex across the Color Line," at 188–96.

38. Williamson, *New People* at 88–91; F. James Davis, *Who Is Black?: One Nation's Definition* 49 (1991); Ernest Porterfield, *Black and White Mixed Marriages* 12, 32–33 (1978).

39. Williamson, *New People* at 92, quoting letter from William Howard to James Gregorie, Jan. 12, 1868, *Gregorie-Elliott Papers,* Southern Historical Collection, University of North Carolina, Chapel Hill.

40. Hodes, *White Women, Black Men* at 148–59; Hodes, "Sex across the Color Line," at 196–212.

41. Donna L. Franklin, *Ensuring Inequality: The Structural Transformation of the African-American Family* 64 (1997); D'Emilio and Freedman, *Intimate Matters* at 220–21.

42. D'Emilio and Freedman, *Intimate Matters* at 106–7.

43. Williamson, *New People* at 96–98.

44. See Ronald Takaki, *Strangers from a Different Shore* 12–15 (paperback ed. 1989). This chapter focuses on groups like the Chinese and Japanese who arrived in substantial numbers before World War II. Because restrictions on intermarriage began to disappear after World War II, the experience of groups like Koreans, Samoans, and Indochinese, who mainly arrived after 1945, are not discussed. Sil Dong Kim, "Interracially Married Korean Women Immigrants: A Study in Marginality" 61–63, 64–66 (Ph.D. diss., 1979); Lee Houchins and Chang-Su Houchins, "The Korean Experience in America, 1903–24," in *The Asian Americans: The Historical Experience* 129–56 (Norris Hundley Jr. ed., 1976); Verona Gordon, "Culturally Sensitive Nursing Care for Indochinese Refugees," in *Asian and Pacific American Experiences: Women's Perspectives* 206 (Nobuya Tsuchida ed., 1982).

45. Three Chinese arrived in California in 1848; by 1852, about twenty-five thousand resided there. Chinese laborers were imported to work on the railroads in the 1860s, and the Chinese comprised one-fourth of the state's workforce by 1870. Takaki, *Strangers from a Different Shore* at 79. The population of Chinese in the United States grew from 34,933 in 1860 to 107,488 in 1890. Megumi Dick Osumi, "Asians and California's Anti-Miscegenation Laws," in *Asian and Pacific American Experiences* (Tsuchida ed.), at 1, 2–3; Kim, "Interracially Married Korean Women Immigrants," at 58–59.

46. Act of March 26, 1790, ch. 3, 1 Stat. 103. For a fuller discussion of the role of race in the naturalization process, see generally Ian Haney López, *White By Law: The Legal Construction of Race* (1996).

47. Corrine K. Hoexter, *From Canton to California: The Epic of Chinese Immigration* 44 (1976). For an article focusing on Asian efforts to obtain citizenship, see Charles J. McClain, "Tortuous Path, Elusive Goal: The Asian Quest for American Citizenship," 2 *Asian L.J.* 33 (1995).

48. Charles J. McClain, *In Search of Equality: The Chinese Struggle against Discrimination in Nineteenth-Century America* 70–73 (1994).

49. *In re Ah Yup,* 1 F. Cas. 223, 223–25, 5 Sawy. 155, 157–59 (1878) (No. 104). A congressman from California also introduced a bill to make clear that no Chinese could become a citizen, but the need for the bill was obviated by the federal court's decision. Twenty years later, the U.S. Attorney General's Office issued opinions that cast doubt on the citizenship of Chinese who received certificates of naturalization before their ineligibility for citizenship was settled. 21 Op. Att'y Gen. 37 (1898).

50. Act of May 6, 1882, ch. 126, 22 Stat. 58, §§ 1, 14, 15; McClain, *In Search of Equality* at 147–50, 191–92, 201–3; Elmer Sandmeyer, *The Anti-Chinese Movement in California* 93–95 (1939). The U.S. Supreme Court upheld the Chinese Exclusion Act in 1889 based on Congress's plenary power to regulate immigration. Chinese Exclusion Case, *Chae Chan Ping v. United States,* 130 U.S. 581, 608–10 (1889). Later, a federal court reinforced the racial categorization of Chinese under the law by denying entry to British nationals from Hong Kong because they were still "laborers of the Chinese race." *In re Ah Lung,* the Chinese Laborer from Hong Kong, 18 F. 28 (C.C.D. Cal. 1883). For a description of events leading up to the *Ah Lung* decision, see McClain, *In Search of Equality* at 155–56.

51. Takaki, *Strangers from a Different Shore* at 111–12.

52. Act of May 6, 1882, ch. 126, 22 Stat. 58, §§ 1, 14, 15; McClain, *In Search of Equality* at 147–50, 191–92, 201–3; Sandmeyer, *The Anti-Chinese Movement in California* at 93–95.

53. Immigration and Nationality Act, Pub. L. No. 414, 66 Stat. 163 (1952), *as amended,* 8 U.S.C. §§ 1101 et seq.

54. Kim, "Interracially Married Korean Women Immigrants," at 59–60; Osumi, "Asians and California's Anti-Miscegenation Laws," in *Asian and Pacific American Experiences* (Tsuchida ed.), at 9.

55. Kim, "Interracially Married Korean Women Immigrants," at 60; Osumi, "Asians and California's Anti-Miscegenation Laws," in *Asian and Pacific American Experiences* (Tsuchida ed.), at 9; Takaki, *Strangers from a Different Shore* at 180–81.

56. See *Ozawa v. United States,* 260 U.S. 178, 183 (1922) (argument on behalf of petitioner citing early instances of Japanese naturalization); see also Bradford Smith, *Americans from Japan* 148 (1948) (describing how some Japanese successfully petitioned for citizenship in the mid- to late 1850s, sometimes by capitalizing on their military service records).

57. Letter to President Theodore Roosevelt from U.S. Attorney General William H. Moody, July 19, 1905; 21 Op. Att'y Gen. 37,581 (1906). Eager to cultivate good relations with Japan, President Roosevelt pressed for legislation that would permit the Japanese to naturalize. His efforts were unsuccessful, however. Raymond A. Esthus, *Theodore Roosevelt and Japan* 147 n. 3 (1966).

58. *Ozawa v. United States,* 260 U.S. 178 (1922).

59. Id. at 198; Takaki, *Strangers from a Different Shore* at 208–9; Smith, *Americans from Japan* at 148.

60. Asian Indians began arriving in the United States in 1907. Unfavorable immigration policies kept their numbers small. In 1909, Congress restricted immigration from India, and less than a decade later, immigration was banned altogether. Takaki, *Strangers from a Different Shore* at 62.

61. Letter from U.S. Secretary of Commerce and Labor Oscar Straus to U.S. Attorney General Charles J. Bonaparte, Jan. 9, 1907; letter from Bonaparte to Straus, Jan. 11, 1907; letter from U.S. Attorney Robert T. Devlin to Bonaparte, Aug. 8, 1907; letter from Bonaparte to Devlin, Aug. 14, 1907; letter from Professor W. F. Willcox to Bonaparte, Sept. 13, 1907; letter from Bonaparte to Willcox, Sept. 16, 1907; letter from Willcox to Bonaparte, Sept. 24, 1907; letter from Bonaparte to Willcox, Sept. 27, 1907.

62. *United States v. Balsara,* 180 F. 694 (2d Cir. 1910); *In re Mozumdar,* 207 F. 115 (E.D. Wash. 1913). For a general discussion of the controversy surrounding the classification of Asian Indians, see Joan M. Jensen, *Message from India: Asian Indian Immigrants in North America* 248–49 (1988); Gary Hess, "The Forgotten Asian Americans: The East Indian Community in the United States," in *The Asian Americans,* at 169–70.

63. 261 U.S. 204 (1923).

64. Id. at 209. For an article criticizing the Court for judging East Indians by "the 'blueness' of [their] Caucasian blood" rather than their personal accomplishments in the United States, see Gurdial Singh, "East Indians in the United States," 30 *Soc. & Soc. Res.* 208, 212 (Jan.–Feb. 1946).

65. Takaki, *Strangers from a Different Shore* at 35–36, 100–101; Dan Caldwell, "The Negroization of the Chinese Stereotype in California," 53 *S. Calif. Q.* 123 (1971).

66. See, e.g., 13 *Cong. Rec.* 3268 (1882) (statement of Senator John Tyler Morgan of Alabama) (likening the problems of assimilating the Chinese and the Indians and arguing for restrictive immigration policies); see generally Takaki, *Strangers from a Different Shore* at 102.

67. Caldwell, "The Negroization of the Chinese Stereotype in California," 53 *S. Calif. Q.* at 128, quoting Hutching's *California Magazine,* vol. I, at 387 (March 1857).

68. Stuart Miller, *The Unwelcome Immigrant: The American Image of the Chinese, 1785–1882* at 169 (1969), quoting *N.Y. Tribune,* Oct. 2, 1854.

69. Osumi, "Asians and California's Anti-Miscegenation Laws," in *Asian and Pacific American Experiences* (Tsuchida ed.), at 6–7; see also Takaki, *Strangers from a Different Shore* at 101.

70. I *Debates and Proceedings of the Constitutional Convention of California 1878–9* at 632 (1880) (E. B. Willis and P. K. Stockton official stenographers).

71. Id. at 225.

72. California Statutes, 23d Sess., ch. 74, § 1, p. 121 (1880) (amending § 69). Significantly, the legislature did not move immediately to make intermarriage illegal, although it easily could have amended a law banning marriages between whites and blacks or mulattoes to include the Chinese. At least one scholar has argued that legislators were concerned about the possibility that such an amendment would void retroactively all marriages between whites and Chinese. Osumi, "Asians and California's Anti-Miscegenation Laws," in *Asian and Pacific American Experiences* (Tsuchida ed.), at 6.

73. California Statutes, 34th Sess., ch. 157, § 20, pp. 335–36 (1901) (amending §§ 60, 69).

74. *Lewis v. Dunne,* 134 Cal. 291, 66 P. 478 (1901) (declaring 1901 amendments to Civil Code invalid for failure to comply with the constitutional requirement of being "re-enacted and published at length as revised" and the requirement that an act's title deal with a definite subject).

75. California Statutes, 36th Sess., ch. 414, § 2, p. 554 (1905) (amending § 60). For a general discussion of the California legislature's efforts to deal with miscegenation among Chinese and whites, see Osumi, "Asians and California's Anti-Miscegenation Laws," in *Asian and Pacific American Experiences* (Tsuchida ed.), at 9, 11, 13−14.

76. Franklin Hichborn, *Story of the Session of the California Legislature of 1909* at 207 n. 90 (1909), quoting Assemblyman Johnson's speech regarding a bill to mandate that the Japanese attend segregated schools.

77. Roger Daniels, *The Politics of Prejudice: The Anti-Japanese Movement in California and the Struggle for Japanese Exclusion* 49 (1978), quoting Chester Harvey Rowell, owner and editor of the *Fresno Republican*.

78. See *Reports of the Senate Immigration Commission, Immigrants in Industries—Part 25: Japanese and Other Immigrant Races in the Pacific Coast and Rocky Mountain States,* 61st Cong., 2d Sess. at vol. I, pp. 162−63 (1911) (noting strong antipathy to Japanese intermarriage in the western United States).

79. Act of Mar. 2, 1907, ch. 2534, 34 Stat. 1228−29, § 3. See generally Candice Lewis Bredbenner, *A Nationality of Her Own: Women, Marriage, and the Law of Citizenship* 16 (1998).

80. Cable Act of 1922, Pub. L. No. 67-346, 42 Stat. 1021−22, *amended by* Act of July 3, 1930, Pub. L. No. 71-499, 46 Stat. 849, *repealed by* Act of Mar. 3, 1931, Pub. L. No. 71-829, 46 Stat. 1511−12; *Chang Chan v. Nagle,* 268 U.S. 346, 353 (1925) (concluding that Chinese women could not rely on marriage to a citizen husband to enter the United States). See also Sucheng Chan, "The Exclusion of Chinese Women, 1870−1943," in *Chinese Immigrants and American Law* 36 (Charles J. McClain ed., 1994); Bredbenner, *A Nationality of Her Own* at 124−29, 134−35 (describing denationalization of American women under principle of "derivative citizenship").

81. Takaki, *Strangers from a Different Shore* at 36−37; Chan, "The Exclusion of Chinese Women," in *Chinese Immigrants and American Law* (McClain ed.), at 2−5.

82. D'Emilio and Freedman, *Intimate Matters* at 135; Takaki, *Strangers from a Different Shore* at 121−23.

83. For an account of a wealthy and successful Chinese businessman who entered into a contract with his white female lover that pledged their lifelong allegiance to one another, although interracial marriages were illegal, see Lisa See, *On Gold Mountain: The One-Hundred-Year Odyssey of My Chinese-American Family* 56 (paperback ed. 1995). Meanwhile, unbeknownst to his white "wife," the Chinese businessman had a wife in China. He justified the arrangement on the ground that he had seen his Chinese wife only once, their marriage had never been consummated, and some men in his home country kept country wives to care for aging parents and city wives for companionship. Id. at 55.

84. Spickard, *Mixed Blood* at 47−48.

85. Act of March 3, 1875, ch. 141, 18 Stat. 477−78; see generally George Anthony Peffer, "Forbidden Families: Emigration Experiences of Chinese Women Under the Page Law, 1875−1882," 6 *J. American Ethnic History* 28 (1986); Chan, "The Exclusion of Chinese Women," in *Chinese Immigrants and American Law* (McClain ed.), at 97−109.

86. Case of the Chinese Wife, *In re Ah Moy,* 21 F. 785 (1884), *writ of error dismissed as moot,* 113 U.S. 216 (1885) (wife of Chinese laborer); for cases dealing with the rights of the wives of Chinese merchants, see *In re Chung Toy Ho and Wong Choy Sin,* 42 F. 398 (D. Or. 1890); *United States v. Chung Shee,* 71 F. 277 (S.D. Cal. 1895); *United States*

v. Gue Lim, 83 F. 136 (N.D. Wash. 1897), aff'd, 176 U.S. 459 (1900); *Ex parte Chan Shee,* 236 F. 579 (N.D. Cal. 1916); *Chew Hoy Quong v. White,* 244 F. 749 (9th Cir. 1917), rev'd and remanded, 249 F. 869 (1918). For a description of these cases, see Chan, "The Exclusion of Chinese Women," in *Chinese Immigrants and American Law* (McClain ed.), at 18–26.

87. Osumi, "Asians and California's Anti-Miscenegation Laws," in *Asian and Pacific American Experiences* (Tsuchida ed.), at 8; Takaki, *Strangers from a Different Shore* at 254.

88. Osumi, "Asians and California's Anti-Miscenegation Laws," in *Asian and Pacific American Experiences* (Tsuchida ed.), at 8.

89. Takaki, *Strangers from a Different Shore* at 234–35.

90. Act of May 26, 1924, ch. 190, 43 Stat. 153, §§ 3–4.

91. *Cheung Sum Shee v. Nagle,* 268 U.S. 336 (1925) (merchants); *Chang Chan v. Nagle,* 268 U.S. 346 (1925) (native-born Chinese). Congress later amended the law in response to vigorous lobbying by native-born Chinese. House Comm. on Immigration and Naturalization, *Hearings on H.R. 2404, H.R. 5654, H.R. 10524,* 71st Cong., 2d Sess. 544–46 (1930) (testimony of Kenneth F. Fung, Executive Secretary, Chinese American Citizens' Alliance, and Florence P. Kahn, Representative from California). The new law allowed native-born Chinese to bring their wives to the United States if the marriage had been consummated before 1924. Act of June 13, 1930, ch. 476, 46 Stat. 581.

92. Takaki, *Strangers from a Different Shore* at 234–35.

93. Spickard, *Mixed Blood* at 26–27.

94. Yuji Ichioka, *The Issei: The World of the First Generation Japanese Immigrants, 1885–1924* at 60–61, 146–50 (1988); Takaki, *Strangers from a Different Shore* at 197–98; Spickard, *Mixed Blood* at 27. For a description of one Japanese colony of farmers in the San Joaquin Valley that was founded by a businessman and publisher who strongly endorsed the development of ethnic enclaves, see Kesa Noda, *Yamato Colony, 1906–1960* (1981).

95. Spickard, *Mixed Blood* at 27–28; Takaki, *Strangers from a Different Shore* at 46, 202–3; Osumi, "Asians and California's Anti-Miscegenation Laws," in *Asian and Pacific American Experiences* (Tsuchida ed.), at 14. The agreement remained in place until 1921 when a "Ladies' Agreement" was reached to prohibit emigration of "picture brides," that is, women from Japan chosen for arranged marriages with immigrant husbands. In effect, the Ladies' Agreement stopped the flow of Japanese immigration altogether. Takaki, *Strangers from a Different Shore* at 208.

96. Spickard, *Mixed Blood* at 26–27; see also Takaki, *Strangers from a Different Shore* at 46–47.

97. Spickard, *Mixed Blood* at 28–29.

98. Takaki, *Strangers from a Different Shore* at 47.

99. Senate Committee on Immigration, *Japanese Immigration Legislation: Hearings on S. 2576,* 68th Cong., 1st Sess. 5 (1924) (statement of Mr. V. S. McClatchy of Sacramento, California).

100. Id.

101. Osumi, "Asians and California's Anti-Miscegenation Laws," in *Asian and Pacific American Experiences* (Tsuchida ed.), at 13, quoting *Grizzly Bear,* July 1923, at 27.

102. Spickard, *Mixed Blood* at 47–48.

103. By 1930, there were 45,208 Filipinos in the United States, of whom 30,470 resided in California. Osumi, "Asians and California's Anti-Miscegenation Laws," in *Asian*

and Pacific American Experiences (Tsuchida ed.), at 16, citing 1930 U.S. Census, vol. III, pt. 1, at 120.

104. Id. at 23; Takaki, *Strangers from a Different Shore* at 58.

105. For a personal account of life in the Filipino bachelor communities, see Carlos Bulosan, *America Is in the Heart* (1946).

106. Manuel Buaken, *I Have Lived with the American People* 169–70 (1948), quoting *Evening Pajaronian,* Jan. 8, 1930.

107. C. M. Goethe, "Filipino Immigration Viewed as a Peril," *Current History* 353, 354 (June 1931), reprinted in *Letters in Exile: An Introductory Reader on the History of Filipinos in America* 72 (1976). Elsewhere, the author characterized white women who involved themselves with Filipino men as "near-moron[s]." Id.

108. H. Brett Melendy, *Asians in America: Filipinos, Koreans, and East Indians* 52–55 (1977) (describing the application of antimiscegenation laws to Filipinos and race riots in California).

109. Takaki, *Strangers from a Different Shore* at 326.

110. Sylvain Lazarus, "Lovers' Departure," *Time,* Apr. 13, 1936, at 17.

111. Takaki, *Strangers from a Different Shore* at 329.

112. Ernest Ilustre, "Great Lovers," *Time,* Apr. 27, 1936, at 4.

113. California Office of the Attorney General, Opinion No. 5641 (June 8, 1926).

114. Osumi, "Asians and California's Anti-Miscegenation Laws," in *Asian and Pacific American Experiences* (Tsuchida ed.), at 18–19.

115. *Robinson v. Lampton,* No. 2496504 (Sup. Ct. L.A. County 1930).

116. For a Filipino's personal account of the tensions surrounding the California courts' treatment of intermarriage, see Bulosan, *America Is in the Heart* at 143.

117. *Roldan v. Los Angeles County,* 129 Cal. App. 267, 18 P.2d 706 (1933); *Visco v. Los Angeles County,* No. 319408 (Sup. Ct. L.A. County 1931) (holding that California law did not bar marriage of a Filipino to a "Mexican Indian girl" and noting in dictum that a Filipino could also marry a white woman); *Laddaran v. Laddaran,* No. 095459 (Sup. Ct. L.A. County 1931) (upholding validity of Filipino–white intermarriage); *Murrillo v. Murillo,* No. D97715 (Sup. Ct. L.A. County 1931) (same). For an article chronicling these legal decisions and concluding that efforts to stop race-mixing would prove futile, see Nellie Foster, "Legal Status of Filipino Intermarriages in California," 16 *Soc. & Soc. Res.* 441 (May–June 1932).

118. *Roldan v. Los Angeles County,* 129 Cal. App. 267, 18 P.2d 706 (1933).

119. Calif. Stat., 50th Sess., ch. 104, pp. 561–62 (1933) (amending §§ 60, 69).

120. *Perez v. Sharp,* 32 Cal. 2d 711, 198 P.2d 17 (1948). See chapter 5 for a discussion of the California Supreme Court's decision to strike down the state's antimiscegenation law.

121. *People v. Godines,* 17 Cal. App. 2d 721, 62 P.2d 787 (1936).

122. Osumi, "Asians and California's Anti-Miscegenation Laws," in *Asian and Pacific American Experiences* (Tsuchida ed.), at 22; see also "Anti-Miscegenation Laws and the Filipino," in *Letters in Exile* at 63.

123. Leti Volpp, "American Mestizo: Filipinos and Anti-Miscegenation Laws in California," 33 *U.C. Davis L. Rev.* 795 (2000) (noting that relations between Filipino men and Mexican women did not prompt serious opposition and that in one case in Los Angeles, a court permitted a Filipino–Mexican marriage because the Mexican wife was denied her status as a white woman).

124. Takaki, *Strangers from a Different Shore* at 341–43.

CHAPTER THREE

1. Martha Hodes, *White Women, Black Men: Illicit Sex in the Nineteenth-Century South* 35–38 (1997); see also Ariela J. Gross, "Litigating Whiteness: Trials of Racial Determination in the Nineteenth Century South," 108 *Yale L.J.* 109 (1998) (describing trials over racial identity in cases involving racially defined crimes, disputes over slave status, inheritance law, and allegations of slander in the antebellum South).

2. William Loren Katz, *Black Indians: A Hidden Heritage* 102–14 (paperback ed. 1986). For a general discussion of intermarriage among blacks and Native Americans, see Jack D. Forbes, *Africans and Native Americans: The Language of Race and the Evolution of Black–Red Peoples* (2d ed. 1993). For an account of some of the offspring of blacks and Native Americans, see William Loren Katz and Paula A. Franklin, *Proudly Red and Black: Stores of African and Native Americans* (1993).

3. Jack Weatherford, *Native Roots: How the Indians Enriched America* 279 (paperback ed. 1991).

4. Katz, *Black Indians* at 109.

5. Id. at 110–11.

6. For a fuller discussion of the rise of state-mandated segregation after Reconstruction, see chapter 5.

7. John D'Emilio and Estelle B. Freedman, *Intimate Matters: A History of Sexuality in America* 171–221 (1988) (describing the challenges to traditional sexual mores that urbanization and industrialization brought and the social reform movement that arose in response).

8. Lawrence Friedman, "Crimes of Mobility," 43 *Stan. L. Rev.* 637, 640–50 (1991).

9. Joel Williamson, *New People: Miscegenation and Mulattoes in the United States* 101 (1980). Some also claimed to be Native Americans, rather than blacks. Virginia R. Dominguez, *White by Definition: Social Classification in Creole Louisiana* 200–204 (1986).

10. Paul R. Spickard, *Mixed Blood: Intermarriage and Ethnic Identity in Twentieth-Century America* 336 (1989); Edward Byron Reuter, *Race Mixture: Studies in Intermarriage and Miscegenation* 69–71 (1931); St. Clair Drake and Horace R. Cayton, *Black Metropolis: A Study of Negro Life in a Northern City* 159–63 (paperback ed. 1993).

11. Kathy Peiss, "Love across the Color Line," in *Love across the Color Line: The Letters of Alice Hanley to Channing Lewis* 77–80 (Helen Lefkowitz Horowitz and Kathy Peiss eds., 1996) (paperback ed.).

12. *Ferrall v. Ferrall,* 153 N.C. 174, 69 S.E. 60 (1910); see also Eva Saks, "Representing Miscegenation Law," 8 *Raritan* 39, 51 (1988).

13. 153 N.C. at 178–79, 69 S.E. at 61–62; see also Saks, "Representing Miscegenation Law," 8 *Raritan* at 51–52.

14. 153 N.C. at 180, 69 S.E. at 62 (concurring opinion of Clark, C.J.).

15. Spickard, *Mixed Blood* at 337.

16. Drake and Cayton, *Black Metropolis* at 165.

17. Id.

18. For a fuller discussion of developments after World War II, see chapter 5.

19. Dominguez, *White by Definition* at 36–37.

20. Id. at 37–45.

21. Calvin Trillin, "American Chronicles: Black or White," *New Yorker,* Apr. 14, 1986, at 62; Dominguez, *White by Definition* at 2–3, 53.

22. Weatherford, *Native Roots* at 274; see also Gary D. Sandefur and Trudy McKinnell, "American Indian Intermarriage," 15 *Soc. Sci. Research* 347, 349 (1986).

23. Weatherford, *Native Roots* at 277.

24. Id. at 278; Sandefur and McKinnell, "American Indian Intermarriage," 15 *Soc. Sci. Research* at 349–50.

25. Quoted in Julie Schimmel, "Inventing 'the Indian,'" in *The West as America: Reinterpreting Images of the Frontier, 1820–1920* at 149, 174 (William H. Truettner ed., 1991).

26. Weatherford, *Native Roots* at 272–73. Some scholars have argued that the degree of sexual exploitation of Native American women, particularly by French fur traders, has been greatly exaggerated. Jacqueline Peterson, "Women Dreaming: The Religiopsychology of Indian White Marriages and the Rise of a Metis Culture," in *Western Women: Their Land, Their Lives* 49, 52 (Lillian Schissel, Vicki L. Ruiz, and Janice Monk eds., 1988).

27. Christian F. Feest, "Pride and Prejudice: The Pocahontas Myth and the Pamunkey," in *The Invented Indian: Cultural Fictions and Government Policies* 49, 49–50 (James A. Clifton ed., 1990).

28. Virginia Code § 20-54 (1960 Repl. Vol.) The statute was declared unconstitutional in *Loving v. Virginia,* 388 U.S. 1 (1966), which discussed in a footnote the historical underpinnings of the rule regarding intermarriage with Native Americans. Id. at 5 n. 4.

29. Dominguez, *White by Definition* at 34.

30. Because the Mexican-origin population is the largest and most longstanding in the United States, better historical materials are available for this group than for other Latinos, such as Puerto Ricans, Cubans, or Central and South Americans. As a result, this chapter focuses on the Mexican-origin population in the Southwest.

31. Suzanne Oboler, *Ethnic Labels, Latino Lives: Identity and the Politics of (Re)Presentation in the United States* 21 (paperback ed. 1995); Ramón A. Gutiérrez, *When Jesus Came, the Corn Mothers Went Away: Marriage, Sexuality, and Power in New Mexico, 1500–1846* at 285 (paperback ed. 1991).

32. Oboler, *Ethnic Labels, Latino Lives* at 21, 23.

33. Rebecca McDowell Craver, *The Impact of Intimacy: Mexican–Anglo Intermarriage in New Mexico, 1821–1846* at 27–28.

34. Id. at 28–29.

35. Edward Murguia, *Chicano Intermarriage: A Theoretical and Empirical Study* 13, 18–22, 31–36, 45 (1982); Tomás Almaguer, *Racial Fault Lines: The Historical Origins of White Supremacy in California* 58–60 (paperback ed. 1994).

36. Juan Gomez-Quinones, *Roots of Chicano Politics, 1600–1940* at 243 (paperback ed. 1994); Almaguer, *Racial Fault Lines* at 59–60 (noting that most intermarriages involved white men and Mexican women, and these women were described as being of "Caucasian origin").

37. Matthew C. Field, *Matt Field on the Santa Fe Trail* 178–79 (John E. Sunder ed., 1960).

38. Craver, *The Impact of Intimacy* at 46–47.

39. Gomez-Quinones, *Roots of Chicano Politics* at 243–45; see also Almaguer, *Racial Fault Lines* at 60–62 (noting that the suitability of Mexican women as spouses typically was linked to their privileged class positions).

40. Craver, *The Impact of Intimacy* at 47.

41. Gomez-Quinones, *Roots of Chicano Politics* at 244–45.

42. Dominguez, *White by Definition* at 56–89; Adrienne Davis, "The Private Law of Race and Sex: An Antebellum Perspective," 51 *Stan. L. Rev.* 221 (1999).

43. Williamson, *New People* at 24.

44. Id. at 51, 67–70.

45. Id. at 112–14; Hyman Alterman, *Counting People: The Census in History* 275–76 (1969); Sharon M. Lee, "Racial Classifications in the U.S. Census: 1890–1990," 16 *Ethnic and Racial Studies* 75, 77 (1993).

46. Williamson, *New People* at 77.

47. 163 U.S. 537 (1896).

48. Margo J. Anderson, *The American Census: A Social History* 82 (1988); Carlos A. Fernandez, "Government Clarification of Multiracial/Multiethnic People," in *The Multiracial Experience: Racial Borders as the New Frontier* 15, 22 (Maria P. P. Root ed., 1996) (paperback ed.).

49. Peter Nabokov, *Native American Testimony: A Chronicle of Indian–White Relations from Prophecy to Present, 1492–1992* at 82 (paperback ed. 1991).

50. See M. Annette Jaimes, "Federal Indian Identification Policy: A Usurpation of Indigenous Sovereignty in North America," in *The State of Native America: Genocide, Colonization, and Resistance* 123, 129–32, 136–37 (M. Annette Jaimes ed., 1992) (describing internal dissension among Indians due to blood quantum requirements)

51. Dawes Act, ch. 119, 24 Stat. 388–91 (1887).

52. Patricia Penn Hilden, *When Nickels Were Indians: An Urban, Mixed-Blood Story* 151 (paperback ed. 1995).

53. Linda J. Lacey, "The White Man's Law and the American Indian Family in the Assimilation Era," 40 *Ark. L. Rev.* 327, 354–55 (1986).

54. Spickard, *Mixed Blood* at 53–56.

55. Id.

56. Treaty of Peace, Friendship, Limits, and Settlement with the Republic of Mexico, 9 Stat. 922–43 (Feb. 2, 1848). See also Almaguer, *Racial Fault Lines* at 54–57 (describing the Mexican-origin population's formal status as white but the limited protection this offered to the working class); Ronald Takaki, *A Different Mirror: A History of Multicultural America* 177–84 (1993) (discussing the alienation and isolation of Mexican-origin persons in the Southwest despite treaty protections).

57. *In re Rodriguez*, 81 F. 337, 350–55 (W.D. Tex. 1897).

58. Almaguer, *Racial Fault Lines* at 54–55; Takaki, *A Different Mirror* at 169.

59. J. Ross Browne, Report of the Debates in the Convention of California on the Formation of the State Constitution in September and October, 1849, at 72–73 (1850).

60. Id. at 63. See generally Almaguer, *Racial Fault Lines* at 54 (describing Californios' lobbying for inclusion at the California constitutional convention).

61. Peter W. Bardaglio, *Reconstructing the Household: Families, Sex, and the Law in the Nineteenth-Century South* 177 (1995); David D. Smits, " 'Squaw Men,' 'Half-Breeds,' and Amalgamators: Late Nineteenth-Century Anglo-American Attitudes toward Indian–White Race-Mixing," 15 *Am. Ind. Cult. and Res. J.* 29, 31–32 (1991).

62. Takaki, *A Different Mirror* at 330, citing Mark Reisler, *By the Sweat of Their Brow: Mexican Immigrant Labor in the United States, 1900–1940* at 153, 155, 156, 205 (1976).

63. David Montejano, *Anglos and Mexicans in the Making of Texas, 1836–1986* at 181

(paperback ed. 1987), quoting William Leonard, "Where Both Bullets and Ballots Are Dangerous," *Survey,* Oct. 28, 1916, at 86–87.

64. Id. at 158, quoting Max S. Handman, "Economic Reasons for the Coming of the Mexican Immigrant," 35 *Am. J. Soc.* 601, 609–10 (1930).

65. Karen Isaksen Leonard, *Making Ethnic Choices: California's Punjabi Mexican Americans* 68–69 (1992). In 1947, when the California Supreme Court invalidated the state's antimiscegenation law, it noted that "Mexicans" and "Hindus" were not covered. *Perez v. Sharp,* 32 Cal. 2d 711, 721, 198 P.2d 17, 22–23 (1948). Leonard's description of the early Asian Indian experience belies the court's claim regarding Hindus, however.

66. Leonard, *Making Ethnic Choices* at 62–63, quoting *El Centro Progress,* Apr. 15, 1918.

67. Id. at 62, quoting *Holtville Tribune,* Mar. 16 and Nov. 10, 1916.

68. Id. at 68.

69. Id. at 70–71. By contrast, the law clearly permitted the children of Mexican–Punjabi unions to hold property. Id. at 70.

70. Neil Foley, *The White Scourge: Mexicans, Blacks, and Poor Whites in Texas Cotton Culture* 208 (1997), quoting interview with Judge Wildenthal.

71. Id. at 208–9, quoting interviews with John Asker and Bob Lemmons, the black man who was prosecuted for miscegenation. Asker reportedly said that he liked Mexicans, but "You can't make a rose out of an onion." Id. at 277 n. 15.

CHAPTER FOUR

1. John D'Emilio and Estelle B. Freedman, *Intimate Matters: A History of Sexuality in America* 130–38 (1988).

2. Id. at 110.

3. Ellen K. Rothman, *Hands and Hearts: A History of Courtship in America* 186 (1984).

4. Id. at 187–88, 202, 246–47, 284.

5. Robert A. Woods and Albert J. Kennedy (eds.), *Young Working Girls: A Summary of Evidence from Two Thousand Social Workers* 54, 66, 106 (1913); *Report and Recommendations for the Wisconsin Legislative Committee to Investigate the White Slave Traffic and Kindred Subjects* 44 (1914); D'Emilio and Freedman, *Intimate Matters* at 183–84.

6. Kathy Peiss, *Cheap Amusements: Working Women and Leisure in Turn-of-the-Century New York* 50–51 (1986); Woods and Kennedy, *Young Working Girls* at 26–27; D'Emilio and Freedman, *Intimate Matters* at 194–201.

7. D'Emilio and Freedman, *Intimate Matters* at 136–37.

8. See, e.g., Virginia Brooks, *Little Lost Sister* (1914) (play); H. M. Lytle, *Tragedies of the White Slaves* (1912) (book); Edward Janney, *The White Slave Traffic in America* (1911) (book); Clifford G. Roe, *The Prodigal Daughter: The White Slave Evil and the Remedy* (1911) (book). See generally D'Emilio and Freedman, *Intimate Matters* at 208–9; Ruth Rosen, *The Lost Sisterhood: Prostitution in America, 1900–1918* at 112–36 (1982); Mark Thomas Connelly, *The Response to Prostitution in the Progressive Era* 114–35 (1980).

9. D'Emilio and Freedman, *Intimate Matters* at 209; Francesco Cordasco, *The White Slave Trade and the Immigrant* 58, 71–72, 80 (1981); Connelly, *The Response to Prostitution in the Progressive Era* at 56.

10. *White Slave Traffic Act,* ch. 395, 36 Stat. 825 (1910), *as amended,* 18 U.S.C. §§ 2421–2424; D'Emilio and Freedman, *Intimate Matters* at 209–10.

11. D'Emilio and Freedman, *Intimate Matters* at 210–11.

12. Irving David Steinhardt, *Ten Sex Talks for Boys* (1914); D'Emilio and Freedman, *Intimate Matters* at 206.

13. D'Emilio and Freedman, *Intimate Matters* at 211, quoting *Report of the Vice Commission of Philadelphia* 5 (1913).

14. Jervis Anderson, *This Was Harlem: A Cultural Portrait, 1900–1950* at 168–69 (1982); D'Emilio and Freedman, *Intimate Matters* at 296.

15. Kevin J. Mumford, *Interzones: Black/White Sex Districts in Chicago and New York in the Early Twentieth Century* 101 (paperback ed. 1997).

16. Id. at 31, quoting *Annual Report of the Committee of Fifteen* 12 (1923).

17. Id., quoting *Baltimore African-American* (April 10, 1920).

18. Id. at 30, citing *Pittsburgh Courier* 1 (October 17, 1923).

19. Id. at 30–31.

20. Id. at 32, quoting *New York Age* 1 (July 4, 1923).

21. Id., quoting *Pittsburgh Courier* (October 4, 1925).

22. Hazel V. Carby, "Policing the Black Woman's Body in an Urban Context," 18 *Critical Inquiry* 738, 745–46 (1992).

23. Mumford, *Interzones* at 57.

24. Id. at 58.

25. Id. at 100–101.

26. Id. at 62–63.

27. Id. at 64.

28. Id. at 98–99, 101–6.

29. Id. at 107.

30. Carby, "Policing the Black Woman's Body in an Urban Context," 18 *Critical Inquiry* at 745–46.

31. Mumford, *Interzones* at 113–14.

32. D'Emilio and Freedman, *Intimate Matters* at 202–23; Mumford, *Interzones* at 6–12.

33. Mumford, *Interzones* at 12–13.

34. For a description of Mexican women in the Southwest as attractive but "liberal to a fault," see George W. Kendall, I *Narrative of the Texan Santa Fe Expedition* 321 (1844). For an account of Mexican wives as a source of pleasures of the "baser sort" but no "intellectual enjoyment," see Lewis H. Garrard, *Wah-to-Yah and the Taos Trail* 171 (1955). For a fuller discussion of the marital expectations of Mexican Catholics, see chapter 3.

35. D'Emilio and Freedman, *Intimate Matters* at 92–93.

36. Id. at 135; Ronald Takaki, *Strangers from a Different Shore: A History of Asian Americans* 41–42 (paperback ed. 1989).

37. D'Emilio and Freedman, *Intimate Matters* at 151.

38. Donna L. Franklin, *Ensuring Inequality: The Structural Transformation of the African-American Family* 31, 34–35 (1997).

39. James Oliver Horton, "Freedom's Yoke: Gender Conventions Among Antebellum Free Blacks," 12 *Feminist Studies* 51, 70 (1986).

40. Charles S. Johnson, *Shadow of the Plantation* 74 (1934).

41. Franklin, *Ensuring Inequality* at 31–33.

42. Id. at 81–85.

43. D'Emilio and Freedman, *Intimate Matters* at 187.

44. W. E. B. Du Bois, T*he Philadelphia Negro* 166 (paperback ed. 1996).

45. Franklin, *Ensuring Inequality* at 76.

46. Id. at 78–81.

47. D'Emilio and Freedman, *Intimate Matters* at 302–18.

48. Daniel P. Moynihan, *The Negro Family: The Case for National Action* (1965); Franklin, *Ensuring Inequality* at 161–69; see also Blanche Bernstein, "Since the Moynihan Report . . . ," in *The Black Family: Essays and Studies* 15 (Robert Staples ed., 3d ed. 1986) (claiming that problems identified in the Moynihan report have only intensified over time).

49. Moynihan, *The Negro Family* at 29–48; see also Franklin, *Ensuring Inequality* at 161–62.

50. Franklin, *Ensuring Inequality* at 165–66, 201–5.

51. Robert F. Berkhofer Jr., *The White Man's Indian: Images of the American Indian from Columbus to the Present* 58–59 (1979).

52. Robert E. Bieder, *Science Encounters the Indian, 1820–1889: The Early Years of American Ethnology* 219–20 (1986).

53. Id. at 223.

54. Linda J. Lacey, "The White Man's Law and the American Indian Family in the Assimilation Era," 40 *Ark. L. Rev.* 327, 347–50 (1986).

55. Id. at 333–34, quoting E. Shaw, *Thirty-Two Years Work Among Indians 1877–1909* at 4 (n.d.).

56. Patricia Albers and Beatrice Medicine, *The Hidden Half* 34–35 (1983) (citations omitted).

57. *Americanizing the American Indian: Writings by the "Friends of the Indian" 1880–1900* at 50–51 (Frances Paul Prucha ed., 1973), quoting Merrill Gates, "Land and Law as Agents in Educating Indians," *Seventeenth Annual Report of the Board of Indian Commissioners* 17–19, 26–35 (1885).

58. H.R. Exec. Doc. No. 1, pt. 5, 48th Cong., 1st Sess. xi (1883).

59. *United States v. Quivers,* 241 U.S. 602 (1916) (adultery); *Kobogum v. Jackson Iron Co.,* 76 Mich. 498, 43 N.W. 602 (1889) (polygamy); *Earl v. Godley,* 42 Minn. 361, 44 N.W. 602 (1890) (marriage).

60. H.R. Exec. Doc. No. 1, 52d Cong., 2d Sess. 28–31 (1892); William T. Hagan, *Indian Police and Judges; Experiments in Acculturation and Control* 109–10 (1966).

61. Dawes Act, ch. 119, 24 Stat. 388–91 (1887).

62. *Americanizing the American Indian* (Prucha ed.), at 334, quoting Merrill Gates, *Proceedings of the Fourteenth Annual Meeting of the Lake Mohonk Conference of Friends of the Indian* 8–13 (1896) (emphasis in original).

63. Patricia Penn Hilden, *When Nickels Were Indians: An Urban Mixed-Blood Story* 1 (paperback ed. 1995), quoting Estelle Reel, U.S. Office of Indian Affairs, *Course of Study for the Indian Schools of the United States: Industrial and Literary* 189 (1901).

64. Id. at 1.

65. *Americanizing the American Indian* (Prucha ed.), at 243, quoting Gen. T. J. Morgan, *A Plea for the Papoose: An Address at Albany, N.Y.* (n.d.).

66. Edward H. Spicer, *Cycles of Conquest: The Impact of Spain, Mexico and the United States on the Indians of the Southwest, 1533–1960* at 489–90 (paperback ed. 1962).

67. Peter Nabokov, *Native American Testimony: A Chronicle of Indian–White Relations from Prophecy to the Present, 1492–1992* at 224 (paperback ed. 1991).

CHAPTER FIVE

1. Martha Hodes, *White Women, Black Men: Illicit Sex in the Nineteenth-Century South* 143–48, 166–75 (1997); Martha Hodes, "Sex across the Color Line: White Women, Black Men in the Nineteenth Century American South" 188–96 (Ph.D. diss., 1991). See generally Reva Siegel, "Why Equal Protection No Longer Protects: The Evolving Forms of Status-Enforcing State Action," 49 *Stan. L. Rev.* 1111, 1121–23 (1997).

2. Paul R. Spickard, *Mixed Blood: Intermarriage and Ethnic Identity in Twentieth-Century America* 374 (1989).

3. Peter W. Bardaglio, *Reconstructing the Household: Families, Sex, and the Law in the Nineteenth-Century South* 177, 180 (1995).

4. 48 Ala. 195 (1872).

5. Id. at 197.

6. Id.

7. 58 Ala. 190 (1877).

8. Id. at 194.

9. Id. at 192, 194–197. Despite the Alabama Supreme Court's new position on the nature of marriage, prominent black scholars like W. E. B. Du Bois continued to insist that "marriage is a private contract, and that given two persons of proper age and economic ability who agree to enter into that relation, it does not concern anyone but themselves as to whether one of them be white, black, or red." W. E. B. Du Bois, *The Philadelphia Negro: A Social Study* 358 (paperback ed. 1996) (originally published in 1899).

10. Michael Grossberg, *Governing the Hearth: Law and the Family in Nineteenth-Century America* 65 (1985).

11. Id. at 67–69.

12. Id. at 69–75.

13. Id. at 76.

14. Id. at 77–78.

15. Id. at 83–95, 105–16.

16. W. W. Wright, "Amalgamation," 29 *De Bow's Review* 1, 14 (1860) (emphasis in original).

17. 69 Ala. 231 (1881).

18. Ala. Rev. Code §§ 3598, 3602 (1867).

19. 69 Ala. at 232.

20. Id.

21. 106 U.S. 583 (1882).

22. Brief and Argument for Appellee at 2–3, 14, *Pace v. Alabama,* 106 U.S. 583 (1882) (No. 908) (October Term, 1882).

23. 106 U.S. at 585.

24. Bardaglio, *Reconstructing the Household* at 185–86. For a discussion of states' preeminent role in domestic relations law despite an expanding national presence, see Anne C. Dailey, "Federalism and Families," 143 *U. Pa. L. Rev.* 1787, 1819–25 (1995).

25. Brief of Plaintiff in Error at 5, *Pace v. Alabama,* 106 U.S. 583 (1882) (No. 908) (October Term, 1882).

26. Grossberg, *Governing the Hearth* at 138.

27. Isaac Franklin Russell, "The Indian before the Law," 18 *Yale L.J.* 328, 331 (1908–9).

28. Grossberg, *Governing the Hearth* at 138. See chapter 2 for a fuller discussion of the historical regulation of Asian–white intermarriage.

29. Gilbert T. Stephenson, *Race Distinctions in American Law* 78 (1910).

30. Edward Byron Reuter, *Race Mixture: Studies in Intermarriage and Miscegenation* 81–101 (1931).

31. 163 U.S. 537 (1896).

32. Siegel, "Why Equal Protection No Longer Protects," *49 Stan. L. Rev.* at 1119–29.

33. J. Harvie Wilkinson III, *From Brown to Bakke: The Supreme Court and School Integration, 1954–1978* at 17 (paperback ed. 1979).

34. Grossberg, *Governing the Hearth* at 140; Stephen Trombley, *The Right to Reproduce: A History of Coercive Sterilization* (1988). For a description of the eugenic roots of Virginia's Racial Integrity Act, which banned miscegenation, see Paul A. Lombardo, "Miscegenation, Eugenics, and Racism: Footnotes to *Loving v. Virginia*," 21 *U.C. Davis L. Rev.* 421 (1988).

35. Grossberg, *Governing the Hearth* at 151.

36. 274 U.S. 200 (1927).

37. Id. at 207.

38. Id.

39. Id. at 208.

40. *Meyer v. Nebraska*, 262 U.S. 390 (1923); *Bartels v. Iowa*, 262 U.S. 404 (1923); *Pierce v. Society of Sisters*, 268 U.S. 510 (1925); *Farrington v. Tokushige*, 273 U.S. 284 (1927).

41. 262 U.S. at 399.

42. Id. at 402.

43. *Bartels v. Iowa*, 262 U.S. 404, 412 (1923) (dissenting opinion of Justice Holmes in which Justice Sutherland concurred).

44. 316 U.S. 535 (1942).

45. Id. at 536–37.

46. Id.

47. Id. at 541.

48. Id.

49. Id. at 537–43.

50. See Steven F. Lawson, *Running for Freedom: Civil Rights and Black Politics in America since 1941* at 1–30 (1991).

51. Brief of N.A.A.C.P. Legal Defense and Educational Fund, Inc. as Amicus Curiae at 17–18, *Loving v. Virginia*, 388 U.S. 1 (1967) (No. 395) (October Term, 1966). According to one study, of the thirty-one states with antimiscegenation laws at the end of World War II, fifteen had eliminated the statutes by 1967. Robert J. Sickels, *Race, Marriage, and the Law* 64 (1972). For a case discussing the Oregon legislature's 1951 repeal of a ban on interracial marriage, see *In re Crawford*, 242 Or. 259, 409 P.2d 330 (1965).

52. 32 Cal. 2d 711, 198 P.2d 17 (1948).

53. Cal. Civ. Code §§ 60, 69 (1933).

54. 32 Cal. 2d at 715, 198 P.2d at 18–21.

55. Id. at 717, 198 P.2d at 21. The petitioners also contended that the statutes violated the First Amendment because they prohibited the free exercise of their Roman Catholic faith, which permitted such marriages. The court's decision did not focus heavily on

the free exercise claim because the First Amendment protects beliefs, not conduct. Id. at 713, 198 P.2d at 18.

56. Id. at 715–16, 198 P.2d at 19–20.

57. Id. at 716, 198 P.2d at 20.

58. See Respondent's Supplemental Brief in Opposition to Writ of Mandate in the Supreme Court of the State of California, at 61–116, *Perez v. Moroney* sub nom. *Perez v. Sharp,* 32 Cal. 2d 711, 198 P.2d 17 (1948) (L.A. No. 20305) (setting forth biological and sociological objections to interracial marriage).

59. 32 Cal. 2d at 720, 198 P.2d at 22.

60. Id. at 718, 198 P.2d at 21.

61. For example, "Hindus" and "Mexicans" were not covered. Id. at 721, 198 P.2d at 22–23. But see chapter 3 for a discussion of restrictions on Asian Indian intermarriage in California.

62. Id. at 721–22, 198 P.2d at 23.

63. Id. at 722, 198 P.2d at 23. The court also distinguished cases involving adultery or fornication, noting that these were not fundamental rights like marriage. Id. at 726, 198 P.2d at 26.

64. Id. at 724, 198 P.2d at 25.

65. Id.

66. Id. at 725, 198 P.2d at 25.

67. Id. at 727, 198 P.2d at 26. The opinion noted that if the state's reasoning were adopted, it could support a ban on interreligious marriages as well. Id.

68. Id.

69. Id. at 728–32, 198 P.2d at 27–29. Two justices concurred separately. Justice Jesse W. Carter summarized the constitutional history leading up to passage of the Thirteenth, Fourteenth, and Fifteenth Amendments and contended that the statutes had always been unconstitutional because they were the products of "ignorance, prejudice, and intolerance." Id. at 732–40, 198 P.2d at 29–34. Justice Douglas L. Edmonds adopted a First Amendment rationale for striking down the legislation. Id. at 740–42, 198 P.2d at 34–35.

70. Id. at 742–59, 198 P.2d at 35–45.

71. Id. at 760, 198 P.2d at 46.

72. Id. at 760–63, 198 P.2d at 45–47.

73. Id. at 758, 198 P.2d at 45 (citing W. E. Castle, Bussey Institution, Harvard University).

74. Id. at 759, 198 P.2d at 45, quoting John La Farge, *The Race Question and the Negro* 196–97 (1943).

75. At least one state court judge noted in dictum that the *Perez* decision cast doubt on the validity of antimiscegenation laws. *Wilkins v. Zelichowski,* 43 N.J. Super. 598, 129 A.2d 459 (1957).

76. Sickels, *Race, Marriage, and the Law* at 68.

77. Id.

78. Id.

79. Id. at 72.

80. Id. at 112.

81. 347 U.S. 483 (1954).

82. *Jackson v. Alabama,* 348 U.S. 888 (1954).

83. Brief and Argument in Opposition to Petition for Writ of Certiorari, at 14, 16–

17, *Jackson v. Alabama,* 348 U.S. 888 (1954) (No. 118, Misc.) (October Term, 1954); Sickels, *Race, Marriage, and the Law* at 3; Peter Wallenstein, "Personal Liberty and Private Law: Race, Marriage, and the Law of Freedom: Alabama and Virginia, 1860's–1960's," 70 *Chi.-Kent L. Rev.* 371, 415–16 (1994) (citing personal papers of Justice William O. Douglas); Philip Elman, "The Solicitor General's Office, Justice Frankfurter and Civil Rights Litigation, 1946–1960: An Oral History," 100 *Harv. L. Rev.* 817, 845–47 (1987) (concluding that "the last thing in the world the Justices wanted to deal with at that time was the question of interracial marriage").

84. Ed Cray, *Chief Justice: A Biography of Earl Warren* 450 (1997), quoting Gerald Gunther, now a constitutional law professor at Stanford.

85. 350 U.S. 891 (1955), *appeal reconsidered,* 350 U.S. 985 (1956).

86. The Virginia statute provided: "It shall hereafter be unlawful for any white person in this State to marry any save a white person, or a person with no other admixture of blood than white and American Indian. For the purpose of this chapter, the term 'white' shall apply only to such person as has no trace whatever of any blood other than Caucasian; but persons who have one-sixteenth or less of the blood of the American Indian and have no other non-Caucasic blood shall be deemed to be white persons." The Virginia law went on to declare that all marriages between a white person and a "colored" person were absolutely void; the law explicitly applied to persons who left the state in order to marry and who intended to return afterward. Violation of the provision was a felony punishable by a penitentiary sentence of one to five years. *Naim v. Naim,* 197 Va. 80, 81–82, 87 S.E.2d 749, 750–51 (1955).

87. Lucas A. Powe, *The Warren Court and American Politics* (2000). For a fuller discussion of restrictions on Asian immigration, see chapter 2.

88. Statement as to Jurisdiction by Appellant Ham Say Naim, at 7–8; Sickels, *Race, Marriage, and the Law* at 103; Wallenstein, "Personal Liberty and Private Law," 70 *Chi.-Kent L. Rev.* at 417. On appeal, David Carliner of the American Civil Liberties Union represented the husband. A number of organizations filed amicus briefs aligning themselves with the husband's cause; these included the American Jewish Congress, the Association of American Indian Affairs, the Association of Immigration and Nationality Lawyers, and the Japanese American Citizens League. The Virginia state attorney general filed an amicus brief on behalf of the wife at the court's invitation. Sickels, *Race, Marriage, and the Law* at 104.

89. 197 Va. at 89–90, 87 S.E.2d at 756; Sickels, *Race, Marriage, and the Law* at 103–4.

90. 197 Va. at 80, 87 S.E.2d at 752–54.

91. 197 Va. 134, 90 S.E.2d 849 (1956); "Virginia's Top Tribunal Rejects Order of U.S. Supreme Court," *Richmond Times-Dispatch,* Jan. 19, 1956, at 12.

92. Cray, *Chief Justice* at 310.

93. Powe, *The Warren Court and American Politics* at 72 (criticizing *Naim v. Naim,* 350 U.S. 891 (1955), *appeal reconsidered,* 350 U.S. 985 [1956]).

94. Walter F. Murphy, *Elements of Judicial Strategy* 193 (1964); Cray, *Chief Justice* at 451; Memorandum from Justice John Marshall Harlan to Other Supreme Court Justices (Nov. 4, 1955) (John Marshall Harlan Papers, Box 11, Mudd Library, Princeton University); Wallenstein, "Personal Liberty and Private Law," 70 *Chi.-Kent L. Rev.* at 416–19.

95. Civil Rights Act of 1964, Pub. L. No. 88-352, 78 Stat. 241 (1964), codified at 42

U.S.C. §§ 2000 et seq. For a description of the events surrounding passage of the Act, see Robert D. Loevy, *To End All Segregation: The Politics of the Passage of the Civil Rights Act of 1964* (1990).

96. Wilkinson, *From Brown to Bakke* at 102–8.

97. Id. at 108–27.

98. The Court reaffirmed its support for the principle of parental freedom in *Meyer* when it decided *Wisconsin v. Yoder,* 406 U.S. 205 (1972). There, the Court held that the Amish could preserve their way of life and bring up their children as they saw fit by keeping teenagers out of high school in defiance of compulsory education laws. Id. at 209–13, 215–29, 232–34.

99. 381 U.S. 479 (1965).

100. Id. at 485–86.

101. Id. at 486.

102. Id. at 485.

103. Id. at 507–31.

104. *Eisenstadt v. Baird,* 405 U.S. 438 (1972).

105. Id. at 448–49. The penalty of five years in prison for doctors who provided married couples with contraceptives also was extreme. Id. at 449. The Court further rejected the argument that the statute was a public health measure, for it could find no reason to distinguish between married and unmarried persons on this ground. Id. at 450–52.

106. Id. at 452–53. By citing *Skinner* as authority for this proposition, the Court indicated that it was expanding the constitutional protections for sexual autonomy. Id. at 453–54. In a subsequent case, the Court followed the reasoning in *Griswold* and *Baird* to strike down a New York law limiting minors' access to nonprescription contraceptives. *Carey v. Population Services International,* 431 U.S. 678 (1977). Even more controversial was the Court's decision that the right to privacy encompassed a woman's decision to terminate a pregnancy. *Roe v. Wade,* 410 U.S. 113, 153 (1973). The Court's continued commitment to protecting the right to legalized abortion despite widespread controversy is powerful evidence of the ongoing vitality of the constitutional right to privacy. For a description of the Court's internal dissension over the propriety of *Roe,* see Bernard Schwartz, *Decision: How the Supreme Court Decides Cases* 36–64 (1996).

107. 405 U.S. at 465–72.

108. 379 U.S. 184 (1964); for a discussion of the politics that influenced the timing of the Court's decisions holding antimiscegenation laws unconstitutional, see Wallenstein, "Personal Liberty and Private Law," 70 *Chi.-Kent L. Rev.* at 435–37.

109. Sickels, *Race, Marriage, and the Law* at 101.

110. *McLaughlin v. State,* 153 So. 2d 1, 1–2 (Fla. 1963); Sickels, *Race, Marriage, and the Law* at 101.

111. Transcript of Proceedings at 55, 84, *McLaughlin v. Florida,* 379 U.S. 184 (1964) (No. 585) (October Term, 1963).

112. Id. at 23, 26, 36, 41, 46, 82, (testimony of Mrs. Dora Goodnick, landlady; Detective Stanley Marcus; Detective Nicholas Valeriani; and Josephine DeCesare, Secretary, City Manager's Office, Miami Beach).

113. Id. at 58 (testimony of Detective Valeriani).

114. Id. at 33, 60 (objections of Mr. Graves); Motion for New Trial, *State v. McLaughlin,* No. 62-1385 (July 3, 1962).

115. The statute provided for penalties of imprisonment not to exceed one year or of a fine not to exceed five hundred dollars. 153 So. 2d at 1 n. 1. The couple was sentenced to thirty days in jail and fined one hundred and fifty dollars each. They had served most of the sentence before being released on bond pending appeal. 153 So. 2d at 2; Sickels, *Race, Marriage, and the Law* at 101.

116. 379 U.S. at 187 n. 6, 195; Sickels, *Race, Marriage, and the Law* at 101.

117. 153 So. 2d at 2.

118. Id. at 2–3; Sickels, *Race, Marriage, and the Law* at 101.

119. Alexander Bickel, *New Republic,* May 30, 1964, at 4–5. In light of this assertion about the civil rights movement's agenda, it is interesting to note that the National Association for the Advancement of Colored People (NAACP) Legal Defense and Education Fund represented McLaughlin on appeal to the Court.

120. 379 U.S. at 187 n. 6, 195–96. Justice Harlan, in concurrence, agreed that the Court need not reach the validity of the interracial marriage ban. He concluded that the interracial adultery statute was not necessary to the ban's enforcement and thus could be considered separately on its own merits. Id. at 197–98.

121. In a later decision, the U.S. Supreme Court made clear that its substantive due process jurisprudence did not "stand for the proposition that any kind of private sexual conduct between consenting adults is insulated from state proscription. . . ." *Bowers v. Hardwick,* 478 U.S. 186, 191 (1986). The Court focused only on consensual homosexual sodomy, noting that it had "[n]o connection [with] family, marriage, or procreation," id., and that it was neither "implicit in the concept of ordered liberty" nor "deeply rooted in this Nation's history and tradition," id. at 194. The constitutional limits on regulation of consensual heterosexual acts, including oral and anal intercourse, were not addressed. Id. at 188 n. 2.

122. 379 U.S. at 187; Sickels, *Race, Marriage, and the Law* at 102. Interestingly, Justice White's opinion makes it impossible to determine whether the black cohabitant was male or female, although the courts below had made the gender and race of each cohabitant clear. Presumably, the Court was reluctant openly to empower black men to live with white women without benefit of marriage.

123. 379 U.S. at 188.

124. Id. at 191–92.

125. Id. at 193.

126. Justices Potter Stewart and William O. Douglas went even further in their concurrence, rejecting Florida's justification altogether and insisting that there was no conceivable purpose that could justify the Florida law. Id. at 198. In their view, "it is simply not possible for a state law to be valid under our constitution which makes the criminality of an act depend upon the race of the actor." Id.

127. Id. at 194.

128. Id.

129. In response to Justice White's draft opinion indicating that only cross-racial adultery and fornication dispensed with the requirement of proof of intercourse, Justice Frankfurter wrote that he wondered whether Justice White was "such a man of the world that he does not know that when a couple cohabit, I don't know for how long they did so in the Florida case they certainly fornicated. . . . [H]as he never heard of Taft C.J.'s famous sentence that what everybody knows judges are also supposed to know." Schwartz, *Decision,* at 59–60.

130. Brief for Appellants at 27–30, *McLaughlin v. Florida,* 379 U.S. 184 (1964) (No. 585) (October Term, 1963).

131. Response to Jurisdictional Statement at 14–15, *McLaughlin v. Florida,* 379 U.S. 184 (1964) (No. 585) (October Term, 1963); Brief of Appellee at 56–59, *McLaughlin v. Florida,* 379 U.S. 184 (1964) (No. 585) (October Term, 1963).

132. 379 U.S. at 187–88 n. 6.

133. Sickels, *Race, Marriage, and the Law* at 102–3.

134. 388 U.S. 1 (1967).

135. Sickels, *Race, Marriage, and the Law* at 76.

136. Id.

137. Id. For an account of one family's attempt to address its mixed origins, which led some members to pass as white and others to identify themselves as black, see Shirlee Taylor Haizlip, *The Sweeter the Juice: A Family Memoir in Black and White* (1994).

138. 388 U.S. at 2–3; Sickels, *Race, Marriage, and the Law* at 78.

139. 388 U.S. at 3; Sickels, *Race, Marriage, and the Law* at 18.

140. In 1963, the Lovings wrote to U.S. Attorney General Robert F. Kennedy, seeking his help. Although sympathetic, Kennedy felt that there was nothing his office could do. He referred the Lovings to the ACLU, which appointed attorneys to represent the couple in contesting their conviction. Sickels, *Race, Marriage, and the Law* at 78–79.

141. Id. at 79.

142. 388 U.S. at 3; Sickels, *Race, Marriage, and the Law* at 80.

143. The judges rejected the ACLU's claim that the Virginia courts had long made clear their support for antimiscegenation laws and that an appeal therefore would be futile. 388 U.S. at 3; Sickels, *Race, Marriage, and the Law* at 81.

144. 388 U.S. at 3; Sickels, *Race, Marriage, and the Law* at 81.

145. *Loving v. Commonwealth,* 207 Va. 924, 931, 147 S.E.2d 78, 83 (1966).

146. Id. at 926–29, 147 S.E.2d at 80–82.

147. Id. at 929, 147 S.E.2d at 82. The Racial Integrity Act, which was the basis for the Lovings' conviction, had been sponsored by two powerful Virginians, John Powell and Walter Plecker, who were both eugenicists and members of the white supremacist Anglo Saxon Clubs of America. Powell used his influence to spearhead a letter-writing and editorial campaign for the institution of eugenic legislation; Plecker, from his platform as a prominent physician in the State Bureau of Vital Statistics, argued for the scientific legitimacy of laws that restricted racial mixing. In fact, Powell and Plecker took an active role in ensuring vigorous enforcement of the Racial Integrity Act once it passed, especially when it faced early challenges. Lombardo, "Miscegenation, Eugenics, and Racism," 21 *U.C. Davis L. Rev.* at 424–50. For a history of Virginia's antimiscegenation law, see generally Walter Wadlington, "The *Loving* Case: Virginia's Anti-Miscegenation Statute in Historical Perspective," 52 *Va. L. Rev.* 1189 (1966).

148. 388 U.S. at 2. The case was argued for the ACLU by David Carliner, who had represented the Chinese husband in *Naim,* and Melvin Wulf. The Japanese American Citizens League, the National Association for the Advancement of Colored People, the NAACP Legal Defense and Educational Fund, and various Catholic organizations filed amicus briefs on the Lovings' behalf. The state of Virginia was represented by Attorney General Button, and the state of North Carolina filed an amicus brief in support of Virginia's case. Sickels, *Race, Marriage, and the Law* at 83, 85.

149. 388 U.S. at 9–10; Sickels, *Race, Marriage, and the Law* at 83–84, 104–5, 106.

150. Sickels, *Race, Marriage, and the Law* at 105, 106–7.

151. Brief and Appendix on Behalf of Appellee at 7, *Loving v. Virginia*, 388 U.S. 1 (1967) (No. 395) (October Term, 1966). Or as the U.S. Supreme Court put it: "On the question [of eugenics], the State argues, the scientific evidence is substantially in doubt and, consequently, this Court should defer to the wisdom of the state legislature in adopting its policy of discouraging interracial marriages." 388 U.S. at 8.

152. *May It Please the Court* 282–83 (Peter Irons and Stephanie Guitton eds., 1993).

153. Id. at 283.

154. Cray, *Chief Justice* at 450.

155. *May It Please the Court* (Irons and Guitton eds.), at 284.

156. 388 U.S. at 10.

157. Id. at 11–12.

158. Id. at 7–12; Sickels, *Race, Marriage, and the Law* at 108–10. Interestingly, in contrast to the *McLaughlin* decision, the *Loving* opinion made clear the race of the white husband and black wife. Presumably, the Court was more comfortable explicitly empowering a white man to marry a black woman than empowering a black man to cohabit with a white woman.

159. 388 U.S. at 12.

160. Id. The Court thus echoed the California Supreme Court's reasoning in *Perez* some twenty years before, although it alluded to that decision only briefly in a footnote collecting state laws on antimiscegenation. Id. at 6 n. 5.

161. Cray, *Chief Justice* at 452–53.

162. For the most famous expression of these concerns about forced association in the name of equality, see Herbert Wechsler, "Toward Neutral Principles of Constitutional Law," 73 *Harv. L. Rev.* 1 (1959).

163. For a discussion of how the substantive due process analysis interacted with equal protection concerns in *Loving*, see Michael W. Dowdle, "The Descent of Antidiscrimination: On the Intellectual Origins of the Current Equal Protection Jurisprudence," 66 *N.Y.U. L. Rev.* 1165, 1225–27 (1991).

164. Brief of the National Association for the Advancement of Colored People as Amicus Curiae, at 7–9, *Loving v. Virginia*, 388 U.S. 1 (1967) (No. 395) (October Term, 1966); Brief of Amici Curiae Japanese American Citizens League at 17–20, *Loving v. Virginia*, 388 U.S. 1 (1967) (No. 395) (October Term, 1966).

165. Powe, *The Warren Court and American Politics* at 286, 294–95; Andrew Kull, *The Color-Blind Constitution* 170 (1992).

CHAPTER SIX

1. 388 U.S. 1 (1967). This decision is discussed at length in chapter 5.

2. Robert J. Sickels, *Race, Marriage, and the Law* 112–13 (1972). Despite the *Loving* decision, Alabama retained the antimiscegenation provision in its post-Reconstruction state constitution. Recently, the legislature voted to remove the clause, now a dead letter, and the voters will decide whether to do so in a November 2000 referendum. Hendrik Hertzberg, "Comment: Bad News for Bigots," *New Yorker*, Mar. 13, 2000, at 29–30. Even when an antimiscegenation law is not on the books, an interracial couple occasionally faces obstacles to getting married. A pastor in southern Ohio recently denied a request by a white woman and a black man to marry in his church because the Bible

forbids interracial marriages. Dennis M. Mahoney, "Pastor Shuts Door on Interracial Couple," *Columbus Dispatch,* July 8, 2000, at 1A. The couple eventually exchanged their wedding vows at a church in a nearby community. Rita Price, "Wedding Bells Ring for Interracial Couple," *Columbus Dispatch,* July 16, 2000, at 1A.

3. By contrast, demographic work in the 1950s focused mainly on interreligious marriage to determine whether Protestants, Catholics, and Jews would eliminate their differences through a triple melting pot. Mildred Kornacker, "Cultural Significance of Intermarriage: A Comparative Approach," 1 *Int'l J. Soc. Family* 147, 152–53 (1971).

4. See, e.g., D. Y. Yuan, "Significant Demographic Characteristics of Chinese Who Intermarry in the United States," 3 *California Sociologist* 184, 184 (1980); Ralph B. Cazares, Edward Murguia, and W. Parker Frisbie, "Mexican American Intermarriage in a Nonmetropolitan Context," 65 *Soc. Sci. Q.* 626, 626 (1984).

5. Thomas P. Monahan, "An Overview of Statistics on Interracial Marriage in the United States, with Data on Its Extent from 1963–1970," 38 *J. Marriage & the Family* 223, 224 (1976).

6. One caveat should be noted in connection with these terms. Like government agencies, researchers typically rely on self-identification to determine a person's race or ethnicity. The categories that scholars use generally do not recognize mixed-race origins, so a marriage could be classified as interracial when one party is white and the other is of mixed origin but is classified as nonwhite. For instance, a man whose mother is white and father is black will be categorized as black. Despite his white ancestry, this man's marriage to a white woman will be treated as interracial. For a fuller discussion of the problems of racial classification schemes, see chapter 8.

7. House Committee on Government Reform and Oversight, Subcommittee on Government Management, Information and Technology, *Prepared Testimony of Professor Mary C. Waters, Department of Sociology, Harvard University,* May 22, 1997 (Federal News Service); "I, Thee, We, Them," *Economist,* June 20, 1998, at 31.

8. David Heer, "Negro–White Marriage in the United States," 28 *J. Marriage & the Family* 262, 265–67 (1966). By 1960, there were 51,409 black–white couples in the United States, a figure which represented only a little more than 0.1 percent of the total number of married couples, or 1.7 percent of those marriages involving a black. Sophia F. McDowell, "Black–White Intermarriage in the United States," 1 *Int'l J. Soc. Family* 49, 53–54 (1971).

9. Yisrael Ellman, "Intermarriage in the United States: A Comparative Study of Jews and Other Ethnic and Religious Groups," 49 *Jewish Social Studies* 1, 3 (1987). For example, David Heer reports a 26 percent increase in black–white intermarriages between 1960 and 1970. David Heer, "The Prevalence of Black–White Marriage in the United States, 1960 and 1970," 36 *J. Marriage & the Family* 246, 247 (1974).

10. Ellman, "Intermarriage in the United States," 49 *Jewish Social Studies* at 3; Barbara Foley Wilson, "Marriage's Melting Pot," 7 *Am. Demographics* 34, 38 (1984).

11. Jack Kroll (with Vern E. Smith and Andrew Murr), "Spiking a Fever," *Newsweek,* June 10, 1991, at 44, 46.

12. Ellman, "Intermarriage in the United States," 49 *Jewish Social Studies* at 3; Wilson, "Marriage's Melting Pot," 7 *Am. Demographics* at 45.

13. Ernest Porterfield, *Black and White Mixed Marriages* 33 (1978).

14. Heer, "Negro–White Marriage in the United States," 28 *J. Marriage & the Family* at 267.

15. Heer, "The Prevalence of Black–White Marriage in the United States, 1960 and 1970," 36 *J. Marriage & the Family* at 247; Wilson, "Marriage's Melting Pot," 7 *Am. Demographics* at 34.

16. Ellman, "Intermarriage in the United States," 49 *Jewish Social Studies* at 3; Kroll, "Spiking a Fever," *Newsweek,* June 10, 1991, at 46.

17. For a full description of the history of black–white relationships during slavery, see chapter 2.

18. William Julius Wilson, T*he Truly Disadvantaged* 90–92 (paperback ed. 1987); Robert Staples, "Beyond the Black Family: The Trend toward Singlehood," in *The Black Family: Essays and Studies* 99 (Robert Staples ed., 3d ed. 1986); Graham B. Spanier and Paul C. Glick, "Mate Selection Differentials between Whites and Blacks in the United States," in id. at 114. But cf. Robert G. Wood, "Marriage Rates and Marriageable Men: A Test of the Wilson Hypothesis," 30 *J. Hum. Resources* 163 (1995) (finding that drops in the income and employment levels of black men account for only a fraction of the decline in marriage rates).

19. Charles E. Smith, "Negro–White Intermarriage: Forbidden Sexual Union," 2 *J. Sex Research* 169, 170–72 (1966); Calvin C. Hernton, *Sex and Racism in America* 59–60, 123–27 (1965); William H. Grier and Price M. Cobbs, *Black Rage* 41, 87 (1968); Charles Herbert Stember, *Sexual Racism* 159–65 (1976).

20. Paul R. Spickard, *Mixed Blood: Intermarriage and Ethnic Identity in Twentieth-Century America* 252–59 (1989); bell hooks, *Feminist Theory: From Margin to Center* 13–14 (1984).

21. Nikki Giovanni, "Woman Poem," in Nikki Giovanni, *Black Feeling, Black Talk, Black Judgement* 78 (1970).

22. Kathy Russell, Midge Wilson, and Ronald Hall, *The Color Complex: The Politics of Skin Color among African Americans* 117 (paperback ed. 1992).

23. See Grier and Cobbs, *Black Rage* at 49, 63; Hernton, *Sex and Racism in America* at 136–42.

24. Michele Wallace, *Black Macho and the Myth of the Superwoman* 117 (paperback ed. 1990); Russell, Wilson, and Hall, *The Color Complex* at 118 ("some African-American women . . . believe the feminist movement is responsible for the recent increase in marriages between Black females and White males" because white women have alienated their male counterparts).

25. *Prepared Testimony of Professor Mary C. Waters.*

26. As in chapter 2, this discussion focuses on Chinese, Japanese, and Koreans because these Asian American subgroups have resided in the United States in substantial numbers for a relatively long period of time. Far less research on other Asian American subgroups' experience with intermarriage is available because their numbers were quite small until recently.

27. Yuan, "Significant Demographic Characteristics of Chinese Who Intermarry in the United States," 3 *California Sociologist* at 186. Importantly, the Chinese also consider interethnic marriages to other Asian groups, such as the Japanese and Koreans, a form of exogamy. Id. at 184–85. However, the focus here is on Chinese–white intermarriage to make possible comparisons with the statistics presented on blacks and Latinos. The rate of intermarriage among Chinese and blacks or Chinese and Latinos is negligible. Id. at 185–86.

28. John N. Tinker, "Intermarriage and Assimilation in a Plural Society: Japanese-

Americans in the United States," 5 *Marriage & Family Rev.* 61, 63 (1982); Betty Lee Sung, *Chinese American Intermarriage* 17 (1990).

29. Spickard, *Mixed Blood* at 55–58. See chapter 3 for a discussion of the treatment of intermarried Japanese during World War II.

30. Harry H. L. Kitano and Lynn Kyung Chai, "Korean Interracial Marriage," 5 *Marriage & Family Rev.* 75, 78–79, 81, 84, 86–87 (1982); see also Harry H. L. Kitano, Wai-tsang Yeung, Lynn Chai, and Herbert Hatanaka, "Asian-American Interracial Marriage," 46 *J. Marriage & the Family* 179, 185 (1984).

31. John Leland and Gregory Beals (with John McCormick, Allison Samuels, Nadine Joseph, and Yahlin Chang), "In Living Colors," *Newsweek,* May 5, 1997, at 58.

32. Tinker, "Intermarriage and Assimilation in a Plural Society," 5 *Marriage & Family Rev.* at 65–67; Harry H. L. Kitano and Wai-tsang Yeung, "Chinese Interracial Marriage," 5 *Marriage & Family Rev.* 35, 38–39, 43–45 (1982) (findings based on marital statistics for Los Angeles County for the years 1975, 1977, and 1979); Yuan, "Significant Demographic Characteristics of Chinese Who Intermarry in the United States," 3 *California Sociologist* at 187–92; Kitano, Yeung, Chai, and Hatanaka, "Asian-American Interracial Marriage," 46 *J. Marriage & the Family* at 185; Kitano and Chai, "Korean Interracial Marriage," 5 *Marriage & Family Rev.* at 78–79, 81, 84, 86–87 (1982).

33. Sean-Shong Hwang, Rogelio Saenz, and Benigno E. Aguirre, "Structural and Individual Determinants of Outmarriage among Chinese Americans, Filipino Americans, and Japanese Americans in California," 64 *Sociological Inquiry* 396, 407–8 (1994).

34. Norimitsu Onishi, "Japanese in America Looking Beyond Past to Shape Future," *N.Y. Times,* Dec. 25, 1995, § 1, at p. 1.

35. Yuan, "Significant Demographic Characteristics of Chinese Who Intermarry in the United States," 3 *California Sociologist* at 187–92 (nationwide 20 percent sample based on 1970 census); Kitano and Yeung, "Chinese Interracial Marriage," 5 *Marriage & Family Rev.* at 38–39, 43–45 (findings based on marital statistics for Los Angeles County for the years 1975, 1977, and 1979); Kitano and Chai, "Korean Interracial Marriage," 5 *Marriage & Family Rev.* at 78–79, 81, 84, 86–87 (data for 1975, 1977, and 1979 from Los Angeles County); Kitano, Yeung, Chai, and Hatanaka, "Asian-American Interracial Marriage," 46 *J. Marriage & the Family* at 180–81, 183 (data for 1975, 1977, ad 1979 in Los Angeles County plus data for 1970–80 from Hawaii). However, one study of 1980 census data for California has reported that the rates of outmarriage among men and women of Chinese descent are approximately equivalent, although Japanese, Korean, and Vietnamese women marry out at a higher rate than their male counterparts. Robert M. Jiobu, *Ethnicity & Assimilation: Blacks, Chinese, Filipinos, Japanese, Korean, Mexicans, Vietnamese and Whites* 161 (paperback ed. 1988). Another study of marriage license applications in New York City during 1972–82 also found approximately equal outmarriage rates for Chinese men and women. Sung, *Chinese American Intermarriage* at 10–11.

36. See chapter 2 for a full account of these historical circumstances.

37. Indeed, Asian American women who marry out are less well educated than those who marry in, while education has no effect on Asian American male outmarriage rates. Sean-Shong Hwang, Rogelio Saenz, and Benigno Aguirre, "The SES Selectivity of Interracially Married Asians," 29 *Int'l Migration Rev.* 469, 481–82, 486 (1995).

38. Yuan, "Significant Demographic Characteristics of Chinese Who Intermarry in the United States," 3 *California Sociologist* at 191; Tinker, "Intermarriage and Assimilation in a Plural Society," 5 *Marriage & Family Rev.* at 69–71.

39. Spickard, *Mixed Blood* at 129–31 ("Many of the men were looking for the docile Asian women that American stereotypes had led them to expect. . . ."); Yuan, "Significant Demographic Characteristics of Chinese Who Intermarry in the United States," 3 *California Sociologist* at 192 ("[T]he stereotypical image of an 'Oriental doll' still exists in the minds of many Caucasian males. . . ."); Kitano and Chai, "Korean Interracial Marriage," 5 *Marriage & Family Rev.* at 88 ("The current Asian female stereotype is that they make good wives. The definition of 'good' may include everything from being obedient, to taking care of the husband to not talking back. . . ."); Joan Walsh, "Asian Women, Caucasian Men," *S.F. Examiner,* Dec. 2, 1990, at 11 (*Image Magazine*) (describing fantasies of the submissive Asian female who is exotic or caters to men).

40. Sumi K. Cho, "Converging Stereotypes in Racialized Sexual Harassment: Where the Model Minority Meets Suzie Wong," in *Critical Race Feminism: A Reader* 203, 204–6 (Adrien Katherine Wing ed., 1997) ("Asian Pacific women suffer greater harassment due to racialized ascriptions [exotic, hyper-eroticized, masochistic, desirous of sexual domination]. . . .").

41. Thomas J. Espenshade and Wenzhen Ye, "Differential Fertility within an Ethnic Minority: The Effect of 'Trying Harder' among Chinese-American Women," 41 *Soc. Probs.* 97, 109 (1994).

42. Ben Fong-Torres, "Why Are There No Male Asian Anchormen on TV?" in *Men's Lives* 208, 210 (Michael S. Kimmel and Michael A. Messner eds., 3d ed. 1995).

43. David Mura, *Where the Body Meets Memory: An Odyssey of Race, Sexuality & Identity* 83 (1996).

44. *Prepared Testimony of Professor Mary C. Waters.*

45. For a description of the status of Native Americans under antimiscegenation laws, see chapter 3.

46. Gary D. Sandefur and Trudy McKinnell, "American Indian Intermarriage," 15 *Soc. Sci. Research* 347, 347–48 (1986).

47. Id. at 348, 356, 360.

48. Karl Eschbach, "The Enduring and Vanishing American Indian: American Indian Population Growth and Intermarriage in 1990," 18 *Ethnic and Racial Studies* 89, 95 (1995).

49. Sandefur and McKinnell, "American Indian Intermarriage," 15 *Soc. Sci. Research* at 348, 356, 360.

50. Eschbach, "The Enduring and Vanishing American Indian," 18 *Ethnic and Racial Studies* at 89.

51. Id. at 90–92, 103.

52. Sandefur and McKinnell, "American Indian Intermarriage," 15 *Soc. Sci. Research* at 360.

53. Eschbach, "The Enduring and Vanishing American Indian," 18 *Ethnic and Racial Studies* at 96–97, 102–5.

54. Ellman, "Intermarriage in the United States," 49 *Jewish Social Studies* at 3.

55. Richard D. Alba and Reid M. Golden, "Patterns of Ethnic Marriage in the U.S.," 65 *Social Forces* 202, 202–3 (1986).

56. Cazares, Murguia, and Frisbie, "Mexican American Intermarriage in a Nonmetropolitan Context," 65 *Soc. Sci. Q.* at 631–33; Edward Murguia and Ralph B. Cazares, "Intermarriage of Mexican Americans," 5 *Marriage & Fam. Rev.* 91, 95 (1982); Celestino Fernandez and Louis Holscher, "Chicano–Anglo Intermarriage in Arizona, 1960–

1980: An Exploratory Study of Eight Counties," 5 *Hisp. J. Behav. Sci.* 291, 300–302 (1983).

57. Jiobu, *Ethnicity & Assimilation* at 153–54.

58. Greta A. Gilbertson, Joseph P. Fitzpatrick, and Lijun Yang, "Hispanic Outmarriage in New York City—New Evidence from 1991," 30 *Int'l Migration Rev.* 445, 450 (1996).

59. Id. at 454.

60. Murguia and Cazares, "Intermarriage of Mexican Americans," 5 *Marriage & Fam. Rev.* at 95; Fernandez and Holscher, "Chicano–Anglo Intermarriage in Arizona, 1960–1980," 5 *Hisp. J. Behav. Sci.* at 300; Cazares, Murguia, and Frisbie, "Mexican American Intermarriage in a Nonmetropolitan Context," 65 *Soc. Sci. Q.* at 626; Carlos H. Arce and Armando J. Abney-Guardado, "Demographic and Cultural Correlates of Chicano Intermarriage," 5 *California Sociologist* 41, 44, 48 (1982).

61. Gloria Cuadraz, "Experiences of Multiple Marginality: A Case Study of Chicana 'Scholarship Women'" (unpublished manuscript on file with author).

62. Ricardo Pau-Llosa, "Romancing the Exiliado," in *Muy Macho: Latino Men Confront Their Manhood* 111, 115 (Ray Gonzalez ed., paperback ed. 1996).

63. Id. at 123.

64. Alba and Golden, "Patterns of Ethnic Marriage in the U.S.," 65 *Social Forces* at 202–3 (using 1980 census data). See also Jiobu, *Ethnicity & Assimilation* at 161 (reporting that among people of Mexican origin, females and males outmarry at approximately equal rates, but among blacks, females marry out at a lower rate than males).

65. Nelly Salgado de Snyder and Amado M. Padilla, "Interethnic Marriages of Mexican Americans after Nearly Two Decades," Spanish Speaking Mental Health Research Center, Occasional Paper No. 15, 1981, at 12, 15–16 (on file with author); Nelly Salgado de Snyder and Amado M. Padilla, "Cultural and Ethnic Maintenance of Interethnically Married Mexican Americans," 41 *Hum. Org.* 359, 361 (1982). Indeed, in evaluating the reasons why Latina women may marry out at higher rates than their male counterparts, one cannot discount the significance of women traditionally adopting an Anglo surname while men typically confer a Spanish surname on their Anglo wives. The same observation applies to Asian American groups as well.

66. Salgado de Snyder and Padilla, "Interethnic Marriages of Mexican Americans after Nearly Two Decades," at 17–18; Salgado de Snyder and Padilla, "Cultural and Ethnic Maintenance of Interethnically Married Mexican Americans," 41 *Hum. Org.* at 362.

67. See Randall Kennedy, "How Are We Doing with *Loving*?: Race, Law, and Intermarriage," 77 *Boston U. L. Rev.* 815, 817–18 (1997).

68. Art Shriberg and Carol Lloyd, "Interracial Marriages Still Taboo," *Tampa Tribune,* June 5, 1997, at 1. Moreover, during a recent flap over a ban on interracial dating at Bob Jones University, observers noted that virtually no one defended the school's policy, although only a few decades before, a number of states had antimiscegenation laws. Hertzberg, "Comment: Bad News for Bigots," *New Yorker,* Mar. 3, 2000, at 29–30.

69. For a sampling of views on the meaning of equal treatment in employment, see "Title VII Symposium: A Critique of Epstein's Forbidden Grounds," 31 *U.S.D. L. Rev.* 1–277 (1994); John J. Donohue III, "Employment Discrimination Law in Perspective: Three Concepts of Equality," 92 *Mich. L. Rev.* 2583 (1994).

70. As the European social critic Denis de Rougemont explained, romantic individualism was "one of the most pathological experiments that a civilized society has ever imagined, namely the basing of marriage, which is lasting, upon romance which is a passing fancy." Denis De Rougemont, "The Crisis of the Modern Couple," in *The Family: Its Function and Destiny* (Ruth Nanda Anshen ed., 1949).

71. Milton Gordon, *Assimilation in American Life* 69–73, 80 (paperback ed. 1964) (classifying large-scale intermarriage as a process of assimilation).

72. Robert K. Merton, "Intermarriage and the Social Structure: Fact and Theory," 4 *Psychiatry* 361 (1941).

73. Id. at 366–67. Indeed, marrying down can be the subject of considerable criticism from one's peers. When Henry Ford II left his first wife, the daughter of a well-to-do Long Island couple listed prominently in the Social Register, for an Italian jet-setter and later a Detroit model who had dropped out of high school, one of his in-laws remarked acidly that he had gone "from class, to brass, to ass." Robert Lacey, *Ford: The Men and the Machine* 551 (paperback ed. 1986).

74. Merton, "Intermarriage and the Social Structure," 4 *Psychiatry* at 372–73. Merton hypothesized that because of gender differences in access to education and employment, a black man was more likely than a black woman to attain high class status and marry out. Id. at 374. Moreover, he believed that because of white men's superior caste and class status, they were more likely than black men to engage in interracial affairs with impunity. Id.

75. Merton believed that interracial couples with partners of equal class status were comprised of pariahs or radicals who rejected collectively imposed hierarchies of caste and class. Id. at 371–72. Confronted with one instance in which a white woman married down in terms of both caste and class, Merton could only attribute the choice to irrational lust: "[This case] is consistent with our interpretation that the upper class White woman in a union of this sort . . . believed that her Negro husband is 'the only man who can satisfy her sexually.' " Id. at 373. Merton's views were similar to those expressed in a 1945 study of Chicago, which characterized most black–white intermarriage as involving intellectuals, bohemians, radicals, and figures from the "sporting world." St. Clair Drake and Horace R. Cayton, *Black Metropolis: A Study of a Negro Life in a Northern City* 148 (paperback ed. 1998).

Interestingly, Merton's views are echoed in part in a 1991 article by Beth Austin in the *Chicago Tribune:*

> Some people marry out to make the statement that where they've come from is not where they're going. They're saying they were never comfortable in their old lives, and they want something new and different for themselves and their families. By marrying out, they are really marrying into something they've always yearned for. . . . Some people marry out to tell the world that they are rebels . . . and have no interest in a conventional, no-risk marriage[, and] . . . some people marry out because they've found someone whose exterior differences are far outweighed by inner qualities that make them feel truly at home.

Beth Austin, "Regarding Your Marriage, Your Honor," *Chicago Tribune,* Oct. 6, 1991, § 6, at p. 11 (Hersay Column), excerpted in Russell, Wilson, and Hall, *The Color Complex* at 118.

76. Frank M. Ahern, Robert E. Cole, Ronald C. Johnson, and Brenda Wong, "Personality Attributes of Males and Females Marrying within vs. across Racial/Ethnic Groups," 11 *Behavior Genetics* 181, 187–93 (1981).

77. Gordon, *Assimilation in American Life* at 215–16 (describing intermarriage rates among Catholics in the United States during the late 1940s and 1950s); see also Kornacker, "Cultural Significance of Intermarriage," 1 *Int'l J. Soc. Family* at 152–53.

78. Grier and Cobbs, *Black Rage* at 87–88; Stember, *Sexual Racism* at 152; Hernton, *Sex and Racism in America* at 84–85.

79. Grier and Cobbs, *Black Rage* at 91; Hernton, *Sex and Racism in America* at 75; Stember, *Sexual Racism* at 110–11.

80. Hernton, *Sex and Racism in America* at 43–50; Grier and Cobbs, *Black Rage* at 93–95; Stember, *Sexual Racism* at 180–86. In these accounts, white women were especially apt to have trouble reentering society if they had children by a black mate. Grace Halsell, *Black/White Sex* 183–202 (1972).

81. Michelene Wandor, "Lilith Re-Tells Esther's Story," in *Ain't I a Woman* (Illona Linthwaite ed., 1990).

82. Phyllis Rose, *Jazz Cleopatra: Josephine Baker in Her Time* 44 (1989).

83. Gerald R. Leslie, *The Family in Social Context* 535 (1967). Despite these calls for recognition of romantic complexity, some scholars continue to seek rational accounts of intimacy. For an effort to apply an economic model to sexuality, see Richard A. Posner, *Sex and Reason* (paperback ed. 1992).

84. Rubin found that when people had high scores on the romanticism scale, their love for another was apt to result in a long-term commitment; when people had low scores on the romanticism scale, love did not necessarily produce a lasting relationship. Zick Rubin, *Liking and Loving: An Invitation to Social Psychology* 234–35 (1973).

85. Many people do specify the race of a desirable partner in personal ads, however, and this practice is not universally condemned as racist. See Note, "Racial Steering in the Romantic Marketplace," 107 *Harv. L. Rev.* 877 (1994) (condemning such ads as racially harmful but concluding that they are protected by the First Amendment).

86. See Gary Peller, "Notes Toward a Postmodern Nationalism," 1992 *U. Ill. L. Rev.* 1095, 1095–97 (describing how an ideology of colorblindness is linked to a vision of human beings who happen to be white or nonwhite).

87. See James H. Liu, Susan Miller Campbell, and Heather Condie, "Ethnocentrism in Dating Preferences for an American Sample: The Ingroup Bias in Social Context," 25 *European J. Soc. Psychol.* 95 (1995) (racial and ethnic group members rate those in their own group as more attractive and similar to them in terms of culture, values, personality, and communication when compared to members of other groups; the difference is most marked for those whose families and friends would disapprove of an interracial or interethnic relationship).

88. "Elie Wiesel's Own Words: A Testament to Survival," *L.A. Times,* Oct. 19, 1986, pt. 6, at p.1 (View).

89. See, e.g., Gary Peller, "Race Consciousness," 1990 *Duke L.J.* 758, 846 (arguing that the equation of black nationalism with reverse racism is "just plain wrong"); but cf. Linz Audain, "Critical Cultural Law and Economics, the Culture of Deindividualization, the Paradox of Blackness," 70 *Ind. L.J.* 709, 731–33 (1995) (arguing that some preferences for all-black social organizations to fight racism are themselves racist).

90. In a similar vein, nonwhite students on college campuses have been able to create racial and ethnic organizations and theme houses to preserve a sense of identity and comfort, while white students feel that they would be accused of being racists if they

took similar steps. Institute for the Study of Social Change, The Diversity Project: An Interim Report to the Chancellor 24–25, 50–51, 74–76, 81–86 (June 1990).

91. For articles touching on black communities' efforts to preserve themselves as discrete social entities, see Doreen Carvajal, "O. C. Social Group Trades Glitz for Shining Examples; Adolescence: Black Debs' Ball Is No More. Now, Both Boys and Girls Are Recognized in a Sociable Atmosphere," *L.A. Times,* Feb. 27, 1994, at A1 (describing how cotillions for black women were expanded to a seven-month program of workshops on career development and African American history and culture as well as social events and field trips that include both black male and female adolescents in the predominantly white Orange County area); Clara Germani, "D.C. Suburb is a Dream Come True for Many Blacks," *Christian Science Monitor,* Apr. 10, 1991, at Z10 (describing preference of some black middle-class couples for Prince George's County, a predominantly black suburb, over integrated suburbs in which blacks constitute a minority).

92. Paul C. Rosenblatt, Terri A. Karis, and Richard D. Powell, *Multiracial Couples: Black & White Voices* 30–31 (1995).

93. Richard Buttny, "Legitimation Techniques for Intermarriage: Accounts of Motives for Intermarriage from U.S. Servicemen and Philippine Women," 35 *Comm. Q.* 125, 135, 139–40 (1987).

94. Id. at 136.

95. Id. at 136–38. Although these women typically spoke English fluently and were familiar with Western popular culture, the servicemen probably were aware of cultural differences, especially those related to the Filipinas' extended and sometimes quite traditional families. The tendency to discount these distinctions may have reflected in part the servicemen's tacit assumption that their wives would bear the burden of making cultural adjustments, especially after their return to the United States. See Bok-Lim C. Kim, "Asian Wives of U.S. Servicemen: Women in Shadows," 4 *Amerasia* 91, 103–10 (1977) (describing serious adjustment problems of Asian women who marry servicemen and return to the United States).

96. Buttny, "Legitimation Techniques for Intermarriage," 35 *Comm. Q.* at 138.

97. Id. at 138–39. The results in the study of American servicemen and Filipina wives are consistent with those in other countries. In a study of college students in Israel, they tended to assume that money and status were highly important to spouses marrying persons of Western origin, a background associated with greater prestige and material resources. Women were especially likely to be perceived as marrying up for materialistic reasons. Love was seen as a less significant factor for women, but not men, marrying spouses of Western origin. Aharon Bizman, "Perceived Causes and Compatibility of Interethnic Marriage," 11 *Int'l J. Intercultural Relations* 387, 391–94 (1987).

98. For example, demographic data typically have shown that the smaller the group, the more likely it is to intermarry, even when there are strong in-group pressures toward endogamy. Peter M. Blau, Terry C. Blum, and Joseph E. Schwartz, "Heterogeneity and Intermarriage," 47 *Am. Soc. Rev.* 45, 51–54 (1982). Group size may also account for why white rates of outmarriage most closely approximate those that would be expected at random. Jiobu, *Ethnicity & Assimilation* at 160.

99. Jiobu, *Ethnicity & Assimilation* at 160.

100. Id. at 56–58; Peter M. Blau, Carolyn Beeker, and Kevin M. Fitzpatrick, "Intersecting Social Affiliations and Intermarriage," 62 *Social Forces* 585, 598 (1984); Terry C.

Blum, "Racial Inequality and Salience: An Examination of Blau's Theory of Social Structure," 62 *Soc. Forces* 607, 611–14 (1984); Heer, "Negro–White Marriage in the United States," 28 *J. Marriage & the Family* at 270. See also Alba and Golden, "Patterns of Ethnic Marriage in the U.S.," 65 *Social Forces* at 270 (socioeconomic factors, such as education, influence homogamy among ethnic groups); Steven Martin Cohen, "Socioeconomic Determinants of Intraethnic Marriage and Friendship," 55 *Social Forces* 997, 1003 (1977) (small but noticeable association between social class, especially educational attainment, and marriage outside the ethnic group where a group includes large numbers of unassimilated members along with assimilated members); Zhenchao Qian, "Breaking the Racial Barriers: Variations in Interracial Marriage Between 1980 and 1990," 34 *Demography* 263, 271–72 (1997) (better educated racial minorities are more likely to intermarry because they are more apt to be in integrated neighborhoods and schools than their less educated counterparts).

101. Sandefur and McKinnell, "American Indian Intermarriage," 15 *Soc. Sci. Research* at 363; Arce and Abney-Guardado, "Demographic and Cultural Correlates of Chicano Intermarriage," 5 *California Sociologist* at 49; Ellman, "Intermarriage in the United States," 49 *Jewish Social Studies* at 3; Wilson, "Marriage's Melting Pot," 7 *Am. Demographics* at 45.

102. Thomas P. Monahan, "The Occupational Class of Couples Entering into Interracial Marriages," 7 *J. Comp. Family Studies* 175, 188–89 (1976); Heer, "The Prevalence of Black–White Marriage in the United States," 36 *J. Marriage & the Family* at 252–56 (Merton's hypothesis suffers from a failure to take into account the number of spouses of a given race available at a particular level of educational attainment); Gary A. Cretser and Joseph J. Leon, "Intermarriage in the U.S.: An Overview of Theory and Research," 5 *Marriage & Fam. Rev.* 3, 5–6 (1982) (summarizing negative research findings regarding Merton's hypothesis).

103. David Mura, "The Internment of Desire," in *Under Western Eyes: Personal Essays from Asian America* 281–82 (Garrett Hongo ed., paperback ed. 1995).

104. See Patricia G. Devine, "Stereotypes and Prejudice: Their Automatic and Controlled Components," 56 *J. Pers. & Soc. Psychol.* 5 (1989) (people are aware of stereotypes, whether or not they personally endorse them, and stereotypical reactions can be triggered even when individuals do not believe the stereotypes themselves).

105. Ruth Frankenberg, *The Social Construction of Whiteness: White Women, Race Matters* 95 (paperback ed. 1993).

106. Id. at 99.

107. Id. at 96.

108. Id. at 94–95, 248.

109. Id. at 94, 260–61.

110. For a discussion of these arguments, see chapter 5.

111. "I, Thee, We, Them," *Economist,* June 20, 1998, at 31.

112. Milton Gordon, *Human Nature, Class, and Ethnicity* 160 (1978).

113. Anecdotal evidence from the popular press reinforces concerns about the isolation experienced by interracial couples. See Michael McQueen, "The Forces That Tear at Interracial Relationships," *Independent Gazette* 2 (1981) ("The world seems determined to make you feel threatened, angry, defensive, ashamed, lonely, even freakish."); Michael McQueen, "Black Woman, White Man," *Washington Post,* Jan. 25, 1981, at C1 ("We know what tribal loyalty means. We know what it is to belong, and we know what it

is to be rejected. We know some of the awful consequences of tolerance, the furies unleashed by those of us who practice what others preach.").

114. John A. Brown, "Casework Contacts with Black–White Couples," 68 *Soc. Casework* 24, 27 (1987). A report on women in interracial relationships who participated in a support group in Berkeley, California, revealed that feelings of isolation and alienation may occur in different settings for white women and black women. White women typically reported that they were not prepared for the slights that they encountered over their choice of a mate in public settings. By contrast, black women had "armored" themselves for such racist treatment, but they were unprepared for and vulnerable to slights from white in-laws in the home, a setting they had treated as an extended, expansive, and accommodating environment. Janette Faulkner, "Women in Interracial Relationships," 2 *Women & Therapy* 191, 195–99 (1983).

115. Bascom W. Ratliff, Harriett Faye Moon, and Gwendolyn A. Bonacci, "Intercultural Marriage: The Korean-American Experience," 59 *Soc. Casework* 221, 223–24 (1978).

116. Jean K. Wagner, "The Role of Intermarriage in the Acculturation of Selected Urban American Indian Women," 18 *Anthropologica* 215, 222–23 (1976). This account is consistent with historical descriptions of whites who joined Native American tribes and became "white Indians" by adopting tribal customs and values. See James Axtell, *The Invasion Within: The Contest of Cultures in Colonial North America* 302–27 (1985).

117. Wagner, "The Role of Intermarriage in the Acculturation of Selected Urban American Indian Women," 18 *Anthropologica* at 225. In addition, the father removed his family from the reservation. Id.

118. Beulah F. Rohrlich, "Dual-Culture Marriage and Communication," 12 *Int'l J. Intercultural Relations* 35, 42 (1988).

119. Clinicians have measured cultural differences by examining (1) the extent of value differences between the cultural groups involved; (2) differences in each spouse's degree of acculturation; (3) religious differences; (4) racial differences; (5) the sex of the spouse from each background to the extent that "sex roles intensify certain cultural characteristics"; (6) socioeconomic differences; (7) familiarity with each other's culture prior to marriage; and (8) the degree to which families have resolved the emotional issues surrounding the marriage before the wedding. Monica McGoldrick and Nydia Garcia Preto, "Ethnic Intermarriage: Implications for Therapy," 23 *Fam. Process* 347, 349–50 (1984). See also Sung, *Chinese American Intermarriage* at 66–67 (describing how divergent cultural expectations can undermine an interracial marriage).

120. McGoldrick and Preto, "Ethnic Intermarriage," 23 *Fam. Process* at 352–55.

121. Id. at 358.

CHAPTER SEVEN

1. *Plyler v. Doe,* 457 U.S. 202 (1982).

2. Gerald Gunther, "The Supreme Court, 1971 Term—Foreword: In Search of Evolving Doctrine on a Changing Court: A Model for a Newer Equal Protection," 86 *Harv. L. Rev.* 1, 8 (1972).

3. For a description of the "best interest of the child" standard, see Carl E. Schneider, "Symposium: One Hundred Years of Uniform State Law: Discretion, Rules, and Law: Child Custody and the UMDA's Best Interest Standard," 89 *Mich. L. Rev.* 2215, 2216, 2219 (1991).

4. See, e.g., *Ward v. Ward*, 216 P.2d 755, 756 (Wash. 1950). This reasoning was subsequently repudiated in *Tucker v. Tucker*, 14 Wash. App. 454, 542 P.2d 789, 790–91 (1975), which said race could be considered as only one factor in custody disputes.

5. Rita J. Simon and Howard Altstein, *Adoption, Race and Identity: From Infancy through Adolescence* 2 (1992).

6. See, e.g., *Fountaine v. Fountaine*, 9 Ill. App. 2d 482, 133 N.E.2d 532, 534–35 (1956) (after the divorce of a black man and white woman, the woman's petition for custody could not be denied solely "because of the racial physical characteristics" of the children, who "had the appearance of colored children").

7. Barbara McLaughlin, "Transracial Adoption in New York State," 60 *Alb. L. Rev.* 501, 507–8 (1996); Margaret Howard, "Transracial Adoption: Analysis of the Best Interests Standard," 59 *N.D. L. Rev.* 503, 510–13 (1984); Elizabeth Bartholet, *Family Bonds: Adoption and the Politics of Parenting* 94 (1993); *Petition of R.M.G.*, 454 A.2d 776, 789 (D.C. App. 1982). See generally Joyce A. Ladner, *Mixed Families: Adopting across Racial Boundaries* 59–64, 68–69 (1977) (describing the history of transracial adoptions in the United States). For a discussion of a 1954 survey on the emerging clash between matching policies and transracial adoptions, see Susan J. Grossman, "A Child of a Different Color: Race as a Factor in Adoption and Custody Proceedings," 17 *Buffalo L. Rev.* 303, 318–25 (1968).

8. See, e.g., *Commonwealth ex rel. Lucas v. Kreisher*, 299 A.2d 243 (Pa. 1973) (holding that white mother's interracial marriage subsequent to divorce in and of itself could not justify denying her custody of her white children).

9. "National Association of Black Social Workers, Position Paper" (Apr. 1972), in Rita J. Simon and Howard Altstein, *Transracial Adoption* 50–52 (1977); Ruth G. McRoy, "An Organizational Dilemma: The Case of Transracial Adoptions," 25 *J. Applied Behav. Sci.* 145, 152 (1989). For an in-depth discussion of the NABSW's opposition, see Ladner, *Mixed Families* at 74–78.

10. Bartholet, *Family Bonds* at 95–96; McLaughlin, "Transracial Adoption in New York State," 60 *Alb. L. Rev.* at 509–10; Elizabeth Bartholet, "Race Separatism in the Family: More on the Transracial Adoption Debate," 2 *Duke J. Gender L. & Pol'y* 99, 99–100 (1995); Howard, "Transracial Adoption," 59 *N.D. L. Rev.* at 509–510; McRoy, "An Organizational Dilemma," 25 *J. Applied Behav. Sci.* at 147.

11. Elizabeth Bartholet, "Correspondence: Private Race Preferences in Family Formation," 107 *Yale L.J.* 2351, 2353–54 (1998); Susan Goldsmith, "The Color of Love: A Minister and His Wife Wanted to Adopt a Drug-Addicted Baby in L.A. but Racial Politics Got in the Way," *New Times*, Apr. 30, 1998 (Features).

12. Howard Alstein and Rita J. Simon, "Introduction," in *Intercountry Adoption: A Multinational Perspective* 1, 14–16 (Howard Alstein and Rita J. Simon eds., 1991) (noting that after the Korean War, Americans adopted large numbers of war orphans, including biracial children of servicemen and Korean women; from the 1950s until the late 1980s, adoptions from Korea were the dominant placement). When Korea altered its policy on foreign adoptions, Americans turned to other countries in Asia, Latin America, and eastern Europe to fill the gap. The countries providing children have fluctuated in recent years, depending on shifts in foreign policies, the economic fortunes of underdeveloped nations, and the outbreak of regional conflicts. Elizabeth Bartholet, "International Adoption: Propriety, Prospects and Pragmatics," 13 *J. Am. Acad. Matrim. Law* 181 (1996); Michelle van Leeuwen, "The Politics of Adoption across Borders: Whose Interests Are

Served? (A Look at the Emerging Market of Infants from China)," 8 *Pac. Rim L. & Pol'y J.* 189, 189–90 (1999); Jorge L. Carro, "Regulation of Intercountry Adoption: Can the Abuses Come to an End?" 18 *Hastings Int'l & Comp. L. Rev.* 121, 125–28 (1994); Lisa M. Katz, "A Modest Proposal? The Convention of Protection of Children and Cooperation in Respect of Intercountry Adoption," 9 *Emory Int'l L. Rev.* 283, 285–88 (1995).

13. Robert M. George, Fred H. Wulczyn, and Allen W. Harden, *Foster Care Dynamics, 1983–1993* (1995); Richard P. Barth, Devon Brooks, and Seema Iyer, *California Adoptions: Current Demographic Profiles and Projections through the End of the Century* (1995); Devon Brooks, Alice Bussiere, Richard P. Barth, and Glendora Patterson, *Adoption and Race: Implementing the Multiethnic Placement Act of 1994 and the Interethnic Adoption Provisions* 3–5 (1997).

14. Kathy S. Stolley, "Statistics on Adoption in the United States," in Center for the Future of Children, 3 *The Future of Children* 26, 34 (spring 1993).

15. Twila L. Perry, "Transracial and International Adoption: Mothers, Hierarchy, Race, and Feminist Legal Theory," 19 *Yale J.L. & Feminism* 101, 145–47 (1998); James S. Bowen, "Cultural Convergence and Divergences: The Nexus between Putative Afro-American Family Values and the Best Interests of the Child," 26 *J. Fam. L.* 487, 490–91 (1987–88); Elizabeth Bartholet, "Where Do Black Children Belong? The Politics of Race-Matching in Adoption," 139 *U. Pa. L. Rev.* 1163, 1179–82, 1207–26 (1991) (describing controversy over transracial placements despite empirical evidence of positive adjustments); Arnold R. Silverman, "Outcomes of Transracial Adoption," in *The Future of Children—Adoption* 104, 107 (Richard E. Behrman ed., 1993); Dong Soo Kim, "Issues in Transracial and Transcultural Adoption," 59 *Soc. Casework* 477, 479 (1978). For a discussion of some of the concerns and recent controversies surrounding international adoptions, see Barbara Tizard, "Intercountry Adoptions: A Review of the Evidence," 32 *J. Child Psychol. & Psychiatry* 743 (1991); Margaret Liu, "International Adoptions: An Overview," 8 *Temple Int'l & Comp. L.J.* 187, 194–95 (1994); Carro, "Regulation of Intercountry Adoption: Can the Abuses Come to an End?" 18 *Hastings Int'l L. Rev.* at 128–42.

16. 466 U.S. 429 (1984).

17. Id. at 431.

18. Id. at 430.

19. Id. at 430–31.

20. Id. at 431.

21. Id. The court of appeals' decision to affirm without opinion denied the Florida Supreme Court jurisdiction to review the case.

22. Id. at 432.

23. Id. at 433–34.

24. "Judge Refuses to Order Girl Returned to Racially Mixed Couple," *UPI,* May 18, 1984; "Judge Withholds Rule on Mixed-Marriage Custody Case," *UPI,* Aug. 28, 1984. Later, alleging that Clarence regularly abused her during their three-year marriage, Linda filed for divorce. An attorney for Anthony Sidoti suggested that the breakup might help her in the custody case because she was "making this effort to get her life straightened out." "Palmores May Divorce," *UPI,* Dec. 27, 1984.

25. See Note, "Black Identity and Child Placement: The Best Interests of Black and Biracial Children," 92 *Mich. L. Rev.* 925, 931–32 (1994); Twila L. Perry, "Race and Child Placement: The Best Interests Test and the Cost of Discretion," 29 *J. Fam. L.* 51, 59–60 (1990–91).

26. See, e.g., *In re Marriage of Kramer,* 297 N.W.2d 359 (Iowa 1980) (court rejected trial court's consideration of race in weighing white mother's sexual relations with a black male but upheld the award of custody to the white father based on the mother's "search[ ] for a more carefree life-style, without regard to its effect on the children."); see also *Boone v. Boone,* 90 N.M. 466, 565 P.2d 337 (1977) (overturning trial court's custody determination, which had been based on findings that their mother was in an "immoral relationship" and that "the fact that [her boyfriend] is Black does not excuse the relationship."); *Commonwealth ex rel. Myers v. Myers,* 300 A.2d 587 (Pa. 1976) (overturning custody award to white father based on white mother's immoral conduct on the ground that the decision was racially motivated because the mother's boyfriend was black); *Edel v. Edel,* 293 N.W.2d 792 (Mich. Ct. App. 1980) (invalidating trial court decision that placed excessive weight on race of white mother's boyfriend in awarding custody to white father but noting that trial court could reach same decision on remand on other grounds). See generally Note, "Transracial Adoption: A Critical View of the Courts' Present Standards," 28 *J. Fam. L.* 303, 314–15 (1989–90); Renee Romano, " 'Bad Mothers': White Women, Racial Transgressions, and Custody Disputes, 1945–1985" (unpublished manuscript on file with author).

27. *Compos v. McKeithen,* 341 F. Supp. 264 (E.D. La. 1972). See also *In re Gomez,* 424 S.W.2d 656 (Tex. Civ. App. 1967) (striking down similar statute on equal protection grounds).

28. Bartholet, *Family Bonds* at 100; Bartholet, "Where Do Black Children Belong?" 139 *U. Pa. L. Rev.* at 1230; Bowen, "Cultural Convergence and Divergences," 26 *J. Fam L.* at 515. See also *In re Davis,* 465 A.2d 614, 621–29 (Pa. 1983) (trial court's failure to consider race as a factor in an adoption suit was harmless error).

29. Bartholet, "Where Do Black Children Belong?" 139 *U. Pa. L. Rev.* at 1184, 1188, 1195; Bowen, "Cultural Convergence and Divergences," 26 *J. Fam L.* at 514.

30. Bartholet, *Family Bonds* at 101–6; Bartholet, "Where Do Black Children Belong?" 139 *U. Pa. L. Rev.* at 1207–26; Note, "Black Identity and Child Placement," 92 *Mich. L. Rev.* at 937.

31. Bartholet, *Family Bonds* at 95, 96–99.

32. See, e.g., *Drummond v. Fulton County Department of Family & Children's Services,* 563 F.2d 1200 (5th Cir. 1977) (en banc); *DeWees v. Stevenson,* 779 F. Supp. 25 (E.D. Pa. 1991); *In re Petition of R.M.G.,* 454 A.2d 776 (D.C. App. 1982); *In re D.I.S. for the Adoption of S.A.O.,* 494 A.2d 1316 (D.C. App. 1985).

33. *Drummond v. Fulton County Department of Family & Children's Services,* 563 F.2d 1200, 1206–11 (5th Cir. 1977) (en banc). In *Smith v. Organization of Foster Families of Equality and Reform,* 431 U.S. 816, 844–45 (1977), Justice William Brennan in a plurality opinion suggested that foster families might be entitled to some constitutional protection if they had forged strong psychological bonds during a long-term placement. However, the Court had never affirmed this dictum in a later holding. Jehnna Irene Hanan, "The Best Interest of the Child: Eliminating Discrimination in the Screening of Adoptive Parents," 27 Golden Gate U.L. Rev. 167, 181–83 (1997).

34. Marla Gottlieb Zwas, "Kinship Foster Care: A Relatively Permanent Solution," 20 *Fordham Urb. L.J.* 343, 343 (1993); Roger J. R. Levesque, "The Failures of Foster Care Reform: Revolutionizing the Most Radical Blueprint," 6 *Md. J. Contemp. L. Issues* 1, 8–9, 25 (1995); Randi Mandelbaum, "Trying to Fit Square Pegs into Round Holes: The Need for a New Funding Scheme for Kinship Caregivers," 22 *Fordham Urb. L.J.*

907, 910–12 (1995); Jill Duerr Berrick and Barbara Needell, "Recent Trends in Kinship Care: Public Policy, Finances, and Outcomes for Children," in *The Foster Care Crisis: Translating Research Into Practice and Policy* 152 (Patrick A. Curtis, Grady Dale Jr., and Joshua C. Kendall eds., 1999).

35. Carol Stack, *All Our Kin: Strategies for Survival in a Black Community* 162–89 (1974); Meredith Minkler and Kathleen Roe, *Grandmothers as Caregivers: Raising Children of the Crack Cocaine Epidemic* (1993); Child Welfare League of America, *Kinship Care: A National Bridge* (1994); Allen W. Harden, Rebecca Clark, and Karen Maguire, *Formal and Informal Kinship Care* (n.d.) (blacks are most likely to live in kinship care settings, and the gap in their use as compared to other racial and ethnic groups widened between 1983 and 1993).

36. *Miller v. Youakim,* 440 U.S. 125, 145–46 (1979) (Marshall, J.).

37. Levesque, "The Failures of Foster Care Reform: Revolutionizing the Most Radical Blueprint," 6 *Md. J. Contemp. L. Issues* at 25–26; Zwas, "Kinship Foster Care," 20 *Fordham Urb. L.J.* at 354–64.

38. Zwas, "Kinship Foster Care," 20 *Fordham Urb. L.J.* at 364–67; Berrick and Needell, "Recent Trends in Kinship Care," in *Foster Care Crisis* (Curtis, Dale, and Kendall eds.), at 161, 164–66.

39. Child Welfare League of America, *Kinship Care* at 65–70; Zwas, "Kinship Foster Care," 20 *Fordham Urb. L.J.* at 370–71; Mandelbaum, "Trying to Fit Square Pegs into Round Holes," 22 *Fordham Urb. L.J.* at 931.

40. Bartholet, *Family Bonds* at 106–10; Bartholet, "Where Do Black Children Belong?" 139 *U. Pa. L. Rev.* at 1243–45, 1248–54.

41. *Petition of R.M.G.,* 454 A.2d 776 (D.C. App. 1982).

42. Id. at 786.

43. *In re D.I.S. for the Adoption of S.A.O.,* 494 A.2d 1316 (D.C. App. 1985).

44. For articles criticizing the use of an intermediate standard of review in transracial adoption cases, see Shari O'Brien, "Race in Adoption Proceedings: The Pernicious Factor," 21 *Tulsa L.J.* 485, 495–96 (1986); Davidson M. Pattiz, "Racial Preference in Adoption: An Equal Protection Challenge," 82 *Geo. L.J.* 2571, 2575–85 (1994). For a defense of an intermediate standard, see Zanita E. Fenton, "In a World Not Their Own: The Adoption of Black Children," 10 *Harv. Blackletter J.* 39 (1993).

45. Howard M. Metzenbaum Multiethnic Placement Act of 1994, Pub. L. No. 103-382, 108 Stat. 4056, codified at 42 U.S.C. § 5115a. For an explanation of Senator Metzenbaum's motivations in introducing the Act, see Senator Howard M. Metzenbaum, "S. 1224—In Support of the Multiethnic Placement Act of 1993," 2 *Duke J. Gender L. & Pol'y* 165 (1997).

46. Marla E. Selmann, "For the Sake of the Child: Moving toward Uniformity in Adoption Law," 69 *Wash. L. Rev.* 841, 857–62 (1994). See also Jo Beth Eubanks, "Comment: Transracial Adoption in Texas: Should the Best Interests Standard Be Color-Blind?" 24 *St. Mary's L.J.* 1225 (1993); Timothy P. Glynn, "Note: The Role of Race in Adoption Proceedings: A Constitutional Critique of the Minnesota Preference Statute," 77 *Minn. L. Rev.* 925 (1993); Pattiz, "Racial Preference in Adoption," 82 *Geo. L.J.* at 2585–2609.

47. Elizabeth Bartholet, "Adoption Is About Family, Not Race," *Chicago Tribune,* Nov. 5, 1993, at 23 (Perspective); Ellen Goodman, "In the Effort to Racially Match in Adoptions, the Children Can Be the Losers," *Boston Globe,* Dec. 5, 1993, at 77; Randall

Kennedy, "Kids Need Parents—Of Any Race," *Wall Street Journal,* Nov. 9, 1993, at A22. For a more detailed description of the controversy surrounding the bill, see Michelle M. Mini, "Breaking Down the Barriers to Transracial Adoptions: Can the Multiethnic Placement Act Meet This Challenge?" 22 *Hofstra L. Rev.* 897, 956–66 (1994); Barbara Bennett Woodhouse, "'Are You My Mother?': Conceptualizing Children's Identity Rights in Transracial Adoptions," 2 *Duke J. Gender L. & Pol'y* 107, 120–22 (1997).

48. S. 1224 (amended by Senate Subcommittee on Labor on Oct. 6, 1993). Congress declined to adopt the more lenient approach offered by a less prominent bill introduced without cosponsors by Representative Luis V. Gutierrez in the House. H.R. 3307, 103d Cong., 1st Sess. (Oct. 19, 1993). This bill provided: "In determining the placement of a child for foster care or adoption, in a case in which an individual of the same race, color, or national origin as the child is not available to be the parent of the child, an entity that receives Federal assistance may not give greater weight to any difference between the race, color, or national origin of the child and that of any prospective parent of the child than the entity gives to any other factor used in determining the best interests of the child." Id. § 2(a). This bill also exempted the Indian Child Welfare Act from its coverage. Id. § 2(b).

49. 42 U.S.C. § 5115a(a)(1)(A).

50. 42 U.S.C. § 5115a(a)(1)(B).

51. 42 U.S.C. § 5115a(a)(2). The Act establishes a private right of action in federal district court for those aggrieved by an alleged violation of the Act. 42 U.S.C. § 5115a(b).

52. 42 U.S.C. § 5115a(c).

53. Dept. of Health and Human Services, *Policy Guidance on the Use of Race, Color, or National Origin as Considerations in Adoption and Foster Care Placements,* 60 Fed. Reg. 20272 (Apr. 25, 1995). See also Carla M. Curtis and Rudolph Alexander Jr., "The Multiethnic Placement Act: Implications for Social Work Practice," 13 *Child & Adolescent Soc. Work J.* 401, 404–9 (1996); Robert L. Jackson, "New Federal Rules on Interracial Adoptions: Agencies Receiving Aid May Not Delay or Deny," *S.F. Chronicle,* Apr. 25, 1995, at A1.

54. Dept. of Health and Human Services, *Policy Guidance on the Use of Race, Color, or National Origin as Considerations in Adoption and Foster Care Placements* at 20273.

55. Id. at 20273–74.

56. Id. at 20274.

57. Pub. L. No. 188, 104th Cong., 2d Sess. (1996), codified at 42 U.S.C. § 1996b.

58. See Administration on Children, Youth, and Families, *Information Memorandum: Guidance for Federal Legislation—The Small Business Job Protection Act of 1996 (P.L. 104-188) Section 1808, "Removal of Barriers to Interethnic Adoption,"* ACYF-IM-CB-97-04 (U.S. Dept. of Health and Human Services, June 5, 1997), reprinted in Joan Heifetz Hollinger and The ABA Center on Children and the Law, *A Guide to the Multiethnic Placement Act of 1994 as Amended by the Interethnic Adoption Provisions of 1996* at C-1 to C-8 (1998).

59. Administration for Children, Youth, and Families, *Information Memorandum: Information on Implementation of Federal Legislation—Questions and Answers that Clarify the Practice and Implementation of Section 471(a)(18) of title IV-E of the Social Security Act,* ACYF-IM-CB-98-03 (U.S. Dept. of Health and Human Services, May 11, 1998), reprinted in Hollinger and The ABA Center on Children and the Law, *A Guide to the Multiethnic Placement Act of 1994* at D-1 to D-11.

60. Id.

61. Id.

62. Id.

63. 42 U.S.C. § 5115a(f). See Bowen, "Cultural Convergence and Divergences," 26 *J. Fam L.* at 522–27, 533–44 (proposing an Afro-American Child Welfare Act modeled on the Indian Child Welfare Act but noting congressional lack of receptivity to such an idea); Jacinda T. Townsend, "Reclaiming Self-Determination: A Call for Intraracial Adoption," 2 *Duke J. Gender L. & Pol'y* 173, 182–87 (1997) (same). But see Christine M. Metteer, "A Law unto Itself: The Indian Child Welfare Act as Inapplicable and Inappropriate to the Transracial/Race-Matching Adoption Controversy," 38 *Brandeis L.J.* 47, 66–81 (1999–2000) (defending the sui generis treatment of tribes under ICWA).

64. Donna J. Goldsmith, "Individual vs. Collective Rights: The Indian Child Welfare Act," 13 *Harv. Women's L.J.* 1, 3 (1990).

65. Subcomm. on Indian Affairs, Indian Child Welfare Program: Hearings, 93d Cong., 2d Sess. 3 (1974) (statement of William Byler).

66. See, e.g., id. at 46 (testimony of Dr. Joseph Westermeyer) (when native American children raised in white homes reached adolescence, "they were finding that society was putting on them an identity which they didn't possess and taking from them an identity they did possess"). In fact, however, the limited empirical evidence available suggests that Native American children make successful adjustments when placed at an early age in white adoptive homes. David Fanshel, *Far from the Reservation* 50–57, 322–23 (1972).

67. Pub. L. No. 95-608, 92 Stat. 3069, codified as amended at 25 U.S.C. §§ 1901–1963. For a fuller discussion of the Act's provisions, see Michael C. Snyder, "An Overview of the Indian Child Welfare Act," 7 *St. Thomas L. Rev.* 815 (1995).

68. 25 U.S.C. § 1901(3) ("there is no resource that is more vital to the continued existence and integrity of Indian tribes than their children"). See generally Philip P. Frickey, "Congressional Intent, Practical Reasoning, and the Dynamic Nature of Federal Indian Law," 78 *Calif. L. Rev.* 1137, 1195–96 (1990); Jeanne Louise Carriere, "Representing the Native American: Culture, Jurisdiction, and the Indian Child Welfare Act," 79 *Iowa L. Rev.* 587, 594 (1994); Goldsmith, "Individual vs. Collective Rights," 13 *Harv. Women's L.J.* at 3.

69. 25 U.S.C. § 1902. At least one scholar has unsuccessfully called on legislatures to pass a statutory analog, an Afro-American Child Welfare Act, that would openly encourage placement of black children with black families. Bowen, "Cultural Convergence and Divergences," 26 *J. Fam. L.* at 522–27, 533–44.

70. S. Rep. No. 597, 95th Cong., 1st Sess. 43–45 (1977); 124 Cong. Rec. 38102–38103 (1978) (remarks of Rep. Lagomarsino). See Peter Hayes, "Transracial Adoption: Politics and Ideology," 72 *Child Welfare* 301, 305–6 (1993) (collectivist arguments that equate group welfare and child's best interest falsely deny potential conflicts of interest). For an article criticizing ICWA's insensitivity to the rights of Indian parents, see Christine D. Bakeis, "The Indian Child Welfare Act of 1978: Violating Personal Rights for the Sake of the Tribe," 10 *N.D. J.L. Ethics & Pub. Pol'y* 543 (1996).

71. 25 U.S.C. § 1911(a). Even before ICWA was passed, the U.S. Supreme Court had held that a tribal court had exclusive jurisdiction of an adoption proceeding when all the parties were members of the tribe residing on a reservation. *Fisher v. District Court,* 424 U.S. 382 (1976).

72. 490 U.S. 30 (1989) (Brennan, J. writing for the majority).

73. Id. at 49–53 (quoting S. Rep. No. 597).

74. Id. at 57–65 (dissenting opinion of Stevens, J., joined by Rehnquist, C.J., and Kennedy, J.).

75. 25 U.S.C. §§ 1911(b), 1912(a), 1913(a). See also Michelle L. Lehmann, "The Indian Child Welfare Act of 1978: Does It Apply to the Adoption of an Illegitimate Indian Child?" 38 *Cath. U. L. Rev.* 511, 522 (1989) (describing different notice requirements for voluntary and involuntary proceedings).

76. 25 U.S.C. § 1911(b). Guidelines promulgated by the Bureau of Indian Affairs have explicitly recognized the right of a child over twelve years of age to object to transfer, and a state court may consider the child's limited contacts with the reservation if the child is over five years of age. The guidelines permit state courts to evaluate not only the child's ties to the reservation but also the socioeconomic conditions and adequacy of social services on the reservation. Bureau of Indian Affairs Guidelines, 44 Fed. Reg. 67591.

77. *In re Adoption of Baby Boy L.,* 643 P.2d 168, 177–78 (Kan. 1982) (upholding non-Indian parent's right to object to transfer); *In re G.L.O.C.,* 668 P.2d 235, 238 (Mont. 1983) (same). See Michael E. Connelly, "Tribal Jurisdiction under Section 1911(b) of the Indian Child Welfare Act of 1878 [*sic*]: Are the States Respecting Indian Sovereignty?" 23 *N.M. L. Rev.* 479, 485–86 (1993) (general description of parental objections to transfer); Catherine M. Brooks, "The Indian Child Welfare Act in Nebraska: Fifteen Years, A Foundation for the Future," 27 *Creighton L. Rev.* 661, 695–98 (1993–94) (describing case in which issue of non-Indian parent's objections was not reached because offspring were not accepted for membership by tribe).

78. Connelly, "Tribal Jurisdiction under Section 1911(b) of the Indian Child Welfare Act of 1878 [*sic*]," 23 *N.M. L. Rev.* at 484–85.

79. 25 U.S.C. § 1915(a), (b).

80. Id. § 1911(c).

81. Erik W. Aamot-Snapp, "When Judicial Flexibility Becomes Abuse of Discretion: Eliminating the 'Good Cause' Exception in Indian Child Welfare Act Adoptive Placements," 79 *Minn. L. Rev.* 1167, 1178–80, 1182–88 (1995); Denise L. Stiffarm, "The Indian Child Welfare Act: Guiding the Determination of Good Cause to Depart from the Statutory Placement Preferences," 70 *Wash. L. Rev.* 1151, 1164–66 (1995); Goldsmith, "Individual vs. Collective Rights," 13 *Harv. Women's L.J.* at 4–5.

82. See *In re M.E.M.,* 635 P.2d 1313, 1317 (Mont. 1981) (termination of parental rights); *In re T.S.,* 801 P.2d 77, 80–82 (Mont. 1990), cert. denied sub nom. *King Island Native Community v. Montana Department of Family Services,* 500 U.S. 917 (1991) (child custody); *In re Adoption of T.R.M.,* 525 N.E.2d 298, 307–8 (Ind. 1988), cert. denied, 490 U.S. 1069 (1989) (adoption); *In re N.L.,* 754 P.2d 863, 869 (Okla. 1988) (temporary custody and preadoptive placement); *In re J.J.,* 454 N.W.2d 317, 329–31 (S.D. 1990) (termination of custodial rights); *In re Robert T.,* 200 Cal. App. 3d 657, 665, 246 Cal. Rptr. 168, 174–75 (1988) (termination of parental rights); *In re C.W.,* 239 Neb. 817, 479 N.W.2d 105, 115–17 (1992) (termination of parental rights). Some courts have rejected use of the best interest test to judge the propriety of transfer and limited the good cause exception to situations in which a transfer to tribal court would lead to substantial inconvenience in litigating the case. See *In re Armell,* 194 Ill. App. 3d 31, 550 N.E.2d 1060, 1065, appeal denied, 555 N.E.2d 374 (Ill.), cert. denied, 498 U.S. 940 (1990) (neglect and dependency proceedings); *In re C.E.H.,* 837 S.W.2d 947, 954 (Mo. Ct. App. 1992)

(termination of parental rights); *In re Guardianship of Ashley Elizabeth R.,* 116 N.M. 416, 863 P.2d 451, 456 (1993) (guardianship proceeding). See generally Carriere, "Representing the Native American," 79 *Iowa L. Rev.* at 615–32; Connelly, "Tribal Jurisdiction under Section 1911(b) of the Indian Child Welfare Act of 1878 [*sic*]," 23 *N.M. L. Rev.* at 492–96.

83. See, e.g., *In re Adoption of Baby Boy L.,* 643 P.2d. 168 (Kan. 1982); *In re Adoption of Baby Boy D.,* 742 P.2d 1059 (Okla. 1985); *Claymore v. Serr,* 405 N.W. 2d 650 (S.D. 1987); *In re Crews,* 825 P.2d 305 (Wash. 1992). See generally Toni Hahn Davis, "The Existing Indian Family Exception to the Indian Child Welfare Act," 69 *N.D. L. Rev.* 465 (1993); Christine Metteer, "The Existing Indian Family Exception: An Impediment to the Trust Responsibility to Preserve Tribal Existence and Culture as Manifested in the Indian Child Welfare Act," 30 *Loyola L.A. L. Rev.* 647, 656 (1997); Brian D. Gallagher, "Indian Child Welfare Act of 1978: The Congressional Foray into the Adoption Process," 15 *N. Ill. U. L. Rev.* 1, 96–104 (1994); Wendy Therese Parnell, "The Existing Indian Family Exception: Denying Tribal Rights Protected by the Indian Child Welfare Act," 34 *S.D. L. Rev.* 381, 397–437 (1997).

84. *In re Bridget R.,* 41 Cal. App. 4th 1483, 49 Cal. Rptr. 2d 507 (1996), cert. denied sub nom. *Cindy R. v. James R.,* 519 U.S. 1060 (1997), and cert. denied sub nom. *Dry Creek Rancheria v. Bridget R.,* 520 U.S. 1181 (1997).

85. 41 Cal. App. 4th at 1492–96, 49 Cal. Rptr. at 516–19. The biological mother's Yaqui heritage was not considered because she did not claim tribal membership. Id. at 1492 n. 4, 49 Cal. Rptr. 2d at 516 n. 4.

86. Id. at 1502–8, 49 Cal. Rptr. 2d at 522–27.

87. Id. at 1492, 49 Cal. Rptr. 2d at 516.

88. Id. at 1508–10, 49 Cal. Rptr. 2d at 527–28. For a subsequent California court of appeals decision that agreed with the *Bridget R.* analysis of the constitutional problems with ICWA but criticized the decision for an excessively narrow interpretation of the existing Indian family exception, see *In re Alexandria Y.,* 45 Cal. App. 4th 1483, 53 Cal. Rptr. 2d 679 (1996). For a decision that applied *Bridget R.*'s reasoning to a dependency proceeding, see *Crystal R. v. Superior Court,* 59 Cal. App. 4th 703, 69 Cal. Rptr. 414 (1997), petition for review denied, 1998 Cal. LEXIS 1124 (Feb. 18, 1998) (No. S067048). But cf. *Alicia S. v. Mishiola,* 1998 Cal. App. LEXIS 575 (1998) (rejecting the existing Indian family doctrine set forth in *Bridget R.*).

89. S. 764, 104th Cong., 1st Sess. (1995); H.R. 1448, 104th Cong., 1st Sess. (1995).

90. 141 Cong. Rec. S6277 (daily ed. May 8, 1995) (remarks of Sen. John Glenn of Ohio).

91. S. 764, 104th Cong., 1st Sess. §§ 2(a), 2(b)(3), 3; 141 Cong. Rec. S6277 (daily ed. May 8, 1995) (remarks of Sen Glenn).

92. H.R. 3286, 104th Cong., 2d Sess. §§ 301–303 (1996). Membership had to be adjudicated at the time of the custody proceeding, adults who became tribal members after the age of eighteen could do so only upon written consent, and no admission to membership would be given retroactive effect under ICWA. Id. Over the strong objections of tribal representatives and some members of Congress, the House of Representatives approved the changes in the Adoption Promotion and Stability Act, but the Senate subsequently rejected the bill. Eric Schmitt, "Adoption Bill Facing Battle Over a Provision on Indians," *N.Y. Times,* May 8, 1996, at A17; Eric Schmitt, "House Endorses Break on Taxes for Adoptions," *N.Y. Times,* May 11, 1996, at A1; Jonathan Riskind, "Pryce Starts Over on Indian Adoption," *Columbus Dispatch,* June 19, 1997, at 4B; David Whit-

ney, "Deal Loosens Tribal Grip on Native Adoptions," *Anchorage Daily News,* July 25, 1996, at 1B.

93. H.R. 1957, 105th Cong., 1st Sess. (1997).

94. S. 1213, 106th Cong., 1st Sess. (1999); H.R. 1082, 105th Cong., 1st Sess. (1997); S. 569, 105th Cong., 1st Sess. (1997). A similar bill failed to win House approval in 1996, but a Senate panel approved the 1997 bill after the House and Senate held a joint hearing on the proposed legislation. House Resources Committee and Senate Committee on Indian Affairs, *Hearings on Amendments to the Indian Child Welfare Act of 1978,* 105th Cong., 1st Sess. (June 18, 1997); Roger K. Lowe, "Indian Adoption Bill Dies in House, Pryce Says She'll Push for More Reform," *Columbus Dispatch,* Oct. 1, 1996, at 3A; "Panel OKs Measure on Adoption of Native American Kids," *National Journal's Congress Daily,* July 31, 1997. See generally Sloan Philips, "The Indian Child Welfare Act in the Face of Extinction," 21 *Am. Ind. L. Rev.* 351 (1997) (describing congressional reform efforts and prospect of ongoing attacks on ICWA).

95. Note, "Custody Disputes following the Dissolution of Interracial Marriages: Best Interests of the Child or Judicial Racism?" 19 *J. Fam. L.* 97, 105–11 (1980–81); *Compos v. McKeithen,* 341 F. Supp. 264, 266 (E.D. La. 1972) (describing Louisiana's argument that "it is not normal or natural for white parents to beget a black child" so the legislature could prohibit transracial adoptions); *Drummond v. Fulton County Department of Family & Children's Services,* 563 F.2d 1200, 1205–6 (5th Cir. 1977) (en banc) (agency could consider such "factors as age, hair color, eye color and facial features of parents and child" as well as race to decide how "to place the child where he can most easily become a normal family member"). See generally Bartholet, *Family Bonds* at 93, 95; Kathy Russell, Midge Wilson, and Ronald Hall, *The Color Complex: The Politics of Skin Color Among African Americans* 99–100 (paperback ed. 1992) (describing how adoption agencies tried to match the skin tone of black infants with that of prospective black parents).

96. *Farmer v. Farmer,* 109 Misc. 2d 137, 439 N.Y.S.2d 584, 588–89 (1981) (collecting cases).

97. Although a slight majority of domestic adoptions are classified as "related," this category primarily includes adoptions by stepparents. Kathy S. Stolley, "Statistics on Adoption in the United States," in Center for the Future of Children, 3 *The Future of Children* at 19. Moreover, about one in six adoptions is international and typically involves unrelated adoptive parents and children. Id. However, it should be noted that statistical records on adoptions are regrettably incomplete and unsystematic.

98. Some prospective parents also report that a "good match is important because people would think the child is yours and not adopted." Sandra L. Lobar and Suzanne Phillips, "Parents Who Utilize Private Infant Adoption: An Ethnographic Analysis," 19 *Issues in Comprehensive Pediatric Nursing* 65, 70 (1996) (in-depth interviews with ten adoptive parents). Prospective parents who pursue private adoptions, whether through an agency or independently, are more apt than those who use public agencies to report that they did so only after unsuccessful efforts to become pregnant. Marianne Berry, Richard P. Barth, and Barbara Needell, "Preparation, Support, and Satisfaction of Adoptive Families in Agency and Independent Adoptions," 13 *Child & Adolescent Soc. Work J.* 157, 166 (1966) (large-scale survey of adoptive families in California).

99. Susan R. Harris, "Race, Search, and My Baby Self: Reflections of a Transracial Adoptee," 9 *Yale J. L. & Feminism* 5, 11–12 (1997).

100. Ruth-Arlene W. Howe, "Transracial Adoption (TRA): Old Prejudices and Discrimination Float under a New Halo," 6 *B.U. Pub. Int'l L.J.* 409, 429–32 (1997).

101. See note 13 above and accompanying text.

102. 843 F. Supp. 356 (W.D. Tenn. 1993).

103. Id. at 357.

104. Id. at 365.

105. Id.

106. Id.

107. Note, "Custody Disputes following the Dissolution of Interracial Marriages," 19 *J. Fam. L.* at 111–36.

108. See notes 86–88 above and accompanying text.

109. *In re Petition of R.M.G.*, 454 A.2d 776, 782 (D.C. App. 1982).

110. *Drummond v. Fulton County Department of Family & Children's Services*, 563 F.2d 1200, 1205 (5th Cir. 1977) (en banc).

111. Id.; *In re D.I.S. for the Adoption of S.A.O.*, 494 A.2d 1316 (D.C. App. 1985). Some judges have argued that social biases also ought to be considered, but this approach was rejected in *Palmore* for custody disputes. *Drummond v. Fulton County Department of Family & Children's Services*, 563 F.2d at 1211–12 (concurrence of Brown, C.J.) ("Granted that society and the community should not harbor attitudes against interracial mixture, the subject of the foster home placement and even adoption is the child, whose life will be affected by community values and prejudices as they exist, not what they ought to be.").

112. *DeWees v. Stevenson*, 779 F. Supp. 25 (E.D. Pa. 1991). Two years before the child was placed in their home, Mrs. DeWees informed agency workers that she did not want to take black foster children because she feared that people would think that she or her daughter was "sleeping with a black man." Id. at 26. Later, she indicated that the real reason was her doubt about whether she would know how to care for a black child. Id.

113. Id. at 27.

114. Id.

115. Id.

116. Id. at 28–29.

117. Id. at 29.

118. For a complete discussion of the Court's approach to interracial marriage in *Loving v. Virginia*, 388 U.S. 1 (1967), see chapter 5.

119. Attachment theory indicates that children bond with adults who are their caretakers, regardless of whether they are biologically related or physically similar. John Bowlby, *The Making and Breaking of Affectional Bonds* (1979); John Bowlby, *Attachment and Loss* (1982). This theory of parent–child bonding has been highly influential in child welfare and placement policy. Joseph Goldstein, Anna Freud, and Albert J. Solnit, *Beyond the Best Interests of the Child* 19, 31–35 (1973) (arguing that a stable relationship with a "psychological parent" is the single most important factor in a child's adjustment).

120. Indeed, one study of black transracial adoptees found that where race played a role in unsuccessful placements, the children were more rather than less closely matched to their parents' appearance. Presumably, the phenotypical matching prompted some white parents to deny the child's racial background by minimizing or ignoring it. Lucille J. Grow and Deborah Shapiro, *Black Children—White Parents* 5–18, 25–28, 224–25, 236 (1974).

121. For a discussion of the stigma that still attaches to adoption despite extensive evidence that adoptive parenting is at least as successful as biological parenting, see Bartholet, *Family Bonds* at 164–86.

122. Fanshel, *Far from the Reservation;* Grow and Shapiro, *Black Children—White Parents;* Ruth G. McRoy and Louis A. Zurcher, *Transracial and Inracial Adoptees* (1983); Joan F. Shireman, *Growing Up Adopted: An Examination of Major Issues* (1988); Simon and Altstein, *Adoption, Race and Identity;* Estela Andujo, "Ethnic Identity of Trans-ethnically Adopted Hispanic Adolescents," 33 *Soc. Work* 531 (1988); William Feigelman and Arnold R. Silverman, "The Long-Term Effects of Transracial Adoption," 58 *Soc. Serv. Rev.* 588 (1984); Dong Soo Kim, "How They Fared in American Homes: A Follow-Up Study of Adopted Korean Children in the United States," 6 *Children Today* 2 (March/April 1977); Joan F. Shireman and Penny R. Johnson, "A Longitudinal Study of Black Adoptions: Single Parent, Transracial, and Traditional," 31 *Soc. Work* 172 (1986); Silverman, "Outcomes of Transracial Adoption," in *The Future of Children—Adoption* (Behrman ed.), at 117; Karen Vroegh, *Transracial Adoption: How It Is 17 Years Later* (Apr. 2, 1992).

123. See Hawley Fogg-Davis, "A Race-Conscious Argument for Transracial Adoption," 6 *B.U. Pub. Int'l L.J.* 385, 398–401 (1997).

124. Kathryn D. Gray, "Fathers' Participation in Child Custody Arrangements among Hispanic, Non-Hispanic White, and Intermarried Families," 23 *J. Comp. Fam. Studies* 55 (1992). The failure to account for cultural differences after divorce may have serious consequences for children. For example, patterns of cultural divergence in marriage and childrearing could account for higher rates of abduction of children following the divorce of interracial as compared to same-race couples. Rebecca L. Hegar and Geoffrey L. Grief, "Parental Abduction of Children from Interracial and Cross-Cultural Marriages," 25 *J. Comp. Fam. Stud.* 135 (1994).

125. According to one recruiter at a Chicago agency, "We have families who say I'll take Hispanic, American Indian, anything but black." She estimates that only about 5 percent of white families express an interest in adopting a black child. Tamar Lewin, "New Families Redraw Racial Boundaries," *N.Y. Times,* Oct. 27, 1998, at A1, col. 1. At least one author has argued that any accommodation of prospective parents' racial preferences reinforces racist attitudes and should be banned, whether or not the practice is constitutional. R. Richard Banks, "The Color of Desire: Fulfilling Adoptive Parents' Racial Preferences through Discriminatory State Action," 107 *Yale L.J.* 875 (1998). Because disregarding parental wishes seems unlikely to reform them and because children might find themselves in unsuitable or rejecting settings, I do not advocate this strategy but instead urge officials to establish an appropriate distinction between empirical and normative views of segregation in the family.

126. See Leslie Doty Hollingsworth, "Sociodemographic Influences in the Prediction of Attitudes toward Transracial Adoption," 81 *Families in Society* 92 (2000) (approximately 71 percent of adults approve of transracial adoption, but only 57.4 percent of black females and 66.2 percent of white males do).

127. Indeed, one need not even choose a spouse of the same race. In Italy, a black woman married to a white man chose to have herself implanted with a fertilized ovum from a white donor so that she could bear a white child. Ezra E.H. Griffith, "Culture and the Debate on Adoption of Black Children by White Families," 14 *Rev. of Psychiatry* 543, 543–44 (1995).

128. In fact, the deregulatory ethic in family law has intensified in recent years, leaving individuals free to break up families through divorce, build new families through remarriage, and live together and form families without the benefit of marriage. Consequently, any effort to shut down independent adoptions would represent a significant departure from this trend toward privatization of family law. See generally Jana B. Singer, "The Privatization of Family Law," 1992 *Wis. L. Rev.* 1449.

129. According to a survey of 2,238 families who adopted children in California through public agencies, private agencies, or independent adoptions in 1988–89, the cost of an independent adoption was $5,766 compared to $5,218 for private agency adoption and $645 for public agency adoption. Berry, Barth, and Needell, "Preparation, Support, and Satisfaction of Adoptive Families in Agency and Independent Adoptions," 13 *Child & Adolescent Soc. Work* at 163.

130. International adoptions may be done through a U.S.-based private agency or independently. Margaret Liu, "International Adoptions: An Overview," 8 *Temple Int'l & Comp. L.J.* at 198–99. For a description of some of the abuses that have occurred in the international adoption process and the limited success of regulatory efforts, see Carro, "Regulation of Intercountry Adoption: Can the Abuses Come to an End?" 18 *Hastings Int'l L. Rev.* at 128–55.

131. For an article arguing that "an adoption market already exists, however distasteful that may seem," see Margaret F. Brinig, "The Effect of Transaction Costs on the Market for Babies," 18 *Seton Hall. Legis. J.* 553, 554 (1994). At least some scholars have defended a market model for adoptions. See, e.g., Elizabeth Landes and Richard A. Posner, "The Economics of the Baby Shortage," 7 *J. Legal Stud.* 323 (1978); Richard A. Posner, "The Regulation of the Market in Adoptions," 67 *B.U. L. Rev.* 59 (1987). However, their views have met with considerable resistance. Brinig, "The Effect of Transaction Costs on the Market for Babies," at 554 n. 2 (collecting critiques of Posner's position).

132. To some extent, these dangers of endorsement are already attenuated by the shortage of white children available for adoption. White, middle-class parents with a strong preference for a child of the same race are likely to turn to independent adoptions. This way, white adoptive parents avoid long delays, and their placement preference can be matched with those of biological parents under agreements unfettered by agency censure or support. See Susan A. Munson, "Independent Adoption: In Whose Best Interest?" 26 *Seton Hall L. Rev.* 803, 809–14 (1996) (describing the rise in independent adoptions and some of the reasons for it).

133. See *In re Petition of R.M.G.*, 454 A.2d at 796–99, 803–6 (dissent of Newman, J.) (criticizing the majority's equation of race with racial attitudes and insisting that if attitudes were the only consideration, they would have to be considered in same-race and transracial placements alike).

134. Perry, "Transracial and International Adoption: Mothers, Hierarchy, Race, and Feminist Legal Theory," 19 *Yale J.L. & Feminism* at 41–49.

135. Rita J. Simon and Howard Altstein, *Transracial Adoptees and Their Families: A Study of Identity and Commitment* 62–63, 80–82 (1987). The same flexible attitudes toward race characterize blacks who are transracially adopted rather than placed in a same-race family. Joan F. Shireman, *Growing Up Adopted: An Examination of Major Issues* 27 (1988); Shireman and Johnson, "A Longitudinal Study of Black Adoptions," 31 *Soc. Work* at 172. Transracial adoptees also are more likely to identify themselves as mixed-race

than are same-race adoptees. In part, this difference may be due to a greater willingness among agencies to consider transracial placements for children with a white and a black biological parent than for children with two black biological parents. Vroegh, *Transracial Adoption* at i, 5, 11–12, 17–18. See also Peter L. Benson, Anu R. Sharma, and Eugene C. Roehlkepartain, *Growing Up Adopted: A Portrait of Adolescents and Their Families* 108 (1994) (describing how transracial adoptees develop "a kind of multicultural competency" that helps them to get along with people of varying races).

136. Francis Wardle, "Are You Sensitive to Interracial Children's Special Identity Needs?" 42 *Young Children* 53, 55 (1987). See also Ruth G. McRoy, Louis A. Zurcher, Michael Lauderdale, and Rosalie Anderson, "The Identity of Transracial Adoptees," 15 *Soc. Casework* 34, 38 (1984); Ruth G. McRoy, Louis A. Zurcher, Michael Lauderdale, and Rosalie Anderson, "Self-Esteem and Racial Identity in Transracial and Inracial Adoptees," 27 *Soc. Work* 522, 535 (1982); Andujo, "Ethnic Identity of Transethnically Adopted Hispanic Adolescents," 33 *Soc. Work* at 533–34.

137. Kathlyn Gay, *The Rainbow Effect: Interracial Families* 25 (1987).

138. Bartholet, "Where Do Black Children Belong?" 139 *U. Pa. L. Rev.* at 1211–23; Bowen, "Cultural Convergence and Divergences," 26 *J. Fam L.* at 498–501, 505–11. See Silverman, "Outcomes of Transracial Adoption," in *The Future of Children—Adoption* (Behrman ed.), at 14, for a recent account of empirical studies indicating that transracial placements can have positive outcomes for adoptees, outcomes clearly superior to long-term foster care or institutionalization.

139. Bartholet, "Where Do Black Children Belong?" 139 *U. Pa. L. Rev.* at 1201–4; Bowen, "Cultural Convergence and Divergences," 26 *J. Fam L.* at 490–94; McLaughlin, "Transracial Adoption in New York State," 60 *Alb. L. Rev.* at 504; Rebecca Varan, "Designating the Adoptive Family: In Support of the Adoption Antidiscrimination Act of 1995," 30 *John Marshall L. Rev.* 543, 596 (1997).

140. Grow and Shapiro, *Black Children—White Parents* at 5–18, 25–28, 224–25, 236; McRoy and Zurcher, *Transracial and Inracial Adoptees* at 16–27, 126–27, 135–36; McRoy et al., "Self-Esteem and Racial Identity in Transracial and Inracial Adoptees," 27 *Soc. Work* at 522, 525; McRoy et al., "The Identity of Transracial Adoptees," 15 *Soc. Casework* at 38; Andujo, "Ethnic Identity of Transethnically Adopted Hispanic Adolescents," 33 *Soc. Work* at 531–34.

141. See Fogg-Davis, "A Race-Conscious Argument for Transracial Adoption," 6 *B.U. Pub. Int'l L.J.* at 405–7 (arguing for a flexible, dialogic notion of race); Griffith, "Culture and the Debate on Adoption of Black Children by White Families," 14 *Rev. of Psychiatry* at 558–63 (warning against an oversimplistic reification of black culture).

142. In the absence of a judicially recognized constitutional interest in preserving de facto families, some states have passed statutes according weight to established emotional bonds with a child. See, e.g., Cal. Fam. Code § 8710; Me. Rev. Stat. Ann. § 9-308(b)(1), (2). See also Hanan, "The Best Interest of the Child: Eliminating Discrimination in the Screening of Adoptive Parents," 27 *Golden Gate U.L. Rev.* at 211–13.

143. For a recent adoption dispute in which white foster parents of a child of black and Hispanic origin have argued that bonds of attachment count more than ties of blood, see Lewin, "New Families Redraw Racial Boundaries," *N.Y. Times,* Oct. 27, 1998, at A1, col. 1. The child's black kin contend, however, that the child welfare agency failed to give them fair consideration as an adoptive home. For a discussion of procedural issues in the case, see *In re Justin,* 711 A.2d 1146 (R.I. 1998).

144. Karen Angel, "Just a Good Family/Law Lessens Requirement for Same-Race Adoption," *Newsday*, Aug. 3, 1997, at A8 (describing black couple's racial discrimination lawsuit based on an agency's refusal to allow them to adopt white foster children in their care).

145. Brooks et al., *California Adoptions* at 5–6 (race is routinely considered in placing white children and transracial placements are rare for them).

146. Judith Stacey, *Brave New Families: Stories of Domestic Upheaval in Late Twentieth Century America* 17–18 (paperback ed. 1991) (describing the postmodern family as a site of contestation and uncertainty); Angel, "Just a Good Family/Law Lessens Requirement for Same-Race Adoption," *Newsday*, Aug. 3, 1997, at A8.

147. See Woodhouse, " 'Are You My Mother,' " 2 *Duke J. Gender L. & Pol'y* at 107–14, 117–18, 124–25, 127–28 (contrasting approaches that treat children as passive objects like property and those that put a child's needs at the center of adoption policy).

148. H.R. Rep. No. 1136, 95th Cong., 2d Sess. 12 (1978); Goldsmith, "Individual vs. Collective Rights," 13 *Harv. Women's L.J.* at 5 and n. 21, 7–8. See also Catharine A. MacKinnon, *Feminism Unmodified* 63–69 (1987) (arguing that male-dominated tribal processes may be an artifact of contact with white culture and therefore invalid); but cf. Angela P. Harris, "Race and Essentialism in Feminist Legal Theory," 42 *Stan. L. Rev.* 581, 593–95 (1990) (contending that MacKinnon's monolithic theory of gender equality cannot account adequately for racial difference).

149. See Judith Resnik, "Dependent Sovereigns: Indian Tribes, States, and the Federal Courts," 56 *U. Chi. L. Rev.* 671, 751 (1989) ("Some deep-seated emotional respect for group governance may be at work here, some sense that these self-contained communities [have] traditions and customs [that] must sometimes be respected and preserved.").

150. This approach to coverage of nonreservation Indians avoids the error of equating tribal sovereignty with geographical territory. Federal policy eliminated many tribes' communal properties, so such an approach would penalize Indians for past government actions that undercut their territorial claims. A membership-based approach permits tribes to influence the evolution of culture and values among those who voluntarily affiliate with the tribe and are recognized as members. By continuing to apply a conclusive presumption of tribal jurisdiction to reservation Indians, tribes' authority over their territorial lands also is preserved. See Allison M. Dussias, "Geographically-Based and Membership-Based Views of Indian Tribal Sovereignty: The Supreme Court's Changing Vision," 55 *U. Pitt. L. Rev.* 1 (1993) (comparing geographical definitions of tribal sovereignty to definitions based on voluntary membership and arguing that the U.S. Supreme Court has applied these approaches in a selective manner that undercuts tribal authority).

151. ICWA already offers some heightened protections to Indian parents who consent to a voluntary change in placement. See 25 U.S.C. § 1913 (requiring that when a parent consents to a foster care placement or termination of parental rights, the consent must be in writing and the judge must certify that the parent fully understood the terms and consequences of the consent, that the parent must later be permitted to withdraw the consent, and that the parent can collaterally attack an adoption decree based on fraud or duress).

152. A Navajo tribal court has adopted this approach, but state courts have not. Stan Watts, "Voluntary Adoption under the Indian Child Welfare Act of 1978: Balancing the Interest of the Children, Families, and Tribes," 63 *S. Cal. L. Rev.* 213, 215, 253–55 (1989). See also Gilbert A. Holmes, "The Extended Family System in the Black Commu-

nity: A Child-Centered Model for Adoption Policy," 68 *Temple L. Rev.* 1649 (1995) (making similar arguments based on black models of the family).

153. H.R. 1452, 105th Cong., 1st Sess. (1997); S. 822, 105th Cong., 1st Sess (1997). See also Madeleine L. Kurtz, "The Purchase of Families into Foster Care: Two Case Studies and the Lessons They Teach," 26 *Conn. L. Rev.* 1453, 1518–24 (1994) (calling for general reforms to kinship care programs to accord appropriate respect to extended family networks); Carol B. Stack, "Cultural Perspectives on Child Welfare," 12 *N.Y.U. Rev. L. & Soc. Change* 539, 546–47 (1983–84) (permanency planning should not unduly interfere with kinship networks); Peggy C. Davis, "Use and Abuse of the Power to Sever Family Bonds," 12 *N.Y.U. Rev. L. & Soc. Change* 557, 570–71 (1983–84) (noting the need for the child welfare system to recognize the success of extended kinship networks in parenting, especially in the black community).

154. Pub. L. No. 89, §§ 301(a)(3)(c), 303, 105th Cong., 1st Sess. (1997), codified at 42 U.S.C. §§ 1320a-9(a)(3)(c), 5113. In addition, Congress has authorized grants to develop kinship care programs for abused or neglected children in not more than ten states. 42 U.S.C. § 5106(a)(3)(B).

CHAPTER EIGHT

1. 388 U.S. 1 (1967). The Court's rationale for the decision is set forth in chapter 5.

2. Douglas S. Massey and Nancy A. Denton, *American Apartheid: Segregation and the Making of the Underclass* 60–114 (1993) (noting that segregation, particularly of blacks and whites, has remained largely unchanged despite legislative reform and improved economic opportunity for nonwhites); see also Benjamin De Mott, *The Trouble with Friendship: Why Americans Can't Think Straight about Race* 7–56 (1995) (describing popular portrayals of black–white friendships as "privatizing, historyless fantasies").

3. Katheryn A. Ocampo, Martha E. Bernal, and George P. Knight, "Gender, Race, and Ethnicity: The Sequencing of Social Constancies," in *Ethnic Identity: Formation and Transmission among Hispanics and Other Minorities* 15–19 (Martha E. Bernal and George P. Knight eds., 1993) (paperback ed.).

4. Robyn M. Holmes, *How Young Children Perceive Race* 40–46 (1995).

5. Id. at 94–99, 101–2.

6. Id. at 99–101, 102–4.

7. Francis Wardle, "Are You Sensitive to Interracial Children's Special Identity Needs?" 42 *Young Children* 53, 55 (1987).

8. Kathlyn Gay, *The Rainbow Effect: Interracial Families* 65 (1987).

9. Id. at 66.

10. Id. at 25 (1987), quoting Geoff Geiger, "The Journey from 'Other,'" 8(2) *I-Pride Newsletter* 1 (Apr. 1986).

11. Jewelle Taylor Gibbs, "Identity and Marginality: Issues in the Treatment of Biracial Adolescents," 57 *Amer. J. Orthopsychiat.* 265, 269–70 (1987).

12. Id. at 271. For additional discussion of the identity problems encountered by biracial offspring of black–white marriages, see Dorcas D. Bowles, "Bi-racial Identity: Children Born to African-American and White Couples," 21 *Clinical Soc. Work J.* 417 (1993).

13. For a range of personal accounts about coping with a biracial identity, see Lise Funderberg, *Black, White, Other: Biracial Americans Talk about Race and Identity* (1994).

14. Nelly Salgado de Snyder, Cynthia M. Lopez, and Amado M. Padilla, "Ethnic Identity and Cultural Awareness among the Offspring of Mexican Interethnic Marriages," 2 *J. Early Adolescence* 277, 279–81 (1982). It should be noted that more females than males expressed a preference for Mexican-origin spouses. Id. at 280. Another study has shown that intermarriage leads to a decline in the use of languages other than English among offspring. Gillian Stevens, "Nativity, Intermarriage, and Mother-Tongue Shift," 50 *Am. Soc. Rev.* 74 (1985). The study by Salgado de Snyder, Lopez, and Padilla (cited earlier in this note, at 280) relied entirely on self-reported use of Spanish and made no attempt to measure fluency independently.

15. Salgado de Snyder, Lopez, and Padilla, "Ethnic Identity and Cultural Awareness among the Offspring of Mexican Interethnic Marriages," 2 *J. Early Adolescence* at 281–82. See also Ronald C. Johnson and Craig T. Nagoshi, "The Adjustment of Offspring of Within-Group and Interracial/Intercultural Marriages: A Comparison of Personality Factor Scores," 48 *J. Marriage & the Family* 279, 282–83 (1986) (reporting that offspring of cross-ethnic marriages were as well adjusted as those of within-ethnic marriages, at least in the tolerant environment of Hawaii where such unions are commonplace).

16. Michael Omi and Howard Winant, *Racial Formation in the United States: From the 1960's to the 1980's* at 60 (1986).

17. James McBride, *The Color of Water: A Black Man's Tribute to His White Mother* 22 (1996).

18. Judy Scales-Trent, *Notes of a White Black Woman: Race, Color, Community* 183 (1995).

19. Henry Louis Gates Jr., "White Like Me," *New Yorker,* June 17, 1996, at 66, 76.

20. Id. at 70–71.

21. Id. at 78.

22. Leonard M. Baynes, "Who Is Black Enough for You?: An Analysis of Northwestern University Law School's Struggle Over Minority Faculty Hiring," 2 *Mich. J. Race & L.* 205, 207 n. 6, 218 (1997).

23. Id. at 208–9.

24. Id. at 210–211.

25. Id. at 226.

26. Id. For a similar account of contested identity involving a female professor from Puerto Rico who grew up with a white mother and black father, see Lisa Levitt, "Mixed Messages; Multi-Ethnic Children Have Hard Time Deciding Who They Are in Society That Likes Categories," *Rocky Mountain News,* Mar. 22, 1998, at F16R.

27. Latinos and Native Americans report similar stories of being asked to prove their authenticity because their origins do not seem pure enough. Deborah A. Ramirez, "Multiracial Identity in a Color-Conscious World," in *The Multiracial Experience: Racial Borders as the New Frontier* 49, 49–50 (Maria P. P. Root ed., 1996) (paperback ed.); Terry P. Wilson, "Blood Quantum: Native American Mixed Bloods," in *Racially Mixed People in America* 108, 123–24 (Maria P. P. Root ed., 1992).

28. Lisa Jones, "Are We Tiger Woods Yet? America Buys Social Change," *Village Voice,* July 22, 1997, at 36.

29. Scales-Trent, *Notes of a White Black Woman* at 101–2.

30. Annharte, "Emilia I Shoulda Said Something Political," in *Miscegenation Blues: Voices of Mixed Race Women* 178, 181 (Carol Camper ed., 1994) (paperback ed.). See also Christine B. Hickman, "The Devil and the One Drop Rule: Racial Categories, African

Americans, and the U.S. Census," 95 *Mich. L. Rev.* 1161, 1258 (1997) ("the attempt to find common ground among multiracial people by asserting that they are natural mediators is an unpersuasive form of stereotyping").

31. Maria P. P. Root, "A Bill of Rights for Racially Mixed People," in *The Multiracial Experience* (Root ed.), at 3, 7.

32. Id. at 7–14.

33. For a brief overview of the controversies leading up to changes in racial classifications on the census, see National Research Council, *Modernizing the U.S. Census* 140–55 (Barry Edmonston and Charles Schultze eds., 1995).

34. See General Accounting Office, *Decennial Census—Overview of Historical Census Issues,* May 22, 1998 (RPT-Number: GAO/GGD-98-103).

35. Hyman Alterman, *Counting People: The Census in History* 266–69 (1969); Margo J. Anderson, *The American Census: A Social History* 7–14 (1988).

36. Alterman, *Counting People* at 275–76; Sharon M. Lee, "Racial Classifications in the US Census: 1890–1990," 16 *Ethnic and Racial Studies* 75, 77–78 (1993).

37. Lee, "Racial Classifications in the US Census," 16 *Ethnic and Racial Studies* at 77–80.

38. Alterman, *Counting People* at 275, 291–301.

39. Id. at 285; Lee, "Racial Classifications in the US Census," 16 *Ethnic and Racial Studies* at 79; Juan Gomez-Quinones, *Roots of Chicano Politics, 1600–1940* at 373–76 (paperback ed. 1994). See also David Montejano, *Anglos and Mexicans in the Making of Texas, 1836–1986* at 182–88 (paperback ed. 1987).

40. Lee, "Racial Classifications in the US Census," 16 *Ethnic and Racial Studies* at 79. Before then, enumerators could second-guess a person's racial identity.

41. The disparities among Asian subgroups already have prompted a lively debate about the utility of lumping them together in a single racial category. Michael Omi, "Racial Identity and the State: The Dilemmas of Classification," 15 *Law and Inequality* 7, 17–18 (1997); Lee, "Racial Classifications in the US Census," 16 *Ethnic and Racial Studies* at 84–86, 88–90. But cf. House Committee on Post Office and Civil Service, *Review of Federal Measurements of Race and Ethnicity: Hearings before the Subcomm. on Census, Statistics and Postal Personnel* [hereinafter 1993 House Hearings], 103d Cong., 1st Sess. 194–95 (1993) (remarks of Henry Der, National Coalition for an Accurate Count of Asians and Pacific Islanders, expressing strong support for listing of various subgroups under Asian and Pacific Islander designation and urging that if any changes are made, more subgroups should be added to this category). The Office of Management and Budget will now treat Native Hawaiians and Pacific Islanders separately from other Asian Americans because of their distinct socioeconomic characteristics. Office of Management and Budget, *Revisions to the Standards for the Classification of Federal Data on Race and Ethnicity* [hereinafter OMB Revisions] (1997).

42. Office of Management and Budget, Directive No. 15, *Race and Ethnic Standards for Federal Statistics and Administrative Reporting,* 43 Fed. Reg. 19260, 19269 (1977).

43. Reynolds Farley, "The New Census Question about Ancestry: What Did It Tell Us?" 28 *Demography* 411, 412 (1991).

44. Deborah A. Ramirez, "Multicultural Empowerment: It's Not Just Black and White Anymore," 47 *Stan. L. Rev.* 957, 960–62 (1995).

45. Hickman, "The Devil and the One Drop Rule," 95 *Mich. L. Rev.* at 1247.

46. For a discussion of patterns of intermarriage for these groups, see chapter 6.

47. Mary C. Waters, *Ethnic Options: Choosing Identities in America* 148–55 (1990);

Farley, "The New Census Question about Ancestry," 28 *Demography* at 411, 412–14, 416–17, 420–21, 424–26.

48. Executive Office of the President, Office of Management and Budget, Office of Information and Regulatory Affairs, *Recommendations from the Interagency Committee for the Review of the Racial and Ethnic Standards to the Office of Management and Budget Concerning Changes to the Standards for the Classification of Federal Data on Race and Ethnicity—Part II* [hereinafter Interagency Committee Recommendations], 62 Fed. Reg. 36874, 36937 (1997).

49. Carl M. Cannon, "More than 1 Answer for Race on Census Form Is Proposed; But Clinton Opposes Multiracial Category," *Baltimore Sun,* July 9, 1997, at 3A.

50. 1993 House Hearings at 107 (testimony of Susan Graham, executive director of Project RACE); 133 (prepared statement of Carlos Fernandez, president of Association of Multiethnic Americans); 161 (testimony of Maj. Marvin Arnold, Ph.D.).

51. Frank James, "Panel Rejects Pleas to Add 'Multiracial' as Official Category," *Chicago Tribune,* July 9, 1997, at 3.

52. Scott Shepard, "Congress Hears Controversy over Multiracial Category," *Atlanta Journal and Constitution,* July 26, 1997, at 5A.

53. Timothy P. Johnson et al., "Dimensions of Self Identification among Multiracial and Multiethnic Respondents in Survey Interviews" (n.d.) (describing study of sixty-nine multiracial and multiethnic women done for the Bureau of the Census, which concluded that most wanted to be able to express their mixed origins and that a substantial number sought a way to identify their multiple origins rather than to identify simply as multiracial); Tabulation Working Group, Interagency Committee for the Review of Standards for Data on Race and Ethnicity, *Draft Provisional Guidance on the Implementation of the 1997 Standards for Federal Data on Race and Ethnicity* [hereinafter Tabulation Working Group], Feb. 17, 1999, at I.A. (noting that "[i]n keeping with the spirit of the new standards, agencies cannot collect multiple responses and then report and publish data using only the five single race categories").

54. Tabulation Working Group at I.D.

55. Id. at IV.A.

56. Id. at IV.B.

57. Office of Management and Budget, *Bulletin No. 00-02 to the Heads of Executive Departments and Establishments, Guidance on Aggregation and Allocation of Data on Race for Use in Civil Rights Monitoring* (Mar. 9, 2000).

58. Id.

59. Id.

60. Steven A. Holmes, "New Policy on Census Says Those Listed as White and Minority Will Be Counted as Minority," *New York Times,* Mar. 11, 2000, at A7, col. 1.

61. Tabulation Working Group at III.A., IV.C.

62. Michael Lind, "The Beige and the Black," *N.Y. Times,* Aug. 16, 1998, § 6, at p. 38, col. 1 (Magazine).

63. Roger Sanjek, "Intermarriage and the Future of Races in the United States," in *Race* 103, 117 (Steven Gregory and Roger Sanjek eds., 1994).

64. Id. at 110–14.

65. See Robert M. Jiobu, *Ethnicity and Assimilation: Blacks, Chinese, Filipinos, Japanese, Koreans, Mexicans, Vietnamese, and Whites* 153–77 (1988); Nancy A. Denton and Douglas S. Massey, "Trends in the Residential Segregation of Blacks, Hispanics, and

Asian-Americans by Socioeconomic Status and Generation," 69 *Soc. Sci. Q.* 797, 798 (1988); Douglas S. Massey and Nancy A. Denton, "Trends in the Residential Segregation of Blacks, Hispanics, and Asian-Americans: 1970–1980," 52 *Am. Soc. Rev.* 802, 820 (1987); Douglas S. Massey and Eric Fong, "Segregation and Neighborhood Quality: Blacks, Hispanics, and Asians in the San Francisco Metropolitan Area," 69 *Soc. Forces* 15, 28 (1990).

66. For a fuller discussion of the history of black–white sexual and marital relations, see chapter 2.

67. For an interesting exploration of evolving racial identity among Americans with one black and one white parent, see Kathleen Odell Korgen, *From Black to Biracial: Transforming Racial Identity among Americans* (1998).

68. Alterman, *Counting People* at 275–76; Lee, "Racial Classifications in the US Census," 16 *Ethnic and Racial Studies* at 77.

69. 1993 House Hearings, at 273. See also Trina Grillo, "Anti-Essentialism and Intersectionality: Tools to Dismantle the Master's House," 10 *Berkeley Women's L.J.* 16, 25–27 (1995) (expressing the desire for a way to recognize biracial identity without undermining the black community); Tanya Katerí Hernández, " 'Multiracial' Discourse: Racial Classifications in an Era of Color-Blind Jurisprudence," 57 *Maryland L. Rev.* 97, 121–39 (1998) (decrying cooptation of blacks with some white ancestry through creation of multiracial category).

70. Steven A. Holmes, "Panel Balks at Multiracial Census Category," *N.Y. Times,* July 9, 1997, at A12.

71. For a more complete discussion of intermarriage patterns among Asian Americans, see chapter 6.

72. Sanjek, "Intermarriage and the Future of Races in the United States," in *Race* (Gregory and Sanjek eds.), at 106–8; Waters, *Ethnic Options* at 148–55.

73. For a description of how the "Hispanic origin" question was added to the census, see Anderson, *The American Census* at 221–25; Harvey M. Choldin, "Statistics and Politics: The 'Hispanic Issue' in the 1980 Census," 23 *Demography* 403, 405–10 (1986); Lee, "Racial Classifications in the US Census," 16 *Ethnic and Racial Studies* at 79, 86–90.

74. Gabrielle Sandor, "The 'Other' Americans," 16 *American Demographics* 36, 38–39 (1994); Christopher A. Ford, "Administering Identity: The Determination of 'Race' in Race-Conscious Law," 82 *Calif. L. Rev.* 1231, 1242–43 (1994).

75. Nancy A. Denton and Douglas S. Massey, "Racial Identity among Caribbean Hispanics: The Effect of Double Minority Status on Residential Segregation," 54 *Am. Soc. Rev.* 790, 798–805 (1989) (based on studies of residential patterns in ten major metropolitan areas using 1980 census data).

76. David Lauter, "Where to Draw the Lines?: Changes in American Society Make It Trickier to Define the Beneficiaries and Goals of Affirmative Action. Thirty Years Ago, Determining Who Was a Minority Was Less Complex," *L.A. Times,* Mar. 28, 1995, at A1 (citing Professor Mary C. Waters of Harvard University). For similar reasons, Latinos are apt to resist changes that appear to convert Hispanic origin from an ethnic to a racial categorization. Interagency Committee Recommendations at 36918–19 (citing the opposition of Raul Yzaguirre, president of the National Council of La Raza, to treating Hispanic origin as a racial identification).

77. OMB Revisions (rejecting request that multiple responses be allowed on the Hispanic origin question).

78. Elizabeth Martin, Theresa DeMaio, and Pamela C. Campanelli, "Context Effects for Census Measures of Race and Hispanic Origin," 54 *Pub. Op. Q.* 551, 562–63 (1990); Clara Rodriguez, "Race, Culture, and Latino 'Otherness' in the 1980 Census," 73 *Soc. Sci. Q.* 930, 931–32 (1992); Sandor, "The 'Other' Americans," 16 *American Demographics* at 38–39; Ford, "Administering Identity," 82 *Calif. L. Rev.* at 1242–43.

79. C. Mathew Snipp, "Who Are American Indians? Some Observations about the Perils and Pitfalls of Data for Race and Ethnicity," 5 *Pop. Res. & Pol'y Rev.* 237–52 (1986).

80. Ford, "Administering Identity," 82 *Calif. L. Rev.* at 1244.

81. Russell Thornton, "Tribal Membership Requirements and the Demography of 'Old' and 'New' Native Americans," 16 *Pop. Res. & Pol'y Rev.* 33, 34–35 (1997); Sanjek, "Intermarriage and the Future of Races in the United States," in *Race* (Gregory and Sanjek eds.), at 106; Farley, "The New Census Question about Ancestry," 28 *Demography* at 412–14, 416, 420–21, 426.

82. Thornton, "Tribal Membership Requirements and the Demography of 'Old' and 'New' Native Americans," 16 *Pop. Res. & Pol'y Rev.* at 38–40; Wilson, "Blood Quantum," in *Racially Mixed People in America* (Root ed.), at 122–24.

83. *Morton v. Mancari,* 417 U.S. 535 (1974).

84. Ancestry as manifested in blood quantum requirements is a necessary, though not sufficient, condition for being labeled "Indian." A white man cannot become a member of a tribe solely through intermarriage and adoption of Indian customs. *United States v. Rogers,* 45 U.S. (4 How.) 567 (1846).

85. Judith Resnik, "Dependent Sovereigns: Indian Tribes, States, and the Federal Courts," 56 *U. Chi. L. Rev.* 671, 715–18 (1989).

86. Thornton, "Tribal Membership Requirements and the Demography of 'Old' and 'New' Native Americans," 16 *Pop. Res. & Pol'y Rev.* at 39.

87. Id. at 36–37; Wilson, "Blood Quantum," in *Racially Mixed People in America* (Root ed.), at 122.

88. See, e.g., *Santa Clara Pueblo v. Martinez,* 436 U.S. 49 (1978) (refusing to overturn tribal rule denying membership to children of women who married out); Resnik, "Dependent Sovereigns," 56 *U. Chi. L. Rev.* at 715–16 (describing how the Santa Clara Pueblo tribe was influenced by internal needs and external constraints to limit membership through the outmarriage rule; the action was a response to a rise in mixed marriages and a consequent strain on tribal resources).

89. For a full discussion of the Indian Child Welfare Act and the problems of membership that have arisen, see chapter 7.

90. Paul C. Rosenblatt, Terri A. Karis, and Richard D. Powell, *Multiracial Couples: Black & White Voices* 19–20 (1995).

91. Harold L. Hodgkinson, "What Should We Call People?: Race, Class, and the Census for the Year 2000," 77 *Phi Delta Kappan* 173, 174–76 (1995); Anthony Flint, "Don't Classify by Race, Urge Scientists," *Boston Globe,* Mar. 5, 1995, at B1 (urging the elimination of racial categories because of their lack of scientific validity); Shawn Foster, "Falling through Racial Cracks; Race: People Defy Categorization," *Salt Lake Tribune,* Nov. 27, 1995, at D1 (citing Yehudi Webster, Sociology Department, California State University at Los Angeles); "Redefining Race," *Investor's Business Daily,* Oct. 30, 1995, at A4 (citing Jorge Amselle, Center for Equal Opportunity, Washington, D.C.).

92. Hodgkinson, "What Should We Call People?" 77 *Phi Delta Kappan* at 176.

93. Sanjek, "Intermarriage and the Future of Race in the United States," in *Race* (Gregory and Sanjek eds.), at 114.

94. Bijan Gilanshah, "Multiracial Minorities: Erasing the Color Line," 12 *Law & Inequality* 183, 197–98 (1993).

95. Barry Bearak, "Questions of Race Run Deep for Foe of Preferences," *N.Y. Times,* July 27, 1997, at A1, A10.

96. Bureau of the Census, *Findings on Questions on Race and Hispanic Origin Tested in the 1996 National Content Survey* (n.d.); Ellyn Ferguson, "What Is Your Race?: Americans Can Check Numerous Answers on 2000 Census Form," *Gannett News Service,* March 25, 1998, at ARC.

97. Jon Michael Spencer, *The New Colored People: The Mixed-Race Movement in America* 147 (1997).

98. Joel Perlmann, "Multiracials, Intermarriage, Ethnicity," 34(6) *Society* 20 (1997) (the Bureau of the Census must not adopt a classification scheme that sends a message that racial groups are wholly isolated from one another).

99. Nancy A. Denton, "Racial Identity and Census Categories: Can Incorrect Categories Yield Correct Information?" 15 *Law & Ineq. J.* 83, 89 (1997) (distinguishing between individual identity and social identity in use of social categories on the census); Linda Hamilton Krieger, "The Content of Our Categories: A Cognitive Bias Approach to Discrimination and Equal Employment Opportunity," 47 *Stan. L. Rev.* 1161, 1186–1217 (1995) (describing how the very process of categorization reduces the ability to appreciate complexity and individual differences).

100. 1993 House Hearings at 1 (remarks of Chairman Thomas C. Sawyer, House Committee on Post Office and Civil Service, Subcommittee on Census, Statistics, and Postal Personnel).

101. Sandor, "The 'Other' Americans," 16 *American Demographics* at 40; Ford, "Administering Identity," 82 *Calif. L. Rev.* at 1243.

102. See OMB Revisions (urging retention of information about multiple racial responses in ways that permit shifting racial identities to be monitored); Steven A. Holmes, "U.S. Officials Are Struggling to Measure Multiracial Heritages," *N.Y. Times,* June 14, 1998, at § 1, p. 32 (preserving information about combined racial responses will describe the "rich mosaic" of American identities but lead to a proliferation of categories); Martha Minow, "Forget 'Multiracial' and Count Each Component; Census: People, Not the Government, Should Define Who They Are for the Most Accurate Racial Portrait of America," *L.A. Times,* Aug. 13, 1997, at B7 (arguing that checking multiple boxes is superior to using a single multiracial category because it provides more accurate information about identity).

103. Steven A. Holmes, "People Can Claim One or More Races on Federal Forms," *N.Y. Times,* Oct. 30, 1997, at A1 (most respondents who identify themselves as mixed-race have Asian or Native American rather than black ancestry); Ellis Cose, "Census and the Complex Issue of Race," 34(6) *Society* 9 (1997) (arguing that many blacks might reject a multiracial classification to insist on their blackness).

104. For a discussion of some of these issues, see Kenneth E. Payson, "Check One Box: Reconsidering Directive No. 15 and the Classification of Mixed-Race People," 84 *Calif. L. Rev.* 1273, 1242, 1258–63, 1282–84 (1996).

105. P. S. Deloria and Robert Laurence, "What's an Indian? A Conversation about Law School Admissions, Indian Tribal Sovereignty, and Affirmative Action," 44 *Ark. L.*

Rev. 1107, 1114 (1991); Luis Angel Toro, "'A People Distinct from Others': Race and Identity in Federal Indian Law and the Hispanic Classification in OMB Directive No. 15," 26 *Tex. Tech. L. Rev.* 1219, 1253–59 (1995); Ford, "Administering Identity," 82 *Calif. L. Rev.* at 1263–67.

106. See Paul Brest and Miranda Oshige, "Affirmative Action for Whom?" 47 *Stan. L. Rev.* 855, 877–97 (1995) (describing degrees of disadvantage for different groups and their eligibility for affirmative action).

107. Bureau of the Census, *Money Income in the United States: 1996,* at vii, Current Population Reports P60-197 (Sept. 1997) (reporting that Asian Americans had highest median household income followed by non-Hispanic whites, Hispanics, and blacks); Bureau of the Census, *Asian and Pacific Islander Americans: A Profile,* Statistical Brief 93-12 (July 1993) (Asian Americans have higher rates of educational attainment than whites).

108. See text at notes 63 and 64 in this chapter.

109. See chapter 6 for a discussion of how outmarriage rates increase intergeneration-ally for Asian Americans, particularly as they acculturate and achieve high levels of education and income.

110. For a discussion of the one-drop rule, see chapter 2.

111. Stephen Magagnini, "The Big Count: Local Governments Are Revving Up for Some Changes in Census 2000," 64 *Planning* 13 (1998) (most blacks who select a multiracial option do not live in predominantly black neighborhoods and hence would have little impact on voting districts or poverty rates); Rochelle L. Stanfield, "Blending of America," 29 *National Journal* 1780 (1997) (middle-class, college-educated blacks are moving to the suburbs and intermarrying but others are not). See chapter 6 for further evidence that outmarriage rates increase among blacks as they attain increased levels of education and employment.

112. Julie C. Lythcott-Haims, "Where Do Mixed Babies Belong?: Racial Classification in America and Its Implications for Transracial Adoption," 29 *Harv. C.R.–C.L. L. Rev.* 531, 539–40 (1994), citing Carl N. Degler, *Neither Black Nor White: Slavery and Race Relations in Brazil and the United States* 185 (1986).

113. Malcolm X, *Autobiography of Malcolm X* 2 (1965).

114. Kwame Anthony Appiah, *In My Father's House: Africa in the Philosophy of Culture* 32 (1992).

115. Hickman, "The Devil and the One Drop Rule," 95 *Mich. L. Rev.* at 1247.

116. "No 'Silly' Boxes for Connerly," *Sacramento Bee,* Oct. 13, 1997, at A12.

117. Lind, "The Beige and the Black," *N.Y. Times,* Aug. 16, 1998, § 6, at p. 38, col. 1 (Magazine).

CHAPTER NINE

1. Gregory Howard Williams, *Life on the Color Line: The True Story of a White Boy Who Discovered He Was Black* (1995).

2. Id. at 256–57.

3. Id. at 259, 268.

4. Other mixed-race persons with ambiguous phenotypical appearance report that they are often asked "What are you?" They answer by explaining their ancestry in a conversation that very often resembles the one that Williams might have after voluntarily

revealing his heritage. Kenneth E. Payson, "Check One Box: Reconsidering Directive No. 15 and the Classification of Mixed-Race People," 84 *Calif. L. Rev.* 1233, 1233–34 (1996).

5. Kathy Russell, Midge Wilson, and Ronald Hall, *The Color Complex: The Politics of Skin Color among African Americans* 94–106 (paperback ed. 1992).

6. Williams, *Life on the Color Line* at 272.

7. Id.

8. See David C. Williams, "The Borders of the Equal Protection Clause: Indians as Peoples," 38 *UCLA L. Rev.* 759, 759–63 (1991); Carole Goldberg-Ambrose, "Not 'Strictly' Racial: A Response to 'Indians as Peoples,'" 39 *UCLA L. Rev.* 169, 184–85 (1991); Randall Kennedy, "Yes and No," *The American Prospect* 116 (1992).

9. Leslie Espinoza and Angela P. Harris, "Embracing the Tar-Baby—LatCrit Theory and the Sticky Mess of Race," 85 *Calif. L. Rev.* 1585, 1596–1605 (1997) (making case for black exceptionalism); John Calmore, "Exploring Michael Omi's 'Messy' World of Race: An Essay for 'Naked People Longing to Swim Free,'" 15 *Law & Ineq. J.* 25, 61–62 (1997) (arguing for singular experience of black Americans); William Julius Wilson, *The Truly Disadvantaged: The Inner City, the Underclass and Public Policy* 143–44 (1987) (describing adverse impact on inner city of flight of the black middle class).

10. Rachel F. Moran, "Unrepresented," 55 *Representations* 139, 141–49 (1996) (describing how inconsistent racialization of Latinos has harmed their status in immigration debates without advancing their case in the civil rights arena).

11. Sharon M. Lee, "Racial Classifications in the US Census: 1890–1990," 16 *Ethnic and Racial Studies* 75, 77–80 (1993).

12. Id. at 85–86.

13. Deborah Ramirez, "Multicultural Empowerment: It's Not Just Black and White Anymore," 47 *Stan. L. Rev.* 957, 958 n. 5 (1995) (contending that Latinos should be identified as a multiracial population with distinct national origins and ethnicities); Miranda Oshige McGowan, "Diversity of What?" 55 *Representations* 129, 133–34 (1996) (questioning utility of racial categories as applied to Asian Americans and Latinos who primarily focus on national origin and ethnicity to identify themselves). But cf. Ian Haney López, "Race, Ethnicity, Erasure: The Salience of Race to LatCrit Theory," 85 *Calif. L. Rev.* 1143, 1188–92, 1203–8 (1998) (contending that Latinos must acknowledge their racialization as an element of their ongoing subordination).

14. Rachel F. Moran, "Foreword—Demography and Distrust: The Latino Challenge to Civil Rights and Immigration Policy in the 1990's and Beyond," 8 *La Raza L.J.* 1, 19–21 (1995); Mari Matsuda, "When the First Quail Calls: Multiple Consciousness as Jurisprudential Method," 11 *Women's Rts. L. Rep.* 7 (1989); Robert S. Chang and Keith Aoki, "Centering the Immigrant in the InterNational Imagination," 85 *Calif. L. Rev.* 1395, 1408–9, 1417–22 (1998). For a discussion of how Native Americans identify themselves on the census, see chapter 8.

15. See Donna L. Franklin, *Ensuring Inequality: The Structural Transformation of the African-American Family* 3–26 (1997) (arguing that even if slaves shared some rudiments of an African heritage, they developed kinship structures and cultural practices that were an adaptive response to their conditions of servitude).

16. Michael Omi and Howard Winant, *Racial Formation in the United States* 55 (1994) (criticizing simplistic definitions of race that elide its powerful social consequences).

17. Williams, *Life on the Color Line* at 33.

18. Id. at 157.

19. Wislawa Symborska, "Love at First Sight," in *Poems: New and Collected, 1957–1997* at 245 (1998).

20. 388 U.S. 1 (1967). For a description of the decision and the events leading up to it, see chapter 5.

21. Reva B. Siegel, "The Racial Rhetorics of Colorblind Constitutionalism: The Case of *Hopwood v. Texas*," in *Race and Representation: Affirmative Action* 29, 57–61 (Robert Post and Michael Rogin eds., 1998).

22. For a complete discussion of the submersion of race in romantic complexity, see chapter 6.

23. 25 U.S.C. §§ 1901–1963. For an analysis of the Act's provisions, see chapter 7.

24. Elizabeth Bartholet, "Where Do Black Children Belong?: The Politics of Race Matching in Adoption," 139 *U. Pa. L. Rev.* 1163, 1172, 1209, 1232 (1991).

25. For a discussion of the statistics on race and placement in adoptive homes, see chapter 7.

26. U.S. Dept. of Health and Human Services, Administration for Children, Youth, and Families, *Removals of Barriers to Interethnic Adoption, Information Memorandum: Guidance for Federal Legislation—The Small Business Job Protection Act of 1996 (P.L. 104-188), Section 1808,* ACYF-IM-CB-97-04 (June 5, 1997), reprinted in Joan Heifetz Hollinger and the ABA Center on Children and the Law, *A Guide to the Multiethnic Placement Act of 1994 as Amended by the Interethnic Adoption Provisions of 1996,* at B-1 (1998); U.S. Dept. of Health and Human Services Administration for Children, Youth, and Families, *Information Memorandum: Information on Implementation of Federal Legislation—Questions and Answers that Clarify the Practice and Implementation of Section 471(a)(18) of Title IV-E of the Social Security Act,* ACYF-IM-CB-98-03 (May 11, 1998), reprinted in Joan Heifetz Hollinger and the ABA Center on Children and the Law, at D-1.

27. See Elizabeth Bartholet, "Correspondence: Private Race Preferences in Family Formation," 107 *Yale L.J.* 2351, 2354 (1998).

28. For a discussion of the special importance of ensuring that blacks enjoy the freedom to forge family ties without moralizing messages from the state, see Peggy Cooper Davis, "Contested Images of Family Values: The Role of the State," 107 *Harv. L. Rev.* 1348 (1994).

29. For an analysis of the use of open adoptions in placing Native American children, see chapter 7.

30. Williams, *Life on the Color Line* at 277.

31. Id.

32. Id. at 282.

33. Id. at 257.

34. Id. at 186.

35. Id. at 187.

36. Id.

37. Id. at 258, 268–69, 282–83.

38. Herbert Wechsler, "Toward Neutral Principles of Constitutional Law," 73 *Harv. L. Rev.* 1, 34 (1959).

39. For a complete set of statistics on intermarriage, see chapter 6.

40. Alan F. Westin and Barry Mahoney, *The Trial of Martin Luther King* 41 (1974).

41. For a discussion of how to draw the line between racist acts and racist thoughts, see Richard Delgado, "Words That Wound: A Tort Action for Racial Insults, Epithets, and Name-Calling," 17 *Harv. C.R.–C.L. L. Rev.* 133, 172–79 (1982) (arguing that expressions of racist sentiment can be punished as conduct that harms individuals without violating freedom of speech); Robert C. Post, "Racist Speech, Democracy, and the First Amendment," 32 *Wm. & Mary L. Rev.* 267, 271 (1991) (noting the lability of the distinction between punishable racist remarks and the free exchange of ideas and expressing concern that hate speech regulation may undermine the possibilities for democratic discourse). Here, too, the debate over racial equality and free speech is complicated by the interdependency of two constitutional principles typically understood as separate and independent. Because certain kinds of ideological discourse reinforce race in ways that impede equality, race and speech are in some respects constitutive of one another. As a result, concerns about freedom cannot be wholly disconnected from demands for equal treatment.

42. For a fuller discussion of this history, see chapter 5.

43. 163 U.S. 537, 544 (1896). For a discussion of *Plessy* and its links to current equal protection jurisprudence, see Siegel, "The Racial Rhetorics of Colorblind Constitutionalism," in *Race and Representation* (Post and Rogin eds.), at 49–52.

44. Wechsler, "Toward Neutral Principles of Constitutional Law," 73 *Harv. L. Rev.* at 34; Dorothy Roberts, "The Priority Paradigm: Private Choices and the Limits of Equality," 57 *U. Pitt. L. Rev.* 363, 363–64 (1996).

45. James S. Liebman, "Desegregating Politics: 'All-Out' Desegregation Explained," 90 *Colum. L. Rev.* 1463, 1504–8 (1990).

46. Neil Gotanda, "A Critique of 'Our Constitution is Color-Blind,'" 44 *Stan. L. Rev.* 1, 43–46 (1991) (describing characterization of racism as irrational); Richard Delgado, "Rodrigo's Tenth Chronicle: Merit and Affirmative Action," 83 *Geo. L.J.* 1711, 1723 (1995) (noting that racism is an irrational consideration that undermines efficiency and the objective evaluation of merit); Mary E. Becker, "Needed in the Nineties: Improved Individual and Structural Remedies for Racial and Sexual Disadvantages in Employment," 79 *Geo. L.J.* 1659, 1664 (1991) (contrasting irrational racism or sexism and reasoned distinctions among blacks and whites or men and women).

47. See Charles R. Lawrence III, "The Id, the Ego, and Equal Protection: Reckoning with Unconscious Racism," 39 *Stan. L. Rev.* 317, 318–26 (1987); Joel Kovel, *White Racism: A Psychohistory* 34 (1970). See also David A. J. Richards, "Liberal Political Culture and the Marginalized Voice: Interpretive Responsibility and the American Law School," 45 *Stan. L. Rev.* 1955, 1963 (1993) (noting that the characterization of racism as an irrational prejudice that undermines equal citizenship and public reason is rooted in abolitionist discourse).

48. 42 U.S.C. §§ 2000a(b)(1), (e); 42 U.S.C. § 2000e (b).

49. See, e.g., *Freeman v. Pitts,* 503 U.S. 467, 495 (1992) (noting that public educators are not responsible for rectifying school segregation due to private preferences and economics); *Board of Education of Oklahoma City v. Dowell,* 498 U.S. 237, 242–43 (1991) (same); *Wygant v. Jackson Board of Education,* 476 U.S. 267, 276 (1986) (employers are not required to remedy amorphous societal discrimination); *City of Richmond v. J.A. Croson Company,* 488 U.S. 469, 479–80 (1989) (racial disparities in the proportion of minority contractors can be due to "past societal discrimination in educa-

tion and economic opportunities as well as both black and white career and entrepreneurial choices").

50. Interview with Stan Sharoff, Denver Assistant District Attorney (Oct. 10, 1991); see also Carole Bass, "*Sheff v. O'Neill:* Doubting Desegregation; Critics Charge that Integration Gets Minority Children Nowhere Fast," *Conn. L. Tribune,* Jan. 10, 1994, at 1.

51. See chapter 1 for a discussion of the special nature of intimate choices and their insusceptibility to rational analysis.

52. 438 U.S. 265 (1978).

53. Id. at 312, citing *Keyishian v. Board of Regents,* 385 U.S. 589 (1967).

54. See, e.g., *Hopwood v. Texas,* 861 F. Supp. 551 (W.D. Tex. 1994), rev'd and remanded, 78 F.3d 932 (5th Cir.1996), rehearing en banc denied, 84 F.3d 720, cert. denied sub nom. *Thurgood Marshall Legal Society v. Hopwood,* 518 U.S. 1033 (1996), on remand, 999 F. Supp. 872 (W.D. Tex. 1998); *Coalition for Economic Equity v. Wilson,* 946 F. Supp. 1480 (N.D. Cal. 1996), vacated and remanded, 122 F.3d 692 (9th Cir.), cert. denied, 522 U.S. 963 (1997). See generally Richard D. Kahlenberg, *The Remedy: Class, Race, and Affirmative Action* (1996) (attacking race-based remedies and urging class-based methods of promoting equality); Christopher Edley Jr., *Not All Black and White: Affirmative Action, Race, and American Values* (1996) (noting recent attacks on affirmative action and arguing that programs be mended rather than ended).

55. See Charles Fried, "Affirmative Action after *City of Richmond v. J.A. Croson Co.:* A Response to the Scholars' Statement," 99 *Yale L.J.* 155 (1989) (citing remedial purpose as the sole permissible justification for affirmative action in employment); Lisa E. Chang, "Remedial Purpose and Affirmative Action: False Limits and Real Harms," 16 *Yale L. & Pol'y Rev.* 59, 61–75 (1997) (describing and questioning trend to recognize only corrective justice rationale for affirmative action in education and employment).

56. For a description of residential segregation, see Douglas S. Massey and Nancy A. Denton, *American Apartheid: Segregation and the Making of the Underclass* 60–82 (1993). For an analysis of marital segregation, see chapter 6.

57. Richard Sennett, *The Fall of Public Man* 295 (paperback ed. 1976).

58. Id. at 310.

59. See, e.g., Linda F. Wightman, "The Threat to Diversity in Legal Education: An Empirical Analysis of the Consequences of Abandoning Race as a Factor in Law School Admission Decisions," 72 *N.Y.U. L. Rev.* 1 (1997) (describing adverse impact on diversity of strict reliance on grade point average and Law School Admissions Test score); Stephane Baldi and Debra Branch McBrier, "Do the Determinants of Promotion Differ for Blacks and Whites?: Evidence from the U.S. Labor Market," 24(4) *Work & Occupations* 478 (1997) (blacks continue to have less education than whites, and even with affirmative action, they tend to work in different types of firms than whites and to be treated differently with respect to promotion).

11/2022
ρ 2001
C 19